'Gordon Corrigan has set out to expose this popular view, or myth, as quite simply not in accordance with fact. To this task he brings a mass of evidence, coupled with an ability to write clear, crisp, highly readable narrative . . . *Mud, Blood and Poppycock* should be in every school library – and studied with an open mind by all who teach the young about the Great War'   Correlli Barnett, *Daily Mail*

'This is no mere hagiography or turgid, blow-by-blow account of battles which, frankly, often seem repetitive. Corrigan's book is a fascinating read because he sets it up as a trial by jury. Each chapter (and they can be read in what order you please) takes a specific "myth" of the Great War and subjects it to a test of evidence. The result – even if you want to disagree with Corrigan's overall thesis – is gripping'

George Kerevan, *Scotsman*

'Corrigan peppers his book with statements that read outrageously at first but which he then backs up with devastating statistics'

Andrew Roberts, *Mail on Sunday*

'Corrigan has fashioned a pugnacious case, stripping away many of the misunderstandings and falsehoods that have settled as if they were established truths in the popular imagination'

Graham Stewart, *Spectator*

'A welcome addition to the revisionist view of World War One . . . Corrigan shows how the British embraced new military technology and developed dynamic new tactics to overcome the stalemate of trench warfare. A good argumentative tone is struck throughout the book'

Tim Newark, *Military Illustrated*

Gordon Corrigan was educated at the Royal School Armagh and the Royal Military Academy Sandhurst. He was a regular officer of the Royal Gurkha Rifles before retiring from the Army in 1998. His last appointment was command of the Gurkha Centre in Hampshire, training recruits and running courses for the Brigade of Gurkhas, for which he was awarded the MBE. He is now a freelance military historian. He is a visiting lecturer at the Joint Services Command and Staff College, writes, conducts battlefield tours and has appeared on and presented television documentaries dealing with various aspects of military history. His published works include a history of the Indian Corps on the Western Front during the Great War and a military biography of the Duke of Wellington. He describes his hobbies as Gurkhas, horses, the *Times* crossword, pricking the pompous and long lunches. He has two grown-up children and lives with his wife, who was a regular officer of the Women's Royal Army Corps and Adjutant General's Corps, in a windmill in Kent.

BY GORDON CORRIGAN

Mud, Blood and Poppycock

Sepoys in the Trenches

Wellington – A Military Life

MUD, BLOOD AND POPPYCOCK

Britain and the First World War

GORDON CORRIGAN

CASSELL

To Shelagh Lea: friend, artist and adviser, who did not live
to see the results of her invaluable contribution to this book

Cassell Military Paperbacks

Cassell
Wellington House, 125 Strand, London WC2R 0BB

Distributed in the USA by
Sterling Publishing Co. Inc.
387 Park Avenue South
New York, NY 10016-8810

Third Impression 2004

Copyright © Gordon Corrigan 2003

First published in 2003
by Cassell
This Cassell Military Paperbacks edition 2004

Cartography by Peter Harper

British Library Cataloguing-in-Publication Data
A catalogue record for this book is available from the British Library

ISBN 0 304 36659 5

Printed and bound in Great Britain by
Cox & Wyman Ltd., Reading, Berks.

www.orionbooks.co.uk

CONTENTS

MAPS AND DIAGRAMS

INTRODUCTION

Everyone knows – because it is endlessly repeated in newspapers, books and on radio and television – that if the British dead of the First World War were to be instantly resurrected and then formed up and marched past the Cenotaph, the column would take four and a half days to pass. Actually it wouldn't. The British lost 704,208 dead in the Great War, and if they were to form up in three ranks and march at the standard British army speed of 120 thirty-inch paces to the minute, they would pass in one day, fifteen hours and seven minutes. It is still an impressive statistic, but utterly meaningless. It is about as useful as saying that if all the paper clips used in the City of London in a year were laid end to end they would reach to the moon, or to New York, or halfway round the world. The figure is quoted, usually around 11 November each year, to illustrate the scale of British casualties in the war of 1914–18. It might mean more if it were coupled with the fact that the French dead, in the same formation, would take three days, five hours and thirty-seven minutes to complete the manoeuvre, and the Germans four days, eighteen hours and sixteen minutes. Even this would not help very much, because the French population was six million fewer than that of Great Britain, and the German population fifteen million more.

The popular British view of the Great War is of a useless slaughter of hundreds of thousands of patriotic volunteers, flung against barbed wire and machine guns by stupid generals who never went anywhere near the front line. When these young men could do no more, they were hauled before kangaroo courts, given no opportunity to defend themselves, and then taken out and shot at dawn. The facts are that over 200 British generals were killed, wounded or captured in the war, and that of the five million men who passed through the British Army 2,300 were sentenced to death by military courts, of whom ninety per cent were pardoned.

A recent schoolchildren's visit to the Western Front required the children to visit the British cemeteries in France and Belgium and answer questions, one of which was 'Why are there so few officers' graves?' The answer sought, according to the teacher present, was that the officers took no part in the attack, being safely behind the lines enjoying a good breakfast while their men went to their deaths.[1] The teacher – and by extension much of the British public – was presumably unaware that the four companies of an infantry battalion going into the attack, 640 soldiers in all, would be led by around twenty-three officers, assuming the battalion was fully up to strength with no one away on leave or courses. Between 1914 and 1918 twelve per cent of all other ranks were killed, and seventeen per cent of the officers.

The Great War, the Kaiser's War, the First World War, call it what you will, is of contemporary interest to the British people because nearly every family in Britain had somebody killed in it. Or did they? According to the official census reports, there were approximately 9,800,000 households in Britain in 1914.[2] Statistically then, only one family in fourteen lost a member. Even allowing for extended family groupings, to include uncles, cousins and in-laws, this is not every family in Britain. Perhaps everyone knew somebody who was killed? In certain parts of the country that is undoubtedly true, largely because of the way in which we recruited our infantry, but there were large swathes of the nation from where no one was killed.

It cannot be a comfort to those widows, sons, daughters, brothers and sisters, all ageing now, who remember a loved one killed in the war, when they are told, as they all too often are, that their menfolk died in vain and that their sacrifice was a pointless waste. It is, however, not surprising that the general public attitude should be thus. As experience of war recedes – and anyone who was old enough to take part in the Second World War is in their mid-seventies now – and when no one under the age of sixty has any experience of National Service, it cannot be surprising that the great majority of the British people have no understanding of war or any insight into what an army does and how it operates. We live in a liberal society, where individual rights are given ever greater priority and legislation outlaws any form of discrimination on the grounds of race, gender, sexual orientation, age or disability. The British army of today, let alone that of nearly a century ago, seems a strange body indeed. As standards of health and material well-being increase, and as governments become more and more accountable to the electorate, so concepts of compulsion, unthinking obedience to orders, constant risk of death or maiming, and subordination of the individual to the corporate aim appear increasingly alien. It is said that the army should reflect society, but what an army does, and what in the final analysis it is for, do not reflect society. The army defends society but it cannot share its values, for if it does it cannot do its job. An army at war may be more representative of society than one at peace, but even then it does not reflect it, being largely composed of young, physically fit males. An army may well be used for humanitarian purposes, ranging from flood relief to the distribution of food, and from peace-making to peacekeeping. Its structure, skills, mobility and discipline make it very good at these tasks, but an army exists to fight wars when and if these occur. A war is not a moral crusade, whatever the propagandists at the time may say; it is a trial of strength with each army striving its utmost to destroy the other by all means open to it. Some years ago the British army's small-arms training manual was titled *Shoot to Kill*. This led to protests from libertarians who claimed that such a title instilled aggression. Quite. Should the army have entitled its pamphlet *Shoot to Miss*? Soldiers are aggressive: they have to be because their job is to kill other soldiers and to do it efficiently and without moral scruple. In war individual morality must be subject to the priorities of the state, for if it is not then the army will lose, and all those hard-won human rights will count for naught.

Given the prevalent outlook of democratic western societies, it is perhaps not to be wondered at that politicians and others objected when in

December 2000 the British Chief of the Defence Staff pointed out that there is no place in the armed forces for the disabled. A compassionate society will, and should, legislate to prevent discrimination on the grounds of disablement, race, gender and sexual orientation. It will, rightly, introduce laws to regulate health and safety at work, to limit the hours worked by employees, and to encourage a climate in which promotion, dismissal, disciplinary procedures, orders and instructions can be challenged. But a society which seriously considers the extension of this culture to cover the armed forces, and in which the deterrent effect on a terrorist bomber of a sentry in a wheelchair is not instantly ludicrous, is unlikely to comprehend the military imperatives of the Great War. Even the humblest signaller, storeman or clerk may be required in the future, as he has been in the past, to pick up a rifle and defend himself, his comrades or his equipment. Soldiers must react instantly to orders, for if they take time to debate them, or to apply their own individual concepts of right and wrong, sense and nonsense, the moment for action will have passed. It is sometimes better to follow what in hindsight turns out not to have been the best course, than to do nothing at all.

Britain has a long history of opposition to whoever is in power, and has never been easily, or complaisantly, governed. This was in many ways a good thing, as dissent has always been able to be expressed and, apart from the Civil Wars of 1638 to 1651, we have been spared rebellion, uprising, oppression and dictatorship as experienced by most of our European neighbours. There has been no successful invasion of Britain since 1066, and since then the old order has never been swept away completely and permanently; it has merely adapted. Sniping at the establishment can go too far, however, and while it is always easy (and fun) to drag the mighty down, it is more difficult to raise someone into their place. British society has always been class-ridden. As officers, by appointment if not by birth, occupy a higher social stratum than that of the men they command, civilians have found them an easy target, and the more senior the easier. Everyone chuckles when a senior politician, or a member of the Royal Family, or an air marshal is caught putting his organ where he shouldn't; newspapers expend large sums of money trying to excavate the dirty laundry of pop stars, sporting figures and vicars. The first person to win £1 million in a recent television quiz show was widely reviled because she was upper middle-class, as if it were only artisans who should be allowed a dip in the bran tub. Criticism of the management of war comes naturally.

It is easy for the public to criticise, and by extension to believe the worst, of the Great War. It is almost impossible for modern Britain even to begin to understand what war is or was like. A society most of whose members have never slept elsewhere than in a bed cannot comprehend that one can be quite comfortable in a hole in the ground. A society in which any distance of more than a mile is an occasion for getting out the car can scarcely conceive that a march of twenty miles carrying seventy pounds or so is no great hardship for trained troops, or that all-in stew cooked with scant regard to the health and safety at work regulations can be nourishing and tasty.

Because everybody thinks something does not mean that they are necessarily right. Majority opinion after the Great War was that it had been a just war, and that Britain had played its part in winning it. The army's reputation was high, the commanders were publicly thanked and, as had long been the custom, were granted monetary awards and titles. When the last Commander-in-Chief, Earl Haig, died in 1928, his body lay in state in Edinburgh and 100,000 people filed past the coffin. Seventy years later there was a campaign by a national newspaper to have his equestrian statue in Whitehall demolished. It was in the thirties that critical opinion began to be formed. The publication of Erich Maria Remarque's fictional *All Quiet on the Western Front* in 1929 – which the Nazis burned but the French merely banned – stimulated a spate of anti-war memoirs and novels that had begun a few years before. Poets and writers like Siegfried Sassoon, Robert Graves, Wilfred Owen, Rupert Brooke, Edmund Blunden, C. E. Montague and Frederick Manning wrote convincingly that the war had been futile. They were a minority, but their views were read. Most of them were not new to having their thoughts in print: the majority had already been published before the war, and the public paid attention to what they said after it. Siegfried Sassoon, egged on by pacifists such as Bertrand Russell, published an anti-war diatribe in *The Times* on 31 July 1917; but then he was a patient in a mental hospital at the time, and what he said caused great offence in his old battalion which was still in France. Opposing voices were ignored, and Graham Greenwell, who stated baldly in *An Infant at Arms* that he had thoroughly enjoyed his war, was flayed by the reviewers. Pacifism became fashionable between the wars, and in 1933 the Oxford Union voted overwhelmingly that they would in no circumstances fight for King and Country. Much has been made of that motion, but a properly conducted debate will vote according to the quality of the argument presented, rather than in accordance with the voters' personal intentions. In the event, of course, they did fight. The arrival of the Second World War brought a temporary halt to criticism of the First, but there was a resurgence in the 1960s when anti-establishment fervour became widespread. Writers such as J. F. C. Fuller and Basil Liddell Hart were critical of the way the war had been managed, and particularly of its commanders. Liddell Hart became the leading exponent of the study of the Great War, and anyone who expressed a view contrary to his was unlikely to be widely published or listened to. Unfortunately Liddell Hart had a personal axe to grind. He was evacuated from the battle area on three occasions during the war: once with a fever, once when concussed by an exploding shell, and finally in July 1916 when he incurred flesh wounds and suffered the effects of gas. On the second and third occasions he was sent back to England to recover, and after his second evacuation he did not return to the front. It does now appear that the injuries from his third experience of battle were more psychological than physical.[3] One cannot blame him for that, but having been found wanting in physical courage – at least in his own mind if not in those of others – he sought ways to explain why it is not courage but intellect that wins wars. The generals were clearly men of courage; therefore they must be made to appear without intellect, and all the mistakes and failures could be laid at their doors.[4] Joan Littlewood's production of the play *Oh! What a Lovely War* was made into a film of which the scriptwriter admitted that it was one part himself and three parts Stalin. It was an enormously popular film, well made and highly entertaining, with a superb musical soundtrack, but about as historically useful as *The Wind in the Willows*.[5]

Any study of the British effort in the Great War must be approached from an understanding of what the army was required to do, and why it was where it was in the first place. It is totally unrealistic to impose today's standards on the events of 1914–18. No modern general would throw 200,000 men straight at a well-defended and fortified enemy line north of the River Somme: he would go over it, round it, bypass it or punch through it. The assets to do this – tanks, helicopters, paratroops, tactical nuclear weapons – were not available in 1916. What made the British army attack along the Somme and keep attacking was dictated by what was happening at Verdun, 120 miles to the south-west.

The war was fought between two coalitions, but that of the Central Powers, consisting of Germany, Austria-Hungary, Turkey and Bulgaria, was dominated by Germany, with by far the strongest economy and largest armed forces. On the Allied side, at some stage during the conflict, no fewer than twenty-four countries were technically at war with Germany, or with Germany and one or more of her allies. Some of these Allies or Associated Powers were of little account: Luxembourg, with its army of 150 royal guards who doubled as the nation's postmen in time of peace, had no opportunity to play any part, being occupied by Germany in the first few hours of the war. The declaration of war in April 1917 by Panama, with no armed forces at all, is unlikely to have caused General Ludendorff to break out in a cold sweat; nor would that in May 1918 by Costa Rica, with a standing army of 600 men and a navy of two patrol craft commanded by an admiral, have kept the Kaiser lying awake at night. Liberia (from August 1917) and Haiti (from July 1918) cannot seriously have expected to save Europe by their efforts. These countries, along with Guatemala (April 1917), Cuba (April 1917), Nicaragua (May 1917), Brazil (October 1917) and Honduras (July 1918), came into the war on the coat-tails of the American declaration of war against Germany in April 1917 and against Austria-Hungary in December. They made no military contribution but their formal entry into the war did allow German investments and assets in their countries, and German ships in their ports, to be seized. Even Siam declared war in July 1917. China, which joined in August 1917, was utterly unable to do anything, such was the internal state of the country, although she did allow the Allies to recruit labourers for duties behind the lines in Europe; large numbers of these Chinese died during the influenza epidemic of 1918. Italy joined the Allies in May 1915 against Austria-Hungary, largely in the hope of territorial gain, and declared against Germany in August 1916. Her participation was more of a hindrance than a help to the Allies, necessitating the diversion of six French and five British divisions and an American regiment to the Italian Front in 1917 to stave off their host's collapse. Greece entered the war in June 1917, her eye on her traditional enemies, Turkey and the Balkan states. Japan joined the Allies early, in August 1914, with a view to picking up German colonies in China and the Pacific. She took no part on land, but her navy was of help in protecting Allied trade in the Far East from German commerce raiders. Portugal came into the war on the side of her oldest ally in March 1916, and sent two small divisions to the Western Front. The efforts of Serbia (the immediate cause of the war), Montenegro and Romania were directed against Austria-Hungary and confined to their own geographical area.

Within the Allied coalition, the nations that actually mattered were France, Russia, Belgium, the United Kingdom and, neutral until 1917 but of enormous importance to the war effort even before entry, the United States of America. Belgium spent most of the war on the defensive, clinging grimly to that sliver of the country not occupied by Germany, and resisting British and French blandishments to take part in joint offensives. As the ostensible reason for the British declaration of war, however, she was important. On the German side Austria-Hungary was a ramshackle multi-ethnic state whose sole unifying factor was its Habsburg ruler, successor to the Holy Roman Emperor and now Emperor of Austria and King of Hungary. While not quite a German client state, Austria-Hungary was so far inferior to Germany in military and economic strength that, in examining the war in the west, it is reasonable to concentrate on Germany on the one hand and France, Britain and, in time, America on the other.

In the West, at least, this was a coalition war and for most of it Britain was the junior partner on land. Decisions as to the conduct of the war could not be made by British generals – or British politicians – in isolation. Actions looked at through Anglocentric eyes may well seem unnecessary, foolish even, but when examined in the context of the war as a whole the reasons for them become clearer.

The British army of the period 1914–18 was really four armies: the old professional regular army, with its associated reservists; the Territorial

Force, of civilians turned soldiers at weekends and at annual camp; the 'New Armies' raised from volunteers in the first year of the war; and the conscripts, joining the ranks from 1916 onwards. Each of these groups had a different ethos and a different perspective on the war; each had its own aspirations and needed handling in a different way. As a generality, the regular army was rarely found wanting; the Territorial Force lacked equipment and was deficient in some aspects of training, but when committed fought well; the New Armies were enthusiastic and drawn from a higher stratum of society than the regulars, but were – not surprisingly – hopelessly inexperienced and undertrained when first deployed; the conscripts, unlike the other three groups, did not fight as units but were used as individual reinforcements, thus perhaps finding the culture of the army harder to adjust to. Any study of the British army in the Great War must take these factors into account.

My own interest in the war was kindled as a schoolboy by my headmaster, a lofty figure with whom we boys rarely came in contact and who, when Empire Day was replaced by Commonwealth Day, summoned the whole school to announce that it would no longer be celebrated by a half holiday. 'Wilf', as he was known, did little teaching, except to the Upper Sixth A Level mathematics class. As this was in the days when university was but one of the many options open to a public schoolboy, we were a small band of six. I was there because two passes at A Level granted exemption from the Civil Service Commissioners' examination for entry to Sandhurst, and maths seemed a reasonable bet. Of my fellow pupils one was, like myself, trying for Sandhurst; two were whiling the time away before they could take over their fathers' estates; one was destined for the church, and one really was intending to read mathematics, at Cambridge. Apart from the Cambridge candidate (he succeeded in gaining a scholarship), none of us took sums very seriously, a fact that Wilf recognised early in the year. He was not just a dry old mathematician, however. He had been an infantry officer in the Great War and, as a change from quadratic equations, often threw us mathematical problems pertaining to war. 'A brigade consists of a headquarters and four battalions, each of 1,000 men. It has a cyclist company and a company of the Army Service Corps attached. It has an escort of two troops of cavalry. The infantry marches at two miles per hour. The brigade sets off from Cassel at 0900 hours. At what time does the last man reach Poperinge?' This was much more fun than proving that $e = mc^2$, but whatever answer we came up with was always wrong. As Wilf wryly pointed out, the brigade was held up for four hours in Steenvorde because the gendarmes considered that the commander lacked the necessary travel pass. Wilf had enjoyed his war. He had been wounded and he had seen his friends and his men killed, but he did not consider the war to have been unnecessary, or a waste, or badly conducted.

As time went on and I became seriously interested in military history, it seemed to me that much received opinion about the Great War was simply wrong. Anecdotal evidence from old soldiers, and statistics in the Public Record Office, did not seem to support much of the pejorative writings and opinions of modern commentators. It seemed to me that while the Great War was unique in British history, in that it was the first and last occasion when Britain fielded a mass army opposed to the major enemy in the main theatre for the entire period of hostilities, it was neither unnecessary nor badly conducted. Mistakes there surely were, but most were honest errors made by men who were as well trained and as well prepared as they could be, conducting a war the like of which no one on either side had expected. During the recent past, since my retirement from the army in 1998, I have conducted numerous battlefield tours, over half of them to the battlefields of 1914–18. I have tried to explain to my listeners what war is really about, how an army does its business and why much legend of the Great War is simply that: legend. I have myself come to the conclusion that Field Marshal Sir Douglas Haig, far from being the 'butcher and bungler' of popular belief, was the man who took a tiny British army and expanded it, trained it and prepared it until it was the only Allied army capable of defeating the Germans militarily in 1918. Some of my listeners have gone away convinced, some have nodded politely and continued in the comfortable safety of their preconceived ideas. People do not like their illusions shattered.

There is today a 'revisionist' school of military historians who are prepared to regard the war as history rather than as an emotional experience, but most popular reading clings to the old myths of incompetence and unnecessary slaughter. Even John Keegan, in his book *The First World*

War, has as his opening sentence, 'This was a tragic and unnecessary conflict.' To be fair to Sir John, he does not say that British participation in the war was unnecessary. I would argue that the aggressive nature of Germany's war aims made it essential to confront them by force, all other options having been exhausted, but Sir John does say that the efforts of revisionist historians are 'pointless'. I regret having to take issue with Sir John, the doyen of modern military historians. It was he, along with David Chandler, who as a lecturer in military history at the Royal Military Academy Sandhurst in the early sixties first stimulated my latent interest in the history of my profession, and who taught me never to accept historical accounts at face value, but to probe and question and pry and dig until the primary evidence was uncovered. Admiration and respect for Sir John need not prevent occasional disagreement with his conclusions.

I believe that the evidence does not support the popular view of the First World War as being unnecessary, or ineptly conducted by the British. The British regular army in 1914 was 257,000 strong, most of it scattered around the Empire in its primary role of a colonial gendarmerie. The Territorial Force and the Reserves numbered, at least on paper, a further 620,000. Unlike the continental powers Britain had always eschewed conscription and, unlike the French and the Germans, the bulk of the population had no military experience. Once at war expansion was rapid and unprecedented. A nation that does not practise conscription in peace, and then has to expand hugely in war in order to field a mass army, will inevitably suffer casualties and make mistakes while that army is learning its trade. It cannot be otherwise, and it is to the very great credit of the British army of 1914–18 that it did learn its trade and was the only army capable of taking the offensive in 1918.

In this book I have tried to look at some of the prevalent myths of the Great War and to examine the evidence relating to them. Some – the deadly effects of gas, the unimportance of the American army – I find to be without foundation: gas hardly killed anyone once it was known about, and the Americans made a very definite military contribution to the war, particularly at the Second Battle of the Marne. Some myths are partly true: some public schools did suffer heavy casualties amongst their ex-pupils, although not anything like the 'lost generation' of mythology – not all of

Harold Macmillan's friends were killed on the Somme. Some beliefs are simply misunderstood: it is quite true that one quarter of all the shipping from Britain to France during the war carried fodder for horses, but only a very small proportion of this was for cavalry horses: the bulk of British (and French and German) transport for artillery, ammunition, supplies and ambulances was horse-drawn; and in any case, the cavalry was nothing like the useless adornment that is often claimed.

In considering the actions of British commanders during the war I have adopted the standards of judges conducting a judicial review, a legal process where decisions made by ministers, functionaries, tribunals, panels and other quasi-official bodies are subject to challenge in hindsight. In deciding whether decisions taken were reasonable at the time, the judges ask themselves: 'Could a reasonable man, faced with the evidence he was faced with, come to the conclusion that he did, even if we, faced with the same evidence, might have come to a different conclusion?' It seems to me that this is the only approach that can reasonably allow an assessment of the capabilities and competence of those charged with conducting military operations in the world's first total war. In general, British command and leadership on the Western Front emerges unscathed, albeit occasionally bruised, from such an examination, although that in other theatres – such as Gallipoli and Mesopotamia – may not. I have concentrated my attention on the Western Front because it was there that the bulk of the British army fought, and there that the war was to be won or lost. I do not say that other non-European theatres were not important, but I do say that success or failure in them was not, in the long term, germane to eventual victory or defeat. The Eastern Front was, of course, an important theatre of war, but I have largely ignored it because the British army had no involvement there until after the armistice of 1918 was signed. At the same time I recognise that had the Eastern Front not occupied the attention of up to a quarter of all available German divisions until late 1917, the results of the earlier battles on the Western Front might have been very different.

As participants in the war open their archives and release documents previously classified, the sources for a study of the war increase with every passing year. Between 1922 and 1927 the German government published, in forty volumes, what it considered to be all the relevant diplomatic and military correspondence from 1871 to 1914, with the aim of expunging the 'war guilt' that had been attached to Germany since the Versailles Treaty. I have not read these forty volumes, but historians such as Fritz Fischer have, and while Fischer, although a German, is considered by some scholars to be biased against his own government's behaviour before and during the war, much of what he quotes speaks for itself. The principal German military leaders wrote their memoirs after the war, and while these are in some cases selective, and written to justify their own actions, much German military thinking prior to the outbreak of war is revealed. On the Allied side the start point must be the Official Histories. They too may be biased, but they do record what actually happened, even if the thinking behind specific operations is sometimes shaded and mistakes understated. British cabinet papers are now, for the most part, in the public domain, as are many of the more sensitive files dealing with such subjects as military executions. Unit war diaries are an excellent primary source for operational detail. In some cases they were written after the event, in others they were edited before being submitted up the chain of command, but for what actually occurred at unit level they are the most accurate sources available to us. Memoirs, diaries and letters of participants are useful, but must be used with care. A soldier might well complain that he never saw a general in the front line, while the unit war diary records frequent visits by brigade, divisional and corps commanders. These accounts are not necessarily mutually exclusive. Not every soldier in the firing line will see a visitor, while behind the lines the whole unit will be drawn up on parade to see and be seen by the great man. Fortunately for the historian, the British army loves paper; and post-operation reports, casualty returns, strength returns, records of ammunition expenditure, equipment tables, receipts for the issue of stores, training programmes, enlistment records, training notes, citations for awards and records of promotions and postings were meticulously compiled and filed, much of this material still being available today. A particularly useful document is *Statistics of the British Empire in the Great War 1914–1919*, a rich fund of information produced by the War Office after the war. Deaths in the war have now been placed on CD-ROM, making comparisons of the casualty rate in the various geographical districts of the nation an easier task than hitherto. Regimental histories, while they too must be treated with care, usually include accurate records of locations, casualties and decorations, and lists of officers, and sometimes of non-commissioned officers, present at any particular period.

In preparing this book I owe particular thanks to the writings of John Terraine, who ploughed a lonely furrow for many years in his efforts to explain the British participation in the Great War, and to show that all those British deaths had not been in vain. Professor Brian Bond of King's College London, Professor Peter Simkins recently of the Imperial War Museum London, Dr Gary Sheffield of the Joint Services Command and Staff College, Dr John Bourne of the University of Birmingham, and Robin Neillands are all inspirational historians of the war, persuaded by the evidence and without axes to grind. I have been greatly encouraged by my fellow members of the British Commission for Military History, a body with a low public profile but a high reputation for scholarship. Here I must pay particular tribute to Chris McCarthy, for many years the General Secretary of the Commission, who not only motivated me to write my first-ever book, but is the author of *The Somme: The Day-by-Day Account* and *Passchendaele: The Day-by-Day Account*, which lay out, starkly and devoid of emotion, exactly what every division of the British and Empire armies did on each day of those two climactic British battles of the Western Front.

The staffs of the Public Record Office, the British Newspaper Library, the Prince Consort's Library Aldershot, the British Library, the Office of Population Statistics and the Templeman Library of the University of Kent at Canterbury have all been unfailingly helpful in my searches for hard evidence on which to base my conclusions, and Mrs Shelagh Lea has, if it is possible, surpassed herself in producing accurate maps and line drawings from my near-illegible sketches. I am grateful to Tony Cowan for permission to make use of his Cowan Report on Army Postings, a monumental work that traces the career of every officer of the rank of colonel and above who served in the British army from 1914 to 1918. Miss Elspeth Griffith, the archivist of Sedbergh School, and Mr Richard Overton have been of great assistance in supplying me with the details of Old

Sedbergians who served in the war, as have Colonel Tony Lea MC of St Lawrence College, Thanet, and Dr Duncan of the Royal School Armagh. Miss Patricia Hardcastle, of the Catholic Media Office in London and Father O'Donoghe of the Jesuit Provinciate in Ireland have gone to great lengths to help in my investigations into the role of padres in the war, and particularly in my enquiries about Father Willie Doyle MC. To Colonel Andrew Pinion OBE I owe a huge debt for his advice on, and technical knowledge of, artillery in the Great War. Colonel Bob Alexander has helped me greatly by his encyclopaedic knowledge of machine guns and their characteristics. Stuart Sampson has been a mine of information on the law as it stood in 1914, and Colonel Dick Austin as to how it stands today; Simon Jones, of the King's Regiment Museum, has been kind enough to advise me on the history of gas warfare, and Brigadier Douglas Wickenden has, as in the past, been unfailingly helpful in answering my untutored questions on the psychiatric effects of war on its participants. The opinions, and the errors, are mine and mine alone.

My wife Imogen has, as always, been a tower of strength. Her ability to read a map, honed during twenty years' service in the Women's Royal Army Corps and Adjutant General's Corps, has been of immense assistance when conducting reconnaissance of the relevant battles, and she has compiled the index. I am not (quite) pompous enough to believe that it was seventeen years of listening to me pontificating about battles that drove her to seek a history degree, as a full-time student at the age of forty-three, but her academic studies have enabled her to comment on the text and to make observations that had not occurred to me. Angus MacKinnon and Ian Drury of Cassell – about as far removed from the image, so beloved by authors, of the wicked publisher as it is possible to be – and my editor, Anthony Turner, have been encouraging and helpful throughout.

This book may not convince all my readers of the validity of my claims, but if it at least prompts them to ask for the evidence when confronted with yet another fulminatory condemnation of the British war effort of 1914–18, then I shall have achieved my aim.

J. G. H. Corrigan
EASTRY, KENT, 2002

NOTES

1 *Bulletin of the Western Front Association*, no. 56, February 2000.

2 There were official censuses in England, Wales, Scotland and Ireland in 1911, and in England, Wales and Scotland in 1921. The Irish Free State and Northern Ireland held separate censuses in 1926. In all cases the census reports included the number of occupied dwellings, a dwelling being a self contained collection of rooms that were occupied by an individual or group, either a house or a flat. In arriving at the number of households in 1914, I have assumed that the rate of change was constant between 1911 and 1921 for Great Britain, and between 1911 and 1926 for Ireland. This cannot, of course, be entirely accurate, but is probably as near to the correct figure as it is possible to get. Statistics are contained in: *Census of England and Wales 1911, General Report with Appendices*, HMSO, London, 1917; *Census of England and Wales 1921, General Tables*, HMSO, London, 1925; *Report of the Twelfth Decennial Census of Scotland, Vol. II*, HMSO, London, 1913; *Report of the Thirteenth Decennial Census of Scotland*, HMSO, Edinburgh, 1923; *Census of Ireland 1911, Preliminary Report with Abstract of the Enumerators' Summaries*, HMSO, Dublin, 1911; *Preliminary Report on the Census of Northern Ireland 1926*, HMSO, Belfast, 1926; *Saorstát Éireann Census of Population 1926, Vol. IV, Housing*, Dept of Industry and Commerce, Dublin, 1926.

3 The question is examined in detail in Alex Danchev, *Alchemist of War, The Life of Basil Liddell Hart*, Weidenfeld & Nicholson, London, 1998.

4 Professor Brian Bond in *Look to your Front, Studies in the First World War*, Spellmount Publishers, Staplehurst, 1999.

5 For an assessment of British anti-war writing see Professor Brian Bond, 'British Anti-War Writers and Their Critics', in Hugh Cecil and Peter H. Liddle (eds.), *Facing Armageddon*, Leo Cooper, London, 1996.

1

AN UNNECESSARY WAR

In deciding whether any war is necessary or not, one must first define one's terms. In this context I take 'necessary' to mean 'in the British interest'. For the war of 1914–18 we need not ask, 'Was it in the British interest for there to be a war at all?' for clearly it was not. Britain had no territorial ambitions in Europe, nor did she have designs on any of Germany's colonies, albeit that some did become British mandates after the war. Germany was becoming a trading and economic rival to Britain, as was the United States, but at no time did any responsible person in Britain suggest that this rivalry should be settled by war. The question that must be asked and answered is: given that war happened, was it in the British interest to participate?

Germany was a relatively recent arrival on the world stage. In 1864 Prussia, with Austria as a reluctant ally, had detached Schleswig-Holstein from Denmark, and this in turn provided the excuse for war with Austria in 1866. In a seven-week campaign Prussia destroyed Austrian hegemony over the German states and annexed Hanover, Hesse-Cassel, Hesse-Nassau and Frankfurt-am-Main. In 1867 the North German Federation under Prussian leadership was formed, while the South German Federation, for the time being, went its own way. By luring the France of Napoleon III into war in 1870, Prussia annexed one-third of the French province of

Lorraine and all of Alsace, and assumed leadership of the south German states as well. In 1871, while the siege of Paris was still going on, the King of Prussia was proclaimed German Emperor[1] in the Hall of Mirrors at Versailles.

While pre-war France and Britain were parliamentary democracies, with power resting with elected politicians returned on a narrower franchise than today but widely representative nonetheless, the new German Empire was not. It was a federal institution, consisting of four monarchies, six duchies, six principalities and three free cities. Of the monarchies, Prussia was the largest (the others were Bavaria, Württemberg and Saxony), with its capital Berlin also the capital of the empire. There was a relatively toothless federal council, the Bundesrat, including representatives of all the component states but with Prussia having the largest bloc. The imperial constitution had as its senior functionary the Imperial Chancellor, an unelected official who was usually also Prime Minister of Prussia and was appointed and dismissed by the Emperor. The Chancellor presided over the Reichstag, the imperial parliament, but he was not answerable to it nor could he be a member of it. The Chancellor did have to obtain the approval of the Reichstag for the imperial budget and for some imperial legislation, and if he could not do so then he had to dissolve parliament and seek support at the polls. As the most influential group in the Reichstag was that representing Prussia, which had a much narrower franchise than the other German states, the Chancellor could nearly always count on acquiescence from that body. This was changing: in the 1912 general election the Social Democrats gained almost one-third of the seats in the Reichstag, but even if parliament did rebel, which it very rarely did, certain powers were in any case the prerogative of the Crown. These included foreign policy, defence, the declaration of war[2] and the making of peace; functions of state that the Emperor directed through the Chancellor. The heads of imperial ministries were not elected, but were officials appointed by the Emperor on the advice of the Chancellor. The Prussian army and the Imperial Navy (there were no German states' navies) at all times, and the armies of the other German states in time of war, came directly under the Emperor. Imperial authority over the armed forces was exercised through the Military and Naval Cabinets for personnel matters, and through the

General and Naval Staffs for operations. The Prussian Minister for War and the Secretary of State for the Imperial Navy (both appointed officials) represented all the armed forces in the Reichstag, but were responsible only for recruitment, equipment and the vote for the army and navy budgets. Lest budgetary control give the Reichstag a veto over military adventures, the military budget was passed for seven years at a time up to 1893, and for five years at a time thereafter. All this gave Prussia an over-whelming influence in the policies of the German Empire. Prussia's ministers were appointed, rather than nominated by the Diet, and her restricted franchise ensured that that influence was conservative and often militaristic. The other German states were not undemocratic: some had a far-reaching franchise, ministers were appointed by elected parliaments, and many of their governments were what we would now describe as liberal. They accepted Prussian dominance, however, partly from fear of red revolution and partly owing to cultivation of the bourgeoisie by successive imperial chancellors.

Germany, for so long a mosaic of statelets, was now an empire and her population became increasingly nationalistic. It has been suggested that had Otto von Bismarck, the 'Iron Chancellor' who had masterminded German unification, remained in power the First World War might never have happened. He would surely have ensured that Germany did not find herself in a position where she was isolated, surrounded by potential enemies and without allies of any consequence. As it was, Kaiser Wilhelm II, who succeeded his father in 1888 at the age of twenty-nine, dismissed Bismarck in 1890. Bismarck was born in the year of Waterloo, 1815, and so was seventy-five when dispensed with by the young Kaiser. Inevitably he was past his prime, and he died in 1898. His absence from the helm is therefore irrelevant, but does serve to reinforce the fact that the men who were chancellors in the pre-war period were either themselves in favour of an expansionist policy, or lacked the influence over Wilhelm II that Bismarck was able to exercise over his grandfather, the first Emperor.

Since the French Revolution democracy had developed in Western Europe, but the German Empire had eschewed it. While there was a measure of democracy within the German states – a considerable measure in some – all major decisions pertaining to foreign policy and war were made by the Emperor and the armed forces, who were accountable to nobody. We do not have a psychological profile of Kaiser Wilhelm II, but we do know that he was born with a withered arm, had an uncomfortable relationship with his English mother, a daughter of Queen Victoria, and idolised his father despite having been bullied unmercifully by him.[3] Wilhelm's father, Frederick III, eighth King of Prussia and second Emperor of Germany, had a reign of only ninety days in 1888 before dying of cancer of the throat. He had been unsuccessfully treated by English doctors called in by Wilhelm's mother, and Wilhelm seems to have blamed her, and by extension the British, for the death of his adored father. Perhaps if Frederick had lived (and he was only fifty-seven when he died) European history might have taken a different course. Unlike his son, Frederick abhorred war and disliked autocracy. He too would have dismissed Bismarck – as crown prince he had objected to the chancellor's anti-constitutional policies – but thereafter he would have followed a programme of alliance rather than alienation.

Despite being a newcomer to the European stage, the German Empire was economically a very powerful performer on it. The German states had never been interested in overseas possessions – they had enough worries at home – but Wilhelm, egged on by the military-industrial complex, wanted what he considered to be Germany's rightful place in the sun. The Germans were not good colonisers. Their treatment of their African subjects was appalling, even by the standards of the time. The German states had never been naval powers – they had virtually no access to the world's oceans and did not depend upon external trade – but Wilhelm wanted a blue-water navy, both as an antidote to the British Royal Navy and as an imperial symbol. The armies were the direct descendants of those of the old German states, whereas the navy owed its loyalty to the empire and the Kaiser alone. By the outbreak of war it was the second most powerful navy in the world.

Germany's wish to be, and to be recognised as, a great power successively alienated those nations that might otherwise have been expected to be well-disposed towards her. The alliance with Austria-Hungary from 1879, coupled with the abrogation of treaties with Russia, antagonised the Tsar and his government. As Germany's economy grew she found it necessary to have a merchant marine, which provided another excuse for developing a navy to protect it. This, and the Kaiser's bombastic statement in Damascus in 1898 that he saw himself as the protector of all Muslims, irritated both the British and the Russians, who ruled over large Muslim populations. The Kaiser's support for the Boers in the South African War helped to shift British public opinion regarding German ambitions from tolerance to suspicion, if not downright hostility. It was hardly surprising that Germany and France saw each other as rivals, as since 1871 France had always hoped to regain the lost territories of Alsace and Lorraine. In December 1905 there was a workers' revolt in Moscow, put down with considerable bloodshed by the tsarist government. Fearing similar unrest at home, the Kaiser wrote to the Imperial Chancellor, Bülow, telling him: 'Shoot down, behead and eliminate the socialists first, if need be by a bloodbath, then war abroad. But not before, and not à tempo.' Hardly the wise words of a peace-loving constitutionalist. In 1911, when British support for France during the Moroccan crisis resolved colonial rivalries in North Africa in favour of France, the German public, and the Kaiser, saw this as a humiliation of Germany; many Germans became increasingly convinced that in war lay the determination of Germany's world position. In 1912, in the aftermath of the Balkan Wars, the German ambassador in London, Lichnowsky, sent a written report to the Emperor warning that Britain 'could under no circumstances tolerate France being crushed'. In a marginal note the Emperor scribbled, 'She will have to.'

All the evidence – and there is much – points to Imperial Germany preparing for a European war of aggression against France and Russia; and, while there were hopes that Britain might remain neutral, against her too if need be. The Kaiser held mixed views about the British. On the one hand he liked the country, enjoyed his visits there and had adored his grandmother, Queen Victoria. On the other hand he thought that the British were forever putting him down, and saw slights where none were intended. For all his bombast, and his revelling in the idea of war and military glory, when faced with the reality of war the Kaiser recoiled, lost his nerve and tried very hard and at the last moment to avoid it. It was far too late. The Kaiser himself may not have wanted a European war, but he surrounded himself with, or allowed himself to be surrounded by, people who did. He did nothing to discourage them until the moment for restraint had long passed.

After the war the Versailles Treaty made very plain that Germany was entirely responsible for the war. Article 231 said:

> The Allied and Associated Governments affirm, and Germany accepts, the responsibility of Germany and her allies for causing all the loss and damage to which the Allied and Associated Governments and their nationals have been subjected as a consequence of the war imposed upon them by the aggression of Germany and her allies.[4]

But then the Versailles Treaty was written by the victors. It went further:

> The Allied and Associated[5] Powers publicly arraign Wilhelm II of Hohenzollern, former German Emperor, for a supreme offence against international morality and the sanctities of treaties. A special tribunal will be constituted to try the accused ... it will be composed of five judges, one appointed by each of the following Powers: namely, the United States of America, Great Britain, France, Italy and Japan.[6]

'Hang the Kaiser' was a popular slogan in the British general election of 1918, and both the British and French governments made strenuous but unsuccessful efforts to persuade the government of the Netherlands, where Wilhelm had sought refuge after abdicating in 1918, to hand him over for trial. It is difficult to see under what law he could have been tried. Even as late as 1999 it was being argued before the British House of Lords that a head of state could not be put on trial for actions carried out in that capacity – 'acts of state' were not subject to domestic law. Unlike the situation after the Second World War, there was no body of international law hastily cobbled together to allow the indictment of the political and military leaders of a defeated nation.

It is not the purpose of this book to examine the causes of the war in detail, nor to apportion guilt for it. That task has been well undertaken by Fritz Fischer, A. J. P. Taylor and James Joll, amongst others. Fischer, the German, is adamant that Germany's foreign policy aims were annexationist and that she went to war to achieve them.[7] What is undeniable, however, is that Germany, by offering unconditional support to

Austria-Hungary in her dispute with Serbia, precipitated the series of events that led to war. Long before that, at least as early as 1906, Germany had in place a plan for an aggressive war based on the premise that Germany would have to fight Russia and France simultaneously, with Britain as a possible ally of France. It need not have been so, but the young Kaiser had abandoned Bismarck's policy of always having a treaty of non-intervention with Russia, and had alienated Britain and France. There was a view in Germany, held by many of the intelligentsia, that Britain was an 'ageing state' and that the future of the world lay with the younger, vigorous, emerging powers: Germany and the United States.

Ever since unification Germany had plans for war on the continent of Europe. Every country has contingency plans and there is nothing wrong with that, indeed it would be surprising if they did not. The difference, perhaps, is that Germany, or at least many politicians and virtually all the military leaders, believed that a war was inevitable and necessary. The Emperor at the very least condoned those views. Field Marshal Helmuth von Moltke, chief of the German general staff for the victory of 1870–71 and designer of the modern staff system, thought that if war on two fronts came, the German army should first defend against France; then deal with Russia; then turn and counter-attack the French. Moltke's ambitions were limited: he planned to cripple Russia and France, not destroy them by total victory. Moltke retired in 1888. His successor, Waldersee, was more aggressive. He wanted to launch a preventive war against Russia, until reined in by Bismarck, but he did not alter the basic war plan – to attack in the east first. The architect of the plan implemented by Germany in 1914 was Field Marshal Alfred Graf von Schlieffen, who had been Waldersee's quartermaster general before succeeding him as chief. Von Schlieffen was the archetypal German staff officer. Born in 1833, he was commissioned into the Prussian Guard Cavalry. He attended the Prussian staff college and was a staff officer during the war against Austria in 1866 and against France in 1870–71. From 1876 to 1883 he commanded a regiment of uhlans, but for the rest of his service he was a staff officer pure and simple. He joined the Great General Staff in 1883, being successively head of various departments before becoming the Chief of the General Staff in 1891, a position he held until 1906. He was a brilliant if somewhat humourless man, and even today aspiring officers in western armies are reminded of his favourite aphorism: 'No plan survives the first five minutes of encounter with the enemy.' He devoted himself solely to his profession, and was known to give his subordinates theoretical tactical problems on Christmas Eve and require the solutions on his desk by Boxing Day. Were this to have happened in the British army, the officers would have concluded that the old boy was mad, thrown the papers in the bin and gone to the races.

Schlieffen began to question the assumptions of his two great predecessors. He recognised the strength of the reconstituted French army and its forts along the Franco-German border, but considered that they could be bypassed through Belgium. Schlieffen drew up a new war plan, which he refined as his tenure went on. By the time he retired this scheme had achieved a status verging on that of the laws of the Persians and the Medes.

The Schlieffen plan assumed that in the event of war Russia would take longer to mobilise than France. Only one German army would defend the frontiers of East Prussia, while three would stand along the Franco-German boundary. The plan assumed rightly that this was where France would attack, and saw no difficulty in these armies giving ground if need be. Indeed, were the French to make headway in the centre, this would be an advantage to the Germans, as making the intended outflanking movement – the revolving door, as he put it – more certain of success. The main thrust would be carried out by four more German armies, the strongest, which would wheel along the Channel coast through Holland and Belgium, pass to the west of Paris and then swing east, pinning the French armies against their own frontier defences and destroying them. This move, employing seven-eighths of all available German troops, would be completed within six weeks; the armies would then move east and deal with the Russians. There were snags: Schlieffen never did work out how to deal with the strong garrison of Paris; and the fact that the Netherlands and Belgium were likely to be neutral mattered not a jot. Schlieffen's successor was Field Marshal Helmuth von Moltke (1848–1916), known to historians as the Younger Moltke to distinguish him from his uncle of the same name. The younger Moltke made some alterations to the plan. Dutch neutrality would not be violated, and the centre was somewhat strengthened at the expense of the flanking armies. As we now know, the plan did not work; but even if Moltke had not altered some of Schlieffen's arrangements it is doubtful whether the German army could have marched fast enough, or been resupplied in sufficient quantity, to achieve the objectives laid down. The Germans would face – and did face – demolished bridges and destroyed railway lines, while the French could move along interior lines using their own railways. All this is speculation; the point is that this was a plan for unqualified aggression. All general staffs draw up plans for all eventualities, including those where their nation is the aggressor – indeed they would be failing in their duty did they not – but most have defensive plans too. Germany was, of course, vulnerable on all fronts, whereas France and Russia needed only to consider their eastern and western fronts respectively, while Britain could only be invaded by sea, and her navy was by far the most powerful afloat. Despite this, there can be little doubt that Germany's intention, formed at least as far back as 1906, was to attack when the time was ripe.

In 1920 General Erich von Ludendorff published *The General Staff and Its Problems*, in two volumes. Ludendorff had effectively directed the whole of the German war effort from 1916 onwards, and this work was intended to divert blame for the defeat away from the soldiers and on to the politicians. In the foreword Ludendorff insists that the documents he publishes show that a 'peace of understanding' was never obtainable, and that much was concealed from the military supreme command by the Imperial government. We need pay but cursory attention to the apologia, but some of the documents are revealing. Ludendorff was the Director of the Concentration Section of the Great General Staff from 1908 until 1913, when he was moved to the command of a regiment for going outside the chain of command to lobby the Reichstag for an increase in the size of the army. The Concentration Section was responsible for the preparation of the army for mobilisation, and for the direction of mobilisation when it came. Ludendorff was thus in a position to know exactly what ministries and the High Command were planning.

Included in Volume One is a letter, marked 'Secret', from the Chief of the General Staff, von Moltke, to the War Ministry, dated 8 February 1911 (on the subject of ammunition reserves): 'In the war we shall need rapid and decisive victories...If we prepare for the attack on the French fortresses we shall be ready for that on the Russian also...'[8] Moltke says: 'In the war', not 'If war comes', or 'If it were necessary to go on the offensive'.

At least as early as 1910 Germany was preparing to go to war, not only with France and Russia, but with England as well. Ludendorff reproduces a paper dated 1 July 1910, sent by von Moltke to the War Ministry. The report begins: 'The last war game in the General Staff, which was based on the assumption of a war of Germany against France, Russia, and England, combined with the relevant General Staff ride, in which the problem was an English landing in Schleswig-Holstein...'[9] A staff ride was the modern TEWT, or Tactical Exercise Without Troops, where command and staff elements study a problem on the ground without the need to deploy men. The theme of a British landing in Schleswig-Holstein recurs in many of Ludendorff's documents, and it was thought to be likely on the thirteenth day after British mobilisation. Presumably the German staff thinking was that Britain would use her naval power to effect an invasion. The British Admiral Fisher (1841–1920), First Sea Lord (professional head of the navy) from 1904 to 1910, and again from October 1914,[10] regarded the British army as a projectile to be fired by the Royal Navy, and was in favour of a landing somewhere on the Baltic coast in the event of war with Germany. In reality, while British naval superiority could certainly have effected a landing, despite the inshore submarine threat, the regular army could not have provided sufficient men to ensure that any beachhead seized was defended and expanded, rather than being driven back into the sea or simply bottled up and ignored. Moltke saw the threat as real, however, but considered that a further German army could not be made available to deal with it, and that if it came it should be contained by depot troops, those responsible for training and running courses.

The European powers of 1914 were connected in a series of alliances. Germany had been linked to Austria-Hungary since 1879, and this eventually propelled Russia into alliance with France in 1891. Britain hardly considered herself to be a European power at all. Trafalgar in 1805 had given her command of the seas, and Waterloo in 1815 had made her a world power – indeed the only world power for nearly a century. She had long attempted to ensure a balance of power in Europe, whereby no one country might dominate the Continent, and a main plank of her foreign policy was that no potentially hostile power should control the Rhine delta and the Channel ports, Britain's access to the Continent. Hence the British interest in Belgium, in any case largely a British creation, whose neutrality Britain guaranteed. Apart from the commitment to Belgium, Britain had long remained aloof from any European alliances, and for many decades her empire and her navy allowed her to do so, until the rise of potential economic and military rivals had forced her to modify her stance. Anglo-Japanese treaties had been signed in 1902, 1905 and 1911 and the Entente with France in 1904. The agreement with France was designed to resolve colonial rivalries in North Africa, but it also prompted much closer cultural, social and diplomatic exchanges than hitherto, helped along by the Francophile King Edward VII. The Anglo-Russian Entente of 1907, agreed with a Russia still reeling from ignominious defeat by the Japanese in 1904–05, removed the Russian threat to India via Afghanistan and brought Britain into the Triple Entente with France and Russia. None of these accords required Britain to involve herself in a European war: they were understandings only, and in any case had originally nothing to do with Europe.

The blow that sparked off the great conflagration of 1914 was struck in the Balkans, a byword for volatility since the collapse of the Ottoman Empire and Turkish rule which, while autocratic and often cruel, had at least ensured the stability of the area. In June 1914 the Archduke Franz Ferdinand, heir to the Austro-Hungarian throne, with his morganatic wife the Duchess Sophie, was visiting Bosnia, annexed by Austria-Hungary in 1908. There were many Serbs living in Bosnia and both they and Serbia itself objected to the Austrian presence. Franz Ferdinand and his wife were assassinated in Sarajevo on 29 June 1914 by Gavrilo Princip, a Serbian anarchist.

Initially European opinion was sympathetic to Austria. Within the dual monarchy opinion ranged from distress and dismay that the heir should have been murdered, through those who thought Slavs within an empire dominated by German-speakers might now be given more consideration (ironically, Franz Ferdinand had been in favour), to those who saw the killing as an excuse for a showdown that would reassert Austria-Hungary's great-power status, in decline for many years.

On 23 July 1914 Austria issued a note to Serbia. The terms were described by the British Foreign Secretary, Lord Grey, as 'the most formidable document that I had ever seen addressed by one state to another that was independent'. The preamble to the note accused Serbia of conniving at a subversive movement aiming to detach portions of the dual monarchy (Austria-Hungary); tolerating unrestrained language on the part of the press, the glorification of the perpetrators of outrages; the participation of officers and functionaries in subversive agitation; and inciting the Serbian population to hatred of the dual monarchy and contempt of its institutions. Austro-Hungarian investigations had, it was claimed, shown that the Sarajevo assassinations were planned in Belgrade, that the arms and explosives had been provided by Serbian officers, and that the assassins had been inserted into Bosnia by the Serbian frontier authorities. Amongst the demands made by Austria-Hungary were a publication in the Serbian official press, and as a general order to the army, of an admission of culpability in, and an expression of regret for, the assassination. Publications expressing anti-Austrian views were to be banned; all anti-Austrian agitation was to stop and anyone in the education system guilty of spreading it was to be removed. Organisations within Serbia considered by Austria to be subversive were to be suppressed with the assistance of Austrian representatives. Serbian army and frontier officials indicated by Austria as being involved in anti-Austrian activities were to be dismissed; two named officers were to be arrested; anyone on Serbian territory involved in the assassination plot was to be put on trial. In all investigations and subsequent judicial proceedings, Austro-Hungarian officials were to take part. Serbia was given just forty-eight hours to reply.[11]

Germany claimed to have had no prior knowledge of the Austrian note. In fact, as Fischer shows, Germany knew very well what was intended and both the German government, and the Emperor personally, had assured Austria of unconditional support in whatever action she chose to take. Frenzied attempts at mediation between Austria, Serbia and Russia (as the self-proclaimed protector of Slavs) by Britain and, belatedly, by the Kaiser, and efforts to localise a conflict if it could not be prevented altogether, came to naught. The German High Command enquired of their opposite numbers in Vienna what their intentions were, and were told that Austria would invade Serbia with six corps. If Russia then intervened those forces would be diverted from Serbia to face 'the principal opponent'. The British Prime Minister, Asquith, said that if war came, Britain's role would be confined to that of a spectator.

From then on events moved swiftly. At 1500 hours on 25 July 1914 the Serbian government ordered mobilisation, and at 1800 hours on the same day the Serbian Prime Minister personally handed his government's reply, to what was effectively an ultimatum, to the Austro-Hungarian ambassador to Belgrade. The Serbian reply went far closer to meeting Austrian demands than anyone had thought possible. All were accepted save two. The admission and apology would be published in the official press but not as a general order to the army (the Serbian government feared a military uprising if it were), and Serbia could not accept the participation of Austro-Hungarian representatives in the trials that Serbia agreed to convene. The Austrians, knowing that they had a blank cheque signed by Germany in their pocket, chose to take this as a rejection of their demands. The Austro-Hungarian embassy left Belgrade.

On 28 July Austria-Hungary declared war on Serbia. On the following day Germany asked for a guarantee of British neutrality in the event of a European war. Britain had still not decided either way, but to declare neutrality would be to encourage war, and on 30 July she declined to give any such undertaking. Russia ordered partial mobilisation in support of her fellow Slavs on 29 July, and Germany warned that unless this was cancelled, she too would mobilise. On 31 July both Russia and Austria-Hungary ordered full mobilisation, as did Turkey, still smarting after her defeat in the Balkan Wars. On the same day Britain asked France (allied to Russia) and Germany for a guarantee of Belgian neutrality in the event of a European war. This was accepted immediately by France, but ignored by Germany. On 1 August Germany, France and Belgium ordered full mobilisation. On 2 August Britain, in reply to an anxious enquiry, assured France that she would not allow the German fleet to fall on the French coast via the North Sea. On 3 August Germany demanded passage through Belgium, and Belgium made an appeal for help from Britain. Germany invaded France, Belgium, Luxembourg and Russian Poland, and declared war on France and Belgium. Britain ordered mobilisation, and issued an ultimatum to Germany demanding withdrawal from Belgium.

In the lead-up to the outbreak of war Britain had no wish to become involved, and it did seem for a time that she could remain apart. Britain's main concern was her empire and her trade routes, and she might have been prepared to make some allowances to Germany in Europe in exchange for colonial concessions abroad. What Britain could not accept, however, was a Europe dominated by one potentially unfriendly power, particularly if that power subjugated Belgium and controlled Britain's routes to and from the Continent. While two British government ministers resigned over the issue, opinion by early August was that France could not be allowed to be crushed by Germany. If she was, then Germany, with the resources of a defeated France and Russia at her disposal, would pose a threat to the United Kingdom and to the British Empire. Another war would be inevitable, and it would not be a war that Britain alone could necessarily win. In the unlikely event of France winning without the support of the British navy and British money, the opprobrium directed against Britain by her nearest neighbour would not be in the British interest either. Germany had fomented this war; Germany had struck the first blow; Germany had violated neutral countries that were no threat to her. It was necessary, and in the British interest, for Britain to declare war, and at midnight German time (2300 hours British time) on 4 August 1914 she did so.

Prior to August 1914 the German government's war aims were global and general, revolving around Germany's aspirations to great-power status, the need to avoid or break out of encirclement, Germany's rightful place in the (colonial) sun, and the desire for a blue-water navy. A certain amount of anti-British propaganda appeared in the German press from time to time, including a cartoon showing British soldiers leaping out of the Channel tunnel (one was being considered, from Folkestone to Calais, before the war) and invading Germany via Belgium. The declaration of war concentrated minds wonderfully. As early as September 1914, when a short war and a quick victory still looked certain, the Imperial Chancellor, Bethmann Hollweg, was formulating his government's demands for the peace conference. In an internal paper he stated his government's aims as being the security of Germany in the east and the west: to weaken France to the extent that she could never regain world-power status, and to push back Russia as far as possible from Germany's borders. Germany was to be the centre of a Middle-European economic bloc. The French and Belgian iron-ore fields, and ownership of the factories therein, were to be ceded to Germany. The military were to comment on the advisability of demanding the cession of Belfort, the western slopes of the Vosges and the coastal strip from Dunkirk to Boulogne, with fortresses remaining in French hands to be demolished. The French market was to be secured for Germany, and British trade excluded.

As for Belgium, she was to be reduced to a German vassal state, economically a province of Germany, and her forts were to be occupied by German garrisons. The Emperor lodged a suggestion that the portion of Belgium bordering on Germany be resettled by deserving NCOs and men of the German army. He did not use the expression 'final solution' – Germany was still a civilised nation and it would be a further generation before she descended to official genocide – but the existing inhabitants were to be 'cleared', and there was no mention of compensation. Grand Admiral von Tirpitz went further: he wanted Antwerp and the Belgian Channel ports to be annexed and used as bases for the German navy.

When the British government decided to enter the war it was not, of course, aware of the details of German designs for France and Belgium – they had not yet been formulated – but it knew very well that some such plans would soon come to occupy German minds. A victorious Germany, in occupation of the Channel ports and the coastal strip, would pose a threat to Britain that could not be contemplated. Its prevention was not just worth fighting for: it was essential.

In 1914 there were technically a number of German armies, belonging to the various federal states, but all were under unified command and can be considered as one army. Germany relied on conscription, to which every able-bodied male was liable from the age of seventeen years. The conscript first served three years in the *Landsturm*, or part-time Home Guard, followed by two years in the regular army and five years on the regular army reserve. From age twenty-seven he served in the *Landwehr*, a type of territorial force intended to support the regular army, until returning to the *Landsturm* from age thirty-nine to forty-five. In practice not all eligible men served in the regular army – there were far too many for the army's requirements – but as this system had been in place since 1895, and similar if less inclusive schemes before it, virtually the whole of the German male population had received some military training. The standing army's peacetime strength in 1914 was approximately 700,000, with about three million trained adult males available for immediate reinforcement on mobilisation.

Germany's immediate target in the west, France, had a standing army of 820,000, including around 45,000 colonial troops, mostly, but not all, stationed in France. Conscription had been reintroduced after the 1870 war with Prussia and refined in 1905, after which all able-bodied males between twenty and forty-five spent two years with the regular army, eleven years with the regular army reserve and twelve years in the territorial army. In 1913 the French government, realising that the German army was larger and better equipped than its own, increased the period to be spent with the regular army from two years to three. On the outbreak of war the French army could call upon two and three-quarter million reservists.

As this study concentrates on the British way of making war it is apposite to examine how the British army of 1914 came to be as it was. The British had long eschewed conscription. To the general public the navy was England's defence, and the army existed to keep order in the empire and to provide expeditionary forces of modest size when needed. The British regular army in 1914 was 247,432 strong, but one-third of it was in India and there were large garrisons in Ireland (including twenty infantry battalions and three cavalry regiments), Africa, the Middle East and Egypt, with smaller contingents scattered around the globe. The army reserve, of men who had completed their service with the colours but either had a liability for reserve service or volunteered for it, totalled around 210,000, and the Territorial Force around 280,000, including the Channel Islands Militia.

In 1871, in the aftermath of the Franco-Prussian War, there began a series of reorganisations to turn the British army from something which had not changed very much since Wellington into the force that went to war in 1914. Purchase of commissions[12] was abolished, the infantry was grouped into (mainly) two-battalion regiments and given geographical areas from where to recruit, and conditions and equipment were improved. As a result of the South African War, 1899–1902, it was clear that further reform was needed. Britain had never before sent so many troops abroad, and the regular army was simply not large enough to cope. Volunteer, Yeomanry and Militia units volunteered to send contingents overseas, and the Dominions rallied too; but it became clear that the British army must now be prepared to fight sophisticated, well-armed enemies – and Germany was increasingly looking like a possibility – rather than numerous but ill-trained and technologically inferior native hordes. The British army, relying on voluntary enlistment, could never hope to compete against European powers in numbers, but it must be organised and equipped along modern lines, and it must have a realistic reserve.

In 1904 the post of Commander-in-Chief of the British Army was abolished. Ever since the death of Wellington in 1852 its powers had increasingly been arrogated to himself by the Secretary of State, and its administrative and policy-making functions were now assumed by an Army Council, presided over by the Secretary of State and consisting of four military officers, led by the newly created Chief of the General Staff (Chief of the Imperial General Staff from 1910), and two senior civil servants, one responsible for finance. The British army had never before had a staff as such. Staff officers, those persons responsible for training, planning and administration, and for the direction of an army on operations, were found as and when they were needed. The Prussians had invented the modern staff system, and it had manifestly worked in 1870–71. Increasingly it became clear to British military thinkers and policy-makers that the old make-do system of cobbling together a headquarters and staff when needed, from whoever was available, was outdated and unsuited to modern war. An Army Order of November 1905 sanctioned the formation of a General Staff and the process was accelerated on the appointment of Richard Haldane as Secretary of State for War in December 1905. In 1908 a further reorganisation divided the staff into three main branches. In broad terms the General Staff were responsible for operations and training, the Adjutant General's Staff for personnel matters and the Quartermaster General's Staff for administration and logistics. Colloquially, these branches were known as G, A and Q. The latter two branches had existed for a century and a half, under various guises; what was new was their formal and permanent establishment at levels below that of the War Office, and the imposition of a General Staff, whose functions had previously been the responsibility of the Commander-in-Chief at the very top, and of the theatre commander and his quartermaster general at subordinate levels. From now on the A and Q staffs would be subordinate to the General Staff. The Chief of the General Staff would be the professional head of the army, and the senior military adviser to the Secretary of State.

Staff training, previously not regarded as an essential to career progression, began to be taken more seriously, and arrangements were made with the London School of Economics for potential staff officers to be trained in the technical aspects of their likely future employment, including business studies and the management of railways. Although much was copied from the Prussians, one major doctrinal principle would not be adopted. In the German army there was effectively a separation of the staff and command avenues to promotion. There, officers who had done well at the staff college and in their first staff appointment were selected to become members of the Great General Staff. They wore the coveted red stripe on their trouser legs and usually spent the rest of their service as staff officers. Commanders and their chiefs of staff bore joint responsibility for results, and a staff officer who was unhappy about his commander's decisions had the right of direct access to the senior staff officer of his branch at the next higher headquarters. The British army was too small to have separate pools of commanders and staff officers, and such a system would in any case have been unacceptable to the British military ethos. The British staff would remain subordinate to command, and officers would not advance by merit in only one stream; they would alternate between the staff and command, needing recommendations in both spheres to gain promotion. At this stage this was but theory; it would take time to train the necessary staff officers, and the British force that deployed to France on the outbreak of war was short of trained staff officers, and would remain so as expansion of the army ran far ahead of the outputs of the Staff College and wartime staff courses.

British military perception was changing too, and it was becoming evident that the British guarantee of Belgian neutrality might, in view of

the burgeoning power and ambition of Germany, require British intervention in Europe. If this were to occur, or indeed if Britain had to fight
anywhere on the scale of the South African War, expansion of the peacetime army would be necessary; and if conscription was unacceptable, as
it was, then reserves would have to be put on a proper footing.

Britain's immediate reserves consisted of men who had served in the
regular army and who retained a commitment for recall in war. Additionally there were Volunteer units raised during the various invasion scares
of the nineteenth century, Yeomanry (cavalry, with men providing their
own horses) and the remnants of the Militia, a hangover from the
Napoleonic Wars but with the compulsory element long in abeyance. All
were subject to a variety of rules and regulations and manifested a wide
disparity in standards of military effectiveness. The Volunteers, Yeomanry
and Militia could not be forced to serve outside the United Kingdom, and
the individual reserves could not be embodied short of general war.

In 1908 a fundamental reorganisation of the reserves took place.
Lifetime enlistment into the regular army had already been replaced by
enlistment for a specific period, part to be spent with the colours (that is
in the regular army) and the remainder on the reserve. Now the old Militia
became the Special Reserve, formed into units but with the role of providing individual reinforcements to the regular army; and the Volunteers
and Yeomanry became the Territorial Force, intended to mirror the regular
army in organisation and equipment and formed into divisions commanded
by regular officers, but available only as home defence unless its members
had signed for general service. By 1914 only five complete units – three
battalions of infantry, one cavalry regiment and a Royal Engineers company
– had signed.

The need to provide officers for war was not neglected, and universities
that already had Volunteer Corps found these converted into the Officer
Training Corps, and other universities were encouraged to set them up.
The same conversion applied to those schools that had Volunteer units,
the forerunners of today's Combined Cadet Force.[13] The quid pro quo for
the universities and schools was the right to nominate a number of boys
for Sandhurst without further examination.

By 1914 the British regular army had eighty-four infantry battalions at home and seventy-three abroad. The spearhead of the home forces was the Expeditionary Force, available for immediate deployment in the event of a major war. It consisted of six divisions and a cavalry division. Each division was commanded by a major-general and had three brigades, each commanded by a brigadier general.[14] A brigade consisted of four infantry battalions, each commanded by a lieutenant colonel. As divisional troops, in support of the whole formation, were a squadron of horsed cavalry, the divisional artillery, a company of engineers, a signals company (then also part of the Royal Engineers), a supply and transport company of the Army Service Corps, and a field ambulance. This last was not, as its name might suggest, a solitary vehicle with a red cross on its sides, but a medical unit responsible for first-line medical attention and the evacuation of casualties. The divisional artillery consisted of fifty-four eighteen-pounders (the recently introduced standard British field gun), eighteen 4.5-inch howitzers and four sixty-pounders. Altogether, once the division had received its individual reservists, its war establishment was 18,000 all ranks, of which 12,000 were infantry and 4,000 artillerymen. Each infantry battalion had two Maxim medium machine guns.

The cavalry division had four brigades, each with three regiments of horsed cavalry. It too had its own engineers, signallers and administrative and medical support, and twenty thirteen-pounder guns of the Royal Horse Artillery (smaller and lighter than the infantry divisional guns because they had to move at the same speed as the cavalry). Its war establishment was 9,000 men and 10,000 horses. Each cavalry regiment had two medium machine guns of the French Hotchkiss type, as it was lighter than the Maxim.

It was intended that, should the Expeditionary Force deploy, it would be commanded directly by a General Headquarters, the staff for which existed in Aldershot. Each division had its own staff but, as an economy measure, only two of the projected six staff officers were actually provided in peace.[15]

The combat-arm units of the Territorial Force were now organised into fourteen divisions, although a worrying factor was that they were mostly under strength. While they mirrored regular units as closely as possible, their artillery was largely obsolescent, consisting of converted fifteen-pounders, five-inch howitzers from the South African War and 4.7-inch guns. The old Garrison Artillery Militia was re-formed into ammunition supply columns, to ensure rapid resupply of the greater quantities of ammunition needed by modern guns, and by 1912 there were forty-two of these in existence, which could expand to forty-eight in time of war. With training carried out at weekends and at an annual camp, the Territorial Force was not immediately ready for war in 1914, and planning was based on the assumption that its divisions would be ready for deployment six months after war broke out, and then only to relieve regular units in the United Kingdom, unless its members agreed to overseas service.

Given that the British army, like all armies, was almost entirely horse-drawn, large numbers of horses would be needed on mobilisation, and a national census of horses was carried out and the necessary legislation enacted to requisition them for war. Developments in technology were not neglected, and while there were few of the new-fangled and as yet unreliable motor vehicles on peacetime equipment tables, a government subsidy scheme was devised which provided assistance towards the purchase of private vehicles, built to military specifications, that could be requisitioned in wartime, and measures to provide each division of the Expeditionary Force with an entirely lorry-borne supply column were well in hand. The British were generally ahead of European armies in the development of military aviation, although methods of artillery fire control using aircraft lagged behind those of the Germans.

British army training at home was based on an annual cycle. The winter was spent in individual training: weapon-handling, shooting, specialist weapon cadres, route marching, map-reading and signals. In the spring the army moved on to sub-unit training by companies and squadrons, followed by unit training by battalions and regiments. Brigade training occupied the summer, and divisional and army manoeuvres were carried out in the autumn.

On the face of it, the Expeditionary Force was a balanced, well-equipped and well-trained organisation; but there were problems. It could not expand with anything like the speed of the European armies with their huge reserves of manpower provided by conscription. Being all-volunteer, the British army had to take its recruits where and when it could find them, and they trickled in to units in dribs and drabs throughout the year. Unit cohesion was not helped by large drafts departing for India during the trooping season, and there was a constant drain of high quality instructors to the Territorial Force and to depots. In addition the army was seriously deficient in artillery ammunition, particularly high-explosive shells (although to be fair, experience in South Africa had suggested that the majority of artillery shells should be shrapnel); it had no trench mortars (trench warfare was not expected to be a major part of any future war); and while there was a British army hand grenade, each one costing £1 1s. 3d., it was unsuitable for use in confined areas. The most striking deficiency was in those items needed for trench warfare, but again, at this stage there was no indication that the coming war would largely be one of siege operations. There had been some discussions (kept highly secret) between the British military and their counterparts in Belgium (from 1906) and France (from 1911) as to how the British might cooperate in the event of involvement in Europe, but there was no commitment, and this was not the only war for which the Expeditionary Force had to prepare. It might have to fight anywhere: on the borders of India, in Egypt, in the Middle East or in Africa, and commanders and trainers had to keep all options open. The army was specifically forbidden to base field exercises on a German enemy, for Germany was still officially a friendly power.

All in all, despite its problems, the Expeditionary Force, renamed the British Expeditionary Force or BEF when it did deploy to Europe in 1914, was probably the best-trained and best-equipped army this nation has ever sent abroad; but it was pitifully small. When war broke out and the German navy enquired whether it should interfere with British shipping conveying the army to France, the attitude of the German supreme headquarters was that the English might as well be allowed to come across and take part: it would be convenient to get them out of the way early on.

Mobilisation of the British army was necessarily later than that of the French, but on 7, 8 and 9 August the BEF crossed to France and began to concentrate on the left of the French armies in the area of Maubeuge, Le Cateau and Hirson. Although the planned Expeditionary Force consisted of six infantry divisions, only four actually went in the first instance. Field Marshal Lord Kitchener, first soldier of the empire and appointed

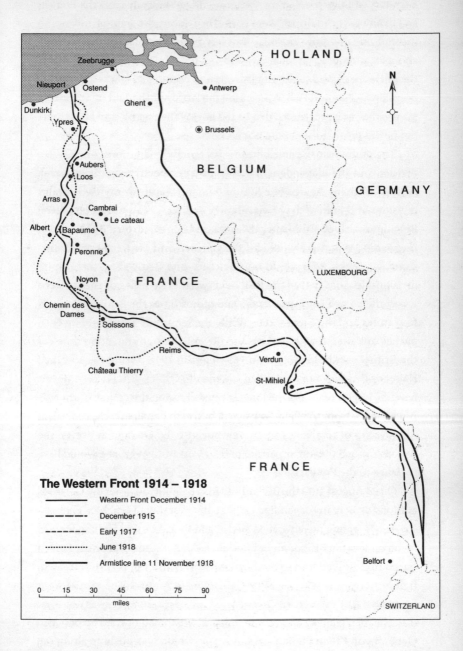

HOLLAND

Zeebrugge

Nieuport
Ostend
● Antwerp

Dunkirk
Ghent ●

Ypres
◉ Brussels

BELGIUM

●Aubers
Loos

GERMANY

Arras
Cambrai
● Le cateau

Albert ●Bapaume

Peronne

LUXEMBOURG

Noyon
FRANCE

Chemin des
Dames
Soissons

Reims
Verdun

Château Thierry
St-Mihiel

FRANCE

The Western Front 1914 – 1918

—————— Western Front December 1914

– – – – – December 1915

– – – – – – Early 1917

· · · · · · · · · June 1918

—————— Armistice line 11 November 1918

Belfort ●

0   15   30   45   60   75   90

miles

SWITZERLAND

Secretary of State for War on 6 August, did not entirely trust the French, and in any case the British were concerned about the state of Ireland, so most of one division – the 6th – was left there. There was some concern about an attempted German invasion and the 4th Division and the rest of the 6th were moved to the English coast to counter it. It was an unlikely possibility – Admiral Fisher, repeating the words of the Earl of St Vincent in an earlier war, proclaimed that he did not say the enemy could not come, but he did say that they could not come by sea.

To put the British contribution – four infantry divisions, one cavalry division and an independent brigade – into perspective, on the outbreak of war Germany fielded one hundred infantry and twenty-two cavalry divisions and France sixty-two infantry and ten cavalry divisions. Even Belgium managed six infantry divisions and one of cavalry. By the end of the war in 1918, there would be 240 German and over 200 French divisions, while the BEF would number fifty-one British and ten empire divisions. In August 1914 the BEF held twenty-five miles of the Western Front, the French 300 miles. At the end of hostilities the British held sixty-four miles and the French 260. While the length of front held by each participant altered with the ebb and flow of the fighting, at no time did the British ever hold more than 123 miles (in 1918 during the so-called Kaiser's offensive), nor the French less than 202 miles. Britain did however have the largest navy and the longest purse. During the course of the war Britain made loans totalling almost £1.5 billion to her allies,[16] the equivalent of one-sixth of total government revenue in 1999. On land, however, she was very much the junior partner and, at least until 1917, she would have to dance to the French tune.

On 23 August 1914 the BEF moved into Belgium and met the Germans at Mons or Bergen (depending on whether you are a French or Flemish-speaker). Fighting there went on all day, and Field Marshal Sir John French, commanding the BEF, thought he could hold. A withdrawal by the French on his right forced him to conform, however, and the British retreated, fighting a rearguard action at Le Cateau on 26 August. The retreat went on and the BEF crossed the River Marne on 3 September. It was now that the Schlieffen plan began to come unstuck. A gap had opened up between General von Kluck's First German Army, which was pushing along the

Channel coast at the extreme right of the plan's wheeling movement, and its neighbour, von Bülow's Second Army. General Joffre, commanding the French army, saw an opportunity and pounced into the gap, severely mauling von Bülow. Von Kluck now had little option but to come to the aid of his fellow army commander, and instead of passing to the west of Paris, as the plan demanded, had to turn in east of Paris, thus exposing the German right flank. The Germans were forced back forty miles to the River Aisne, where they went on the defensive.

Now began what was termed 'the race to the sea'. It was not, of course, a race, but successive attempts by Germans and Allies to turn the other's flank, and each army moved further and further north to achieve it. Neither did, and the race, if race it was, was won by the Allies (just) when they reached the coast at Nieuwpoort, south-west of Ostend, in the first week of October. This was the end of mobile war on the Western Front, the war for which all armies had trained and which all expected. From now on operations developed into what was effectively siege warfare, with the Germans digging in on someone else's territory, while the rightful owners attempted to expel them.

The year 1915 was a learning phase, when both sides adjusted to trench warfare and sought ways of breaking out of it. This necessitated offensives by the Allies (it was their land that was occupied) with British offensives at Neuve-Chapelle in March and Aubers Ridge in May, far larger French attacks in Champagne, and a joint effort at Loos in September. The Germans experimented with the use of gas, in the Franco-British Ypres sector in April, and the Allies retaliated at Loos. Simultaneously the British Territorial Force was arriving at the front, and the first of the New Army divisions were deployed. Away from Europe the joint landings at Gallipoli, well conceived but flawed in execution, were turning to failure.

Nineteen sixteen saw major attempts by the Allies to break the German line, with the joint Somme offensive much affected by a major German attack at Verdun in the French sector. The British New Armies were now fully employed, tanks made their first appearance and conscription was introduced in the UK. The following year rendered the bulk of the French army temporarily unavailable for anything other than static defence after its mutinies in June, and the British fought at Passchendaele perforce alone.

America entered the war on the Allied side and US troops began to arrive in France in large numbers. The final year of the war, 1918, saw a major German offensive in March, prompted by losses at Passchendaele and the imminent threat of American action. This offensive failed: it pushed the French and British back but never split them, and it ran out of steam in the summer. Now the Allies, led by the British, went onto the offensive once more, launching the final advance that was to drive the German army back and lead not to unconditional surrender, but to an armistice and victory for the Allies. The threat of German militarism had been removed, at least for a further generation, the lost French territories were regained and Belgium was once more secure. This was a just war, and a necessary war. The British expenditure in lives and in treasure was great, but there was no alternative, and the price paid, in this author's respectful submission, was worth that outcome.

NOTES

1 The title was German Emperor rather than Emperor of Germany, in order to show that there were other German monarchs, but this was semantics. By 1914 Wilhelm II and his acolytes decided policy for the whole empire.

2 Strictly speaking, the Emperor could declare a defensive war on his sole authority; he had to have the approval of the Bundesrat to declare an aggressive war. In practice it made no difference.

3 This seems to have been a Prussian trait: Frederick the Great was at one time sentenced to death (and subsequently reprieved) by his own father.

4 *The Treaty of Peace between the Allied and Associated Powers and Germany*, signed at Versailles, 28 June 1919, HMSO, London.

5 The USA was an Associated Power, not an Ally. The difference is not entirely semantic, being imposed because the American President Woodrow Wilson wished to appear as an honest broker, distanced from French and British war aims despite having entered the war on the Allied side.

6 Ibid., Clause 227.

7 Fritz Fischer, *Germany's Aims in the First World War*, Chatto and Windus, London, 1967.

8 General Erich von Ludendorff (trans. F. A. Holt, OBE), *The General Staff and Its Problems*, Hutchinson, London, 1920.

9 Ibid.

10 He was recalled to replace Prince Louis of Battenberg, hounded out of office by an upsurge of anti-German public opinion. Battenberg, son of the Grand Duke of Hesse-Darmstadt, had been in the Royal Navy since he was a boy and became First Sea Lord in 1912. There is no evidence whatsoever that he was ever anything but a loyal officer of the British Navy. The family name was changed to Mountbatten in 1917, and his son was Lord Louis

Mountbatten, who became First Sea Lord and subsequently the first Chief of Defence Staff.

11 The full text of the note is in Bernadotte E. Schmidt, *The Coming of the War 1914*, 2 vols., New York, 1930.

12 It would have been abolished much earlier, but the Treasury was unwilling to find the money to compensate those officers who had already paid for their commissions, or to fund the pensions that would have to be paid now that retiring officers could not raise capital by 'selling out'. The system was not all bad – see my *Wellington – A Military Life*, Hambledon & London, London, 2001.

13 Eton College had sent a volunteer contingent to the Boer War, and today is the only CCF to have a battle honour.

14 Today the rank is brigadier, an economy measure introduced in 1921. If brigade commanders were no longer generals then they were not entitled to certain allowances admissible for all generals. The brigadiers carried on doing exactly the same job, with rather less pay and fewer perks. The equivalent ranks today in the (less parsimonious) American and French armies are brigadier general and *général de brigade*.

15 Today's division, with a war establishment of around 15,000 men, is provided with thirty-one staff officers in peace, augmented from the TA watchkeepers' pool in war.

16 To Russia £568 million, to France £425 million, to Italy £345 million and to others £127 million. Much of this was in turn raised by Britain on the American money market. Britain had to repay eventually, but she failed to recover much of the Russian loan and some others also defaulted. The situation led to suspicion in America that the financial and industrial lobby were in favour of American entry into the war on the Allied side to ensure that the loans were repaid.

2

THE LOST GENERATION

The British perception of the Great War is of seemingly endless lists of dead and wounded soldiers, many maimed for life. The war, it has been claimed, led to the loss of the very men who could have prevented the inter-war decline of Britain as a world power, and who would have provided the national leadership missing for much of the rest of the twentieth century. Every town and village has its war memorial, and the names of the dead are seen as evidence of the sacrifice of a whole generation to war.

By 1914 Britain had long ceased to involve herself in large-scale military adventures in Europe. She was a naval power, and while the sinking of a ship of the line with all hands might cost 600 lives, it did not happen very often, and when it did those who lost their lives were professional sailors: drowning was an occupational hazard. In the twenty-two years of war against Revolutionary and Napoleonic France the major British effort on land was in the Iberian Peninsula, where Wellington's army was never more than 100,000 strong, all volunteers who effectively enlisted for life. Total British deaths there were around 40,000. The climactic Battle of Waterloo produced twenty-eight per cent British casualties, but this amounted to only 1,400 British dead. Britain's involvement in the Crimean War, 1854-6, led to the death of over 20,000 British soldiers, four-fifths from disease rather from than Russian bullets. Prior to 1914 the largest number of troops ever sent abroad by Britain was 450,000 to the South African War, 1899–1902; 22,000 of them died, two-thirds from disease.

In contrast the European powers were well accustomed to the losses of war. The combined armies of continental Europe suffered well over three million dead between 1793 and 1815. The Battle of Austerlitz on 2 December 1805 accounted for 4,000 French and 7,000 Russian dead; at Wagram on 5–6 July 1809 the French lost 8,300 killed and the Austrians nearly 6,000; Borodino on 7 September 1812 cost nearly 7,000 French and 10,000 Russian lives. In the Crimea the combined Russian, French and Turkish death toll was 765,000.

Rather than following the European pattern of huge armies raised by conscription, the British employed a small all-volunteer force that could be inserted, supported and supplied by the Royal Navy, and that could as easily be removed should the situation demand.

The British were not accustomed to a heavy butcher's bill. The number of British dead in the Great War, and particularly that on the Western Front, came as a rude shock, for their experience had done nothing to prepare them for it. The table below shows the size of the armies deployed by Britain in her wars of the previous 120 years, those armies

Table 1

War	Dates	UK population	Average strength of army	Army as percentage of the population	Soldiers died	Percentage of population died
French Revolutionary and Napoleonic	1793-1815	17 million	198,587	1.17	60,000	0.35
Crimean	1854-6	28 million	97,864	0.35	20,707	0.07
South African	1899-1902	42 million	208,226	0.5	22,000	0.05

as a percentage of the population, and the percentage of the British population killed.[1]

In the past, the death of soldiers had little impact on the population at large. Now, for the first time in history, the British would wage a war with mass armies deployed against the main enemy for the entire war. It is hardly surprising that the scale of casualties seemed – and by British standards was – horrendous. Britain mobilised around eight million men.

Most of these went to the army, which was, and remains, a manpower-intensive organisation. The Royal Navy, on the other hand, was a technical service; there it was ships that mattered, and a dreadnought of 1914, with ten twelve-inch guns, carried the firepower of six army divisions'-worth of artillery but needed only one twenty-third of the number of men to operate it.[2] In the greatest sea battle of the war, at Jutland in 1916, in which 265 warships took part, combined casualties were fewer than 10,000, of whom around 3,500 were killed. Of the total British deaths in the Great War, only 32,208, or 4.6 per cent, were in the Royal Navy.

Putting the British army deaths for the Great War in the same format as those for previous wars, shown in Table 1 above, we find:

Table 2

War	Dates	UK population	Average strength of army	Army as percentage of the population	Soldiers died	Percentage of population died (including RN and RAF)
First World War	1914-18	45.75 million	3,281,932	7.17	670,202	1.53

The Great War deaths impressed the British far more than had those in any previous conflict, not only because they were thirty-two times greater in absolute numbers than those of the last war the British had fought, (against the Boers), but also because a far greater proportion of the population than ever before was under arms. The deaths were not spread evenly across the population, but occurred mainly in males of military age, those who were between nineteen and thirty-four during the conflict. While there were many deaths of men over the age of thirty-four, and many below nineteen who committed the offence of false enlistment by lying about their age, it was this portion of the population that bore the brunt of the military deaths. As an aside, a mathematical exercise may enable us to arrive at some comparison of the impact of the death rates in British wars on the British armies themselves. If the military deaths in each war are assumed to have been spread evenly over the period of hostilities – which of course they were not – and those casualties are compared to the average strength of the army during the war, we find that the percentage of deaths was just over one per cent during the twenty-two years of the wars against France, 3.5 per cent for the South African War and just over five per cent for the Great War. For the Crimea the figure is almost eleven per cent, which would indicate that for the man on the ground the Crimean War was worse by a factor of two than the Great War.

Enormous though they seem, compared to ally and enemy the British casualties of the Great War were far from excessive – a relative term, of course. One in sixty-five of the British population was killed, one in twenty-eight of the French. In Britain one in every twelve men mobilised was killed; in France one in every six. With the exception of some of the relatively small number of reservists with a liability to reinforce the regular army, Britain mobilised few men over thirty until the last two years of the war. France, with far more men in the population who had received military training, mobilised over three million men who were over thirty when war broke out, and fourteen per cent of them were killed. In addition she conscripted 230,000 men who were under eighteen when the war ended, and 3,600, or 1.6 per cent, of those were killed. Nearly 60,000 Frenchmen aged forty-five when war broke out were mobilised during it. The highest death rate for the French was amongst those born in 1896, who were aged eighteen in 1914: 292,000 were mobilised, mostly in 1914, and twenty-nine per cent of them were killed.

Germany, with a population of 60,300,000 in 1914 and her efficient system of universal conscription, mobilised 13,250,000 men during the course of the war. Nearly fifteen per cent of these were killed, one in thirty-one of the population, one in every seven mobilised. Table 3 below illustrates the comparative cost in lives to the three major western combatants.[3]

Table 3 Country	Population in 1914)	Men mobilised	Men killed (all theatres, all services)	Percentage of men mobilised killed	Percentage of population killed
France	39,000,000	8,500,000	1,391,000	16.4	3.7
United Kingdom	45,750,000	8,375,000	702,410	8.4	1.53
Germany	60,300,000	13,250,000	1,950,000	14.7	3.23

France, with a population six and a half million less than that of the United Kingdom, mobilised more men and suffered nearly twice as many deaths. The demographic effect on France was enormous, particularly in the removal of a large number of young men of breeding age. It led to an acceleration in the decline of an already ageing population, and influenced the course of French politics and military strategy for a generation. Even in the France of today, the death toll of the Great War is manifest in the plethora of war memorials with long lists of men *Morts pour la France*. Every village has one, and the same names occur over and over again, men of successive generations of the same families who died for Napoleon, for Bazaine or MacMahon in 1870, and for Joffre, Nivelle, Pétain and Foch in 1914–18.

The demographic effects on the United Kingdom were far less, as a glance at the population counted by the ten-yearly censuses shows:[4]

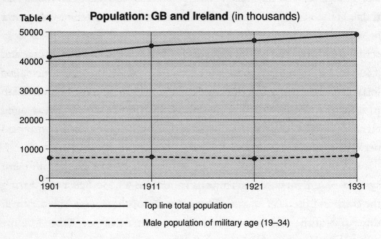

Table 4   **Population: GB and Ireland** (in thousands)

————— Top line total population

------------- Male population of military age (19–34)

The casual observer would be forgiven for failing to notice that between the census of 1911 and that of 1921 the greatest bloodletting in British military history took place. Despite the war deaths the overall male population between 1911 and 1921 actually rose, admittedly at a slightly lower rate than during the previous ten-year period, but at about the same rate as between 1921 and 1931.

A similar exercise may be narrowed down to males of military age, that is those between the ages of fifteen and thirty-four in 1911, all of whom would have been of an age to fight at some time in the war. These same men would have been aged from twenty-five to forty-four at the 1921 census. This group shows a decline of fourteen per cent between 1911 and

1921, but the reduction includes deaths other than those attributable to the war, and net emigration. Examined on the same basis, the period from 1901 to 1911 shows a decline in the equivalent group of eight per cent, and the period from 1921 to 1931 of six per cent. The point is that of all those counted in 1911 and who were of military age between 1914 and 1918, eighty-six per cent of them were still there when they were counted again in 1921. Even if the reduction was entirely due to the war, which it was not, it is far from the loss of a generation.

If the overall population loss in the war was rapidly replaced, which the census figures indicate, then we should examine the losses sustained by that portion of British society that would have been expected to provide the political, commercial, academic and military leadership of the nation after the war. While there were many who rose from humble beginnings to achieve greatness, the largest source of leaders and opinion-formers, after the war as before and during it, was the public schools. At this point readers who, in the words of Cecil Rhodes, failed to win the lottery of life by being born British, should note that British public schools are actually private. They are separate from the state education system, fee-paying and mainly boarding. Then as now, pupils gained entry by passing an examination set and marked by the school. The public schools' ethos was based on the production of a governing class to run nation and empire. During the Great War, and before it, the output of the public schools was a natural source of officers.[5]

Eton College, founded by King Henry VI in 1440, had long been seen as an institution for the nurturing of cabinet ministers, colonial governors and, it has to be admitted, a fair few lounge lizards. Boys who wanted to learn, or could be forced into learning, received an excellent education and contacts that ensured gainful and influential employment. Those who were rich enough not to have to bother at least acquired some manners, and the ability to mix in society. When war came, Old Etonians answered the call. In total 5,650 served, almost all as officers, and 1,157 were killed, a ratio of one in five.[6] Between them they won thirteen Victoria Crosses, the British Empire's highest award for gallantry. Tonbridge School, smaller and slightly less grand than Eton, sent 2,225 of its old boys to the war. They may have collected only one VC, but 415 were killed, the same ratio as that of Eton.[7] Sedbergh School, in Cumbria, sent 1,250 men to the war and 251 were killed, again a ratio of one in every five.[8] St Lawrence College, in Thanet, sent around 650 ex-pupils to the war and 132, or one in five, were killed.[9] The figures for other public schools are similar. Apart from a few schools, such as Pangbourne, which had a long tradition of providing naval officers, the vast majority of these public schoolboys went to the army. Eton sent only 163 to the Royal Navy, where the death rate was trivial in comparison. The Irish gentry fared only slightly better. The Royal School Armagh, a typical Irish public school, sent 235 of its old boys to fight, and forty-three were killed, a ratio of one in six.[10] This may be explained by there being no conscription in Ireland, or perhaps they were just luckier than most.

Oxford and Cambridge, the premier universities in the land, had a similar strike rate to those of the public schools. Seven thousand seven hundred and forty-five Oxford graduates served and 1,542, or one in five, were killed, while Cambridge graduates provided 9,926 men for the armed services, with 2,210, or just over one in five, killed.[11] Even so, eighty per cent came back.

Overall, one in every seven British army officers was killed in the Great War, and one in every eight other ranks, so it would seem that the products of public schools and universities were killed in a rather higher proportion than officers and men from other sources. It is of course true that those who were killed, both officers (who by definition were leaders) and other ranks, were the physically fittest and, at least before conscription, the most strongly motivated sections of the male population. Whether the removal of one in seven of the obvious potential leaders really did lead to a dearth of national direction after the war is doubtful; enough returned unscathed to ensure that life went on.

Not all deaths were caused by enemy action. Men contracted diseases, suffered from heart attacks, were run over by vehicles or suffocated by carbon monoxide produced by heaters, drowned while swimming, caught food poisoning in civilian cafés, and died when home on leave. Ten per cent of British deaths in the Great War were from causes other than enemy action, but the figure varied widely by theatre. Provided one could avoid German bullets and shells, the Western Front was the healthiest place to be, as only nine per cent of deaths were attributable to causes other than the enemy.[12] In Salonika, on the other hand, of the 9,717 British deaths, fifty-five per cent were from disease and accidents. A comparison, by theatre, of deaths caused otherwise than by the enemy is shown below:

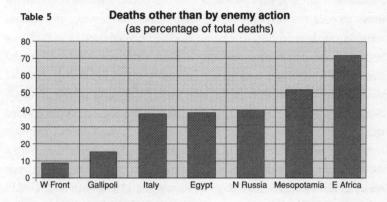

Table 5 — **Deaths other than by enemy action** (as percentage of total deaths)

The epidemic of influenza that spread across the world in 1918 and 1919 affected the armies too. It first made its appearance in America in 1917, but the suspicion that it was the American army, arriving on the Western Front from June 1917 onwards, that imported the disease to Europe is probably unfounded. The first recorded outbreak of this strain of influenza in Europe was in Spain in May 1918. What became known as 'Spanish flu' spread into France, Italy and Germany. It cut swathes through India, and wherever it appeared it seemed to attack those between twenty-five and forty, and the physically fitter specimens at that. On the Western Front there were local outbreaks in April and May 1918, before it subsided to reappear in September. Between 12 October 1918, when the British army made influenza a notifiable disease, and the end of the war in November, there were 45,000 flu admissions to casualty clearing stations, of which 2,584, or six per cent, died. By the end of the year, with the army at peace, there had been a further 1,883 flu deaths, and in 1919, from 1 January to 31 March, 1,088. Other armies were affected too, but the German civilian population, not far above starvation level as a result of the British blockade which continued into 1919 until Germany signed the Armistice, probably suffered more than anyone. Estimates as to how many died from the influenza epidemic worldwide vary greatly. It is often said that it killed more people than the war did, but we shall probably never know.

Up to this point, when asking whether Britain really did lose a generation to the war, we have only considered deaths. Death is definite and quantifiable. A man who dies or is killed has made his contribution; his input to society ceases for ever. Deaths in the belligerent armies and nations can be compared with a reasonable accuracy. Men who are wounded but survive are more difficult to quantify, because not all armies classified their wounded and sick in the same way. In the British army, for example, men posted as 'missing' were included in daily casualty returns. These men might be missing because they had been taken prisoner, killed out of sight of their comrades, blown to pieces, buried under collapsing trenches or simply lost. Many of the missing turned up, hours or days later, or were officially declared by the German government as having been taken prisoner. The British records should then have been amended in hindsight, but this did not always happen. A British soldier who sustained a minor wound that did not preclude him from duty was not recorded as a casualty; in the American army all wounds, however minor, were recorded. The German army reported casualties at much greater intervals than the British, by which time their 'missing' had been accounted for. As the war went on the German army began to misreport their casualties, in order not to hand information to the enemy, and at one stage announced that ninety per cent of all men wounded were returned to duty – a ridiculous claim. A wound could be anything from a cut sustained in opening a tin of jam to a traumatic injury requiring amputation, and the injuries to a man wounded more than once on different occasions were returned as separate casualties.

As for the impact on society after the war, a man who recovered from a wound and retained all his faculties would, in general, be perfectly capable of holding down employment and making his contribution to national life. A man missing an arm or a leg might or might not be capable of carrying on, and a man so badly wounded that he could never lead a normal life would be a net drain on society. The sight of maimed and disfigured men returned from the war would have had an effect on public morale, and on public perception of the war, but it is impossible at this distance to assess the psychological effects of their experiences on the mass of the returned soldiers themselves.

It is probable that the war produced fewer traumas than similar experiences would today. On 21 December 1988 a Pan American Airlines Boeing 747 exploded in mid-air over Lockerbie in Scotland, killing all 270 passengers and crew. Bodies and bits of bodies were strewn over a wide area, and a battalion of British infantry was deployed for a period of some weeks to scour the area and recover body parts, mostly mangled and partly putrefied. The experience was such that many of the young soldiers had to be given counselling, and some had recurrent nightmares and anxiety attacks for months afterwards. Today's youth have little or no experience of death. Bodies are rarely seen, and even the practice of viewing a family member in his or her coffin, tastefully laid out by a professional undertaker, is rare. It is now illegal to kill a pig (or a cow, sheep or goat) for human consumption, even one's own, other than in a properly equipped and licensed abattoir. Blood and guts, human or animal, are alien to today's Britons and disturbing when encountered. This was not the case earlier in the century when family members would assist in the preparation of a body for burial and it was common practice to kill and butcher one's own pig, chicken or sheep. Men and women affected by rickets, or with clubbed feet, harelips or hunchbacks, were a common sight in the first half of the twentieth century, and cripples did not arouse the pity or revulsion that they would today when such conditions have been all but eliminated.

British army statistics compiled by the medical services show that 6,218,540 non-fatal casualties were recorded throughout the war, in all theatres. Of these, sixty-five per cent were classified as 'non-battle casualties', that is those caused by other than enemy action. On the Western Front fifty-seven per cent of non-fatal casualties were unrelated to enemy action.

One way in which non-fatal casualties might be quantified as to their effect on the nation and on the generation that fought the war is to examine the number of pensions paid after the war to men who were incapacitated by their wounds. While it might be argued that a man who had been a marathon runner before the war and now was minus a leg could become a lawyer instead, and thus still make a contribution, it is fair to say that the overwhelming majority of men receiving a war disablement pension were to a greater or lesser extent incapable of performing as they might otherwise have done, and to have been affected by the war. Medical boards began to sit immediately after the war to decide who should qualify for a war disablement pension. The number awarded each year increased, as men came forward or as wounds initially thought to have been cured flared up again. In 1929 the number of men in receipt of pensions reached its peak, and then began to decline as men recovered entirely or began to die off through natural causes.

The British government made monetary awards, either as lump sums or as pensions, to 735,487 men. Many of these awards were for non-battle casualties, but if the man was serving at the time he contracted the disease or suffered the accident, it was considered to be attributable to war service. In all there were 308,622 awards for the effects of wounds, including amputations, and 426,865 for the effects of diseases. Major disabilities for which pensions or gratuities were paid are shown in Table 6:

Table 6

Cause of disablement	Number of awards made	Percentage of the total number awarded
Wounds not involving amputation	278,535	38
Mental illness (ranging from nervous disorder to madness)	67,840	9
Heart problems	48,368	7
Malaria	43,572	6
Tuberculosis	34,884	5
Amputation	33,718	5
Rheumatism	28,992	4
Injury by gas	8,371	1
Blindness	923	0.12

While some of the heart problems and rheumatism might well have arisen anyway, and tuberculosis was present in the British population in or out of uniform, the total of those who died in the war plus those accepted as having been left physically or mentally disabled by it comes to 1,437,897. In the 1930s the British Legion, the ex-servicemen's organisation founded by Field Marshal Earl Haig after the war, organised a campaign to obtain pensions or lump-sum awards for men initially not considered to be eligible, but upon whom the effects of war service surfaced after the government's medical boards had ceased to sit. The British Legion claimed that 100,000 men were so affected. Adding this to our figure of men killed or affected by the war, we arrive at a figure of three per cent of the total population, or nineteen per cent of the males of military age.

What cannot, of course, be ignored is what might be termed the 'ripple effect' that casualties may have had upon subsequent generations. The decline of family fortunes due to the death or incapacitation of the bread-winner; the unborn child who might have become Prime Minister (or a serial murderer); the elimination of an entire male branch of a family; all these must have had an influence on the future of the nation, but the war was imposed upon the population, and what might have been is simply not quantifiable.

In absolute numbers, as a proportion of the population as a whole, and as a proportion of those who fought, the British lost fewer men and had fewer men medically affected as a result of war than had either her chief ally or her main enemy. The British, however, unlike other partici-pants, had no conception of the casualties likely to be caused by war on the European scale. All that said, there was a further major factor that influenced the British perception, then and now, of the loss of a genera-tion. That factor was the way in which the British raised the manpower to fight this war.

By the end of 1914 the BEF had fought on the Mons canal, retreated 200 miles to the Marne, advanced to the Aisne, moved north and fought the First Battle of Ypres. It was still very largely an all-regular army. The first Territorial Force battalion to cross to France did so in September, and by the end of 1914 twenty-three Territorial Force battalions had arrived in theatre, but none joined front-line brigades before November. In August 1914 the BEF had 1,382 men killed; in September 2,717; in October 5,640 regulars and eighteen Territorials. November's bill was 4,656 regulars and thirty-six Territorials, and that of December 2,361 and 105 respectively. In total the BEF deaths for 1914 numbered 16,915, of which 1,230, or just over seven per cent, were officers. Although in the same period 450,000 French soldiers were killed, the tiny British army could not possibly sustain the casualty rate of 1914. This had been obvious to Lord Kitchener very early on, but there was no instant solution. The individual reservists had already been embodied, the two divisions retained in England at the outbreak of war were now present with the BEF, but the bulk of the Territorial Force, with its units intended for home defence and its members not liable to serve overseas unless they volunteered (which virtually all did) was not yet ready to be deployed. There was, of course, the empire. As the law stood in 1914 a declaration of war by Britain automatically applied to the Dominions and colonies, whether they liked it or not, although the Dominion authorities had the right to decide where their troops would be employed. Apart from South Africa, where two former Boer generals led a revolt, promptly put down by two other former Boer generals, the Dominions greeted the declaration of war with enthusiasm, and all assured the mother country that they would supply troops. The difficulty was that in 1914 there were not very many troops to be had. The Canadian and Australian regular armies totalled just 3,000 men each, that of New Zealand 600. These countries did have numbers of men who had received some military training through the local militias, and they would in time make a very valuable contribution to the BEF, but that time was not yet. The only source of more trained regular manpower in 1914 was the Indian army, and two Indian infantry divisions and a cavalry brigade (swiftly expanded to two cavalry divisions) began to arrive in Marseille in September 1914. They arrived in Belgium just in time and in just sufficient strength to block the gaps in a very stretched British line and prevent the Germans from breaking through to the Channel ports.[13]

When war broke out it was clear to Lord Kitchener, although to very few others, that this would not be a short war of manoeuvre, over in a few months. He thought it would last three years and that the British army would need a million men. In the event it lasted four and a quarter years and Britain needed nearly eight and a half million, but even if Kitchener's initial thoughts had been right, the combination of the regular army, individual reservists, the Territorial Force, the Indian army and the Dominions was not going to produce a million men for the Western Front. More soldiers had to be found and they had to be found quickly. Conscription was still politically unacceptable and the men would have to be volunteers.

One option would have been to expand the Territorial Force: it already had a structure with officers, non-commissioned officers and men; it had been training part-time and had at least a rudimentary operational capability; it was already established and accepted around the country; it owned drill halls and had a system of management and administration based on county associations. Each company of the existing four-company battalions could have been the nucleus of a new battalion, which would have had some men who were trained, or at least partly trained, in every platoon. Kitchener decided against this option. He felt that the Territorial Force, which had its original *raison d'être* in home defence and could not be deployed abroad without volunteering, was not the best basis on which to raise the hundreds of new battalions that would be needed. He decided to raise a completely new regular army. It would be composed of men aged between nineteen and thirty who volunteered to enlist for three years or for the duration of the war, whichever was the longer. On 5 August 1914, the day before Kitchener took office, Parliament approved an increase in the establishment of the army by 500,000 men. The famous 'Your King and Country Need You' proclamation was issued on 11 August and recruiting offices were swamped.

The British army recruiting system was designed to process around 30,000 recruits a year. The job could be done in a leisurely fashion, and contracts for clothing, ammunition and equipment were based on that figure. Within ten days the first New Army, of 100,000 men known colloquially as Kitchener 1 or K1, had been enlisted, enough to produce six divisions and supporting units. By 28 August the army had a further hundred thousand – K2 – and in mid-September K3 was in being. It was one thing to find the men, quite another to provide officers and NCOs to command and train them. The rules were changed and discharged private soldiers up to the age of forty and ex-NCOs up to fifty were permitted to re-enlist. Regular officers were taken away from the Territorial Force and officers on leave from India were prevented from returning to the Indian army and attached to New Army units instead. University cadets were granted direct commissions, as were selected senior NCOs from the regular army. There were insufficient barracks to house all the new recruits, and despite emptying all the married quarters by sending the families home and using gymnasia, army schools and empty stables, there was still a shortage of accommodation. At one stage large numbers of men had to be billeted on the local population, something that had not been done since the eighteenth century. Public buildings were taken over, lines of tents were erected, and hutted camps were built. There was a shortage of everything from buttons to boots. Thread for saddlery could not be obtained because the only pre-war supplier was in Belgium, with his output now diverted to Prussian uhlans, and nobody could be found to supply enough khaki cloth to make uniforms. This last difficulty was resolved by buying up large quantities of blue serge from the GPO, and postmen went without uniforms so that soldiers could be clothed. At one stage a recruit who could turn up with his own boots and greatcoat and one suit of clothes was paid ten shillings for doing so.

At the same time the Territorial Force was encouraged to persuade all its members to sign for general service and to expand under the aegis of its county associations. Here it came into direct competition with the New Armies. Government was not yet ready to direct industry – business as usual was the cry – and as the War Office had priority, Territorial Force associations found it difficult to let contracts for clothing, while the removal of its regular officers and NCOs led to problems in training. It became obvious that the regular army recruiting organisation could not cope with the unprecedented rush of young men to the colours. A temporary brake had to be applied to recruiting, and so the physical standards were raised in September 1914; they were lowered again in November when some semblance of order had been restored.

As the regular army simply could not accommodate, clothe and administer all these New Army battalions, the raising of the fourth and fifth New Armies was privatised. Now local authorities, city and county councils, and indeed almost anyone who could form a committee for the purpose, took over the raising of new battalions. They were to recruit, accommodate, clothe and train, but not arm, the battalions in the first instance. The regular army provided such instructors and officers as it could, but these were few. There were hardly any fourth and fifth New Army battalions that were given more than three officers and twelve NCOs, if they were lucky. Few members of this cadre were drawn from the cream of the service. Many were brought out of retirement, some were recovering from wounds sustained at the front, and some were the officers of the Indian army prevented by Kitchener's orders from reporting back to their own battalions and regiments in India. This last measure caused great resentment, for Indian battalions only had eleven combatant British officers, compared to around thirty in a British battalion.

By the time some of the later raisings were carried out the supply of officers and NCOs with some knowledge of what had to be taught was running out. The 13th Battalion the York and Lancaster Regiment (First Barnsley Pals) was commanded by a local solicitor, with the temporary rank of lieutenant colonel. The second-in-command was an alderman of the city, and the adjutant a colliery manager. The company sergeant majors were all retired NCOs, none of whom had served since the Boer War[14] The few experienced men available for the 'pals' battalions could not possibly administer a battalion at home, nor command it in war, entirely alone. Finding officers and NCOs was a constant problem; the men were present, but a platoon of forty men needed an officer to command it, a sergeant to administer and discipline it and four corporals, each assisted by a lance corporal, to command the sections. A company needed a company commander, a company second-in-command, a company sergeant major and a quartermaster sergeant. Initially anyone with a university or grammar-school education was liable to find himself an officer, without any training at all. These men had at least the ability to read orders and to cope with administration. Eventually short officer-training courses of four weeks' duration were run at the Royal Military College Sandhurst. A foreman or chargehand would be a corporal, for he had experience of handling men. It was less difficult in the more technical arms. A man who was a qualified engineer in peace could do much the same job in the Royal Engineers, once he had learned something about man management and how the army did its business. In the infantry, on the other hand, the learning curve was very steep indeed.

The trainers did their best. Men drilled with staves instead of rifles, did small-arms training with Lee-Metford rifles left over from the Boer War and went all over the country on route marches, while artillerymen practised gun drills on lengths of steel piping.

It is sometimes asked why the army, then as now, spent so much time on close-order drill, perfecting the art of turning to the right, left and about,

marching up and down a parade square and performing complicated evo-
lutions that appear to be more relevant to facing Napoleon's Imperial
Guard at Waterloo than to taking on German machine guns. The answer
is that the difference between an armed rabble and an army is discipline.
Soldiers must be trained to react immediately and automatically when
under conditions of high stress, and when there may be no one to tell them
what to do. Contrary to popular opinion, the army did not, and does not,
attempt to stamp out all initiative and ability to think – indeed it prizes
those qualities in a soldier – but it does aim to give the man a rock to cling
to when all around is chaos. Not for nothing are basic tactical manoeuvres
known as battle drills: automatic reactions to certain happenings on the
battlefield, reactions that will occur regardless of the physical and psychological influences to which a man is subjected. The basis of that ability
to react instantly is drill: square-bashing is not a waste of time.

Until inspected by the War Office and found to be 'efficient', when
control passed to the army and the original mentors had their expenditure refunded, the raising, training and administration of the new units
remained with their sponsors. This led to the phenomenon of the 'pals'.
'Join together and serve together' was the guarantee, and men knew
that if they enlisted they would serve alongside their friends, their neighbours and their workmates, rather than being sent off with a lot of people
whom they did not know and with whom they might have little in
common. Employees of the cloth industry joined what was technically
the 21st Battalion the West Yorkshire Regiment, but which was always
known as the Wool Textile Pioneers; the University and Public Schools
Committee found 5,000 of their friends for the Public Schools Brigade,
four battalions of the Royal Fusiliers. The 13th Battalion the Cheshire
Regiment was raised by Lord Leverhulme, who made a personal appeal
to his employees at Port Sunlight. One thousand men responded. Sports
clubs, occupational groups, youth organisations all did their bit.

All this made for tremendous strengths: the men had shared interests,
spoke with the same accents, had the same friends, belonged to the same
clubs, used the same pubs, ate the same food, walked out with each other's
sisters, and were adamant that their battalion would be better than any
other. Once in action a reluctance to let their chums down, and the

consequences of misbehaviour being witnessed by those with whom they would have to live once the war was over, reinforced cohesiveness and bred a determination to 'stick it out' come what may. It also planted a further seed to grow into a myth. When a New Army 'pals' battalion did go into action its casualties – in any case larger than anyone had thought possible – were not distributed evenly across the country, but concentrated in small areas: a few streets, half a dozen villages, three or four factories, a specific sector of employment. The 'pals' were largely an urban phenomenon. Men in rural areas joined up too, but while they might end up in their county regiment they would not necessarily all be in the same battalion and therefore not all killed together if the battalion suffered heavily.

The Americans had long ago recognised that perception of casualties is far worse if the dead and maimed are concentrated in small areas, rather than being spread evenly across the country. After the American War of Independence, the new republic adopted the military system that it understood: that of the British. Regiments and battalions recruited as they had had done in the colonial era, territorially. The American Civil War, fought by Americans on both sides and with regiments raised from specific, often very small, areas, produced enormous casualties. The death toll was greater than in any American war before or since, but owing to its concentration the impact was even heavier. After the war the American army took a deliberate policy decision. Henceforth regular army regiments would contain men from all over the nation, and units of the militia (which became the National Guard) would be recruited statewide. It would not be until after the Great War that this lesson was brought home to the British army.

New Army infantry units became battalions of their local regiment, numbered after Territorial Force battalions of that regiment. While subtitles such as Accrington Pals, Post Office Rifles, Hull Sportsmen, Newcastle Railwaymen, and Edinburgh City were unofficial, they were often retained in brackets.

When these battalions went to war, the overall deaths were not spread evenly across the country, nor were they spread evenly chronologically. The effect on friends, relatives and neighbours at home of heavy casualties at the front was exacerbated by the local men all being in the same regiment, often in the same battalion. The citizens of Bradford mourned the death of 5,442 soldiers, of whom 1,779 were in the West Yorkshire Regiment, and 459 in the two Bradford Pals battalions of that regiment. In Leeds 8,264 men were killed, of whom 3,611 were in the West Yorkshire Regiment, and 252 in the 15th Battalion (Leeds Pals). Durham City lost 1,320 of its sons, 655 in the Durham Light Infantry with 61 in the 18th Battalion (Durham Pals). An examination of the total killed in a representative sample of towns and cities compared with the number in the local infantry regiment shows what the impact on those at home must have been:[15]

Table 7

Residence and local regiment	Total killed	Killed in local regiment	Deaths in local regiment as percentage of total
Leeds (West Yorks)	8,264	3,611	44
Bradford (West Yorks)	5,442	1,779	33
Barnsley (York and Lancaster)	1,633	913	56
Durham City (DLI)	1,320	655	50
Liverpool (King's Liverpool)	14,116	6,514	46
Canterbury (East Kent Regt)	1,882	747	40

In the Second World War the overall death toll of the British army was much lower than it had been in the First. While it is often averred that the generals in the Second War learned their trade in the First and were thus determined to avoid mass casualties, the truth is that the two wars were very different in character, at least as far as the British army was concerned. From beginning to end of the First War, the bulk of the British army was fighting the main enemy in the main theatre of war (the Western Front). Between the evacuation of Europe via Dunkirk and Cherbourg in 1940 and the Normandy invasion of 1944 the British army only fought in peripheral theatres. While those who fought in North Africa, Crete and the Far East in the Second War would object to their efforts being described as peripheral, the fact is that in terms of men deployed, and in the intensity of the fighting, the British army was far less involved in the Second War than it had been in the First. Hence British army casualties between 1939 and 1945 were considerably less than those between 1914 and 1918, and minuscule compared to those of the Russian army, which spent most of the Second War fighting the main enemy on land. While the local regiment was still the major recruiter in the Second World War, the British army had appreciated the inadvisability of filling up its infantry battalions with men drawn from the same small areas. Taking the towns listed in Table 7 above and applying the same exercise to the Second War gives a very different picture: not only are there fewer deaths overall, but, more importantly, a much lower percentage occurred in the local regiment:

Table 8

Residence	Total killed	Killed in local regiment	Deaths in local regiment as percentage of total
Leeds	2,488	127	5
Bradford	1,114	61	5
Barnsley	417	24	6
Durham City	339	84	25
Liverpool	4,086	210	5
Canterbury	270	52	19

The impact of First War casualties was far greater because in a particular area or a particular employment or social group they tended to occur all at once, and those areas or groups were very small. Of the Bradford dead, 345 were killed on one day, 1 July 1916, the opening day of the Somme offensive, and 217 of those were in the two Bradford Pals battalions. In Portadown, little more than a large village, twenty-three men of the 19th Battalion Royal Irish Fusiliers, a New Army battalion formed from the Ulster Volunteer Force, were killed on that same day. The 8th Battalion the London Regiment (Post Office Rifles) had 1,434 men killed between 1915 and 1918. While there were men in that battalion from as far away as Kelso and Nottingham, the vast majority were Londoners and had been Post Office workers before the war.

On the other hand, there were a number of 'thankful villages' where there were no deaths at all. The hamlet of Knowlton, in rural Kent, had a population of thirty-nine in 1914. Of these, twelve – or what must have been all the males of military age – joined up before March 1915. There was no local 'pals' battalion and they were spread between five different regiments. Four joined the Royal East Kent Yeomanry, three the 4th Battalion the Buffs (a Territorial Force battalion), two the 2nd Life Guards, one the King's Royal Rifle Corps and one the 6th Battalion the Buffs. The response to the call by Knowlton's menfolk won the *Weekly*

Despatch competition for the bravest village in England, but it brought them more good fortune still, for not one was killed. Statistically one of the twelve should have died, and if he had, Knowlton would not have considered that it had lost a generation.

There was another group, often lost sight of, which after the old regular army, the reservists, the Territorial Force and the New Armies made up the manpower that Britain called upon to fight the war: the conscripts. Historically it was seen as a freeborn Englishman's right not to be conscripted. Conscription was a foreign practice and thought to give far too much power to the military. Britain had never needed a large army anyway, and although there had been conscription by ballot for the Militia during the Napoleonic Wars, the units thus manned could not serve outside the United Kingdom. As the Great War went on it became increasingly clear to government and army that voluntary recruiting could not sustain the size of the army needed. The initial surge of patriotism that greeted the declaration of war was beginning to recede by the middle of 1915. Those who were attracted by a wage and three square meals a day (a much larger proportion of recruits than is sometimes realised) had already enlisted, and there was now no shortage of civilian employment. Voluntary enlistment was inefficient anyway. Men turned up as it suited them, which was not necessarily when the army wanted them, and no accurate forecasts of available military manpower could be made. There were some recruits, qualified or experienced in specific trades, who would have been of far more use to the war effort if they had stayed at the factory or in the mine.

By 1915 the government was reluctantly examining ways in which manpower as a whole could be directed into areas – industrial as well as military – directly applicable to the prosecution of the war. The average number of men coming into the army each month was 125,000 but it varied widely from month to month, and it was not going to be enough. On 19 May 1915 Lord Kitchener made another appeal to the young men of Britain, asking for 300,000 to enlist. The response was disappointing, for while the figures for May were 10,000 more than the average, those for June were 10,000 below. On 15 July the first step towards compulsion was introduced – the National Registration Act. Under the act the capabilities and occupation of every man in Great Britain – and, interestingly, of every woman too – between the ages of fifteen and sixty-five was recorded. This would allow the authorities to discover exactly how many people were employed in each industry, permitting a calculation as to the number of men needed in munitions work, shipbuilding, agriculture and other activities essential to national survival. It would also show the surplus manpower that would be available to the army and the navy.

Registration duly took place. Men considered essential to their existing civilian occupations were recorded ('starred') as being in 'reserved occupations' and ineligible for military service. Initially there were 1,605,629 men starred, and this rose to 2,574,800 by the end of the war. All those shown to be available were then approached by recruiters, seeking to discover their intentions and to persuade them to enlist, now or later. On 11 October 1915 Lord Derby was appointed Director General of Recruiting, and on 16 October the 'Derby Scheme' was announced. Under this, men not starred as being in reserved occupations essential to the war effort could enlist now, or attest – that is, take the oath of allegiance required by every recruit – with an obligation to report for military service later if required. The attested men would be divided into forty-six groups by age, from eighteen to forty-one, with single and married men in separate groups. Asquith, the Prime Minister, announced that if single men did not come forward voluntarily, then they would be conscripted before attested married men. Concurrent with registration was the introduction of the War Pensions Act which introduced pensions not just for married men, (as had been the case up to then), but for all soldiers who had dependants.

From the outbreak of war until the end of 1914 a total of 1,186,337 men had joined the regular army or the Territorial Force. In 1915 a further 1,280,362 volunteered. Registration had produced 2,184,979 who had attested by the end of that year, but around 650,000 men had avoided both enlisting and attesting. It was now obvious that compulsion would have to be introduced. On 4 January 1916 the Military Service Act was introduced in the House by the Prime Minister. It became law on 27 January and from that date all voluntary enlistment in Great Britain stopped. Ireland was unaffected; it had never been the intention to introduce conscription or registration there, partly because of the unsettled state of the country and partly because the Unionists objected to Catholics being given military training.[16] All men between the ages of eighteen and forty-one in Great Britain who were unmarried and had no dependants were now liable to be conscripted into any branch of the forces, with no choice as to service or arm of it. The exception was that if a man was a volunteer for the navy, then the Admiralty had first call on his services. There were provisions to exempt those found to be medically unfit and conscientious objectors. Initially the number of men obtained was lower than expected, and so on 25 May 1916 compulsion was applied to all single and married men. By July 1916 a mere 43,000 men had been obtained by conscription, while 93,000 failed to turn up when summoned; 748,587 claimed exemption for one reason or another and were under investigation, and 1,433,827 were now starred. Things did get better. Evaders realised that they would have to go eventually, frivolous claims for exemption were dismissed, and further age groups were called up. By the end of the war 2,500,000 men had been conscripted, nearly all for the army. Conscripts were drafted to where they were needed, and as far as possible went to their local regular or Territorial Force regiments. It is not possible, short of examining each man's record individually, to differentiate conscripts and volunteers in the casualty lists. The government, and the army, did their best to avoid making a distinction between those who had come of their own free will and those who were compelled. All had fought, all had done their bit, and to separate them would have been invidious. The soldiers themselves do not seem to have distinguished between the two classes of their comrades, and after the halting of all voluntary enlistment men could claim, often with justification, that they would have volunteered had that avenue been open to them. After the war old soldiers did not advertise the fact that they had been conscripted, and this large body of military manpower has not been researched in any great detail. As men arrived in their units the exigencies of war, shared by all, volunteer and conscript alike, soon welded men together into one battalion family, and origins were soon forgotten or ignored. Because conscripts from a given area were not all placed in the same battalion, their deaths would have been spread more evenly across the country than those of the 'pals' battalions. Conscription was universal, and individual. The men made a vital contribution to the war, particularly on the Western Front, where the BEF was seriously under strength from late 1916 onwards until drafts of conscripts began to arrive to fill up the ranks.

Had conscription and direction and control of manpower been introduced in 1914 – which for very good reasons it could not have been – and had the British infantry been structured in a different way, then death and disablement would have been spread much more evenly across the nation, and any one locality's perception of the toll would have been less shocking than it was. The British nation had never been so involved in a war before, and never had it suffered as it did between 1914 and 1918, but its sufferings were less by far than those of the other combatants. Britain did not lose a generation to the war.

NOTES

1 Figures for the average size of the army are taken from, Major T. J. Mitchell and Miss G. M. Smith, *Official History of the War, Casualties and Medical Statistics*, Imperial War Museum (reprint), London, 1997.

2 A dreadnought, with a crew of twenty-two officers and 1,000 sailors, could fire eight of her ten guns at once, delivering 10,560 lbs' weight of explosive per salvo. A division's artillery (field, howitzers and heavy guns), manned by 4,000 men, produced 1,742 lbs per salvo.

3 French and German figures have been obtained from L'Historial de la Grande Guerre, Péronne, France. British figures are from *Statistics of the Military Effort of the British Empire during the Great War*, War Office, London, 1922.

4 Figures for Great Britain are from *Census Historical Tables 1991*, HMSO, London, 1991. For Ireland the figures are from W. E. Vaughan and A. J. Fitzgerald (eds.), *Irish Historical Statistics – Population*, Royal Irish Academy, Dublin, 1978. Up to and including 1911 Irish censuses were held concurrently with those in Great Britain. Owing to unrest it was not possible to hold an Irish census in 1921, and in both 1926 and 1937 separate censuses were conducted in both the Irish Free State / Éire and Northern Ireland. To obtain the Irish figures for 1921 and 1931, extrapolation from the 1911, 1926 and 1937 tables has been employed.

5 This was relatively new. The public-school system expanded greatly during the Victorian age. Prior to that officers tended to be younger sons of the middle classes, the largest group being the sons of officers, and were generally educated in the grammar schools.

6 Eton War Memorial Council, *List of Etonians Who Fought in the Great War MCMXIV–MCMXIX*, privately published, London, 1921.

7 H. R. Stokoe, *Tonbridge School in the Great War*, Whitefriars Press, London, 1923.

8 Sedbergh School records, courtesy of the Archivist.

9 St Lawrence College records, courtesy of the Bursar.

10 Royal School Armagh records, courtesy of the Headmaster.

11 J. M. Winter, *The Great War and the British People*, Macmillan, London, 1985.

12 French deaths on the Western Front from sickness alone were thirteen per cent of the total.

13 See my *Sepoys in the Trenches, the Indian Corps on the Western Front 1914–1915*, Spellmount Publishers, Staplehurst, 1999.

14 Jon Cooksey, *Barnsley Pals* (3rd impression), Leo Cooper, London, 1996.

15 Figures are from *Soldiers Died in the Great War 1914–19*, and *Army Roll of Honour, Soldiers Died in the Second World War*, CD-ROMs, Naval and Military Press, 1999 and 2000. The figures are for other ranks only, as officers' residence and place of enlistment for WWI are not shown. The comparisons for the two wars are not entirely accurate, as records from WWI very often do not show a man's residence or place of birth, but in all cases do show place of enlistment. World War II records do not show place of enlistment but do show place of birth. I have therefore taken place of enlistment to indicate residence for WWI, and place of birth to show residence for World War II.

16 In World War II conscription, applied in Great Britain before the outbreak of war, was not applied to Northern Ireland because the Unionist government there raised the same objection. It has been claimed that the proportion of the population volunteering for the British forces from the (neutral) south was rather greater than that from the (province of the UK) north!

3

THE HORRORS OF THE TRENCHES

The perception of soldiering in the Great War is of a young patriot enlisting in 1914 to do his bit, and then being shipped off to France. Arriving at one of the Channel Ports he marches all the way up to the front, singing 'Tipperary' and smoking his pipe, forage cap on the back of his head. Reaching the firing line, he is put into a filthy hole in the ground and stays there until 1918. If he survives, he is fed a tasteless and meagre diet of bully beef and biscuits. Most days, if he is not being shelled or bombed, he goes 'over the top' and attacks a German in a similar position a few yards away across no man's land. He never sees a general and rarely changes his lice-infested clothes, while rats gnaw the dead bodies of his comrades.

Real life was very different. The original BEF, composed of pre-war regulars and reservists, did do quite a lot of marching, but they would have been very unlucky to have to tramp all the way from Boulogne to Belgium. As far as possible men moved by train until they were a few miles from the front, and as the war went on and motor lorries became available these too were used to speed up movement. As early as October 1914 London buses were shipped out to the front for use as troop carriers. The pre-war army was in any case well accustomed to marching. They had to be prepared to fight anywhere in the world, and most of the likely places lacked both roads and railways. The regulars' feet had been toughened by regular route marches in peacetime; twenty miles in a day was normal, and forced marches could cover twice that. The reservists were not so lucky. In the army they wore boots, but when most had completed their engagements with the colours they had taken civilian jobs where they wore shoes. Reservists sitting by the side of the road, boots off and feet bleeding, were a common sight in the early days, until the advance into Belgium and the retreat to the Marne hardened their feet. The old sweats rarely sang. It was not a British thing to do, and whilst German and French soldiers were taught marching songs as part of their training, the British regulars thought it was silly, and a waste of breath better kept for marching. When they did sing it was more likely to be an obscene parody, rather than well-crafted and melodious lines about home and mother. The men of the New Armies, untainted by experience, did sing, and so did some of the more naive Territorials, but even that tended to be put on for the cameras or the reporters, well behind the lines.

British armies had always entrenched when necessary. In Wellington's time trenches were usually employed only during sieges, as the Duke preferred to keep his men on a reverse slope from where he could move them to a threatened point. In any case the standard musket was difficult to load lying down, so soldiers fought standing up. As weaponry improved it became increasingly important to shelter soldiers from enemy fire. Colourful clothing and gaudy flags disappeared from the battlefield; breech-loading weapons could be handled from behind cover or lying down; and rifled barrels increased range and accuracy to the extent that anyone not under cover was an easy target. The best way to obtain protection from enemy observation and fire was to disappear into the ground – to occupy a trench. A well-constructed trench allowed the man to move about in safety and to carry out his personal administration, sleep and use his weapon with a modicum of protection. In the early stages of the Great War men dug trenches where and as they could. They used drainage ditches, banks, hedges, folds and dips in the ground. Until October 1914 and the end of the race to the sea the war was still mobile, and the makeshift trenches were adequate until it was time to move on. Once the conflict settled down into what would effectively be siege warfare until 1918, the trench lines became more sophisticated and better constructed, with bunkers and dugouts, drains and fire-steps.

French and German ideas on trench construction differed according to the military philosophy of the two nations. The French military doctrine was one of constant aggression: the offensive was what mattered, and their defence works reflected this. They were largely earthen, used little concrete and were often without revetment. Their primary purpose was to provide a launching pad for the French attacks that, by their ferocity, would drive the invader out into the open, where he would be destroyed. German defences, on the other hand, were stoutly and meticulously constructed. Concrete was used in abundance, and deep dugouts were built; in some cases so well built and so deep that no Allied artillery could affect them, as the British would learn to their cost on the Somme. The Germans were on someone else's territory and, once the Schlieffen plan failed, were content to stay on the defensive while the Allies tried again and again to evict them. Once the initial phase of movement was over, the Germans only mounted three major offensives on the Western Front: at Ypres in 1914, at Verdun in 1916, and the so-called *Kaiserschlacht* of 1918. This is not to say that German soldiers never attacked; they often did, as in the Second Battle of Ypres in 1915, or at Cambrai in 1917, but these were local attacks for immediate tactical objectives: to test new weapons and methods, or to counter-attack to regain lost ground. British soldiers often commented that German trenches were better than their own, and this was generally true. Allied trenches were temporary, even if some of them did not move very much for three years.

The design and dimensions of British entrenchments were based on a good British compromise. The British adopted much from the French methods, but they also used concrete and revetting when available. Unlike the French, the British army was not wedded to the idea of constant attacks. Indeed, in private, some British commanders and politicians thought that Britain should stay on the defensive until her New Armies were ready and then intervene massively, end the war, and dictate the future shape of Europe. In a coalition war this could not be, and the British recognised that trenches would be from where attacks would be launched; but they wanted them to provide sound and comfortable protection too.

As it became clear that action would no longer consist of wide enveloping movements followed by a pursuit by the cavalry, trench systems became more sophisticated. There were usually three lines of trenches. The forward line or front line, or more usually firing line, was the trench nearest the enemy. How far away it was from the opposing line depended on the ground, and often they were not sited to the Allied advantage. In some areas opposing trenches were only twenty yards apart, but this was unusual. The normal distance was between 200 and 500 yards.

In an ideal world, where the defenders had ample warning of the approach of an attacker, the defending commander would decide where he wished to stop the foe and a detailed reconnaissance would be carried out. Factors considered included the ability to dominate the approaches, preferably from higher ground. Dominating meant that the defending troops should be able to observe and fire on the ground over which the attacker must advance. This did not mean that the infantry in the trenches should necessarily be able to fire their rifles at long range. Defending on the forward slope of a ridge or hill facing the enemy line of advance meant that one had a good field of view and fire, but the enemy had the same advantage, and the defenders could not move or carry out routine administrative tasks in daylight. To site defence works on the top of a hill risked creating dead ground over which the enemy could move without being seen. Much reliance was therefore placed on using the reverse-slope position, which prevented the attacker from knowing exactly where the defending trenches were until he had crossed the crest, and allowed much more freedom of movement to the defender. While the reverse slope gave the defender a much shorter field of fire, this could be countered by the use of artillery – which could fire over ridge lines – directed by observers hidden on the forward slopes.

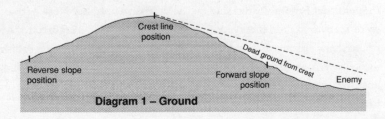

Crest line
position

Dead ground from crest

Reverse slope
position

Forward slope
position

Enemy

Diagram 1 – Ground

Once the commander had decided where he was to defend, detailed reconnaissance by local commanders took place, and the lines of the trenches were marked out by spitlocking (turning the earth with shovels) or with tape. Then the troops arrived and digging started. The procedure for the digging was all laid down: how many diggers per yard of front, the dimension of the trench itself and its parapet and parados, where the fire-step was to be constructed and where the traverses were to go. The parapet was a bank of earth thrown up in front of the trench itself to allow a man to fire his rifle from the trench with a rest for his elbows and as much protection from incoming fire as possible. The French calculated that one foot four inches of packed earth (and incidentally four feet of manure) were required to stop a standard German rifle bullet. This was wildly optimistic and the British tended to make their parapets thicker – about four to five feet of earth. The parados was the equivalent of the parapet, but behind the trench. Its purpose was to stop bullets from carrying on to the next line of trenches, to shield men from the blast of a shell exploding behind them, and to serve as a parapet if the enemy managed to get behind the firing line. As the trench was supposed to be deep enough to allow a man to walk along it fully upright, without showing any part of his body above the parapet, a fire-step had to be

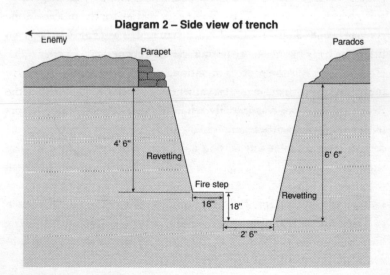

Diagram 2 – Side view of trench

constructed to allow men to fire their weapons from the trench. This was a simple platform in the side of the trench, onto which men stepped when required to defend their position.

As a shell dropping into a trench could spread its blast for many yards on either side, trenches were not simple straight lines. They followed the lie of the ground, with frequent dog-legs and bends, and where they had of necessity to be in a straight line, they had inbuilt traverses. A traverse was a barrier to blast, created by digging the trench in a crenellated shape. Most traverses were reverse, that is they jutted behind the trench, but some were deliberately built forward, to provide the defenders with a flanking-fire position. A traverse every eighteen to thirty feet was normal, and not only limited the effect of a well-aimed shell, but provided an obstacle to enemy movement should the trench be infiltrated. By the same token traverses also provided an interloper with cover, so loopholes were dug through them and they were sited far enough apart to prevent an enemy from throwing a grenade further than into the next trench bay along.

Immediately behind the main firing trench, and anything from ten to twenty yards from it, was a narrower trench running parallel to the main trench. This was the command or supervision trench, designed to allow the commander of that sector to move rapidly along his area of responsibility. It was here that battalion headquarters might have a forward position and where a communal officers' dugout, or shelter, for the officers of the company controlling the sector might be situated. It was linked to the main firing line by frequent short communication trenches.

Revetting was the process of shoring up the sides of the trench, to prevent it caving in during wet weather or as a result of enemy shelling. Revetting material was initially whatever could be obtained: doors from abandoned houses were widely used. As time went on purpose-designed wood, rabbit-wire netting and, eventually, corrugated iron were supplied. Corrugated iron was easier to handle and quicker to install than lengths of wood, but it had to be securely fastened, as a sheet of it sent flying by a shell could act as an airborne guillotine. To enable men to leave the trenches to patrol in no man's land, or to attack the opposing lines, ladders were built into the sides of the trench, or portable versions provided.

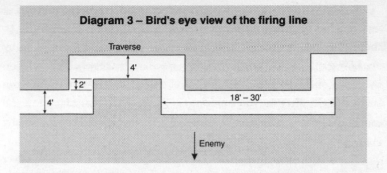

Diagram 3 – Bird's eye view of the firing line

Traverse

4'

2'

4'

18' – 30'

Enemy

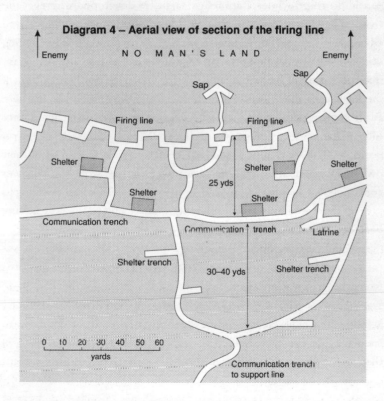

Diagram 4 – Aerial view of section of the firing line

Enemy

NO MAN'S LAND

Enemy

Sap

Sap

Firing line

Firing line

Shelter

Shelter

Shelter

Shelter

25 yds

Shelter

Communication trench

Communication trench

Latrine

Shelter trench

30–40 yds

Shelter trench

0 10 20 30 40 50 60
yards

Communication trench
to support line

Barbed-wire obstacles of varying depths were erected in front of the trenches to slow up enemy movement and, more importantly, to channel attackers into a killing area where they could be fired on by machine guns, rifles or artillery. At first the British army had virtually no wire, and obstacles were primitive and created from wire taken from farmer's fields. In time huge amounts of wire were manufactured and issued, and belts of wire were constructed deep enough to keep the enemy out of grenade-throwing range.

This was the ideal, when defending troops had ample time to select the location of their trenches and to plan and construct them according to laid-down principles. In practice, trenches developed wherever the fighting had come to a halt. Neither side could advance, so they stayed where they were and dug in, often under fire and in positions where getting under cover was the first priority, regardless of fields of fire or reverse slopes. For most of the war the British army was in the northern portion of the Allied lines, in Flanders, where there is a high water-table and few hills. Far from being situated in high, well-drained land, British trenches were often in flat, marshy ground where they could be overlooked by German positions. The alternative would have been to retreat to ground of their own choosing, then fend off the advancing Germans while the ideal was constructed. This was not possible, even if the Allies had been willing to give up yet more ground to German occupation, and so the British army defended as and where it could.

Behind the firing line, and anything from 200 to 500 yards from it, was the support line. This was identical to the firing line and its purpose was to check any local enemy penetration of the firing line. Further back again was the reserve line, which held reserves who could mount a local counter-attack if an enemy succeeded in capturing a portion of the forward trenches. The French tended to do without the reserve line, relying on their artillery instead. As they had far more guns than the British, this tactic was usually successful.

So that troops could move around in the forward positions, and so that rations, ammunition and stores could be brought up and casualties moved back, the three lines of trenches were linked with communication trenches. They might have traverses in them if time permitted; if it did not then they zigzagged forward, which produced the same effect without impeding movement up and down. As time went on more and more communication trenches were built, dummy trenches dug and saps pushed out. A sap was a trench which ran out into no man's land; from it, observation parties would watch the enemy line and raids on the opposition could be mounted.

It was easy to get lost in the network of communication trenches, and so trench maps were issued and signposts erected. British communication trenches had names reminiscent of home – Regent's Street, the Strand – or of something that had happened there – Dud Corner, Sniper Alley.

At first British map-marking convention showed enemy positions in blue and friendly ones in red, but this was changed to conform with the French, who used the reverse system.

Trench maps showing the trenches of one's own side were classified 'secret', and forbidden in the front line – if they were captured during an enemy attack the results could be disastrous.

Despite the tales of rats, lice and general filth, cleanliness and hygiene in the trenches were strictly enforced. The army paid a great deal of attention to its latrines, as indeed it had to. Disease caused by poor hygiene had dogged armies throughout history and dysentery had always been a frequent visitor. By now the army was well aware that if human waste was not disposed of properly, unnecessary casualties would follow. The average man produces 2.4 pounds' weight of faeces and urine per day. In the average company-defended position this is a ton a week, over a frontage of about 200 yards. While a few men on patrol, or larger bodies in a war of movement, might practise cat sanitation and get away with it, men in trenches could not be allowed to drop their trousers where they felt like it. In the forward areas latrines were constructed just behind the trenches, at the end of a communication trench or off the command trench, and out of view of the enemy. They were usually deep pits with wooden seats on top. Disinfectant was provided, and when full the latrine was closed and covered over, the area was marked as 'foul ground' and another latrine was dug. Farther back, the deep-trench latrine, a pit up to sixteen feet deep, was excavated by the Royal Engineers. The deep-trench latrine was an example of perpetual motion, or perhaps cessation of motion, as it never filled unless the entire battalion suffered from diarrhoea. Faeces deposited well out of the light and left alone, without chemicals being thrown on them, break down and dissipate naturally.[1] The army being an hierarchical organisation, there were of course separate latrines for officers, senior NCOs and junior ranks.

The 63rd Royal Naval Division felt the wrath of its commander because its officers did not consider the subject of shit management to be worthy of much attention – there were far more important things to think about. The Royal Naval Division was a creation of Churchill. As First Lord of the Admiralty he found that on mobilisation the Royal Navy, having called up its reserves, had far more men than there were berths on ships. It was thought (correctly as it turned out) that naval casualties would be few; hence the retention of a large number of replacements was unnecessary. The army, on the other hand, did need men and their need for reinforcements could be very great. The Royal Navy produced an infantry division consisting of a brigade of Royal Marines and two brigades of sailors turned soldiers. The division got off to a somewhat shaky start. It took part in an abortive attempt to prevent the Germans from taking Antwerp in October 1914; when it had to withdraw, the 1st Royal Naval Brigade were too slow, failed to get across the River Scheldt, and had about half their number interned in Holland for the duration of the war. The division next took part in the Gallipoli escapade and eventually arrived back on the Western Front in May 1916, when they found themselves transferred from the Admiralty to the War Office. There were problems. The Royal Marines adapted without any great difficulty; they belonged to the Navy but their traditions stemmed from the army and they were trained as soldiers. The sailors, on the other hand, resented what they saw as enforcement of unnecessary army discipline and army ways of doing things. Naval and army discipline are, of course, different. A sailor goes where the captain sails, and cannot absent himself. He has a job to do in the ship and his working environment is much the same in peace as it is in war. A soldier can run away, his working environment changes by the minute once battle is joined and, unlike the sailor who kills anonymously from a distance, the infantry soldier can see the look in the eye of the man whose life he is trying to extinguish. Army and navy training and discipline reflect these differences.

The navy would have liked to have an admiral commanding their division, but this would have been about as sensible as appointing a general to be captain of a battleship. When the division arrived on the Western Front in 1916, Major-General Cameron Shute was appointed General Officer Commanding 63rd (Royal Naval) Division. Shute was a pre-war regular officer, originally of the Welsh Regiment and the Rifle Brigade, and was fifty years old when he took up the post. He had attended the Staff College, at a time when most officers did not, and had been through the mill of staff appointments including Brigadier General Staff Aldershot, one of the really taxing, and important, pre-war staff jobs dealing with troops. He had also commanded his battalion before the war, and a brigade on the Western Front. He was by any standards a well-trained, experienced and competent officer. Shute inspected the various units of the Royal Naval Division on taking over command, and did not like what he saw. Too little attention was being paid to keeping weapons clean, and latrine management was nothing short of a mass outbreak of dysentery waiting to happen. Shute is forgotten in military history except in the words of a poem, supposedly written by A. P. Herbert (who served in the division) and which, like all scurrilous and witty productions, received wide circulation:

The General inspecting the trenches
Exclaimed with a horrified shout,
'I refuse to command a division
Which leaves its excreta about.'

But nobody took any notice,
No one was prepared to refute
That the presence of shit was congenial
Compared with the presence of Shute.

And certain responsible critics
Made haste to reply to his words,
Observing that his staff advisers
Consisted entirely of turds.

For shit may be shot at odd corners
And paper supplied there to suit,
But a shit would be shot without mourners
If somebody shot that shit Shute.

It caused great amusement, but Shute was absolutely right. Dirty weapons will fail to fire when needed, and lack of attention to latrine discipline leads to disease. It would appear that the Royal Naval Division did not fully absorb General Shute's strictures, for in January 1918 the 2nd Battalion Oxfordshire and Buckinghamshire Light Infantry took over a sector of the front from the Nelson Battalion and reported that the state of the trenches was bad. [2]

A general lack of cleanliness compounded by food left lying about, particularly in and around horse lines and abandoned ration dumps, could of course attract rats, and in the early days there were certainly lots of them in evidence. They did scamper around in no man's land and bodies left unrecovered did provide nourishment for them. Bodies were always recovered whenever humanly possible and taken back to the rear for temporary burial, before being given a proper and seemly funeral. Bodies left lying where they fell were not good for morale; they were never left in the trenches for longer than absolutely necessary, nor did the British follow the French practice in the early days of burying their dead in the parapet. Good discipline got rid of rubbish and edible scraps, and rats were rarely a problem in the trenches, although lice, inevitable when men cannot wash properly, sometimes were. On coming out of the line troops had their uniforms fumigated, laundered and ironed, and if necessary exchanged, to reduce the risk of infestation.

The usual procedure in defence was for an infantry battalion to man the firing line and the support line, while the reserve line would contain the brigade reserve, from another battalion, and sometimes the battalion reserve as well. The reserve trenches were rarely fully manned; rather, reserves would be in billets anything up to a mile behind the firing line, ready to be deployed as necessary, either to mount a counter-attack or to man the reserve trenches if an enemy offensive was taking place or imminent. The proportion of men placed in the firing line varied;

sometimes two companies would be in the firing line and two in the support trenches, at other times three might be in the firing line. As the war went on it became increasingly the practice (on both sides) for the firing line to be lightly held, so as to avoid casualties from sporadic shelling and sniping, and to reinforce from the support line if an attack was likely. It was for the brigade staff to allocate stretches of the front to battalions, and a matter for battalions to decide which company went where.

British soldiers did not spend four years of war in the firing line, or even at the front. Men were regularly rotated from the firing line to the support and reserve lines and then back to billets, usually well behind the battle area. The billets were generally civilian houses in villages, appropriated by the army. They varied in standard and there were times when men were accommodated in stables, tents, or huts erected by the Royal Engineers. Here they would recover from the fighting, undergo training, eat freshly prepared food, have hot baths or showers and exchange their worn-out items of clothing. Although French law forbade the sale of spirits in the war zone, this was widely flouted and those who wanted to (which was most) could easily obtain alcohol and the staple of the British soldier, fried eggs and fried potatoes. It is said that the current Belgian obsession with chips with everything stems from their entrepreneurial culinary activities during the war, although this does not explain their curious habit of lacing them with mayonnaise.

The British army took great pains to ensure that men were regularly rotated between front-line positions and billets to the rear. With a division having two of its brigades in the line and one out, and with each brigade having two of its four battalions in the line, a battalion could expect, on average, to spend just ten days a month in the trenches. In practice this varied with the tactical situation: more men would be in the line when a German attack was imminent, or when the British intended to take the offensive. This was balanced by each division's coming out of the line en bloc at intervals, to rest and undergo retraining. Even when a battalion was in the line there were usually only two companies forward, with two in the support or reserve trenches. On occasions the reserve line was not manned, but the troops held in billets ready to occupy the trenches if needed. An examination of five typical regular battalions, stationed on the Western Front for the whole of the war, shows how effective the British system of rotation was. The tables below show the maximum time any soldier of those battalions spent in the trenches – firing, support or reserve – during the month of January in each year of the war. These were typical trench-warfare months, in which nothing very much was happening save the usual programme of trench raids, shelling and sniping. The maximum time is shown because, while adjutants did their best to give all four companies an equal amount of time in the trenches and out of them, when a battalion went into the line for three or five days an equal distribution was not possible; this was corrected when the battalion next went into the line. Also shown is the number of deaths in the battalion from all causes during those months. Deaths in a defensive posture, though a constant drip, were not excessive; it was the major offensives, where men had to cross open ground and expose themselves to enemy fire, that caused the majority of the casualties.

Table 9

1. January 1915 Battalion	Maximum days in trenches	Longest continuous period in trenches (days)	Longest continuous period in firing line (days)	Deaths from from all causes
1st Bn South Wales Borderers	13	6	2	49
1st Bn King's Royal Rifle Corps	13	4	1	28
2nd Bn South Staffordshire Regt	7	1	1	11
1st Bn Black Watch	9	4	4	74
2nd Bn Oxfordshire and Buckinghamshire Light Infantry	7	2	2	5

2. January 1916 Battalion	Maximum days in trenches	Longest continuous period in trenches (days)	Longest continuous period in firing line (days)	Deaths from from all causes
1st Bn South Wales Borderers	6	4	2	2
1st Bn King's Royal Rifle Corps	4	4	1	5
2nd Bn South Staffordshire Regt	8	5	2	3
1st Bn Black Watch	9	6	3	3
2nd Bn Oxfordshire and Buckinghamshire Light Infantry	3	2	1	2

3. January 1917

Battalion	Maximum days in trenches	Longest continuous period in trenches (days)	Longest continuous period in firing line (days)	Deaths from from all causes
1st Bn South Wales Borderers	0	0	0	2
1st Bn King's Royal Rifle Corps	4	4	0	2
2nd Bn South Staffordshire Regt	2	2	2	9
1st Bn Black Watch	0	0	0	3
2nd Bn Oxfordshire and Buckinghamshire Light Infantry	4	4	2	4

4. January 1918

Battalion	Maximum days in trenches	Longest continuous period in trenches (days)	Longest continuous period in firing line (days)	Deaths from from all causes
1st Bn South Wales Borderers	6	4	2	1
1st Bn King's Royal Rifle Corps	8	3	1	1
2nd Bn South Staffordshire Regt	2	1	1	6
1st Bn Black Watch	7	4	2	2
2nd Bn Oxfordshire and Buckinghamshire Light Infantry	7	4	2	2

The so-called horrors of the trenches were very short-lived indeed, and it is unusual to find any battalion spending more than four or five days a month continuously in the firing line.[3] Out of the line there was much to do, but while deaths did occur from accidents, sporadic shelling of billets, premature explosion of grenades in training and air attack, men were relatively safe and comfortable. The 1st Battalion South Wales Borderers were out of the line for the whole of January 1917, and in billets near Beaucourt. Their programme for this month is shown overleaf:

Table 10

1 Jan. Cleaning up after trenches. CO's inspection of billets.

2 Jan. Drill and weapon training, under company sergeants major for other ranks, under regimental sergeant major for officers.

3 Jan. Baths for all.

4 Jan. Fatigues for all.

5 Jan. Battalion drill.

6 Jan. Christmas Day, delayed as the battalion was in the trenches on 25 December 1916. Company and mess parties. Roast pork, Christmas pudding, beer and rum issue.

7 Jan. Church parade and holiday.

8 Jan. Fatigues for all.

9 Jan. Fatigues for all, band concert p.m.

10 Jan. Fatigues, except for signals classes.

11 Jan. Work on camp improvement (the battalion was billeted in huts).

12 Jan. Platoon battle drills training and range firing. Band concert in evening.

13 Jan. Fatigues for all. Concert in evening.

14 Jan. Church of England church parade a.m. Range firing and arms drill (RSM). p.m. battalion cross-country run (won by HQ Company Team II).

15 Jan. Baths for all. Platoon battle drills training. Night exercise. Pay parade.

16 Jan. Fatigues for other ranks, TEWT for officers.

17 Jan. Owing to snow, weapon training in huts.

18 Jan. Range firing.

19 Jan. Fatigues for all. Band concert in evening.

20 Jan. p.m. battalion route march (15 miles, 4 hours 15 minutes).

21 Jan. Church of England church parade, erection of memorial at High Wood to men of battalion killed there during Somme offensive.

22 Jan. Fatigues for all.

23 Jan. Move to new billets at Baizieux.

24 Jan. a.m. signals and scout training; officers TEWT. p.m. battalion drill.

25 Jan. Battalion training.

26 Jan. Divisional attack procedures practised.

27 Jan. Officers' riding lesson. B Company versus D Company football (draw).

28 Jan. Reconnaissance for divisional attack exercise. HQ Company beat C Company at football.

29 Jan. Divisional attack exercise. Officers' riding class. B Company beat D Company at football.

30 Jan. Inspection of gas helmets. Battalion inspection and drill by RSM. Officers' conference. Battalion cross-country run (first man back awarded a tot of rum). B Company beat A Company at football.

31 Jan. Battalion training in moving in artillery formation. Brigade cross-country competition, winners 2nd Bn Royal Munster Fusiliers, 1 SWB equal fourth with Bde HQ.

This constant rotation between firing and support lines, reserve and billets occasioned a great deal of work for brigade staff officers and much effort in traffic control. It was a constant headache for those responsible for allocating billets, and kept adjutants gainfully employed making sure that each company got an equal balance between time at the front and time in billets or reserve. Rotation required more units to hold a given length of front than if units had simply been put in the trenches and left there, and local knowledge of a unit's sector could never be as comprehensive as it would have been had men spent longer in the line. There was always the risk of an enemy attack being launched while a relief was taking place, or when a newly arrived company or battalion had not yet settled in. Sporadic shelling of the communication trenches could cause mayhem if a battalion was moving up them to relieve another battalion at the front.

All these problems were far outweighed by the advantages that rotation had for morale. The firing line was not a fun place to be, but however unpleasant it might be on Tuesday, the soldier knew that on Friday he would be back in a comfortable billet out of range of anything but a speculative shell; in the warm, eating hot food and with a hot bath and clean clothes available. There can be no doubt that regular rotation, never keeping men in the post of most danger for more than a few days at a time, made a very significant contribution to the fact that the British army, alone amongst the major forces on the Western Front, never suffered a collapse of morale. Even when things were at their worst, as during the German offensive in the spring of 1918, British soldiers never seriously doubted that in time things would get better, and that great efforts were being made to look after their comfort and welfare. Their time in the firing line was short enough for them to see relief in sight, and to know that they only had to stick it out for a few days at most before they could move back to comparative civilisation.

This was not the case in the French army, where rotation was only formally introduced at divisional level during the battle for Verdun in 1916, and was even then far less frequent at company level than it was in the British army, and where, before 1917, French official welfare was almost non-existent. Even when the full weight of the enemy was directed against the BEF, men still never spent more than six or at most seven days in the line. This was also the case during British offensives, when a man attacking on the first day would normally be out of the line on Day Two. During the battles of the Somme in 1916 and Passchendaele in 1917, the British kept on attacking for months, but not with the same troops. Battalions were regularly relieved and given time to reconstitute and rest before being committed once more, as we shall see.

There were other attractions, besides egg and chips, that could be enjoyed when in billets. If a battalion was not in reserve or on stand-by for a move, soldiers were allowed to visit villages and towns. An inevitable consequence was venereal disease, long an occupational hazard for soldiers away from home. The French army recognised that young, fit men, away from wives and girlfriends, will inevitably attempt to get rid of their dirty water, particularly when it may be the last chance they will have, and it took steps to provide for it. The inhabitants of the *maisons tolérées* in the rear areas were inspected by medical officers, and access was controlled by the military police. Venereal disease amongst French soldiers was never a serious problem in Europe. The official British view was that such urges could be controlled by good discipline and healthy exercise, with the result that venereal disease took a steady, and unnecessary, toll of the fighting strength of the BEF. Men visited independent prostitutes or enthusiastic amateurs, with the inevitable results. Altogether the army medical services treated 153,531 cases of VD on the Western Front.[4] Thirty-two men per thousand per year, or the equivalent of a platoon in every infantry battalion, caught VD and were unavailable for duty for between twenty-eight to thirty-seven days. This was only marginally better than in the South African War, where the average wastage through VD was thirty-four men per thousand. These figures represent only a small proportion of VD cases, those that were not reported early and could not be treated in battalion regimental aid posts or as outpatients. Contrary to the popular view of French girls being of lax morals and enticing our young soldiers into a life of sin, only forty-five per cent of infections were contracted in France; thirteen per cent came from other countries or were of unknown origin; and a possibly surprising forty-two per cent of all cases were contracted in the United Kingdom, indicating a lowering of moral standards under the pressures of war.[5]

The British army was never quite sure whether catching VD should be regarded as a self-inflicted wound, and thus subject to punishment, or whether it should be regarded in the same light as influenza or any other disease common on the front. While VD undoubtedly is self-inflicted, and absents a man from duty, fear of punishment only encourages men to conceal it until it reaches an untreatable stage.[6] In some cases local commanders came to an agreement with the French and turned a blind eye to their men's doing their bit for inter-allied cooperation. Eventually it was realised that men could not be prevented from having sex, but that opinion at home would never accept the French solution. The Commander-in-Chief was an old enough soldier to accept, albeit with reluctance, that other ranks would contract VD, but was perturbed when officers caught it. In a General Order it was announced that warrant officers and NCOs infected with VD should be considered for reduction in rank, and officers might be required to resign their commissions. This latter was a serious matter, for unlike a relinquishment of a commission in peacetime, which permitted withdrawal to civilian life, a resignation during the war made the one-time officer liable to conscription as a private soldier. It is not known how many officers were required to resign under this provision, but it is likely to have been very few: officers could afford to have the results of their dalliances treated privately without the army finding out.

Flanders, where a large proportion of the BEF spent most of the war, is flat and the water-table is high. Even in good, dry weather water appears after only a few feet of digging. The winter of 1914–15 was exceptionally cold and wet, and flooding of trenches was a problem. Initially this led to large numbers of men contracting trench foot, caused by a lack of circulation in the feet and legs and, if untreated, leading to gangrene and amputation. Most cases were caught before recourse to the knife but, before preventative measures were enforced, many soldiers suffered from bad feet which would affect them for the rest of their lives. The remedies were the issue of whale oil (to be rubbed on the feet before entering the trenches) and thigh-high rubber waders, the loosening of puttees, regular changing of socks, and drainage of trenches. At first drains were soak-pits dug into the floor, but mechanical pumps would later be provided. If all else failed and trenches were uninhabitable in very heavy rain, they were abandoned and men took refuge behind breastworks – grouse-butt-type banks of earth. By the middle of 1915 trench foot had been all but eliminated, except in battalions new to the front, and a high incidence of it was regarded as the fault of officers who had failed to enforce remedial action.

British commanders knew that, while an army might not exactly march on its stomach, in the Napoleonic sense, men who were hungry or whose food intake lacked the ingredients essential to good health would not fight as well as men who were well fed. A balanced diet was provided, and the administrative staff took great pains to ensure that it was delivered. It is now recognised that a fit, active and athletic adult male needs a daily intake of between 3,000 and 3,500 calories. Heavy physical work or exceptionally cold conditions increase the requirement. The British army aimed to give its soldiers at the front a daily intake of 4,193 calories. This was less than the French and more than the Germans, who aimed for 4,466 and 4,038 calories respectively. The difference was that the French ration, despite including almost a pint of wine daily, was of such poor quality that it was one of the causes of the mutinies of 1917. The Germans, however hard they tried, rarely managed to provide the laid-down ration once the blockade by the Royal Navy began to take effect. British soldiers hardly ever went without, and the prescribed daily ration scale per man is shown in the table opposite.

Preserved meat and fresh or frozen were alternatives, as were bread and biscuit, and fresh and dried vegetables. Even if the item of lower calorific valued was issued, the daily intake was still 4,111 calories. It was a balanced and healthy diet. Soldiers rarely went hungry except in the most extreme circumstances, such as the chaos of First Ypres or the withdrawal of spring 1918. Soldiers did not complain about lack of food, although

Table 11 Rations

Item	Daily Ration	Calories
Fresh or frozen meat	18 oz	1,112
Preserved meat (bully beef or equivalent)	16 oz	989
Bread	18 oz	1,184
Biscuit	12 oz	1,653
Bacon	4 oz	349
Cheese	3 oz	352
Fresh vegetables	8 oz	45
Dried vegetables	2 oz	45
Tea	0.63 oz	
Jam	4 oz	296
Sugar	3 oz	335
Salt	0.5 oz	
Mustard	0.005 oz	
Pepper	0.028 oz	
Condensed milk	12 oz	425
Rice	1 oz	34
Oatmeal	0.9 oz	102

they did complain about its monotony. Where possible fresh meat and bread were issued, even in the firing line when a hot meal might be brought up at night, but there were many occasions when the exigencies of the fighting meant that men subsisted perforce on corned beef and biscuits. Nevertheless, while hardly haute cuisine, this was a far better diet than many had been accustomed to at home, where in poorer households meat was eaten but once or twice a week, and it was healthy and filling. The tea issued was enough to provide each man with six pints of army tea a day, and British soldiers have always loved their tea. An item missing from the ration was eggs. There were difficulties in supplying an army of several million men with eggs that would keep fresh long enough to reach the forward lines, but men in billets behind the lines would find eggs on the ration, bought from funds raised by selling swill, and many men bought eggs out of their own pockets.

In 1915 the meat ration was reduced slightly, without detriment to the calorific value, by issuing less bone. On occasions rabbit was issued as the meat ration, and an Army Rabbit Skin Clearing Committee was duly set up to market the skins, an enterprise which brought £123,000, from six million skins, to the welfare funds. Being appointed Chairman of the Committee for Purchase of Army Camp Refuse can hardly have been greeted with delight, but this organisation was responsible for selling fat and bones to contractors. These in turn extracted the glycerine from the fat, and supplied it to munitions factories where it was turned into propellant for shells. In the year 1917 alone, sufficient glycerine to propel fifteen million eighteen-pounder shells was produced by this means.

Great efforts were made to provide something special for Christmas dinner, and if a battalion was in the line for Christmas then it was granted an 'official Christmas' once it was relieved and in billets. The 1st Battalion King's Royal Rifle Corps spent 25 December 1915 in billets, and all companies and messes held parties. The war diary reported that all detachments were visited by the commanding officer and adjutant, who by the time they had completed their rounds, had each drunk twelve glasses of port. The war diary for that day is signed by the assistant adjutant!

It has generally been considered that one indicator of morale and discipline in a unit is its sick rate: that is, the percentage of men reporting sick with ailments due to causes other than enemy action. Before the war it was considered that 0.3 percent daily, or about three men a day in an infantry battalion (750 at peace establishment, but usually below that) was a reasonable sick rate for an army that was in the field, but where there was no epidemic or serious fighting. The rate for 1913 was in fact 0.12 per cent, and the rate after the war, 1920 to 1928, was 0.17 declining to 0.12 per cent, indicating that the army was made of fit, healthy young men. On the Western Front, with total war in full swing, the sick rate for August to December 1914 was 0.26 per cent, declining to 0.24 per cent in 1915 and 0.13 per cent in 1916. It rose slightly to 0.15 per cent in 1917 and 0.16 per cent in 1918, but throughout the war on the Western Front the sick rate was well below acceptable peacetime rates, and not much higher than actual pre-war rates.[8] The conclusion must be that not only did the Army Medical Services have preventative measures well established, with the treatment of sickness well managed, but that, saving shot and shell, the Western Front was a remarkably healthy place to be throughout the war.

While service in the trenches was by no means a sinecure, the welfare of the troops was always a foremost consideration in the mind of commanders. The British army had long taught the maxim of horses first, soldiers second and officers last when it came to comfort and feeding. Tobacco had not acquired the negative cachet that it has now, and most officers and soldiers smoked. In 1914 only one-fifth of the tobacco sold in the UK was in the form of cigarettes, most of the rest being for pipes. By 1918 the proportions had reversed, presumably because cigarettes were easier to issue to soldiers, and were less difficult to light and maintain in operational conditions. Tobacco was widely available and there were frequent issues of free cigarettes and pipe tobacco. Rum was a ration item; that is, there was an entitlement of one modest tot of rum per man per day, provided that the commanding officer considered the weather to be 'inclement' – which he usually did, regardless of the temperature. Officers tended to drink whisky rather than rum, and there was no shortage of either, although drunkenness in the trenches was very rare and severely punished if it occurred.

One very useful provider of welfare was the chaplain, or padre. Each major unit, whether infantry battalion or cavalry regiment, had one; his denomination depended upon the majority religion of the men. In English battalions this was generally Church of England, in Southern Irish regiments Roman Catholic and in Scottish regiments Church of Scotland (Presbyterian). For free-church Christians and Jews, chaplains of their denominations were attached to divisions or corps and acted in a roving capacity. Until the early years of the Napoleonic Wars the British army had paid little attention to the spiritual welfare of its men, largely because it was blindingly obvious that most had little interest in formal religion. This changed during the Peninsular War, when Wellington considered that chaplains of the right calibre could be a steadying influence on his ragamuffin army, and could act as a counter to the spread of Methodism, then regarded as politically dubious. During the Victorian age the growth of the cult of Muscular Christianity increased religious observance in the army, at least on the surface, and by 1914 it was normal for there to be a church parade every Sunday, when the battalion was formed up, inspected and marched to church. In English regiments at least, most regimental or garrison churches were Church of England, so on arrival at the church those not of the established faith were fallen out. Little changes, and this author recalls a massive conversion to various Nonconformist affiliations at Sandhurst in the early 1960s, many officer cadets seeing a return to bed as preferable to sitting through a church service.

As the basic business of an army is killing people, not usually a pleasant affair and with the risk of being killed oneself, all armies dress up the essential nastiness of their trade with bands, medals, colours, gaudy dress uniforms and appeals to patriotism. If the approval of God can be added, then so much the better. It is difficult to quantify the religious feelings of individual soldiers. Church parades were compulsory, and danger tends to concentrate the mind on human mortality. Most people welcome a visit from the priest on their deathbed, in war or in peace, even if they have not set foot inside a church or said a prayer since they left school. As a generality, the soldiers of the regular army had no great depths of belief and tended to pay lip-service to religion because they had to, while the Territorial Force and men of the New Armies took it more seriously. Many officers were genuine believers, including Field Marshal Haig, and a conviction that God was on your side and willed you to win the war must indeed have been a comfort and a solace to the loneliness of command. Most padres not only officiated at formal religious services but acted as welfare officers too, distributing cigarettes, sweets and cups of tea, while providing the soldier with a sympathetic ear to a problem that he might not want to discuss with a regimental officer. Many were popular with the men, probably because they did not stand on ceremony. As the chaplain was not involved in the day-to-day running of the unit or in the decision-making process, and had no real military responsibility, he could afford a familiarity that the regimental officer could not. Many padres were brave men and stretched their non-combatant role to the limit. In all, 163 chaplains were killed, including the Reverend Theodore Bayley Hardy, VC, DSO, MC, padre of the 8th Lincolns, who died of wounds just three weeks before the end of the war.

Hardy was aged fifty-one when war broke out, and was priest-in-charge at the parish of Hutton Roof in the Lake District. He at once volunteered for the Army Chaplains' Department but was rejected as being too old. He continued to badger the authorities and eventually, in August 1916, he was accepted and posted to France, initially to the 8th Lincolns, later taking on the 8th Somersets as well.[9] Hardy's first decoration was the

Distinguished Service Order (DSO), by now being awarded as an acknowl-
edgement of leadership rather than, as earlier, for gallantry on the part of
junior officers.[10] The chaplain had accompanied a party of men who had
gone out into no man's land to rescue soldiers stuck fast in the mud. He
helped with the rescue operation and, despite having a broken arm himself,
tended the wounded, under fire the while. Only a few days later further
acts of personal bravery in tending wounded men attracted the Military
Cross. Between 5 and 27 April 1918, when the Allies were under extreme
pressure during the Kaiser's Offensive, Hardy continually accompanied
patrols and raids against German positions, tending wounded men and
assisting in extricating those caught by German shelling. These aggregated
acts of bravery by Hardy led to the supreme accolade for gallantry: the
award of the Victoria Cross. King George V personally pinned the medal to
Hardy's chest, and the occasion is commemorated in a painting by Terence
Cuneo, now in the Headquarters Mess of the Royal Army Chaplains'
Department.[11] Despite the pleas of his military and religious superiors,
and an offer of a post in England from the King himself, Hardy refused to
leave the front. His luck ran out and he died of wounds received on the
night of 10 October 1918, during the victorious British advance that was
to end the war just a month later.

Precisely because they were clerks in holy orders, whose presence was
felt by some to be incongruous, what chaplains did and how they behaved
was looked at in a different light from the actions of combatant officers
and soldiers. Chaplain Evers, padre of the 9th Loyals, a New Army battalion, was reported on favourably as having helped to carry forward a
machine gun, 'although he did not fire it'.[12] As every soldier might be required to do exactly that, and fire it, there was nothing very courageous
about it, but it was considered by the men to be good form.

A quite remarkable man of the cloth was Chaplain Willie Doyle, padre
to the 8th Battalion the Royal Dublin Fusiliers, a New Army battalion and
part of the 16th (Irish) Division formed from Redmond's Irish Volunteers.
Doyle, a Jesuit, was aged 42 when he became an army chaplain in 1915.
Like so many Jesuits, Doyle was a charismatic leader and would probably
have been as much at home commanding the battalion as being its
spiritual mentor. He was known for being constantly in the firing line,

encouraging the men, ministering to the sick and dying, and on many an occasion bringing up ammunition as well as the Host. He was awarded the Military Cross for bravery on the Somme in 1916, and was highly respected and admired by all, whether of his faith or otherwise. He was killed on 17 or 18 August 1917 during the fighting for Zonnebeke as part of the British offensive known as Third Ypres. Under heavy German shelling the battalion had been forced to withdraw from the Frezenberg Ridge and, according to the battalion war diary, on the way back the dead bodies of Father Doyle and Second Lieutenants Green and Marlow were seen in a dugout near the railway line. None of the bodies were ever recovered, or if they were recovered were not identified, and the men's names are engraved on the Tyne Cot Memorial near Ypres in Belgium. After his death, Father Doyle was the subject of much speculation and rumour. A biography of him, published in 1920 by Professor Alfred O'Rahilly, alleged that Doyle was recommended for the Victoria Cross but that this was turned down because the British would not award their highest gallantry decoration to an Irish nationalist who was a Jesuit to boot.[13] The year of publication of Professor O'Rahilly's book was one when Irish passions were running high. Anti-British sentiment, fanned by the execution of the ringleaders of the 'rising' of Easter 1916 and the deployment of the 'Black and Tans', or auxiliary constabulary, by the British to keep order, was intense. Professor O'Rahilly may not have been altogether detached in his opinions. In fact, Doyle's religious affiliations and political views seem unlikely reasons for the withholding of a decoration. Major-General W. B. Hickie, the commander of the 16th (Irish) Division, and the man who would have rejected or supported a citation for gallantry, was himself a Southern Irish Catholic with nationalist sympathies, (he became a senator in the Irish Free State government after retirement from the army), and decorations had already been awarded to all manner of persons not otherwise noted for their love of the British.[14] Another theory, which has been advanced by the Revd Nigel Cave, not only a Roman Catholic priest but a respected author and historian of the Great War, is that it was Doyle's ecclesiastical superiors who blocked the recommendation, on the grounds that nothing could be above and beyond the call of duty for a Catholic priest. This too cannot hold water. As Father O'Donoghe, the present archivist of the Irish Jesuit

Provinciate has been kind enough to point out to this author, the church authorities had always regarded the award of decorations as a matter for the military alone; they would not have interfered with any recommendations put forward through the chain of command. In any case, Father Doyle had already been awarded the MC, and gallantry decorations had been awarded to, and accepted by, other Jesuit priests.[15]

Although we may never know for sure, it seems that Father Doyle was never recommended for the Victoria Cross; not as any criticism of the man or of his actions, but simply because the criteria for an award were incredibly high. It is unfortunate that Father Doyle's personal file is missing (or as the Public Record Office engagingly puts it, 'search frustrated' – meaning that it cannot be found but is still being looked for). This fact should not encourage conspiracy theorists: among the millions of documents held in the PRO it is hardly remarkable that not all can be found, or that some are irretrievably lost, particularly those gathered in the aftermath of a major war. The war diaries of neither the 8th Royal Dublin Fusiliers, nor 48 Brigade nor the 16th Division make any mention of a recommendation, although this is not conclusive.[16] All we can say is that Father Doyle had a considerable influence on all who knew him, and that he would hardly have approved of the manipulation of his memory for the scoring of political points. Whatever the truth about a recommendation or otherwise for the VC, Father Doyle was an outstanding representative of his church and his order.[17]

After the war there was much discussion as to whether there had been a religious revival in Britain after 1914, emanating from the trenches. This tended to be the view of the theological establishment. The counter-argument was put by those such as Robert Graves, who considered that religion had contributed nothing. Religion is only of use in an army if it enhances morale and thus contributes to operational effectiveness. Looked at in this light, religion certainly helped those who believed. The church supported the official line (as, of course, it had to) and preached that the war was a just cause and worth fighting for. Those who believed drew comfort from the chaplain's presence, and those who did not at least got the occasional packet of cigarettes. Some New Army battalions formed branches of the Christian Union, and the influence of chaplains was probably greatest in Scottish and Irish battalions, where the church had a stronger hold on civilian society than was the case in England. Conversely, German soldiers had the words *Gott mit Uns* engraved on their belt buckles.

As for blood, there was much less of it about than is portrayed. Stories of men wading though blood, rivers running red with blood and the ground being red with blood are, sadly for Hollywood film-makers, just that: stories. Men stop bleeding once they are dead; a little bit of blood goes a long way, as anyone who has ever washed the blood from a small cut will know, and blood turns black fairly quickly once it has been expelled from the body. Men were wounded in the front line not only during Allied or German offensives, but in the steady daily attrition of shelling, sniping, trench raids or patrols in no man's land. When they were wounded the Royal Army Medical Corps came into its own. Each infantry battalion and cavalry regiment had one Regimental Medical Officer (RMO), a qualified doctor of medicine, with a team of medical orderlies and stretcher-bearers. When in the line the RMO set up a Regimental Aid Post, or RAP, which was the first port of call for the sick or wounded. The RAP was usually in the reserve line, but was often much closer – somewhere just behind the support line, or, when it was the British who were doing the attacking, in the firing line itself. The function of the RAP was first aid and diagnostic. A lightly wounded man could be treated and returned to his company or squadron, while more serious cases received sufficient attention to keep them alive until they could be evacuated back to the next line of treatment, the Advanced Dressing Station. These were mobile treatment centres, usually two per brigade, set up by the divisional field ambulance unit and far enough back to be out of the line of fire. At the ADS further treatment was given and weapons were removed, after which the man was moved farther back to the Casualty Clearing Station, normally one per division, and thence to a field, base or UK hospital. The rule was that recovery was always from the rear. That is, it was not for the wounded man's comrades to take him back for treatment – they had their own jobs to do – but for dedicated medical orderlies to come forward and evacuate him. At one stage an instruction was issued that men other than those of the medical staff were not to be recommended for the Victoria Cross for rescuing wounded. The very sound reason for this was that a man who stops to tend a wounded soldier is no longer getting on with what he is supposed to be doing – closing with and killing the enemy. There were occasions when soldiers who took wounded men back for treatment were suspected of using this humanitarian mission as an excuse to avoid combat, and in a few cases this was probably true.

War always stimulates medical advances, and survival rates increased dramatically as the war went on. What was important was speed, and on the Western Front, once wounded men got into the chain of evacuation, that is from the ADS on back, only 7.61 per cent died. In the case of men sick or injured from causes not attributable to the enemy, 0.91 per cent died. In the South African War the figures were 8.39 and 3.39 per cent respectively. Military medicine is concerned with returning men to duty as quickly as possible, and in even the most serious cases, those admitted to hospitals in the UK, 54.03 per cent were returned to duty.[18]

Many medical officers were extremely brave men. In the entire history of the Victoria Cross only three men have ever won the British Empire's highest award for gallantry twice. One of these was Captain Noel Chavasse, of the Royal Army Medical Corps.[19] Chavasse was the son of the Bishop of Liverpool. He graduated from Oxford and joined the Territorial Force in 1913. On the outbreak of war he was the medical officer of the Liverpool Scottish, a Territorial battalion of the King's (Liverpool) Regiment. When the Somme offensive started Chavasse had already won the Military Cross for bravery at Hooge in 1915. On 9 August 1916 the Liverpool Scottish were attacking the village of Guillemont from a position in Trones Wood, during the second phase of the offensive. The battalion suffered heavy casualties and Chavasse spent most of the day and the following night tending the wounded in no man's land, often under enemy observation, and helping to bring casualties back to the RAP. He was himself lightly wounded and was awarded the Victoria Cross. In a subsequent battle during the Third Ypres offensive Chavasse again went out into the open and rescued a number of men from no man's land. This time he was badly wounded in an advanced aid post that he had set up in a dugout, and subsequently died at Brandhoek Casualty Clearing Station. He was awarded a posthumous bar to his VC.

Chavasse was undoubtedly a highly motivated and personally very gallant officer. One has to ask, however, what on earth he was doing out in no man's land. It is not the job of the RMO to recover wounded: that is the task of the battalion stretcher-bearers. The RMO should remain in the RAP because it is there that the wounded will be brought, or there that they will report if they can walk. If the RMO is getting himself involved in the action, he is not present at the RAP when he may be needed. It is precisely for that reason that the army insists that the wounded come or are brought to the doctor, and not the doctor to the wounded. Without in any way attempting to detract from Chavasse's personal heroism and self-sacrifice, this author, cynical old soldier that he may be, cannot help but reflect that if he had been Chavasse's commanding officer, then he might have awarded a rocket rather than the Victoria Cross.

NOTES

1 The author recalls one deep-trench latrine, or DTL, which had been in use by 200 men for at least six years, and would have lasted for years longer had it not been blown up, with interesting results.

2 Public Record Office, Kew, *War Diary 2 Oxs & Bucks*, WO95/1348.

3 The exception was in the two divisions of the Indian Corps, some of whose battalions spent far longer in the trenches, the record being held by a Gurkha battalion that spent three weeks in the trenches without relief. This was because the establishment of an Indian battalion was 250 less than that of a British battalion, while the Indian Corps was expected to hold the same length of front as its British equivalent.

4 Major T. J. Mitchell and Miss G. M. Smith, *Official History of the War, Casualties and Medical Statistics*, Imperial War Museum (reprint), London, 1997.

5 Much the same happened in the Second World War. In 1941 the incidence of syphilis alone increased by 116 per cent amongst British men and by 63 per cent amongst women. Angus Calder, *The People's War*, Jonathan Cape, London, 1969.

6 At one time in the author's Gurkha battalion, a brigade commander of sound morals announced that men who contracted VD would be removed from the promotion roll. The result was that soldiers did not report it but instead visited a Chinese doctor, who charged the men 100 Hong Kong dollars to be injected with what turned out to be Carnation milk. Quite what effect Carnation milk has on the body is not known, but it most certainly does not cure VD, and the rule was eventually rescinded.

7 *General Routine Orders, Part I, Adjutant General's Branch*, GRO 2785, HMSO, 1 January 1918.

8 Mitchell and Smith, *Official History of the War, Casualties and Medical Statistics*, Imperial War Museum (reprint), London, 1997.

9 This was unusual: each battalion was entitled to its own chaplain, but the huge expansion of the army had created a shortage.

10 The introduction of the Military Cross (MC) in 1915 had led to a redefinition of the DSO.

11 The painting shows Hardy wearing a steel helmet, while the contemporary photographs show that he actually wore a service dress cap. This sort of error is all too common in military paintings commissioned long after the event, and is not the fault of the artist, but of those commissioning the painting.

12 Rich Schweitzer, 'The Cross and the Trenches: Religious Faith and Doubt among Some British Soldiers on the Western Front', in *War and Society*, Vol. 16, University of New South Wales, October, 1998.

13 Professor Alfred O'Rahilly, *Father William Doyle, SJ*, Longmans, Green & Co, London, 1920.

14 On the other hand, Tom Johnston and James Hagerty, in *The Cross and the Sword*, Geoffrey Chapman (Cassell), London, 1996, speculate that there was discrimination between the 36th (Ulster) Division and the 16th (Irish) Division in the award of decorations.

15 Southern Irish Roman Catholic priests in World War II refused gallantry awards, but not campaign medals, on the grounds that they were not British citizens. This was a somewhat illogical stance, as Gurkhas, who most certainly did accept gallantry awards, were not British citizens either.

16 *War Diary 8 Royal Dublin Fusiliers*, Public Record Office, Kew, WO95/1974; *War Diary 16th Division (General Staff) May 1917–April 1919*, WO95/1956; *War Diary 16th Division (A&QMG)*, WO95/1957; *War Diary HQ 48 Brigade*, WO95/1973.

17 It is the experience of this author – a member of the Church of England – that the most effective army padres are the Roman Catholic ones, and the best of those are the Jesuits.

18 Mitchell and Smith, *Official History of the War, Casualties and Medical Statistics*, Imperial War Museum (reprint), London, 1997.

19 The others were Lt Martin-Leake (1902 and 1915) and Capt. Charles Upham (1941 and 1942).

4

THE TOOLS OF THE TRADE

The private soldier in his trench in the firing line was the point of a very long spear, which stretched forward from well behind the battle area. Armies are structured for the job they have to do – kill enemy soldiers efficiently. This structure, common to all armies in a greater or lesser degree, and learned from centuries of experience, is based on the assumption that one person can control the actions of about ten other individuals, and that one headquarters can control up to four subordinate units. In 1914 the private soldier in the British infantry was a member of a section, consisting of up to eight privates, riflemen or guardsmen and commanded by a corporal, with a lance corporal to assist him.[1] Four sections were grouped into a platoon, the lowest officer's command, with a lieutenant or second lieutenant assisted by a sergeant. Not every army had commissioned officers this far down the chain of command, and indeed an NCO could quite well command a platoon. The real reason for the presence of a subaltern in the British army platoon was to train him, and to give him experience of small-unit command before he graduated to command of a company, which had four platoons commanded by a major or captain. The battalion, with four companies, a machine-gun section and a headquarters, the whole commanded by a lieutenant colonel, was the soldier's immediate family. Once he joined he would spend his entire service in that battalion, except for possibly being sent away for a year or two as an instructor or recruiter if he became an NCO, or occasionally being transferred to another battalion of the same regiment. Within the battalion everybody knew everybody else, at least by sight. King's Regulations, the application of military law as embodied by Parliament in the Army Act, laid down that a soldier could not be forced to change his regiment. All this made for a closeness and a regimental spirit not always present in other armies where men could be moved around as individuals, but it made for weaknesses too, as we have seen in the system of territorial recruiting. Officers hardly ever changed regiments and most infantry officers' ambitions stretched no farther than command of their own battalion; anything after that was a bonus. In the pre-war regular army a competent officer could expect to reach the rank of lieutenant colonel from the age of forty-five onwards. If appointed to command a battalion his tour was for four years or until the age of fifty-two, whichever came first. This was rather older than today, when the commanding officer of a battalion is thirty-nine or forty on assuming command, which he holds for between two and a half and three years. Promotion in the pre-war army was inevitably slow as, unlike today, most officers joined with the intention of making the army a lifetime career. In the New Army battalions commanding officers were usually even older at the beginning of the war, for they tended to be men called out of retirement or majors previously passed over for command of their own regular battalions.

The next level above the battalion was the brigade, commanded by a brigadier general, with four infantry battalions and certain brigade units such as a transport company of the Army Service Corps and, from 1915, a brigade trench-mortar company. A division, with three brigades, was commanded by a major-general. A division was almost a mini-army, with its own artillery, communications unit, transport, cavalry squadron and field ambulance. Before 1914 the British army rarely had formations above divisions – it was not large enough to need them – and on deployment to Europe in 1914 it had been intended that General Headquarters, the supreme military command in the field, would command the divisions directly. The French, however, with their vastly larger army, were organised into corps, with from two to four divisions in each; so for the sake of conformity the British followed suit, with each corps commanded by a lieutenant general. As the war went on and the BEF expanded, the next level up was required, and armies, commanded by a general and with two or more corps in each, were formed, beginning with the First and Second Armies at Christmas 1914. Despite the substantive ranks established for the commanders of brigades, divisions, corps and armies, the British army is wary of making too many promotions, as it invariably contracts after a war; officers were thus often a rank below that officially sanctioned, or granted local or acting rank until it was certain that they would retain the post.[2]

The organisation of formations of the BEF evolved as the war progressed, particularly after the lessons of the Somme in 1916 had been absorbed. The organisation of a division of 1915 is shown opposite.

Throughout the war it was very rare for battalions to move to another brigade, and brigades were not often transferred to another division. Divisions did move up and down the front, so battalions gained experience of different parts of the line. Corps and armies, on the other hand, tended to be static and divisions moved in and out of them as operational requirements demanded.

The length of front held by a division depended upon the ground and on the prevailing tactical situation, but was generally between 2,000 and 4,000 yards. A brigade held half that, a battalion between 500 and 1,000 yards, and a company frontage was anything from 100 to 250 yards. This gave considerable depth to the position. An enemy attacking had first to penetrate the firing line, then fight through the support line. By then the reserve line would be fully manned and the attacker would have to get through that as well. If he succeeded – and he rarely did – the reserve brigade or a resting division's troops would have been warned for action and further defensive positions would be manned. As the attacker advanced, his supply, evacuation and reinforcement chain got longer and longer, while the defender was pushed back onto his own equivalents. The depth of the positions on each side very largely contributed to the fact that, once the war settled down from the autumn of 1914, very few significant advances were made and a real breakthrough was rarely achieved.

Unless enemy action was imminent, or when a major British offensive

A BRITISH INFANTRY DIVISION IN 1915

DIVISIONAL HEADQUARTERS
(Major General commanding and staff)

1 signal company

ARTILLERY
HQ Divisional artillery
12 batteries of 18pdr guns (total 48 guns)
4 batteries of 4.5" howitzers (total 16)
1 heavy battery (4 x 60pdr)
1 Divisional ammunition column

ENGINEERS
HQ Divisional Engineers
3 field companies Royal Engineers

INFANTRY
3 brigades, total 12 battalions, each battalion 4 x Vickers medium machine guns

MOUNTED TROOPS
1 squadron cavalry, one cyclist company

PIONEERS
1 pioneer battalion

SERVICE AND SUPPORT
3 field ambulances
1 motor ambulance workshop
1 sanitary section
1 mobile veterinary section
Divisional train

TOTAL ALL RANKS: 19,614

was in the offing, a division usually put two of its brigades in the front lines, with the third brigade well out of the battle area resting and retraining. Brigades had two battalions in the front, or 'up' as it was known, and two behind, although some brigades had three of their battalions up. As we have seen, within the battalion the usual deployment was two companies up and two back.

The British army was divided into fighting arms and non-fighting arms. This was not an accurate description: all soldiers were expected to fight when necessary, and most of them did. The terms used today are combat arms and supporting arms. The fighting arms were those that actually directed their activities to killing the enemy: cavalry, artillery, engineers, infantry, the Cyclist Corps and the Royal Flying Corps, with the later addition of the Machine Gun Corps and the Tank Corps. The so-called non-fighting arms were the Army Service Corps (responsible for supplies of all types and most transport not belonging to units), the Royal Army Medical Corps, the Army Veterinary Corps (responsible for the procurement and care of army horses, mules, dogs, pigeons, camels and oxen), the Army Ordnance Corps (mainly technicians who looked after ammunition and machinery), the Army Pay Corps and, from 1917, the Labour Corps.

On 1 September 1914 men in fighting arms on the Western Front made up eighty-three per cent of the total, declining to sixty-six per cent by 1918 as advances in technology produced more and more aids to warfare. This figure is deceptive, as not all the men in a combat unit were there to fight. In an infantry battalion of 1914, at established strength of 1,000 all ranks, 640 were in rifle platoons, that is men available for defending a trench line or mounting an attack, and thirteen were manning the battalion's machine guns. The remainder were there to ensure that the fighting men were launched into battle at the right place and the right time, and had the equipment and support they needed. Overall the proportion of supporter to fighter was probably in the order of 1:1 in 1914 and 3:1 by 1918. This ratio increases when the Labour Corps is included: established in 1917, it had 200,000 men on the Western Front by 1918, making up fourteen per cent of the total strength. The increase in the ratio of support to combat is an inevitable trend in all armies. In Normandy in 1944 it was about 4:1 in the

British army and 5:1 in the US forces (but only about 2.5:1 in the German Wehrmacht). In today's British army it verges on 8:1.

Much of the soldier's time in the trenches was spend in hard labour, for trenches required constant repair if they were not to collapse. During quiet periods, that is when an attack by either side was not imminent, every battalion had a routine laid down for life in the trenches. This routine revolved around security, administration and rest. It had long been the practice in the British army to stand-to every morning at first light and every evening at last light. Stand-to meant that every soldier was either on the fire-step or ready to get onto it, fully clothed with webbing equipment of ammunition pouches and water bottle, weapon loaded and ready to fire. Not only did this ensure that the troops were ready for an enemy attack delivered at these times, as was often the case, it also gave officers an opportunity to move along the line and see each man, check that he was fit and well, that he understood his orders and that he was prepared in all respects for whatever might come.

Each bay, that is the portion of trench between two traverses, was occupied by a section or half-section under its own NCO. By day one of these men would be on the fire-step as a sentry, looking out over no man's land from behind the protection of a sandbagged embrasure, or through a steel shield with an observation slit. Later much use was made of periscopes, which gave sentries absolute protection as they could be operated from within the trench without a man's having to expose his head. The remainder of the group would be improving the trench, pushing saps out towards enemy lines, digging sleeping bays into the bottom of the trench wall or in the command trench, or sleeping to order. There was very little cooking in the firing line as the smoke attracted enemy attention, but there was usually a constant supply of tea and sandwiches. Much time was spent keeping weapons clean and serviceable, and there was an inspection by officers and NCOs of every man's rifle at least once each day, usually after breakfast. Weapon cleaning was done by half-sections, so that at least half the men's rifles were ready to fire if need be. By night sentries were doubled, and men's tours as sentry, generally for two hours, overlapped so that both did not change over at once and there was always at least one man whose eyes had adjusted to darkness.

Radio in 1914 was rudimentary. The Royal Flying Corps did have a spark transmitter in some aircraft, and at corps level there was some radio equipment. No radio was yet small enough and robust enough to be used by the troops in the trenches, and communication was by runner, telephone, semaphore flags, heliograph and even by pigeon and trained dogs. The most common method was by telephone. Lines were laid from forward companies back to battalion headquarters in the support or reserve trenches, and then back to brigade headquarters. Two sets of line were always laid in case enemy shelling cut one, and where possible the line was dug in and protected.

Most work was done at night. The carrying-up of rations, ammunition and water and the digging of major new trench lines or communication trenches was much safer under the cover of darkness. Signallers would check their telephone wires, and parties would go out to ensure that the obstacle belt in front of the firing line had not been damaged by shelling or cut by unseen German patrols.

Throughout the war the largest arm of the service was the infantry, with fifty-four per cent of the total strength of the BEF in 1914, reducing to just over thirty-three per cent in 1918 as other methods, such as tanks and the Machine Gun Corps, were used to help inflict death and destruction. Not surprisingly the infantry had the highest casualty rate of any arm, eighty-three per cent of the total on the Western Front, while the safest combat arm to be in was the cavalry: with an average of just over three per cent of the army's manpower, they sustained less than one per cent of its casualties. The casualties in the Machine Gun Corps were very heavy. Although it was only formed in late 1915, it had about twice the number of casualties of the Royal Engineers, despite having only one-quarter of the number of men.

Each soldier in the BEF, with the exception of medical personnel and chaplains, was armed with a rifle, the .303 calibre Lee-Enfield, probably the best military rifle ever made anywhere, which remained in service in the British regular army with only slight modification until 1960. This rifle, like all rifles, had to be 'zeroed' to the user. Every man holds his rifle in a slightly different way, and every rifle has slight variations in the alignment of its various components. A rifle was a personal issue, which the man was supposed to retain throughout his service, and he had to fire it on a range until, by adjustment of the foresight and backsight, the rifle put the shots where the man aimed. Even the best shot in the army could not be sure of hitting a target with the first few rounds if the rifle was not zeroed to him personally. Much nonsense is talked about the British infantry and its shooting. It is true that the British army spent more time perfecting rifle shooting than any other in Europe – a sensible precaution when it was always smaller than anyone else's, and when, as a long-term volunteer organisation, it could afford the time to develop this important skill. The regular army had a high standard of shooting in 1914, but the so-called 'mad minute', where each man fired fifteen rounds, was very far from accurate and was nothing more than the bringing-down of a lot of lead in a wide area. It probably did confuse the young German reservists into thinking that the British had more machine guns than they actually did, but it would not have fooled them for long, or a regular NCO at all. The usual rapid rate of fire was eight to twelve shots per minute, supposedly aimed, but this could not be sustained for long with a bolt-action rifle: the bolt had to be worked after each shot to eject the spent round and load the next, the sights lined up, the breathing adjusted and the trigger squeezed. Men were trained to fire aimed shots at up to 600 yards' range, and longer in volley fire, but the normal battle shooting range was between 100 and 300 yards. When the rifle was not in use the sights were set to 300 yards. At the beginning of the war the overall standard of shooting was good in the regular army, less good in Territorial Force battalions and only moderate among the New Army men. As time went on the first declined and the latter two improved; by 1918, when much less reliance was placed on individual prowess with the rifle, the general standard was much the same throughout the infantry, the majority qualifying as first- or second-class shots, with a few marksmen and a handful of incorrigible third-class men.

Each man normally took 150 rounds of rifle ammunition with him when he went into the trenches, and more was available in the front line. It would be very unusual indeed for a man to fire off this amount of ammunition, even when engaged in a major offensive or defending against a large-scale attack; but the British had learned the lessons of having insufficient ammunition the hard way, and it was now very rare for a man to run out. It is not possible to quantify the exact rate of ammunition expenditure to kills achieved. At Neuve-Chapelle in March 1915 the British and Indian soldiers fired a total of three million rounds of small-arms ammunition. The total of German killed and wounded is estimated at 16,000, giving a hit rate of one for every 187 rounds fired. This, however, takes no account of casualties caused by bomb guns (trench mortars), machine guns and shelling, or of men hit several times. It is more likely that around 400 rounds of rifle ammunition were fired for every hit, but even this is not the whole picture. Rifle fire is not always aimed at a specific target. Men will be ordered to fire on an area to prevent the enemy using it, or on a line of trenches to keep the enemy heads down, and a strict linkage of rounds fired to enemy casualties is meaningless.

It is a common misconception that it was the machine gun that killed most British soldiers in France and Flanders, but the real killer was artillery. An analysis undertaken by the RAMC showed that just over two per cent of all wounds were caused by grenades, almost thirty-nine per cent by bullets, either rifle or machine-gun, and just over fifty-eight per cent by shells from artillery or trench mortars. The remainder, some 0.32 per cent of the total, were due to other causes, including bayonets.[3]

In the British army the Royal Artillery was divided into three branches: the Royal Horse Artillery, the Royal Field Artillery and the Royal Garrison Artillery. The horse artillery supported the cavalry and the field artillery the infantry. The Royal Garrison Artillery originally manned static guns in fortifications, but by 1914 their main purpose overseas was to man heavy guns, used mainly for bombarding enemy artillery positions (this was known as counter-battery fire). The garrison artillery was also responsible for manning anti-aircraft guns (from September 1914). Curiously, perhaps, mountain artillery also belonged to the Royal Garrison Artillery. This sub-branch consisted of artillery units intended to support the infantry in inhospitable terrain where there were no roads. Their light guns could be dismantled and carried on mules, the criterion being that the guns had to be able to go where a man could go without using his hands to crawl or scramble. There were only three mountain-artillery batteries employed on the Western Front, but others, of both the British and Indian armies, fought in Egypt (two batteries), Gallipoli (four), East Africa (five), Mesopotamia (twelve) and Palestine (fourteen).

Artillery pieces can be broadly classified as field guns, heavy guns and howitzers. The difference between a gun and a howitzer is that the former fires on a relatively flat trajectory, whereas the latter can 'lob': that is, fire a shell at a high angle into the air so that it falls behind an obstacle, beyond a range of hills or into a trench.[4] With artillery of the Great War period, the penalty for this ability to lob was a shorter range than a gun of the same calibre.[5]

It is a common cry of those who belong to the 'butchers and bunglers' school of Great War scholarship (if their activities can be dignified with the term 'scholarship') that the British army always prepared to fight the last war. This is one of the more enduring accusations of those who consider that British generalship was concentrated in the hands of stupid, hidebound traditionalists. Of course British generals – and indeed all generals – prepared to fight the last war. As a crystal ball to foresee the future is not available, it is only by examining the lessons of previous campaigns that any sort of war-fighting doctrine can evolve. General staffs which were unprepared to face problems that had appeared before would be failing in their duty and deserving of censure. Men who examined what had happened in the past and were prepared to meet it can only be praised. In liberal democracies at least, there is little funding for speculative development, and an army that spent too much time and money planning for a future which might not come to pass would be foolish indeed. That said, professional soldiers in all armies took note of current experience and where possible incorporated its fruits, and this was particularly true in regard to artillery.

Consideration as to how a future European war might develop was based on the events of the Franco-Prussian War of 1870–71, the South African War of 1899–1902 and the Russo-Japanese War of 1904–05. All these wars consisted of manoeuvring by armies, interspersed with short set-piece battles, and a few siege operations. The infantry, who would do most of the fighting, needed an artillery gun that could move quickly to their support and fire at enemy infantry and cavalry in the open at the maximum range at which the methods of fire control then available could guarantee hitting a target.

During the first decade of the century most armies re-equipped their artillery with what were known as 'quick-firing' guns. During the last great pan-European conflagration, the Napoleonic Wars, artillery guns had been muzzle-loading and ammunition divided into the ball or shell (what was actually fired at the enemy) and the propellant (the charge that drove the shell from the gun). Guns had been sighted by eye and the recoil of firing drove the gun backwards, from where it had to be hauled back into its firing position and re-aimed before another round could be loaded and fired. Technical development since then had concentrated on increasing rate of fire, accuracy and range. This was achieved through four major innovations: ammunition incorporating a cartridge case, which would increase the rate of firing as well as sealing the breech; a breech mechanism that was easy and quick to operate, thereby increasing the rate of fire; the incorporation of a recoil mechanism inherent to the gun carriage, allowing the gun to remain in position when firing and reducing the time needed to set the sights between firings; and rifled barrels to improve range and accuracy. In most cases the ammunition came in one piece: that is, the shell and the cartridge case containing the propellant were fixed together, rather than separate as they had been formerly; although in some howitzers, where the propellant had to be varied according to the range required, ammunition came separated.

The French were the first to mass-produce a gun that combined all these attributes: the 75-mm model 1897, so called for the year it first came into service. The 75 was breech-loading; its ammunition came with the shell at the end of a brass case in which was the propellant, so it could be loaded in one movement. On firing, the brass case expanded to make a gas-tight seal at the breech. A recoil mechanism absorbed the shock of firing by allowing the barrel to move back, ejecting the spent case as it did so, before returning to the loading-and-firing position. As the gun remained static throughout, a shield could be incorporated to protect the crew from small-arms fire. There was a simple pole trail and the gun could be drawn by six horses. By 1914 the 75 was an artillery legend, but actually almost obsolete. It suited the French doctrine of continuous attack, however, and the French army had a great many of them. Though the British, German and Austrian equivalents were superior in range and weight of shell, there are times when a great many bows and arrows are better than one rifle, and there is a natural reluctance in all armies to admit that what you are equipping your soldiers with may not the best available. And thus the 75, with numerous modifications, remained in service with the French (and American) armies until the early 1940s.

The standard British field gun was the eighteen-pounder, introduced in 1904 and combining the best features of artillery development by other countries and by the Royal Navy. It too was a rifled breech-loader with recoil mechanism and protective shield. It was robust, once the recoil mechanism had been adapted for the very high rate of fire experienced on the Western Front, and accurate. The gun had a dial sight to allow unseen targets to be engaged by laying the gun from a known compass bearing. In 1914 each British division had three brigades (regiments in modern parlance) of eighteen-pounders, each brigade having three batteries of six guns each, or a divisional total of fifty-four guns. By 1915 the requirement to equip the New Armies and the Territorial Force had forced a reduction to forty-eight guns per division, and in 1916 a further reduction to thirty-six allowed the formation of Army Field Artillery Brigades, a centralisation of assets which could then be deployed where the army commander thought they were most needed.

On the outbreak of war artillery training was based on what had gone before, and this had generally been situations where guns could see the target they were firing at. Fire control consisted of the battery commander standing to the upwind flank of his battery with a telescope, watching the fall of shot and correcting the fire until it hit the target. It was thus unnecessary for the guns to be able to fire further than a man with a telescope could see, and the maximum range of the French 75 was 7,500 yards, and of the British eighteen-pounder 6,500, increasing to 9,300 in 1917.[6] In the early stages of the war it was not uncommon for field (and horse) artillery units to bring their guns right up to the infantry forward positions. Partly this was due to the difficulties of communication, but there was also a feeling in the Royal Artillery that guns at the front helped boost infantry morale, as indeed they did. At the end of the movement phase of the war it became obvious that artillery would no longer fire at a target that the gunners could see, and methods of fire control from a distance began to be developed. Guns were placed to the rear and behind cover, usually a ridge line, but often dug in as well, and an observer – the Artillery Observation Officer – was stationed where he could see the target.

In defence guns would be unhitched from their transport – horses – and lined up at a location identified on the map, with all gun barrels pointing in the same direction, specified by a compass bearing. In its simplest form an opportunity shoot might be conducted by the Observation Officer giving the map reference of the target to the gun line by telephone. At the gun line the battery commander, or later the Gun Position Officer, would work out the range to the target and the direction left or right of the known bearing, and the gunners would traverse the guns to point at the target. The elevation would be given, worked out from range tables that gave the number of degrees of elevation required for a given range, and one or two guns would fire one round. Contrary to popular belief, an artillery piece is not a pinpoint weapon but an area one, and the Observation Officer would tell the gun to go right or left, drop or add, until the shells were landing where they were wanted. The officer on the gun line had to know the compass bearing between the guns and the target in order to work out what the observer's 'left one hundred' meant for the guns, and the alteration of elevation and traverse for the guns was applied accordingly. When the firing gun dropped a shell within twenty-five yards of the target, the observer would report 'on target' and the whole battery would fire. Firing off the map was not the best method of bringing artillery fire onto a target, as maps, at least in the early part of the war, were inaccurate. The preferred method was for the row of guns to be positioned at right angles to what was known as the 'zero line', a compass bearing from the centre of the gun line to the target, or to the centre of a designated area. The artillery observer would then work out the range and angle from his position to the target, and from his position to the guns, using a rangefinder. Once these measurements were known, simple trigonometry, incorporated in range tables, allowed the officer on the gun line to work out the range and bearing to the target. Usually two guns would fire at first, one with its range set at 300 yards farther than the second, which fired five seconds later. The aim was to achieve a bracket, that is with one gun dropping its shell ahead of the target, and the other behind it. The observer corrected the fire, by voice or more often by telephone, until the rounds were falling where they should, and the whole battery could then fire onto the target.

The system depended totally on the ability of the observer to communicate with the gun lines, and while the telephone, with lines duplicated and dug in, worked well when the BEF was static in trenches, it was unreliable in the attack, when gunners had to lay a line to the observer who was moving forward with the infantry. All methods were tried, and used, but it would not be until well after this war that a portable radio would allow instantaneous reaction to an infantry request for fire on an opportunity target. Fire plans to support infantry on the move in the Great War were timed, rather than 'on call'. In the course of the conflict fire control became ever more sophisticated, as did the method of aiming the gun. As ranges increased so the flight of the shell was influenced by such factors as wind direction, humidity and atmospheric pressure, and range tables were amended to take account of these.

The lesson of previous wars had been that most field artillery ammunition should be designed to take on infantry, cavalry and other guns in the open, and so British field artillery entered the war with a preponderance of shrapnel shells.[7] The shrapnel shell for the eighteen-pounder had a steel casing filled with 375 lead balls, each about the size of a marble and weighing just under half an ounce, and a bursting charge. On reaching the target the shell exploded in mid-air, scattering the area in front or around it with a hail of lead, rather like a very large shotgun blast. It was widely believed that the fuse, time or percussion, was made under licence from Messrs Krupp of Essen, and that it was not until the arrival of the less than gentlemanly Lloyd George as Minister of Munitions in 1915 that the British government stopped paying royalties for the use of this German invention. As with many good stories there is no evidence whatever for this, and in any case the British had developed a fuse of their own.

Shrapnel was excellent for shooting at troops in the open, but it was less effective for blowing gaps in wire obstacles and for destroying fortified emplacements and collapsing trenchworks. It rapidly became clear that it was high explosive that was needed on the Western Front, and not shrapnel, but with the British armaments industry based on a limited requirement of shells for peacetime training and small colonial campaigns, it would be some time before the BEF could have an unlimited supply of the type of shell they wanted. On the outbreak of war there was no high-explosive shell for the eighteen-pounder, and it was not until October 1914 that an experimental high-explosive shell for this gun was issued. Highly effective as it turned out to be, it could not be issued in quantity for some considerable time; even then it often buried itself in the ground before exploding, thus reducing its effect. It was not until 1917 that the British introduced a 'graze' fuse, which could be set to explode the shell as soon as it came into contact with the target.

Behind the field artillery, and complementary to it, were the howitzers and the 'heavies'. In 1914 each division had one brigade (regiment) of eighteen (reduced to sixteen in 1915) 4.5-inch howitzers, which fired a thirty-five-pound shrapnel shell to a range of 7,300 yards. This was an excellent gun, once sufficient high-explosive shells were made available for it, and a few were still in service in the British army until 1944, the only modification of any significance being the addition of pneumatic tyres. The 4.5 had come into service in 1904, but only 192 had been manufac-tured by 1914, of which 108 were with the BEF, forty-five were in reserve and thirty-nine had gone to Australia, Canada and New Zealand. Some regular and all Territorial Force batteries were initially equipped with older weapons.

A division also had one heavy battery of four sixty-pounder guns. This weapon, dating from 1904, fired a sixty-pound high-explosive or shrapnel shell from a five-inch barrel to a range of 10,300 yards, soon increasing to 12,300 with better ammunition. Again, with industry not geared up to the requirements of total war, only forty-one sixty-pounders had been made by 1914, of which thirteen were in India or Canada. More had to be manufactured quickly, but this was a precision instrument, never designed for mass production. Modifications to enable rapid assembly increased the weight to five tons, too heavy to be drawn by horses, and so wartime versions were towed by traction engines.

Other heavy guns used by the BEF during the war were all howitzers of various types: the biggest was the fifteen-inch, which fired a shell weighing 1,400 pounds out to a maximum range of 10,795 yards, and the

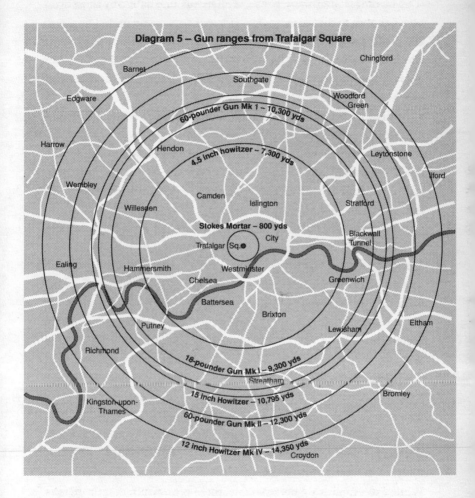

Diagram 5 – Gun ranges from Trafalgar Square

one with the longest range was the twelve-inch Mk IV, which could project its 750-pound shell out to 14,350 yards, or more than eight miles.

The ranges of artillery guns are often misunderstood by those who have not been at the receiving end or have not been supported by them, and the diagram on page 123 shows how far each of the various types of gun could reach were it to be allowed to fire from Trafalgar Square – an unlikely scenario, but one which might help the current obsession with the removal of pigeons.

The German army had similar guns with similar capabilities. In 1914 a British infantry division disposed of seventy-six artillery pieces of all types, while a German division had eighty-four, not a great disparity, but the difference was that the German army was much larger than the British, had no shortage of ammunition, and could call on a much greater corps reserve of artillery than could the British.

British casualties from enemy artillery occurred when high-explosive shells collapsed trenches, suffocating the occupants if they were not blown apart first, or when shrapnel was either fired at troops advancing over open ground or exploded directly over a trench. The British army went into the war in soft cloth forage caps, armour on the battlefield having long disappeared except in the French cavalry, which still wore the helmets with horsehair plumes and the back and breastplates in which they had charged Wellington's squares at Waterloo, with about as much protective effect. The French were the first to issue their infantry with a steel helmet, designed not to stop a rifle bullet (no helmet, then or now, could be made which could stop a bullet and still be light enough to wear) but as a protection against shrapnel and bits blown off trenches. The British followed suit in 1915, initially issuing helmets as trench stores, to be handed over on relief, and then in 1916 making them a personal issue to every man. While exact figures are not available, there is no doubt that the helmet provided protection against spent bullets, splinters and glancing shrapnel, and the incidence of wounds from these sources was considerably less than it would have been without them. Soldiers, then as now, worried most about head wounds (particularly blindness) and having their wedding tackle blown away. The latter anxiety may have been irrational – castration allows a normal life in many respects, and is probably a lot less incapacitating than losing a leg – and in any case not much could be done about it; but the helmet did protect against facial injuries, or men thought it did, which was almost as important.

The roles of the artillery in the BEF were many. One important task was counter-battery fire, in which the position of enemy guns would be identified by sound ranging, from intelligence reports or by guesswork, and British guns would attempt to shell them and make it impossible for them to fire.[8] This was particularly important during the lead-up to and during a British advance, for it was enemy artillery that would cause most casualties to the attacker. The guns would attempt to collapse enemy trenches and destroy emplacements and bunkers, particularly those containing machine guns, and shrapnel would be used to keep the enemy infantry from firing on advancing troops. It was also the task of the guns to create gaps in the enemy wire through which our troops could pass, and here the limitations of shrapnel quickly became apparent. It had been thought that shrapnel could cut wire, and in the early days it seemed that it could. In the artillery bombardment before Neuve-Chapelle in March 1915, a forty-minute affair which was the greatest artillery bombardment by the British up to that time, the artillery supporting the Indian Corps cleared away most of the German wire. It failed to do the same thing on the front of the British division attacking at right angles to the Indians, but that was thought to be because the guns had been late into position and not had time to identify the targets properly and range in on them The truth was that German wire obstacles at that stage of the war were very largely a series of wooden knife-rests with barbed wire attached. The shrapnel blew them out of the way and broke up the wood; it did not actually cut the wire. Later, when wire obstacles were securely fixed to the ground by iron pickets, the flexible wire did not break but simply sprang back into position after being hit by a shrapnel ball. Many of the difficulties for the rest of 1915 and for 1916 were caused by there being insufficient high-explosive shells with an effective fuse to make breaches in the wire.

As more and more artillery, and better, more plentiful and role-designed ammunition became available, so methods of artillery support became more complicated and more helpful to the infantry. If the infantry were attacking a specific portion of the enemy trench the artillery could lay down a curtain of shellfire to the left and right, preventing enemy rein-forcements from moving into the threatened area. A lifting barrage was one where the artillery fired a continuous stream of shells along a certain line ahead of advancing friendly infantry. Once the infantry reached the limit of the danger area (that is, where shells could affect our own troops), firing stopped and the guns altered their elevation and began firing on another line farther ahead. A more sophisticated method – and a better one because there was no halt in the firing – was where the guns fired on two lines, leapfrogging their fire forward: this was known as the rolling, or creeping, barrage. This, however, required a prodigious amount of artillery, with each gun firing four rounds per minute, reverting to three as the advance progressed. Guns could also leave lanes in their barrage, to allow an undamaged approach for cavalry or tanks, or to facilitate the construction of a road by the Royal Engineers.

There were problems. The lifting or rolling barrage left craters, destroyed drainage systems and, particularly where ground had been fought over more than once and when it rained, made crossing the area a real effort for the infantry (although, once fire and movement techniques – about which more later – began to be implemented, it provided more cover for individuals and machine-gun groups). Unless communications between the advancing infantry and the guns, via the observation officers, were perfect, it was very difficult to slow down or speed up the artillery barrage, which was supposed to be moving forward at the same speed as the infantry. If the infantry were held up, either because the defenders had not all been incapacitated or forced to stay below ground, or if the ground was badly cut up, the artillery fire would have moved on well beyond the enemy trenches when the infantry still had a long way to go to reach them. Another problem was that when the infantry had reached the limit of the guns' range, the guns had to move forward before they could give support once more. Eventually this would be solved by leapfrogging batteries, but in the early days there were simply not enough artillery units for this to be effective.

Prior to a major attack the artillery would bombard the enemy trenches in the hope of so devastating the defenders that the infantry could advance without much opposition. At first this ploy worked, but eventually it fell victim to its own predictability. The Germans dug deeper and deeper into the earth, used more and more concrete, and evacuated most of the troops in their firing line into deep shelters until the bombardment ceased or moved on – as it had to once attacking troops got within a hundred yards or so. Sitting in a dugout while an artillery bombardment was going on overhead was not a form of relaxation. Dugouts and trenches collapsed and some men went mad with the noise, but with a bit of luck the Germans could then man their firing line once more, with the attackers exposed and without artillery support. The British tried various permutations, including a very short bombardment, or even no bombardment at all, and the shelling not of the firing line but of the likely areas for reinforcements, headquarters and stores dumps – the idea of the last tactic being to so disorganise the enemy command structure that the infantry could have a straight fight with what was left on the firing line. The trouble with this method was that until well into the war guns still had to range in, that is, fire at the intended target until they were sure of hitting it, after which the details of range, direction and elevation would be noted for use when the time came. This gave the enemy ample warning that something was up. Predicted fire, where initial ranging is not required, was a very black art indeed, requiring all sorts of meteorological information to be entered on the range table, and it was not perfected until the Battle of Cambrai in late 1917.

The artillery increased enormously as the war went on, although as a percentage of the total manpower only from sixteen per cent in 1914 to eighteen per cent in 1918. In 1914 Britain manufactured ninety-one guns or howitzers; in 1918 industry provided 10,680. In 1914 the Royal Artillery had 554 batteries in all theatres; by 1918 there were 1,796. The artillerymen worked very hard, as manning the guns became a twenty-four hour task. Unlike the infantry, whose soldiers were regularly rotated out of the line, a division's guns remained in position as long as any part of that division was in the line, and manpower had to be increased to ensure that there were always crews ready and able to man the guns. Even when a whole division was taken out of the line, the guns were often left in action before being sent off to rejoin their parent division days or weeks later.

On any one day on the Western Front there could be as many as eighty batteries of artillery on the move, which not only caused all sorts of problems of traffic control, but added to the fatigue of the gunners.

It has been calculated that the Royal Artillery fired over 170 million rounds on the Western Front between 1914 and 1918. If only one per cent of those were duds that failed to explode (and the real figure was much higher), then it is not surprising that even today somebody is killed in France or Belgium every year by unexploded shells from the Great War.[9]

It is not possible to distinguish between deaths and wounds caused by bullets fired from machine guns and those caused by rifle rounds, but machine guns were one of the most valuable weapons available to both sides. Armies had long sought a weapon that could project a steady stream of bullets across the battlefield to increase the firepower of the infantry and compensate for inferior numbers. During the Napoleonic Wars the Royal Navy produced a seven-barrelled musket, but it fired all seven barrels at once and, while devastating at close range, took a long time to reload. Trials were held using a number of muskets attached to carts and fired one after the other in rapid succession, but the reloading time and the inherent inaccuracy of smooth-bore weapons ensured that the experiment came to naught. The French were the first, in the Franco-Prussian War, to bring a practical machine gun into service; but the *mitrailleuse* was regarded as an artillery weapon, and was anyway so secret that it played little part in the war. The Gatling, which came into the British service in 1871, was useful against mass charges by unsophisticated enemies encountered in colonial campaigns, but was hand-cranked and liable to jam at awkward moments. In 1884 Hiram Maxim, an American, invented a machine gun that used the recoil of the weapon to load, fire and eject the empty case. It was on his principle that all subsequent machine guns were based. The British army introduced the Maxim into service in 1891 (well in advance of the German army), and as the Maxim, Vickers-Maxim and Vickers, it remained in service with only a few modifications until the early 1960s – almost a record for any firearm.[10] The British Vickers Mark I, as the gun eventually became, was mounted on a tripod and could fire at a cyclical rate of 500 rounds per minute.[11] This was slightly slower than the German Maxim or the French Hotchkiss at

600 rounds per minute, but the Vickers was more robust and less liable to stoppages. Ammunition came in canvas belts of 250 rounds, and as the very high rate of fire caused the barrel to overheat, it was surrounded by a jacket into which water was poured as a coolant. The jacket held around seven pints of water, and as the heating of the barrel turned the water to steam, a tube ran from the jacket to a can, in which the steam condensed back into water that could be used to refill the jacket. A perk of being a machine-gunner was that there was always hot water to make tea. The gun, including the tripod and sights, weighed seventy-three pounds, and each box of ammunition, holding a belt of 250 rounds, weighed a further twenty-two pounds. Each gun team of six men had thirty-two boxes as first-line ammunition, and the total weight of gun and ammunition came to 777 pounds, or just over a third of a ton, without counting the water. The Vickers could, at a pinch, be carried by its crew for short distances, but conveyance was normally by mules. Each infantry battalion started the war with two guns, which operated as a section and had a reserve ammunition supply of four boxes and 15,000 loose rounds in a section cart that was horse- or mule-drawn. A further 10,000 rounds per gun were held in the divisional ammunition column. The Vickers fired the same calibre of ammunition as did the infantry rifle, which simplified manufacture and storage, and meant that in a crisis the machine-gun crews could get ammunition from the riflemen.

As the machine guns of cavalry regiments had to be able to keep up with the troops they were supporting, cavalry machine guns were carried on horses rather than mules. A horse is less good at weight-carrying than is a mule, and so the cavalry was issued with the French Hotchkiss, which was air-cooled and lighter than the Vickers but more prone to stoppages.

A machine gun was not intended to put a number of rounds into the same target, who could quite as efficiently, and a lot more cheaply, be killed by one bullet as by five. The idea was to lay down of a belt of fire across which no enemy could pass unscathed. The weapon was not aimed directly at an enemy soldier; rather, it was sited in a defilade position so that it could produce enfilade fire and thus make full use of its rate of fire and range. It was not fired in the hosepipe fashion so often seen in films, but laid on a fixed line that may have had some traverse to the left and right.

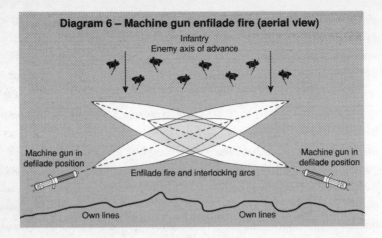

Diagram 6 – Machine gun enfilade fire (aerial view)

Infantry
Enemy axis of advance

Machine gun in
defilade position

Machine gun in
defilade position

Enfilade fire and interlocking arcs

Own lines

Own lines

No two bullets fired from a machine gun follow exactly the same trajectory. They deviate according to the wind, minute variations in the propellant, expansion of the barrel during firing, and vibration of the weapon. When a burst is fired from a machine gun, gravity acts on each bullet, which eventually strikes the ground. A bullet will fall slightly to the right or to the left of those preceding it, a little ahead or a little behind. The area of ground so struck is called the beaten zone. The size of the beaten zone varies according to the range at which the gun is being fired. A Vickers could fire accurately up to 2,800 yards, or well over one and a half miles, and on level ground the beaten zone at that range was twenty-eight yards wide and 215 yards long, centred on the target. In simple terms, anything in that area and not under cover was liable to be hit. The shorter the range the narrower and longer was the beaten zone, and at a fairly typical (for trench warfare) range of 600 yards the beaten zone was three yards wide and 250 yards long. These figures presuppose level ground from gun to target, and they varied if the ground sloped up or down away from the gun. Firing at a target on a one-in-eight, or seven-degree, slope, rising from the gun, reduced the length of the beaten zone to twenty-five yards, and firing downhill correspondingly lengthened it. Range tables were provided which contained all this information, including the adjustments necessary for wind. The longer the range to the target the higher the gun had to be elevated, and firing over the heads of our own advancing infantry was perfectly possible, although the plunging nature of the fire shortened the beaten zone.

It was not only a target within the beaten zone that was at risk, of course. At short ranges anyone between the gun and the target was liable to be hit. The bullets emerged from the gun in an expanding cone, the lowest shot at 600 yards' range being eight minutes of angle from the centre of the cone. The ideal line of fire for a machine gun was therefore level ground all the way out from the gun; in this situation a virtually impenetrable barrier of bullets could be created. Because of the effect of gravity, the barrel of any firearm actually points above the direct line of sight to the target, and at longer ranges men between the gun and the target would not necessarily be hit. If the gunsights were set to 2,800 yards, the maximum effective range of the Vickers, a man standing directly in front of the gun and 200 yards from it was perfectly safe, as the bullets rose well above the line of sight before descending to fall on the target. At maximum range bullets took twelve seconds to travel from the gun to the target, travelling at rather less than the speed of sound.

In a defensive position guns were sited so that the arcs of fire overlapped, either with the two battalion guns interlocking with each other, or with the guns sited together and their arcs of fire interlocking with those of another battalion. At the beginning of the war the British saw the machine gun as being both a defensive and an offensive weapon, its use in the latter role being to support troops advancing over open ground. This firepower was in the hands of the infantry battalions. It was said that the Germans had many more machine guns, and the British army is criticised for this omission. In fact the German regiment of three battalions had the

Diagram 7 – Cone of fire and beaten zone

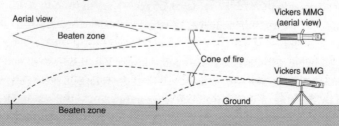

same number of guns as three British battalions – six – but the Germans saw machine guns as primarily defensive weapons, designed to prevent an enemy crossing no man's land. German machine guns were grouped into a regimental machine-gun company, which allowed them to be concentrated and used more efficiently than those of the British, who had delegated control to battalion level. As time went on the British realised the advantages of concentrating their machine guns. Brigade machine-gun companies were often cobbled together by withdrawing guns – increased to four per battalion in February 1915 – from battalions. Eventually this arrangement was formalised with the establishment of the Machine Gun Corps on 22 October 1915. Battalions were compensated for the withdrawal of their heavy firepower by the issue of the Lewis gun, and conversion took place on a rolling programme as Lewis guns were manufactured and issued.

The Lewis gun was a breakthrough in infantry firepower, as it could be carried by one man and could thus provide the infantry platoon with its own intimate fire support, which previous heavier guns could not do. The gun was originally developed in the USA by a Colonel Lewis from a design by Samuel MacLean. Unable to interest the American army, Lewis took the design to Europe and had it adopted first by the Belgians; at the outbreak of war he moved to Britain, where his gun was manufactured by the Birmingham Small Arms Company under licence. The Lewis was air-cooled, had a bipod on the end of the barrel to steady it when it was fired, and had a drum magazine of forty-seven .303 rounds, the same ammunition used by the Vickers and the rifle. Although the cyclical rate of fire was 550 rounds a minute, it was normally fired in bursts of five or ten rounds. The maximum range was 1,500 yards, but 300 to 600 yards was the usual range of engagement. The gun was subsequently adapted for use on aircraft, with a magazine of ninety-seven rounds. In this role, firing incendiary bullets, it was particularly effective against balloons and Zeppelins.

To begin with, in late 1915, each infantry battalion was issued with eight Lewis guns, and with a further eight in the spring of 1916. This meant that by the time of the Somme offensive in July 1916 each platoon had its own portable machine gun. So effective was this gun as a platoon weapon that the British infantry was reorganised in 1917 along functional lines: the Lewis was treated as the main weapon of the platoon, whose role was to support its machine gun and bombers (grenade-throwers) rather than simply to act as forty men with rifles and bayonets.

The Machine Gun Corps, which now provided the heavy machine-gun support, could provide each brigade with a machine-gun company of sixteen guns. In April 1917 a further divisional machine-gun company, also of sixteen guns, was formed. Thus after April 1917 a division could field sixty-four medium machine guns, compared with twenty-four in 1914. As brigades were reduced from four battalions to three in 1917, the firepower available per battalion was even greater.

With warfare conducted mainly from trenches, either as positions to defend or as a jumping-off line whence to mount an attack, it quickly became evident that the infantry needed a means of projecting high explosive a short distance – either into the enemy trench when opportunity arose, or as covering fire for movement outside one's own trench, or to allow an instant response that the artillery could not provide. One of the ways of doing this was with trench mortars, originally called bomb guns or trench howitzers. A trench mortar is a weapon which is portable, can be set up inside a trench, and lobs a high-explosive bomb a short distance. As a mortar was intended for firing at relatively short distances, the pressure in the barrel to propel the shell could be much less than that needed in an artillery piece; hence the shell casing itself could be thinner and lighter than that of an artillery shell. Thus a trench mortar delivered a much greater quantity of explosive on target than an artillery piece of the same calibre. In 1914 the German army had a considerable number of trench mortars, some capable of delivering sixty pounds of explosive over a distance of several hundred yards. As the bombs travelled through the air relatively slowly they could be seen in flight, and this gave an opportunity to dodge them; but if one landed in a trench bay when men could not get out of the way, it left very little of either bay or occupants. The standard German light trench mortar, or *Minenwerfer*, had a barrel of 2.99-inch calibre and delivered eight pounds of explosive on the target. It had a rapid rate of fire, and while a bomb might be in the air for fifteen seconds or so, a good crew could have six bombs in the air at once. The British had no trench mortars in 1914, and one of the tasks of our own artillery was to shell identified trench-mortar positions; this could only be done effectively with howitzers, themselves in short supply.

The French too had few trench mortars, and their initial solution was to raid museums and employ mortars last used in the Napoleonic Wars. It was those great improvisers of warfare, the Indians, who produced the BEF's first effective trench mortar, manufactured in a factory in Béthune.[12] These were crude but effective weapons, although their use of black powder, and hence the emission of clouds of smoke, tended to attract retaliation in kind and made their crews unpopular with the inhabitants of the trench from where they fired their contraptions. The British started to search for a practical trench mortar, and by early 1915 a number of models were in service. Woolwich Arsenal produced a two-inch version that fired the 'toffee apple' shell with twelve pounds of explosive out to a range of 600 yards. The most effective mortar produced during the war was that invented by Wilfred Stokes, which, after many trials and tribulations, was accepted into service in March 1915. It was simple to operate, had few moving parts to go wrong, was fired by a fixed firing-pin in the base of the tube and used smokeless ballistite as the propellant. It projected a cylindrical steel shell with twenty pounds of explosive and had a range of between fifty and 430 yards, later extended to 700 yards and then to 800 with improvements in bomb and propellant. In 1918 experiments were being conducted with the French Brandt mortar shell which would, had the war continued, have given the Stokes a maximum range of 2,500 yards. The three-inch Stokes was operated by the infantry, while its larger brothers, the four-inch and six-inch versions, were the province of the Royal Artillery. The three-inch Stokes was sited in the firing or support line, dug into pits so that no part of it projected above ground level. It was unfortunate that the Stokes mortar pit was of very much the same dimensions as a latrine, and German artillery, firing at targets identified from air photographs, spent much time shelling British latrines, thus increasing the incidence of constipation amongst soldiers in the firing line.

Another method of projecting high explosive a short distance was by a grenade, either thrown by the soldier or projected from his rifle. The

British did have a percussion grenade in 1914, derived from one used by the Japanese in 1904–05, but it had very few of them. This weapon had a sixteen-inch wooden handle and was more dangerous to the thrower than to his opponent, being liable to strike the rear wall of the trench on the backswing and thus to explode. Eventually men were instructed to throw it by the head, in the manner of a darts player, and this consequently reduced the distance at which it could be used. Various types of percussion fuse were used but none were satisfactory, and so improvisation produced the jam-pot, or jam-tin, bomb. The jam-tin bomb was made from discarded empty jam tins, packed with a mixture of explosive and bits of shrapnel, horseshoe nails, broken glass, stones or anything else that could be guaranteed to cause injury if whizzing about, and sealed with a wooden plug with a fuse inserted. The fuse was lit with a match, cigarette or pipe and the device thrown. It was used mainly in trench fighting, when British troops raided a German trench or when the reverse happened, and was thrown from bay to bay over the traverse. It was unreliable on a number of counts: the fuse did not always light in wet weather; if the bomb landed in mud the fuse went out; the missile could be picked up and thrown back if the fuse was too long, and had a disconcerting habit of blowing up in the thrower's hand if the fuse was too short. Nevertheless, it was all that was available to begin with, and it came to be considered almost unpatriotic not to eat as much jam as possible. Further types followed: the Indians produced the Battye bomb, with a handle for throwing it, and commercial manufacture of the jam tin, using shrapnel balls rather than any old scrap iron, was begun. From the end of 1914, when the requirement was identified, to the spring of 1915, a plethora of grenade types was issued, and by the time of the Battle of Loos in September 1915 no fewer than twelve different varieties were in service. Despite all these stopgap measures, the number of grenades reaching the BEF was inadequate: in August 1915 Field Marshal Sir John French, the Commander-in-Chief, told the War Office that the BEF requirement was 63,000 a week. By October of the same year the supply of all types had reached 8,000 a week. The problem was in the manufacture of the detonator, as what was wanted was a timed, rather than an unreliable percussion, fuse. Many of the factories that made timed fuses were German, and thus unavailable to fill British orders, and the firms in England which could make them were already making fuses for the mining industry, itself essential to the war effort. Some of the grenades issued were so dangerous that in some battalions the men who used them were referred to as the Suicide Club. The so-called lemon grenade had a friction igniter, which was set off by pulling a ring at the top of the grenade. Many rings were so stiff that men were instructed to place the grenade between the knees and use both hands to withdraw the ring. As the fuse had a five-second delay before the grenade exploded, any fumbling or dropping of the grenade tended to be fatal. The pitcher grenade had a cast-iron body which was intended to fragment as an anti-personnel feature; unfortunately it flung out its fragments in a circle of 200 yards' radius, thus disposing of the thrower too, if he was not safely under cover. There were so many accidents with this grenade that in September 1915 the Commander-in-Chief ordered that it was not to be used. A similar device, the cricket-ball grenade, was so unreliable that during the fighting at Loos eighteen out of twenty grenades issued failed to ignite, with deleterious results to attempts by the BEF to fight through buildings and fortified areas. One of the major problems of having a diversity of grenades all in service at the same time was training. Men might be trained in one type of grenade and then find themselves having to use another, and there were many accidents due to unfamiliarity, overconfidence or carelessness.

At last, starting in May 1915, the first safe, effective and easily employed grenade began to come into service. This was the Mills bomb, a fragmentation grenade which by the end of 1915 replaced every other grenade in service. Although initially it was not entirely reliable, with a number of modifications it ended the war as the No. 36 Grenade, the most effective grenade used by any army, and remained in service until the 1970s. Weighing between 1 lb. 7 oz. and 1 lb. 9 oz. depending on the version, it could be thrown or bowled twenty or even thirty yards. The Mills bomb did away with matches and pipes in the grenade-throwing industry for ever. It had a spring-loaded striker and a percussion-cap igniter within the body of the grenade. The striker was held away from the igniter by an external lever, which was itself held in position by a split pin. When the soldier wanted to throw the grenade he gripped it with the lever close against the body of the grenade and removed the split pin. Once he threw the weapon the lever was released and the striker hit the cap, which ignited a five-second fuse. The Mills bomb withstood damp and vibration, was easy to use and eventually came in a rifle-grenade version, fired from a cup discharger and propelled by a ballistite cartridge.

The British army started the war with far fewer machine guns and less artillery than the Germans, whose army was structured for a war of conquest, and with virtually no grenades. Once the requirements were identified swift action was taken to supply the infantry – the men who had to close with and defeat the enemy – with the weapons and the support that they needed. Despite the difficulties of converting an industrial base that was not under state control into a machine that could play its part in total war, by 1916 the weapons available to the British infantry were as good as anything the Germans had, and in some cases – such as the Lewis gun and the rifle – better. All that was needed was an understanding of how best to use them, and that could only be learned by experience.

NOTES

1 The British infantry today has a number of ranks all equating to private, including fusilier, highlander, kingsman and ranger (until recently). During the Great War they were privates in the line infantry, Irish and Welsh Guards, and riflemen in rifle regiments. The Grenadier and Scots Guards had guardsmen; the Coldstream Guards had privates until 1918 when they became guardsmen; and all members of the Guards Machine Gun Battalion, part of the Machine Gun Corps, were guardsmen.

2 Substantive rank is permanent and cannot be taken away other than for disciplinary reasons. Acting rank confers the powers of the rank and counts for pay and increments, but the holder can be required to revert to his substantive rank if the post he is holding disappears, or if he is moved to another post that is established in a lower rank. Local rank carries the powers but no pay benefits, and is granted for a specific short-term task, or for a post which the incumbent is not expected to hold for long.

3 Major T. J. Mitchell and Miss G. M. Smith, *Official History of the War, Casualties and Medical Statistics*, Imperial War Museum (reprint), London, 1997.

4 Most modern artillery pieces are designed to be used in both high- and low-angle mode, that is as both guns and howitzers.

5 The calibre is the diameter of the barrel of the weapon. Guns may be described by calibre or by the weight of shell they fire: e.g., six-inch gun, eighteen-pounder gun.

6 The ammunition remained the same, but the trail and cradle were redesigned so that the gun could achieve greater elevation, and hence longer range.

7 Called after Colonel (later Lieutenant General Sir) Henry Shrapnel (1761–1842) who invented a hollow shell filled with musket balls and a bursting charge that had a timed fuse; the shell was first used in 1804. Shrapnel never did get the royalty of 6*d*. a shell promised by the East India Company. The term is still used today, incorrectly, to refer to the fragments of a burst shell casing, which are more properly 'shell splinters'.

8 The French were the first Allied army to use sound ranging, and the British began to experiment with it in October 1915. By the spring of 1916 it was a very effective way of locating enemy guns.

9 Unexploded shells are regularly turned up by ploughing. Farmers stack them by the side of the road and they are removed by the French or Belgian army and blown up. Occasionally even the bomb-disposal experts get killed doing this.

10 In 1914 it was known as the Maxim; then the lock was reversed and it was made under licence by Vickers, hence the Vickers-Maxim, until after more modifications it became the Vickers. Its longevity was not quite a record: the Brown Bess smooth-bore musket was in service for 180 years.

11 The term 'cyclical' means that the gun was capable of firing that number of rounds if the trigger was kept engaged. In practice, bursts of fire were much shorter, ten to twenty rounds being the norm.

12 See my *Sepoys in the Trenches, the Indian Corps on the Western Front 1914–15*, Chapter IV, Spellmount Publishers, Staplehurst, 1999.

5

GOVERNMENT-SPONSORED POLO CLUBS

All the British generals were from cavalry regiments and clung to an outmoded equestrian concept of warfare. Battle, they thought, was fox-hunting with rather less chance of a broken neck. Horses had no place in modern war, and yet twenty-five per cent of all the shipping from England to France was taken up with fodder for these pampered beasts, which spent most of their time standing in stables, being cosseted by their riders who had nothing else to do, and playing no part in the prosecution of the war. Such is the popular conception of the horse in the First World War.

We shall get to the generals later, but it is certainly true that the British army had a great many horses, both on the Western Front and in the other theatres of war. In August 1914, just before war broke out, the army was established for 25,000 horses. As soon as mobilisation was declared this was raised to 165,000. By August 1915, when the war had been going on for a year, the British army had over half a million horses, 368,000 of them on the Western Front. It also had 82,000 mules in France and Belgium. By 1917 the number of equines in all theatres had peaked at 591,324 horses and 231,149 mules, of which 368,149 and 81,731 respectively were on the Western Front. In the more exotic theatres of conflict, in addition to its horses and mules, the British disposed of 47,000 camels, 11,000 oxen and 6,800 donkeys.[1]

As for cavalry, the proportion of the *arme blanche* to other arms was no greater in the British army than in either the French or the German forces, and it got smaller as the war went on. In September 1914 the BEF had two cavalry divisions to support six infantry divisions. By 1918 three cavalry divisions supported sixty-one infantry divisions. In 1914 each infantry division had 5,592 horses, of which only 167 belonged to the divisional cavalry squadron. A cavalry division, despite being composed entirely of mounted men, had, at 9,815, only seventy-five per cent more horses than its infantry counterpart. The fact is that only a minority of horses used by the British army were cavalry horses, and the reason for that was the lack of any other means of transporting a man or stores quickly around the battlefield. The internal combustion engine had been known about since its first experimental inception in 1884, but in 1914 the motor car was still unreliable and incapable of moving off roads. Each regular division of the BEF had, by 1915 when organisations had stabilised, eleven motor cars (used as staff cars and for postal deliveries well behind the lines); four motor lorries, nineteen motorcycles (for despatch riders) and twenty-one motor ambulances (for transport between the casualty clearing station and the hospital, or the port of embarkation). Everything else was horse-drawn.

It was not only cavalrymen who rode horses. Commanders of brigades, divisions, corps and armies rode them too, as being the fastest way to get from place to place. In an infantry battalion the commanding officer, all company commanders and the adjutant were established for horses. The movement of armies in 1914, once they had been delivered to the battle area by rail, motor lorry or bus, was restricted to the speed at which a man could march; and given that the infantryman not actually engaged with the enemy carried, on average, sixty pounds on his back, this was about two miles an hour. An infantry brigade moving out of contact with the enemy took up two and a quarter miles of road, and took over two hours to pass a given point. A division took up fifteen miles of road, and more than seven hours were needed for it to pass. All this needs to be borne in mind when it is asked why it took so long to deploy reserves, and why reactions to changes in the tactical situation seem slow by modern standards. Given that a means of moving the infantry around the battlefield, with speed and protection from small-arms fire, would take a further half-century to become a practicable proposition, and that universal radio communication was thirty years away, anyone who needed to move from place to place, to find out what was happening, to give orders to more than one unit or to deliver urgent information had to have a horse: there was no faster or more efficient way of getting about.

The field artillery had to be able to support the infantry, get its guns to a position from where it could fire at the enemy, and move forward once the infantry had moved to the limit of the guns' range. As this movement was nearly always either off roads or along roads already damaged by shelling, the guns had to be mobile over any terrain. Traction engines were well known and widely used by 1914, but they were very slow and cumbersome. They could be, and were, used to pull the very heavy artillery pieces, those that fired from well behind the immediate area of fighting, but they were quite unsuitable for field artillery supporting the infantry. Only horses would do, and each eighteen-pounder gun was pulled by six draught horses. Horses could get through all but the worst ground, were faster than traction engines and less liable to break down. Each brigade (regiment) of field artillery had 108 horses to pull its guns, but also needed horses to pull the ammunition wagons, and for the battery commanders and observation officers. In the field artillery the gun crews might, on good firm ground, hitch a ride on the gun limbers, the cart attached to the gun and containing the immediate ammunition supply; but generally they marched. Horse artillery, on the other hand, had to be able to keep up with the horsed cavalry, and so their gun crews rode. A field-artillery regiment (with three batteries) had 748 horses, a horse-artillery regiment of only two batteries needed 779. While the use of motor transport for heavy guns underwent enormous expansion between 1914 and 1918, even by the outbreak of the Second World War in 1939 the French and German armies' artillery, other than that in direct support of infantry or in the armoured units, was still largely horse-drawn.

The mule is uncomfortable to ride and cannot cover ground at the speed of a horse, but pound for pound he is a better weight-carrier, and less fussy about what he eats. Transport that did not need to be faster than the marching infantry could be provided by mules, and this included machine guns and battalion ration carts. The mule is an artificial creation, being a cross between a horse and a donkey, and although they come in the usual two sexes, they are sterile and cannot breed. Mules have a reputation for being stubborn, but once trained are capable of sustained spells of hard work, each carrying up to 600 pounds' weight depending on type. The only drawback in war is a tendency for the mule to bray, a sound which carries for miles, particularly at night, and most army mules had their vocal cords surgically removed to prevent an unwitting bray giving their position away to the enemy.

To keep an army in the field for any length of time requires a huge logistic, and hence transportation, effort. Rations, ammunition, clothing, stores of all kinds, had to be supplied to the forward troops to keep them capable of fighting, and most of this was delivered by horse-drawn transport. It was not blind prejudice or love of the horse that made this so, but the unreliability and lack of off-road capability of mechanical transport. As motor vehicles became more reliable, so the army adopted them, and the need to reduce the amount of shipping space taken up by fodder for horses undoubtedly accelerated this process. Unlike hay and oats, petrol is not subject to the depredations of rats and mice, does not deteriorate in hot or damp conditions, and takes up far less space.

In 1912 the British government's Board of Agriculture and Fisheries issued an updated version of its pamphlet *Types of Horses Suitable for Army Remounts*, and this was the bible for all purchases of horses for the army. The army needed four types of horse: for riding, for pulling field guns, for pulling heavy guns and for transport wagons. Each type was further classified according to the work that the animal was required to do. Commanders and staff officers did not have to carry all their possessions with them, so their riding horses could be lighter of bone – and hence capable of more speed – than those required to carry a cavalry trooper. Some officers brought their own horses to the war, often thoroughbreds, but these are fussy animals and in general they did not respond well to conditions in the battle area. Most officers' riding horses were of the light hunter type, averaging fifteen hands two inches (15h. 2) and the government paid up to £100 each for them.[2] Cavalry troopers required a horse that could stand up to the rigours of active service and carry weight. The mounted man had to have with him his own weapons and ammunition, rations for himself and his horse, blankets for himself and his horse, spare horseshoes, and piqueting ropes and pegs for the horse. The total weight carried by the horse could be as much as 400 pounds. These cavalry horses were generally around 15 h. to 15 h. 2 and the guide price was £40. The exceptions were the mounts needed for the Household Cavalry: these, owing to their regiments' ceremonial role, had to be bigger and capable of carrying a man in full-dress gear, including steel breastplate and back-plate. They were 16 h. high and bought for around £70. Artillery horses were 15 h. 2 to 15 h. 3 for the field artillery, rather smaller for horse artillery, and of the light draught type: that is, capable of pulling a gun in a team of six. Again the guide price was £40. To pull the really big guns, such as the sixty-pounder, heavy draught shire horses (or carthorses) were used. They needed twice as much feed as a light hunter but were capable of prodigious amounts of work, albeit only at the walk. Transport horses used by the Army Service Corps, responsible for supplying the army, were of the 'parcel-vanner' type and needed to be able to pull a load at a fast trot, but were not required to canter or gallop. A typical horse of this description was 16 h. high and cost £35 to £40.

During times of peace the army bought black horses for the Household Cavalry, grey for the Scots Greys and black, brown or bay for the rest. Grey horses are not a good idea in war as they stand out from their background, and once the war began any horse that was grey or multicoloured was dyed a dark colour with vegetable dye.

The expansion of the army's horse establishment in August 1914 from 25,000 to 165,000 was accomplished in two weeks, by the simple expedi-ent of impounding horses from the civilian population. Owners of horses who could not show that the animals were needed for agriculture or essen-tial transport found them pressed into military service, with a fixed scale of compensation paid. Around seventeen per cent of the British horse pop-ulation was sequestered in this way. Thereafter the army bought horses where it could, and as the supply in the UK was not inexhaustible, pur-chasing commissions were sent overseas to buy the type of animal the army needed. These purchasing commissions were largely civilian, made up of persons experienced in the judging of horseflesh. Any master of hounds who was not already in the Territorial Force or Yeomanry, or had not enlisted in the New Armies, was liable to find himself a member of a purchasing commission as the army strove to avoid tying up men needed in the field. Apart from the United Kingdom, the main sources of horses were Canada, the United States and the South American countries. Altogether the army bought and shipped to England 428,608 horses and 275,097 mules from Canada and the USA, and 6,000 horses and 1,500 mules from South America. Spanish and Portuguese mules had been the mainstay of Wellington's logistic machinery a century before, and this source provided 3,700 army mules.

Once horses and mules had been purchased they were moved to England in shipping adapted for the purpose. Horses are generally good travellers, but there was an inevitable wastage through sickness and ships sunk by German submarines or surface raiders. Overall the loss on voyage ran at around three per cent, as compared to around four per cent during the South African War. The improvement in horse care is more marked when it is recalled that the Boer republics did not dispose of a navy.

On arrival in England the horses and mules were held in remount depots in Bristol, Liverpool and Southampton for three weeks' quarantine. Once found to be disease-free, they were issued to cavalry, artillery and Army Service Corps regiments in the UK for training; eventually they were moved to smaller remount depots in the various theatres of war, for issue to units as replacements. Horses bought in the UK – 468,323 of them between 1914 and 1918 – were sent straight to training units. Remount depots in England had capacity for 1,200 equines in 1914, and this increased to 60,000 as the war went on, with around 16,000 horses held in depots in France ready for issue.

The time taken to train a horse for military purposes varied, depending on the role of the horse and its age and previous experience. An experienced hunter, carriage or draught horse had only to be trained to ignore the noise of gunfire and, in the case of artillery horses, to work in teams of six. This did not take long – a week or so – and these animals could be issued to units with little delay. An animal with no previous experience took longer. Pre-war the army bought their horses unbroken: that is, animals that had never had a human on their backs or pulled any form of wheeled conveyance. This made sense when there was time for the army to break, back and train its horses from scratch; there would be no existing bad habits, nor were there likely to be work-related injuries concealed by the vendor. Once war was declared the training time had to be reduced and many horses were bought broken and backed, that is, they had been made accustomed to a bridle and saddle, or had been taught to stand in traces (the equipment fitted to the horse to allow it to pull a cart or gun). France had a great many horses, but needed most of them for its own armies. There were few to spare for the British, but some heavy draught horses were bought, mainly of the Percheron type. Mules could be trained fairly quickly: stoical beasts in the main, they had to become accustomed to wearing pack equipment, and had to be introduced to it gradually, so that sores did not develop on shoulders and withers previously unused to bearing weight. Here a few weeks would suffice.

Even an unbroken horse could be prepared for military service in six weeks or so; the human element took a little longer. For the mounted arms in peacetime the army preferred to take recruits who could not ride – there were thus no bad habits to be ironed out – but once the war started any man who declared that he had experience in handling horses was encouraged to enlist in the cavalry, artillery or Army Service Corps. The New Armies were composed of infantry, artillery, engineers and supporting arms, but not cavalry. The British raised hardly any new cavalry regiments during the war, relying on the existing regular regiments and the Yeomanry. The Yeomanry was the cavalry equivalent of the Territorial Force, and men initially provided their own horses, replaced at government expense if they became casualties.

Alone amongst the major participants in this war, the British recognised that the roles of cavalry no longer included shock action against formed bodies of troops. Wire and the machine gun ruled that out. In mobile warfare the cavalry was intended to act as a screen, operating well forward of the infantry to give warning of enemy movement. It could also cover the flanks and gaps between formations. It was well suited for reconnaissance, patrolling and escort duty, as well as being able to provide mounted messengers at a headquarters. In static operations, into which the Great War lapsed from October 1914 onwards, cavalry could still act in the reconnaissance, message-carrying and escort roles, but its main task was to stand by to exploit a breakthrough. Once the infantry and artillery had succeeded in forcing a genuine break in the opposing lines, and had penetrated beyond the last line of fixed defences, the cavalry would pour through and, using their speed, drive well into the enemy's territory, harassing his troops and giving him no opportunity to prepare further defence lines. That was the theory, and that the envisaged breakthrough never occurred should not lead to a conclusion that the means to exploit it should not have existed. It very nearly happened at the Battle of Cambrai in late 1917, and the cavalry were poised to thrust deep into German-held areas; but a failure in communications, and a reluctance to commit the cavalry until it was quite certain that a breakthrough had actually been achieved, prevented what might have been a great victory.

The British had absorbed the lessons of the South African War, in which both Sir John French and Sir Douglas Haig, the two commanders-in-chief of the BEF, had served, and the training of British cavalry, and the roles envisaged for it, were far more modern in outlook than that of enemy or ally. British cavalry by 1914 was effectively mounted infantry. That is, the cavalryman used his horse to get him to where the action was, and there he dismounted, handed his horse to a horse-holder, and fought on his feet. The British cavalry soldier was armed with a sword and a lance for mounted action, these weapons still being more reliable than a revolver or rifle fired from a moving platform; but unlike his French or German equivalent he was also equipped with the same rifle as the infantry, rather than with an inferior carbine.

The British army was the last European army to adopt the lance for its cavalry, doing so in 1816 as a result of experience fighting Napoleon's Polish lancers. Originally sixteen feet long, later reduced to nine, the lance was withdrawn in 1903 before being reissued to all British light cavalry regiments in 1907. By then it was made of bamboo, with a ten-inch steel point. The cavalry sword, the 1908 pattern, was introduced as a result of experience in the South African War and was probably the best cavalry sabre ever issued in any army. Well balanced and with a rubber handgrip, it was withdrawn in 1915. The lance, however, remained, now being issued to all British cavalry regiments whatever their designation.[3]

Contrary to the impression given in paintings and Hollywood films, the lance was not couched under the armpit in the manner of medieval jousting. To strike an opponent in this way would either pull the soldier off his horse or leave him with a transfixed German sitting on the front of his saddle. Rather, the lance was held at the point of balance, slightly away from the body, and the sheer momentum of horse and rider carried the point of the lance into the target. Once the target was pierced it was vital for the lance-wielder to 'watch his point': that is, to bend head and body back in the direction of the lance point as he galloped past his enemy so that the lance could be withdrawn from the target ready to be used again. Men in training quickly found that to remain upright and looking to the front as they rode on allowed the butt of the lance to strike them in the back of the head and bring them to the ground.[4]

Once it became clear that large-scale mounted actions would not take place, the cavalry often took their place in the line without their horses and were issued with bayonets and digging implements like the infantry. There was, of course, a penalty. A cavalry regiment, at 600 men, had 400 men fewer than an infantry battalion, and one man in four was a horse-holder. When a cavalry unit engaged in dismounted action, the horse-holder looked after his own horse and those of three of his comrades. A cavalry regiment in the trenches was therefore the equivalent of only two companies of infantry, or half a battalion. A cavalry brigade of three regiments was the equivalent of one large battalion, and was given that designation for duty in the line, being referred to by its brigade number: thus the 1st Cavalry Brigade would provide the 1st Cavalry Battalion.

The Germans produced eleven cavalry divisions on mobilisation. Rather surprisingly, given the rolling plains of Russia, which were more suited to mounted action than Belgium with its hedges and built-up areas, ten of these divisions were deployed on the Western Front. Having experienced very heavy losses in charges against the Belgians in the early days of the campaign, the German cavalry rarely operated alone, but fell back behind a screen of *Jäger* – light infantrymen – and artillery when threatened. The French thought this cowardly, but it was entirely practical. The French mobilised eleven cavalry divisions on the Western Front. In addition to the Cavalry Corps, of three divisions, each of the five French armies had its own cavalry division. The mounted man has always considered himself to be a cut above those who walk, and this was especially so in the French cavalry, who rarely got off their horses and had no concept of dismounted action. While British cavalry soldiers were accustomed to dismounting and leading their horses for long periods, and had care and grooming of their mounts instilled in them, the French never walked if they could possibly help it, and even when billeted at night often left the saddles on, without loosening the girths. They paid the price of neglect: girth galls, fistular withers, abscesses, sore backs and all manner of equine infections were rife in French cavalry regiments. It was said that you could smell a French cavalry regiment a mile off, echoing what had been said of them by Wellington's soldiers in Spain a hundred years before. Nevertheless most of the animals put up with this treatment, or lack of it, for the French, with about three times as much cavalry as the British, lost only about twice as many horses during the war (roughly 500,000 to the British 250,000). This statistic may not be entirely reliable, however, as the British were much more ready to cast (declare unfit for work and retire) horses than were the French, who tended to work them until they literally dropped. The Intelligence Officer of the British 1st Cavalry Division, Lieutenant Colonel Barrow, was horrified during the move up to the concentration area in 1914 when he entered a farmyard and found a wounded French horse lying on a pile of burning bedding. It was trying, unsuccessfully, to get up, and was literally roasting to death. The yard was full of French troops who took not the slightest notice, and Barrow shot the animal with his pistol.[5]

Apart from the Welsh Horse, and fourteen (reduced to six in 1917) reserve cavalry regiments formed in the UK solely to provided drafts of men and horses, the British raised no new cavalry regiments during the war, although the Household Cavalry (the Life Guards and the Royal Horse Guards) were expanded to produce three composite mounted regiments. All regular cavalry regiments remained horsed throughout the war, with the Yeomanry being used as a source of reinforcement. As time went on much of the Yeomanry was converted to infantry, and there was a constant drain of regular cavalry officers transferring to other arms.

The cavalry were doing their bit, but the constant waiting for a break-through that never came, and dismounted duty in the trenches, did not always appeal to the cavalry spirit. Some cavalry officers transferred to the infantry, many to the Royal Flying Corps, the Tank Corps and the Machine Gun Corps.

The care of the army's horses and mules was the responsibility of the Royal Army Veterinary Corps, which expanded from 508 all ranks in 1914 to 1,668 officers and 41,755 other ranks in 1918. Even this gave but one veterinary surgeon to 354 horses – never mind the mules, dogs and carrier pigeons – which would be perfectly reasonable in private practice but gave the veterinary officer little time for relaxation in war.[6]

The cavalry's great moment, when 12,000 horsemen would erupt through the German defence lines and sweep out into open country and beyond, never came. The depth of the successive lines of defence, the all-pervading wire and the slowness of communications prevented that. There were occasions, however, when the cavalry, in its mounted role, was able to achieve results, albeit on a smaller scale than had been hoped. Phase Two of the Somme offensive began on 14 July 1916 with a night attack by the British, which advanced nearly two miles and captured the German-held villages of Longueval and Bazentin. More importantly, it also captured the valley south of the Longueval–Bazentin road, a valley which was in 'dead ground' – that is, out of sight – from the next objective held by the Germans, the Bois de Fourcaux, known to the British as High Wood. Up into the valley at the trot came the Secunderabad Cavalry Brigade, part of the 2nd Indian Cavalry Division. By early evening it was apparent that German resistance was slackening, and the cavalry were ordered forward to support the infantry. Emerging from a defile the 20th Deccan Horse and the 7th Dragoon Guards galloped through the open cornfields between High Wood and Delville Wood.[7] Speed and surprise worked: those Germans in the open who did not surrender were speared by the troopers' lances. While the horsemen could not penetrate High Wood itself – the trees were too close together and the edges were heavily wired – they did remove the German outpost line, rendering good service to the infantry. The brigade was withdrawn during the night, having taken remarkably few casualties.

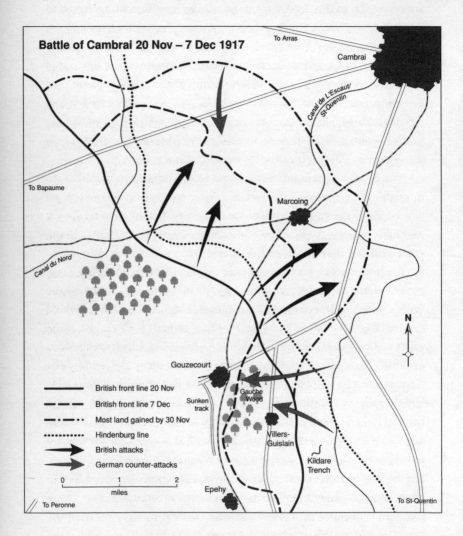

Battle of Cambrai 20 Nov – 7 Dec 1917

To Arras

Cambrai

Canal de L'Escaut/ St-Quentin

To Bapaume

Marcoing

Canal du Nord

N

Gouzecourt

Gauche Wood

Sunken track

Villers-Guislain

Kildare Trench

British front line 20 Nov

British front line 7 Dec

Most land gained by 30 Nov

Hindenburg line

British attacks

German counter-attacks

0   1   2
         miles

To Peronne

Epehy

To St-Quentin

Phase Three of the same offensive was launched on 15 September 1916, the day that also saw the first use of tanks in war. On 26 September a Royal Flying Corps aircraft reported that the Germans in the village of Gueudecourt, which had been attacked several times with no success, seemed to be pulling out. Now was a chance to seize the village before the Germans had time to reorganise themselves further back. Time was of the essence, and a squadron of Fane's Horse, of the Sialkot Brigade in the 1st Indian Cavalry Division, was sent forward. The track leading to the village was being shelled by German artillery, so the squadron spread out and galloped full tilt for the village. Despite the ground being badly pitted with shell holes no horses came down, and on the outskirts the squadron met a few disorientated Germans who were swiftly despatched. Dismounting, the cavalry soldiers took up all-round defence in the village, and held it against German counter-attacks until relieved by the infantry. It was a classic microcosm of what mounted infantry – which is what the cavalry were, in fact if not in name – could do.

On 20 November 1917 the British launched an attack at Cambrai, using 300 tanks and nineteen divisions of infantry on a six-mile front. The cavalry were standing by to exploit the breakthrough when it came, and they did capture Marcoing on the afternoon of the first day. If the cavalry could get beyond the immediate battle area all would be well; the difficulty was in getting through the wire, negotiating the shell holes and getting over the trenches. Measures had been put in train to create a 'cavalry track' clear of obstacles, to allow the cavalry to get forward quickly. The attack was a major success, but petered out after two to three miles when there was no more reserve infantry to exploit the initial penetration. The cavalry were later blamed for not seizing the opportunity to advance when it came, but the real reasons were a lack of communications in an age before battlefield radio, and caution on the part of higher commanders who were reluctant to commit the cavalry until they were absolutely sure that the breakthrough had been achieved. American observers thought that the cavalry had been unfairly criticised. In a report written for American eyes just after the battle, Captain J. P. Hogan, adjutant of the 11th US Engineer Regiment, said:

It seems...that the British had given up the idea of a general advance and that the initial successes exceeded their expectations. The orders to the Cavalry called for them to seize and hold, on the first day, the bridgeheads over the canal at Marcoing and Masnières. They actually did more than this, but there was a universal disposition on the part of British officers to criticise their operations and to claim that they had failed to take advantage of their opportunities.[8]

By 30 November the cavalry had been withdrawn to billets twenty miles from the front, when the Ambala Cavalry Brigade, of the 8th Hussars (British), 8th Hodson's Horse and the Tiwana Lancers were ordered forward for dismounted duty in the trenches. They turned their horses out and handed in their swords and lances. On 1 December 1917 the Germans launched a surprise counter-attack, regaining nearly all the ground that had been taken in November, including the villages of Gouzeaucourt and Villers-Guislain, and also Gauche Wood, a copse between the two villages. The Ambala Cavalry Brigade was ordered to concentrate at Épéhy, two miles south of the captured villages. Horses were hastily brought in, rubbed down and saddled up, and as the regiments rode out of billets at the trot, quartermasters handed out lances and swords. The brigade reached Épéhy by 1100 hours, and at 1300 hours was ordered to attack Gauche Wood. Between Gauche Wood and Gouzeaucourt was a railway line, running north–south to the west of the wood, and a sunken track a further 200 yards west. The 8th Hussars led, and as they debouched from the Gouzeaucourt road they came under fire from the wood. One squadron got into the sunken track; the remainder could make no progress. Hodson's Horse was now ordered forward in support and told to make contact with the Guards Division (which had by now recaptured Gouzeaucourt) and to attack the wood. The regiment found a gap in the wire along the Gouzeaucourt road and trotted through. C Squadron (Punjabi Mussalmans), in the lead, spotted German infantry moving from Gauche Wood towards the sunken track. If the Germans could occupy the sunken track then Gouzeaucourt would be untenable. The squadron broke into a gallop. The squadron commander, one Indian officer and four sowars were killed, but the rest got into the sunken track just before the Germans did, dismounted and began to form a firing line on the lip of the bank.[9] The next squadron through the gap, D (Pathans), took severe casualties among its lead troop from German artillery, but the survivors formed diamond formation (known as 'artillery formation') and galloped for the sunken track, followed by A and B Squadrons and regimental headquarters. At about 1830 hours the Tiwana Lancers arrived and the sunken track was now held by men of the 8th Hussars, Hodson's Horse and the Lancers. They now joined with the 2nd Battalion Grenadier Guards in Gouzeaucourt. A telephone line to brigade headquarters had been laid and orders came for an attack on Gauche Wood at 0700 hours the next morning, 2 December 1917. The Grenadiers would be on the left, the Tiwana Lancers on the right. Hodson's Horse and the Hussars would provide fire from the sunken track, and the attack would be supported by fourteen tanks from H Battalion, 2nd Tank Brigade, and two batteries of Royal Horse Artillery.

By 0700 hours there was no sign of any tanks. The Grenadiers wanted to go anyway, the Tiwana Lancers advised caution. The Grenadiers launched their own attack, which was made with great gallantry but had no chance, being driven back in confusion and with the loss of so many officers that the battalion had to borrow some from the Tiwana Lancers.[10]

At around 0730 hours clouds of smoke, a clanking and a rumbling announced the arrival of the tanks, which promptly opened fire on Hodson's Horse, killing three sowars and nearly killing the commanding officer when he ran out to remonstrate. It was not the tank crews' fault – visibility from tanks of 1917 was difficult, and navigation more so. After a hurried conference of commanding officers, the attack was launched. The Tiwana Lancers led, charging from the sunken track, the Grenadiers followed up and the artillery fired them in. The tanks did little, having difficulty in getting over the railway embankment, but their firepower was useful and the wood was taken; the Lancers and Grenadiers captured twelve German machine guns, a howitzer battery and a large number of prisoners. Despite the confusion about the tanks and the initial abortive solo effort by the Guards, it was a fine example of an all-arms battle in which the cavalry had used the speed of their horses to take the sunken track before the Germans could. All-arms cooperation had worked, and the skirmish was a timely reminder that mounted cavalry was not yet an anachronism on the battlefield, provided its capabilities and limitations were clearly understood.

While the mixed force of cavalry, artillery, infantry and tanks was dealing with Gauche Wood, another cavalry action took place against the village of Villers-Guislain to the east of the wood. Here the Germans had occupied the village and the Lucknow Cavalry Brigade was ordered to retake it. Zero hour was 0600 hours and the assault was to be supported by six tanks, which did turn up, but in the wrong place. The attack went ahead anyway, with Jacob's Horse and the Jodhpur Lancers assaulting dismounted on either side of the road running north to the village. About 460 men of the two regiments pressed forward, but a German machine-gun nest in an abandoned sugar-beet factory opened up and they fell back. The corps commander, who had now arrived, ordered mounted action, in the hope that speed might compensate for lack of firepower to suppress the German machine guns. The 6th Inniskilling Dragoon Guards formed up for mounted action and the horses clattered down the road. They too were quickly stopped. Then, on the right flank, an opportunity appeared. A valley sloped gently down to the first German infantry trenches, which were not a continuous line but a series of outposts, surrounded by wire, that the Germans had taken up in the area of Kildare Trench, an old British trench abandoned when the counter-attack had come in. Four hundred officers and men of Gardner's Horse swept down the grassy slope, not yet cut up by shelling. One officer said the going was better than in the average point-to-point. The Germans opened fire but the horses were now in full gallop down the hill and few bullets found a mark.

The German infantry must have assumed that their hastily thrown-out barbed wire would protect them, for wire is a terrible obstacle to horses. A horse either cannot see wire at all, and runs straight into it, or sees it at the last minute, tries to cat-leap it and lands on it. Either way injuries can be horrific, and a galloping horse is stopped dead in its tracks. Horses can, of course, see the posts and pickets upon which barbed wire is affixed, but a horse – a fairly stupid animal but not entirely devoid of common sense – will not jump a single post: rather, he will attempt to go round it, once again ending up entangled in the wire. Indian cavalrymen, regular volunteers all, had given some thought to the problem of getting horses over wire obstacles, and had trained one or two horses in each troop to jump a single post. As the horse is a herd animal and one will follow where another leads, enough were able to get over the wire to begin spearing the German infantry, who rapidly abandoned their positions pursued by whooping Sikhs.

Having chased the Germans out of their positions in Kildare Trench, the cavalry dismounted and prepared to hold what they had gained. Horse-holders took the horses into as sheltered a position as they could find. Communication with brigade headquarters was established by sending a volunteer – Lance Daffadar (corporal) Gobind Singh – back up the valley on a fast horse. For most of the day Gobind Singh travelled back and forth, reporting the situation to the brigade commander and returning with instructions to the regiment. Three horses were killed under him and he was himself wounded, but he insisted in continuing as the regiment's postman. He was later awarded the Victoria Cross. Once again speed, and the ability of British cavalry to act as mounted infantry when required, had achieved results, even if they were minor in the context of the war as a whole.

The initial successes of Cambrai were greeted with jubilation in England: all had appeared to go well and a considerable advance had been made. The German counter-attack came as a rude shock and attracted much criticism in Parliament and in the press. Inevitably, the government wanted answers: why had not more been achieved by the British attack, and why had the Germans been able to counter-attack with such seeming ease? The truth would appear to be that having achieved a decisive victory the British were content to rest on their laurels, and the army commander failed to realise how exposed the newly won salient was to determined counter-attack.

In February 1918 the British Cavalry Corps was reduced to three cavalry divisions by the removal of the two Indian divisions to Palestine. There the war had become more fluid and was now one of movement, in which cavalry could act both as mounted infantry and as shock troops. Yeoman cavalry were moved from the Middle East to be converted into machine-gun units on the Western Front, and replaced by regular Indian cavalry. The British army now had a much smaller proportion of cavalry in the

BEF than the French or Germans did in their armies, a recognition that the need for this arm was reducing. The remaining cavalry, however, continued to do good work.

In the spring of 1918 the Germans, alarmed by their losses against the British at Passchendaele the previous year, and aware that a potentially huge American army was being built up in France, decided on a Napoleonic gamble. All their assets and all their energies would be directed into one last throw, an offensive designed to split the French and British armies and finally achieve victory in the west. The blow fell on 21 March. The Allies retreated, but while the elastic band of khaki and horizon blue grew dangerously extended, it did not break. With the war now moving away from fixed lines of entrenchments, albeit in the wrong direction for the Allies, there was once more a role for mounted cavalry.

The Germans captured Noyon, and Compiègne was under threat. On 29 March Montdidier fell and the German advance continued towards Beauvais. The German thrust line then swung right between Montdidier and Breteuil and pressed on towards Amiens. If continued this would take the German army through Abbeville to the coast, thus pushing the British north against the Channel and cutting them off from the French. The British 2nd Cavalry Division had spent most of the winter dismounted in the trenches. It had been a desperately cold winter and a combination of German U-boats and a poor harvest had necessitated the reduction of the cavalry ration to nine pounds of hard feed a day: enough to keep a hack, or even a light hunter, but insufficient to keep a cavalry horse fully fit in cold weather. Nevertheless, the threat to Amiens was such that the division was rushed forward, horses still munching from their nosebags as they marched. On 30 March the Germans occupied the woods to the north of the village of Moreuil, and the French withdrew from the village. This was serious, as Moreuil was only just south of the junction between the British and the French. If the Germans were allowed to concentrate here, then not only might the integrity of the Allied line be at risk, but the north–south railway could not be used by the Allies and Amiens itself would be under threat from a thrust down the main road from Moreuil. Once again immediate action was called for: men had to be moved swiftly to the threatened area in order to act before the Germans could consolidate and while they were still vulnerable. The 3rd British Cavalry Brigade (4th Hussars, 5th Lancers and 16th Lancers) and the Canadian Cavalry Brigade (Lord Strathcona's Horse, Royal Canadian Dragoons and Fort Garry Horse) were ordered to clear the Germans out of the woods and to secure the British line as far as Moreuil.

The Germans, who had been feeding men into Moreuil Wood from the south-east, had to be prevented from advancing out of the wood, and if possible driven from it. The two cavalry brigades crossed the River Avre and the Canadians advanced at the trot against the north-west corner of the wood. They came under heavy machine-gun fire but, supported by their own machine-gun squadron armed with Hotchkiss guns, the lead squadron got as far as the edge of the wood, although they could not penetrate far through the trees. The second squadron galloped along the west side of the wood, dismounted, formed a firing line and opened fire into the wood, while the third squadron did the same along the northern edge. The 4th Hussars followed up and made contact with the French to the south, while the 5th and 16th Lancers reinforced the Canadian firing line. Fighting went on all day on 30 March and on one occasion a squadron of Lord Strathcona's Horse, working its way round the north-east end of the wood, came upon a German infantry battalion that had left the cover of the trees and was attempting to press forward towards the Amiens road. There was no time to dismount or to draw rifles; the squadron commander ordered his bugler to blow 'charge', and the men lowered their lances and kicked their horses into a canter. The Germans had no time to form a firing line and were caught flat-footed. Many were killed by sword and lance thrusts and the rest disintegrated and fled back into the trees.[11] The cavalry held the line until relieved by infantry in the small hours of 31 March. The Germans never did manage to advance beyond the woods, and this was as far as the 'Kaiser's offensive' got in that part of the line. Had the cavalry, and their horses, not been available, it is quite possible – indeed probable, given the state of the French army in the area – that the Germans would have been able to press on over the railway and the main road, and bring up significant reinforcements to Moreuil village long before Allied infantry could reach it.

There were occasions when lack of cavalry made a difference to the result. In January 1917 the Italians – who had entered the war on the Allied side because the Allies had offered them more in territorial concessions than the Central Powers could offer to keep them neutral – were making progress against the Austro-Hungarians. Germany, previously reluctant to take troops away from the Western Front to help her Austrian under-strapper, now had troops to spare as a result of withdrawing to the Hindenburg Line. A new Fourteenth Austrian Army was formed, of thirty-five divisions. The army commander and seven of these divisions were German, as was most of the artillery. On 24 October the Fourteenth Army, spearheaded by German units, erupted out of Tolmino, captured Caporetto, poured across the River Isonzo, and established itself on the foothills of the main Italian defence line, the Kolvorat Ridge. Small German mountain infantry units, including one led by Lieutenant Erwin Rommel, penetrated the Italian positions in thick mist, and by 26 October the Italians were in full retreat to the River Tagliamento, thirty-five miles to the rear. Here was an opportunity for the German cavalry to pursue, and had they done so the Italians could never have reached and crossed the Tagliamento; but there was no German cavalry to be had. Most of it was on the Eastern Front, and those cavalry units that were available had been left far behind as being unlikely to be needed. It was a close-run thing for the Italians, but they eventually managed to retire from the Tagliamento in some order, and by 10 November were reasonably safe behind the River Piave, a further sixty-five miles to the rear. It was a great victory for the Germans, who took 180,000 prisoners of the Italian Second Army, but it could have been greater – it might even have forced Italy out of the war altogether, if only there had been cavalry to cut off the retreat to the Tagliamento.

During the 'Kaiser's offensive' on the Western Front in 1918 there were many occasions where the timely and speedy use of cavalry could have helped the German cause, particularly when the French and British had withdrawn from their forward defence positions and were in full retreat. That there was then no cavalry available to the Germans was due to greed. The Treaty of Brest-Litovsk in March 1918 saw Russia withdraw from the war, and the whole of the Ukraine, Russian Poland, Finland, the Baltic provinces and the Caucasus were effectively annexed by Germany. To control this huge tranche of territory the Germans left a million men in the east, including most of their cavalry. A little less greed and that cavalry could have been deployed to the Western Front, where they might have made a difference.

Germany's offensive of 1918 ran out of steam and depleted her resources without achieving its aim of splitting the Allies. Now the Allies went over to the offensive, and by September had pushed the Germans back to the Hindenburg Line, from where the 'Kaiser's offensive' had been launched. This was accomplished by a series of attacks all along the German line. It was a new concept, made practicable by more and better mechanical transport that allowed the shifting of Allied resources along the front at a pace that would have been impossible a year earlier. It was still hoped that once a gap had been created the cavalry could pour through, but as long as the Allies were advancing over ground that had already been fought over many times, the debris of war, and particularly the wire, prevented mass cavalry operations. On 27 September 1918 the British launched an attack between Cambrai and Saint-Quentin, and after nine days had crossed the formidable Canal du Nord, pierced the Hindenburg Line and penetrated into open country beyond the last German defences. Soon there would be a chance for the cavalry. Squadrons were detached to the leading infantry divisions while the rest of the Cavalry Corps followed close behind. By now the much-vaunted German system of command and control was breaking down, morale amongst the troops was low, the home population was not far from starvation, and the American First Army was in the field. It was apparent to even the most rigid Prussian that Germany had lost the war. The Armistice followed, and the cavalry never did get their chance.

By the end of the war there had been staggering advances in the reliability and cross-country performance of mechanically propelled vehicles. Lorries could carry men and supplies; light tanks and armoured cars mounted with machine guns could do most of the work of the cavalry. Between the wars the horse would be all but banished from the battlefield. The horse had been essential in 1914, and while its usefulness had diminished as the war went on and technology improved, it had been far from a useless encumbrance to modern war.

The British army was fully mechanised by 1939, but in the wet and cold winter of 1939–40 it was found impossible for lorries to supply many of the forward troops along narrow Belgian and French lanes whose surfaces had been cut up and damaged by heavy rain and blocked by snow. The answer? Mule companies of the Royal Indian Army Service Corps.

NOTES

1 *Statistics of the Military Effort of the British Empire during the Great War*, War Office, London, 1922.

2 Horses are traditionally measured in hands, one hand equalling four inches. Measurement is done from the highest point of the withers (the area of the spine just in front of the saddle) vertically to the ground, without shoes. Polo ponies were then limited to 14 h. 2, so the army often bought animals that had been intended for polo but which grew too big, and were sold off cheaply.

3 The Indian cavalry retained their swords, except for sergeants and above, who were issued with revolvers.

4 As this author discovered when he first took up tent-pegging.

5 The Marquess of Anglesey, *A History of the British Cavalry*, Vol. 7, Leo Cooper, London, 1996.

6 *Statistics of the Military Effort of the British Empire during the Great War*, War Office, London, 1922.

7 An Indian cavalry brigade had one British regiment and two Indian regiments.

8 *The USA in the World War 1917–19*, Vol. 4, United States Army Center of Military History, Fort McNair DC, 1988–92.

9 A sowar was a private soldier of Indian cavalry.

10 Indian squadrons of cavalry, like companies of infantry, had one British officer in command. A second British officer, usually a lieutenant or second lieutenant, was attached as a 'squadron officer' to assist the commander and to learn his trade. It was these squadron officers who were borrowed by the Guards. The thought of guardsmen being led by officers of Indian cavalry is intriguing, but it obviously worked.

11 The Canadian cavalry, unlike the British, had retained swords for all ranks.

6

FRIGHTFULNESS

One of the abiding images of the Great War is of lines of soldiers, eyes bandaged, shuffling along in a slow crocodile, each with his hand on the shoulder of the man in front. Tales abound of thousands of young men drowning with lungs full of fluid, choking to death, bodies covered in angry blisters, or permanently blinded. Gas was, and is, regarded as a barbaric way of making war; it is uncivilised, unsporting, and somehow unfair. Death by shooting, bayoneting, bombing or shellfire is acceptable; death by insidious and undetectable vapour is not. The first use of gas, by the Germans, was a deliberate breach of the laws of war and typical of a savage and unprincipled enemy.

This was the conception propagated by the British and French when gas was first used on the Western Front, and it has remained with us ever since. In fact, gas was never a war-winning weapon, casualties were far less than has been stated, and the British – not the Germans – became the masters of its use.

The first recorded use of gas in the war was at what became known as the Second Battle of Ypres, in 1915.[1] In the spring of that year the Ypres salient was a relatively quiet sector. North of the salient to the Channel coast the line was held by the Belgian army, determined to remain on the defensive and hold what little remained of unoccupied Belgium.

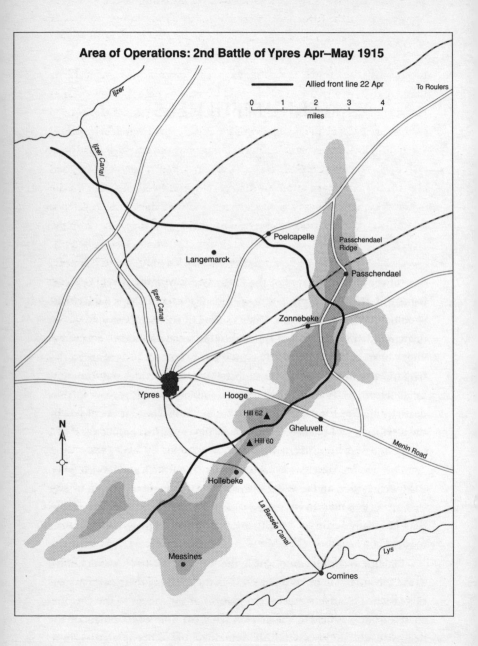

Area of Operations: 2nd Battle of Ypres Apr–May 1915

Allied front line 22 Apr

0   1   2   3   4
miles

To Roulers

Ijzer

Ijzer Canal

Ijzer Canal

Poelcapelle

Langemarck

Passchendael Ridge

Passchendael

Zonnebeke

Ypres

Hooge

Hill 62

Gheluvelt

Hill 60

Menin Road

N

Hollebeke

La Bassée Canal

Lys

Messines

Comines

The Belgians' task was made easier by their flooding of the sluices at Nieuwpoort on the River Ijzer, which created an almost insuperable water obstacle between their positions and the Germans'. The north of the salient itself was held by a French Territorial division, and the defence was then taken up by the French 45th Algerian Division from the canal as far as Langemarck, where the newly arrived Canadians held the line as far as Passchendaele. From Passchendaele round the salient and then south to the La Bassée Canal, the remainder of the British sector was held by British and Indian divisions. French Territorials, Algerians and Canadians had been placed where they were precisely because things were quiet – it was a good area for them to learn about trench warfare and to adapt to life on the Western Front. As far as the French were concerned there was no defence in depth: most of the troops were strung out along the firing line, with the artillery – mainly the 75-mm standard French field gun – close up behind.

On 22 April 1915 – a fine spring day, with a mild south-westerly breeze, according to the weather reports – there was heavier than usual German shelling of the Ypres salient, particularly in the northern sector. All German shelling then suddenly stopped, and at about 1700 hours the men of the Algerian Division saw what appeared to be a bank of greenish-yellow smoke moving slowly towards them from the German lines, all along the French front. British observers, some way behind the French lines, thought the cloud looked like a bluish-white mist, and felt a tickling in their throats and a watering of the eyes. The cloud gradually enveloped the French lines and then, quite suddenly, men could be seen running back out of the cloud coughing and spluttering, many without weapons. In a very short time the whole of the Algerian Division – twelve battalions and ten batteries of artillery – broke, and a disorganised mob streamed rearwards, finally rallying about a mile and a half north of Ypres. At the northern tip of the salient a French Territorial battalion stood fast on the bridge over the canal, and the Canadians too, with a battalion of French Tirailleurs (light infantry), held their ground for the moment. There was now a gap about three miles wide in the Allied lines, with very little to prevent a German advance on Ypres itself.

Fortunately for the defenders, the Germans were almost as surprised as the Allies by the success of the new weapon. German infantry, some equipped with a very primitive protective mask, and some with nothing at all, followed up for about two and a half miles, but they lacked the reserves to mount a major offensive, and their soldiers were wary of moving too fast lest they too became affected by the gas.

The Germans had installed nearly 6,000 cylinders of chlorine in their front-line positions, waited until the wind was favourable, and then turned on the taps. The Algerians, with no warning and no protection, understandably ran. Later investigations showed that those men who dived into bunkers or lay in the bottom of trenches, and the wounded lying on the ground, were particularly badly affected, as were those who fled, keeping pace with the gas and gulping it in as they ran. Those who remained on the fire-step (not many) and those who stood up on the parapet (even fewer) were less affected as the heavier-than-air gas swirled round them and moved on.

The Allied reaction was one of public indignation and private panic. The Germans were accused of a flagrant breach of the laws of war, and the Allies exaggerated their casualties to demonstrate German beastliness. The *Daily Mail* of 26 April 1915 thundered:

> His methods of warfare do not bear comparison with those of even a savage but high-minded people like the Zulus, but rather recall the hideous and unbridled violence of the Mahdi's hordes. His savagery, however, is not of the assegai and shield order. It is the cold-blooded employment of every device of modern science, asphyxiating bombs, incendiary discs and the like, irrespective of the laws of civilised warfare. When baffled his malice is that of an angry gorilla, senselessly slaying and destroying everything in its path.

As the gorilla is a mild-mannered vegetarian, this was not perhaps the best comparison to make, but the thrust is clear.

In fact the casualties suffered by the Algerians were very much fewer than was stated at the time. Unfortunately, what really happened and what was said to have happened have become confused, and even in 1939 Major-General Sir Henry Thuillier, formerly Director of Gas Services at GHQ of the BEF, was claiming 20,000 casualties including 5,000 deaths on that first day of gas warfare.[2] This figure seems to have been accepted without question, but as a French division at full strength numbered barely 15,000 it is clearly an exaggeration. The German chemist Fritz Haber visited the ground an hour after the attack and reported that he saw some men killed by gas, but 'not many'.[3] The Chief Medical Officer of the German Fourth Army visited the trenches on 23 April and found a number of men with breathing difficulties due to the effects of gas. The majority recovered. Altogether around 200 French soldiers were treated in German Fourth Army hospitals, of whom twelve died. The German XXIII Reserve Corps reported that forty gas casualties were treated in their hospitals, of whom eighteen were Germans who showed no medical symptoms at all, four were Germans who were severely affected, five were French and were recovering, and eight were French who were badly affected and of whom one died.[4] One German officer gas casualty, Leutnant Telle, stated that there were no French dead in their trenches, but that they had run away 'like a flock of sheep'. It was also reported that of 800 French gas-affected soldiers in a German prisoner-of-war camp on 22 April, all were coughing badly and some were very ill. Haber cites a French record that shows that of 625 gas casualties undergoing treatment on 24 April, three died of congestion of the lungs.[5] A reasonable estimate for the gas casualties of the attack on 22 April is around 1,500 at most, of whom around 200 may have died.[6]

The laws of war regarding gas were contained in the Hague Convention of 1899 (modified in 1907), to which Britain, France and Germany were signatories, and which prohibited 'the use of projectiles the sole object of which is the diffusion of asphyxiating gases'. Germany could – and did – argue that this prohibition applied to shells, not to the diffusion of gases by other means such as cylinders. The Allies maintained that this was mere trifling with words and that the intent of the clause was to prohibit the use of gases in war, however delivered. Allied protests were, of course, partly motivated by the discovery that the enemy had a weapon which they had not; but that the Germans felt at least some ambivalence is suggested by their (untrue) claims that the British had used gas shells against them to the east of Ypres in April, and by the lack of any mention of the use of gas in German official news releases about the battle. The Germans also claimed that the French army had frequently used gas grenades before the war (they were actually tear-gas grenades, not prohibited by the convention, and they were used by the French police, not the army).

There do appear to have been some intelligence indications as to what the Germans were planning: shortly before the April attack a German prisoner was found in possession of a cloth bag containing a piece of cotton waste impregnated with chemicals, and a British report mentioned some cylinders found in German trenches after the capture of Hill 60, to the south of the salient, on 17 and 18 April, but although a warning about the possible use of gas was issued by the British V Corps (General Plumer), no protection was available and the intelligence was sketchy anyway.[7]

Chlorine attacks the respiratory organs, and if no preventative action is taken, death is by asphyxiation. The immediate problem for the Allies was to provide some protection for the troops. A party of chemists arrived from England, pronounced that the gas was indeed chlorine, and recommended the use of a pad of cotton waste dipped in hyposulphite and carbonate of soda. The pad was to be sewn to a gauze veil and tied over the mouth and nose with tapes. This would provide some protection until something more soldier-proof could be introduced. Manufacture of this first gas mask began, many of them sewn by the women of England who used the veils from their hats and provided jolly red, white and blue ribbons. By 15 May all soldiers were issued with the mask, contained in a waterproof bag; in the intervening period they made do with old socks, handkerchiefs or any other piece of cloth soaked in bicarbonate of soda or chloride of lime. Some adopted the simple precaution of urinating on a cloth and using that as a mask – unpleasant, but as urine contains ammonia, which is alkaline, and as chlorine is acidic, it did provide some protection. The Indian Sappers and Miners were convinced that chewing tobacco provided protection, but this may have been a joke directed against the Sikhs, to whom tobacco is forbidden.

More German gas attacks in May achieved little: surprise was gone and the improvised gas mask proved effective. On 6 July the British smoke helmet, known as the 'hypo helmet', was issued. This was a flannelette hood that covered the head completely, being tucked into the neck of the tunic. It was impregnated with hyposulphite of soda and had eyepieces of mica, later of celluloid. This was hot and uncomfortable, and made the issuing and hearing of verbal orders difficult, but as the man breathed in through the impregnated cloth it conferred complete protection against chlorine. In November 1915 the hypo helmet was replaced by the P helmet, a similar hood, but with glass eyepieces (the celluloid had a tendency to mist up) and a mouthpiece outlet valve. In addition to the hyposulphite, phenate was added as a protection against phosgene, which it was thought that the Germans might use next – and in December 1915, they did.

While protective equipment was being made and issued to the troops, the question of whether or not to retaliate in kind was being discussed. The army in the field was in no doubt: gas had been used against them, and they wanted to use a similar – and if possible more effective – weapon against the Germans. At home the public and the government were divided. Some felt that it would be wrong to descend to the level of the enemy; others felt that as the law had been breached by one side, the gloves were now off.[8] It took the Cabinet three weeks to make a decision, and this may have had as much to do with fears that the British chemical industry was not as advanced as that of Germany – if we could not beat them, why bother to make the effort? – as it had with the moral question.

After assurances by the British chemical industry and following representations by the army, the Cabinet agreed that gas could now be used by the British, and manufacture began. In May 1915 the formation of four Special Companies Royal Engineers was authorised. This organisation was commanded by the then Lieutenant Colonel C. H. Foulkes, DSO, RE and was responsible for the waging of chemical warfare. At the same time a Gas Defence Organisation was established, commanded by a doctor, Lieutenant Colonel S. L. Cummins, CMG, of the Royal Army Medical Corps, which was responsible for gas intelligence and the laboratory examination of all enemy chemical weapons. The Defence Organisation liaised closely with the Medical Branch at the War Office, which was responsible for the production of respirators and other protective equipment.

One of the first acts of General Sir Douglas Haig, who assumed command of the BEF in December 1915, was to ask, on 5 January 1916, for this organisation to be expanded into a Special Brigade, to consist of four battalions responsible for the discharge of gas by cylinder and for the deployment of smokescreens, and an additional four companies, each to be equipped with forty-eight Stokes four-inch mortars to fire gas shells, and four sections armed with flame-projectors. The men for the brigade were to come from volunteers already in France and by drafting suitably qualified men from England. By the end of May 1916, just in time to take part in the Somme offensive, the brigade was in being, with 208 officers and 5,306 men.

Prior to the expansion of the special companies into a brigade, the British employed chlorine gas for the first time at the Battle of Loos in September 1915. As at Ypres, the method of diffusion was by cylinders, and although in the south the gas was initially effective, in the north the wind changed and the gas blew back towards the attackers. Amongst British soldiers affected by their own gas when it blew back on them, there was widespread disillusionment as to the protective qualities of their issued smoke helmets. Many of those who reported to aid posts claiming to have been gassed had in fact been affected by exertion, fear, hysteria or a belief that the smell of the protective chemicals in which the flannel of their smoke helmets had been dipped was actually the smell of gas. On 19 October 1915 a Headquarters First Army order titled 'Information Regarding Asphyxiating Gas', classified secret and signed by the Major-General General Staff (Major-General Butler) said, *inter alia*:

> A large number of men reported sick at the dressing stations and field ambulances purporting to be suffering from the effects of gas. Nearly all these men, however, were merely out of breath from running and were suffering from excitement and fright; they required no treatment and were discharged at once. A considerable proportion of them were recognised as habitual malingerers.

While it appears that the order may never have actually been issued, the thinking is clear.[9]

There was a major problem with the use of gas cylinders: it all depended on the wind. The Allies did have the advantage, as the wind tended to blow west to east about twice as often as it blew east to west. For this reason, while between 1915 and 1918 the Germans launched eleven gas attacks using cylinders, the British launched 150. Despite the advantage of the prevailing wind, to base offensive plans entirely around the weather, which was fickle anyway, was not the best way of waging war; and the greater the distance between the opposing trenches the less effective the gas was when it arrived at its destination. A better and more reliable method of delivering noxious vapours would be found.

In December 1915 the Germans, as predicted, used phosgene gas. Phosgene is a compound of carbon monoxide and chlorine and was more effective than chlorine because, although it too attacked the respiratory system, a dangerous dose was not easily detectable, and even if it was detected it did not necessarily cause discomfort to begin with. When the Germans did launch their first phosgene attack, at Ypres, the British were well prepared and had ample warning. Even so, 1,069 casualties were inflicted, of which 120 died. These deaths were largely caused by soldiers not donning their respirators quickly enough. The attack, however, achieved nothing.

The way was now clear for the British to retaliate with phosgene, but there were two problems: the Cabinet once again took a long time to decide that retaliation in kind was acceptable, and in any case phosgene was a by-product of the cloth-dyeing industry, which was thriving in Germany but had almost ceased in the United Kingdom. Eventually the Cabinet agreed to the use of phosgene, and the British found that the French manufactured ample supplies of it. An initial difficulty was that the production process was commercially secret; this was obviated by the British obtaining phosgene from the French in exchange for chlorine, with British cylinders being filled in a factory in Calais, until the British could obtain the licences to make phosgene for themselves. At first cylinders were filled with a mix of chlorine and phosgene in order to create sufficient pressure for the phosgene to diffuse, and this continued until a reliable phosgene shell was produced.

The first serious use of shells containing gas – a method of delivery that did not depend upon the wind – was by the Germans at Hill 60 in late April 1915. These initially contained a form of tear gas, an irritant but not a lethal one, followed up by a more toxic variant and finally by shells containing a form of phosgene (diphosgene) in mid-1916. Once the Germans had used shells containing gas, the way was open for the British to do the same. The British armaments industry was, however, having enough trouble providing high-explosive and shrapnel shells, and the first British gas shell contained only tear gas. After much badgering of the War Office by Sir Douglas Haig, and following the inevitable crisis of conscience in the Cabinet, a few so-called lethal British shells appeared at the end of 1916, containing a mixture of prussic acid and arsenious chloride. They were generally thought to be ineffective and of little use except to make the Germans put on their respirators.

The last major form of gas to be used on the Western Front was mustard gas, or dichlorethyl sulphide. This was first employed by the Germans at Ypres in July 1917, and was far more dangerous than anything used hitherto. Mustard gas was very difficult to detect, having no characteristic smell, but was highly toxic if inhaled in even small quantities, as well as having a blistering effect on the skin. It also caused conjunctivitis and (painful but usually temporary) blindness. An additional problem was that ground impregnated with mustard gas remained toxic long after the initial shelling had ceased. British respirators provided complete protection to the eyes and the respiratory system, but did not prevent the blistering effect on the skin. The only complete protection would have been to issue soldiers with a suit that completely covered the body, similar to the present-day nuclear, biological and chemical warfare suit (known irreverently as the 'Noddy suit'), and while materials such as asbestos and oilskin were considered, the technology to produce an all-enveloping suit that would not unduly restrict movement did not exist in 1917.

This first attack by mustard gas was unexpected by the British, and for the first few days many soldiers failed to put on their respirators in time and died as a result. Once soldiers were warned, however, deaths were negligible, although there were large numbers of temporary casualties from the blistering effects of the gas. Although the results were painful, nearly all the men affected recovered and were able to return to duty within a few weeks. Among those caught without wearing respirators in a mustard-gas attack, one immediate reaction was to cover the eyes with a bandage soaked in water as a temporary relief for the pain: it was this that gave rise to the belief that huge numbers of men were blinded.

The British now began to manufacture mustard-gas shells, and although the French got in first, by September 1918 the British had large stocks of mustard-gas shells and the means of delivery. Had the war lasted another year, this gas, unlike its predecessors, might well have had a decisive affect on the war.

There were two reasons why the British, although never the first to use a particular type of gas, were better at using it than the Germans: British protection and British delivery. A smoke helmet, gas mask or respirator works on a simple principle: all the air breathed into a man's lungs must come through a filter, which removes the toxic elements. Although the flannel-hood types of helmet were efficient and saved lives, when the Germans introduced a new type of gas the whole assembly had to be replaced. Far better would be a method of retaining the breathing apparatus but having an easily changed filter attached to it. As different types of gas came along, so filters to protect against them could be quickly developed and issued, and affixed to a man's existing mask. The more gases that were likely to be encountered, the more filters would be needed; so there would come a point where the filter, if attached to or near the mouth or face, would not only be unwieldy and interfere with the wearer's performance, but would be heavy enough to pull the mask away from his face. Hence the British produced the box respirator. The soldier wore a light mask that covered his mouth, nose and eyes, and this was attached by a flexible rubber tube to a canister containing the filters, the canister being carried in a canvas bag on the man's chest. A considerable weight could be carried in this way, and the British respirator proved more than equal to anything the Germans or the wind could throw, fire or blow at it. If a new gas came along, a filter could be made to counter it and added to the filters already in the bag on the chest. The Germans, on the other hand, were very short of rubber, being prevented from importing it by the Royal Navy's blockade, and were forced to have all their filters attached directly to the mask, with a severe limitation on the weight that could be carried. German filters had a shorter life than did those of the British, and the British would often fire smoke shells to force the Germans to don their masks, then fire various types of gas at them until the filters were no longer effective. Not a great number of Germans were killed, but such tactics did force them to withdraw from positions once they were no longer protected.

Gas shells for artillery were expensive, and as they had to be strong enough to withstand the pressures of being fired from an artillery piece, they were limited in the amount of gas they could hold. One British solution was the Livens projector, invented by Major W. H. Livens of the Royal Engineers. The projector was a simple metal tube about four feet in length and eight inches in diameter, closed and rounded at one end. It came with a detachable steel baseplate to prevent it being driven too far into the mud when fired. The tube was half buried in the ground, the elevation and direction being calculated to deliver the gas where desired. The projectile was of steel and contained thirty pounds of phosgene and a bursting charge of TNT. The propellant was cordite and range was determined by the amount of cordite used. The device was fired by an electrically initiated charge in the bottom of the projector. Used in massed batteries of twenty-five or so, with the wires to their propellent charges all connected to one firing device, the Livens projector could deliver a lot of gas quickly and at a high concentration in a specific area at up to a mile's range. It was cheap, easy to operate and very effective for local use, as – in contrast to the cylinder-release method – there was no warning of the gas's approach.

One striking British development, which might have had a major effect on the Western Front had it been ready before the Armistice in 1918, was not lethal at all. The idea was to use diphenyl chlorarsine in a smoke cloud whose particles would be so fine as to penetrate the German respirator. The chemical had no long-lasting deleterious affects but produced an intense irritation of the mouth, nose, eyes and throat, pains in the chest, difficulty in breathing, and vomiting. It rendered those exposed to it completely helpless for a limited period. The Germans had tried diphenyl chlorarsine, but gave up when it became apparent that their method of delivery – by artillery shell – did not produce a cloud whose particles were fine enough to penetrate the Allied respirators. The British discovered that a sufficiently fine cloud could be produced by heat distillation, rather than by an explosive bursting charge. They intended to use a derivative of the substance delivered by canisters placed on the parapet of their own trenches. Each canister had a heating element below the chemical, and the fuse would be lit when the wind was blowing in the right direction. The aim was to follow up such an attack with infantry, who could seize the opposing defence lines when their occupants were incapacitated. British box respirators were adapted by the addition of cheesecloth filters to stop the particles, and preparations were well in hand when the war came to an end.

Through better methods of protection, and through the development of ever more efficient means of delivering successively more noxious gases, the British rapidly became the leaders in gas warfare; the Germans never regained their early advantage. The British launched a total of 768 gas attacks between 1915 and 1918, using 88,000 cylinders, 197,000 Livens projector drums, 178,000 Stokes gas bombs, 5,700 tons of gas of various types and a huge quantity of artillery shells firing gas. The British were, however, sufficiently sensitive to public opinion at home and in the neutral countries to take care that they never initiated a new form of gas warfare. They predicted it, prepared for it and manufactured the chemicals for it, but they always waited until the Germans had used it first; then they replied in kind, nearly always with more devastating effect.

While there can be no doubt that gas came as a terrible shock initially, when the Allies had no conception of what it was or how to protect themselves against it, it never became more than a useful tactical expedient for either side. The wearing of gas masks was uncomfortable and inconvenient, and although gas did cause casualties it never conferred more than a temporary local advantage to the user. Throughout the course of the war the British lost 487,994 dead from all causes on the Western Front. Of these deaths 5,899, or 1.2 per cent of the total, were attributable to gas.[10] In July 1917 the Germans shelled the Ypres salient with 50,000 rounds of mustard gas, the nastiest gas then available. Two and a half thousand soldiers were gassed, but only eighty-seven died. During the next three weeks a further 14,726 men were gassed, of whom 500 died, many as a result of failing to don their respirators in time. Despite the tales of the great numbers of men whose lives were cut short or subsequently ruined by their having been gassed, of the pensions awarded for injury caused by war service, only one in a hundred was to a gas victim, and only 0.12 per cent were for blindness from all causes. Although fatalities due to gas were far fewer than claimed at the time and since, an injured man causes more problems to his own side than does one who is dead. Bodies are relatively easily disposed of; injured men have to be evacuated, cared for, fed and housed. To have to deal with large numbers of men incapacitated, albeit temporarily, by gas was a very real administrative burden for both sides. In that the British inflicted more gas casualties than they sustained, gas warfare was to the Allied advantage overall, but gas was never a decisive weapon. The cynic might say that if it had really been any good, it would never have been banned.

If being killed or injured by an undetectable vapour that arrived with no warning was regarded as unpleasant, being roasted to death was seen as being even more so. As with gas, the Germans were the first to use flame as a weapon, firstly against the French at Malancourt in February 1915 and then against the British in July of the same year. The 8th Battalion the Rifle Brigade, a New Army battalion, arrived on the Western Front on 20 May 1915. At 0200 hours on 30 July the men moved into the front lines at Hooge, on the Ypres salient. Here the opposing lines were very close together, separated only by the Menin road, and at 0315 hours the battalion was subject to a German mortar attack, following which the German parapet suddenly erupted in gouts of flame and thick smoke directed at the Rifle Brigade. A number of men were burned, and many were later reported missing (probably burned). The battalion were driven out of their trenches and the position was not stabilised until late afternoon. Eight officers and 169 other ranks of the Rifle Brigade were killed that day, although how many by mortar fire, how many by flame and how many in the subsequent fighting is not clear. As to exactly what type of flame-projector was involved, sources are confused. The British official view was that portable devices were used, but the war diary of the battalion indicates that the flame was projected by means of pipes laid to the German parapet and fed from containers of a pressurised mix of oil and petrol that was ignited at the mouth of the pipe. As the Germans seem to have made no attempt to advance under cover of flame, it is likely that the apparatus was static, or at least not man-portable. The Germans eventually produced three types of *Flammenwerfer*: the small and medium varieties came as cylindrical devices strapped to a man's back with the flame projected from a flexible nozzle, while the large variant was only portable in sections.

The British, having made the usual protestations about beastliness and unfairness, promptly opened a factory in Wembley to manufacture flame-projectors of their own. Each of the flame sections of the Special Brigade RE had, by late June 1916, one large and four portable contraptions. The main limitation of these weapons was their range – not much more than around thirty yards for the large version, and less for the portable. While they could have been of great help to an attacker for the clearing of dugouts and bunkers, they had to be carried across no man's land first, and the operator was an easy target owing to both his inability to move quickly and his distinctive silhouette. A solution might have been to fit the devices in tanks, as was done with the 'crocodile' in the Second World War, but the vulnerability of such a weapon to an artillery strike might have made it difficult to persuade crews to man it.

Flame-projectors were used increasingly but sporadically by both sides until the end of the war, with mixed results. Concurrently with their attack on the 8th Rifle Brigade, the Germans managed to gain a foothold on Hill 62 – an area of vital ground to the defenders of the Ypres salient – by the use of flame-throwers; but difficulty in following up prevented them from exploiting the advantage gained, and the area was recaptured by the British on 9 August. In June 1916 the Germans again attacked in the same area with flame, but a stout defence by Princess Patricia's Canadian Light Infantry prevented them holding the ground taken.[11]

On the opening day of the Somme offensive, 1 July 1916, there was an area of mine craters, occupied by the Germans and forward of their main line, on the British 18 Division's front. This potential obstruction was neutralised by the use of a large flame-projector positioned at the end of a sap, the operation being supervised by the redoubtable Major Livens, RE, inventor of the gas-projector. The sap itself had been created using another British invention, the 'pipe-pusher'. This device used a hydraulic jack to push a pipe full of ammonal explosive in the horizontal direction required at a depth of four to five feet below ground. Once the requisite distance was reached, the explosive content of the pipe was detonated and the resultant ditch turned quickly into a communication trench.

Flame-throwers continued to be used sporadically by each side, but there is little mention of them in either of the two great mobile offensives: that of the Germans in spring 1918 and that of the Allies in August of the same year, when the portable versions might have been useful for clearing bunkers and (for the Germans) as an anti-tank weapon. The reasons appear to be the difficulty flame-thrower operators had in keeping up with the infantry, and the weapon's very limited range – about twenty-five yards. It would take a further war to produce a flame-thrower that was sufficiently portable, effective and plentiful to be of any great benefit in battle.

Mining, or tunnelling, was a military art that dated back centuries. Wellington had used sappers to mine under the walls of Burgos Castle in 1812, with mixed success. In this war it was, once again, the Germans who initiated tunnelling as a technique on the Western Front. In December 1914 the Sirhind Brigade, part of the Lahore Division of the Indian Corps, was holding a sector of the front just north of Richebourg-l'Avoué. This brigade was new to France, having disembarked at Marseille from Egypt on 1 December, and arrived in the battle area still wearing tropical uniforms six days later. On 19 December the brigade was involved in severe fighting north-east of Givenchy as part of Sir John French's harassing attacks all along the British front. The Sirhind Brigade had briefly taken parts of the German lines, but by shortly after dusk the men were back in their own trenches and there seemed to be a lull in the pace of operations. For some time there had been rumours about German tunnelling, and reports from the Royal Flying Corps had indicated that there were attempts to hide excavated spoil behind the German lines. No definite evidence as to what this meant was forthcoming, and the men who had paid a short visit to the German positions on 19 December saw no signs of tunnelling from there. All night it poured with rain, so heavily that fire-steps were washed away and such pumps that were available were overwhelmed by the torrents of water. At first light on 20 December German artillery and trench mortars began a bombardment all along the Indian Corps line, and two German infantry attacks were made on Givenchy and La Quinque Rue, only to be beaten off.

At about 0900 hours there was a series of terrific explosions along the Sirhind Brigade front, and earth, revetting material and bodies went flying into the air. A company of the 1st Battalion 1st Gurkha Rifles and half a

company of the 1st Battalion Highland Light Infantry were simply obliterated: blown to pieces or buried in collapsing trenches. Strong German
infantry attacks followed and the fighting went on all day, with the Sirhind
Brigade eventually driven back to their reserve lines where they held on
grimly with ever-depleting manpower. The situation was not restored until
timely support could be given by Haig's I Corps on 22 December.

We now know that the Germans had tunnelled under the Indian lines
and had placed charges of gunpowder (old-fashioned black powder, the
material Wellington had used at Burgos a century before) at the end of
their tunnels. Ten of these charges were successfully detonated, each of
110 pounds of explosive. By later standards this was a paltry amount – a
mere squib – but its total surprise, and the shock it created, precipitated
what almost became a major German success. While nobody liked being
shot at or shelled, at least you knew it was coming. The thought that one
might be going innocuously about one's business – eating a sandwich,
cleaning a rifle, reading a book, sitting on the latrine, or lying fast asleep
– when at any moment and without warning one's whole world might
erupt in noise, debris, death and destruction was not good for morale. The
mining war had begun.

Ever since the siege of Port Arthur in the Russo-Japanese War the
British army had studied mining in a modern context, but there were no
dedicated tunnelling units in the BEF, and the existing Royal Engineer
field companies were far too busy with other vital matters to devote
large numbers of men to the activity. On 3 December Lieutenant General
Sir Henry Rawlinson, General Officer Commanding IV Corps, had asked
for a mining battalion to be formed, and the events of 20 December
hastened thinking on the matter. On 28 December action to form
tunnelling units began: brigades were to form their own mining sections
as a temporary measure and the War Office agreed to send out 500 men
experienced in tunnelling. The driving spirit was Major J. Norton-
Griffiths, an MP with mining interests who had managed to circumvent
Kitchener's dislike of private armies and who was now an officer of
the 2nd King Edward's Horse, largely raised by him. Norton-Griffiths
took charge of the recruitment of miners, many of them so-called
clay-kickers, that is, experienced in tunnelling through clay rather than

rock. Norton-Griffiths was not a professional soldier – indeed with his political connections he was regarded as somewhat of a nuisance – but as so often happens in war, the coming of the hour brought forth the man. Norton-Griffiths bounced around between England and France, using his own London office as the recruiting centre for miners, and by the middle of 1915 there were twenty tunnelling companies on the Western Front. In most cases the company commander was a regular officer of the Royal Engineers while the company officers were mining or colliery engineers, civil engineers or men with previous experience of mining or tunnelling. As most of the soldiers were recruited straight from civilian employment, with only a rudimentary training in the peculiarities of army life, there were misunderstandings. Norton-Griffiths had recruited men at varying rates of pay, dependent upon their mining qualifications. On one occasion representatives of the men informed their company commander that they were concerned about the eroding of pay differentials and that they intended to down tools until the dispute was resolved. The company commander explained that this procedure might be all very well in the mines of Lancashire. The army, however, in its quaint way, would regard it as mutiny, which carried the death penalty. Work was instantly resumed.

At the height of the war on the Western Front there were twenty-five British tunnelling companies, three Canadian, three Australian and one from New Zealand. As each company numbered up to a thousand men, this was the equivalent of two divisions burrowing away far underground, fighting their own private war, with those above them entirely oblivious to what was going on except when one of the more impressive mines was blown.

There were two types of mining carried out by both sides: defensive and offensive. Defensive mining, as practised by the British, consisted of sinking a number of shafts along a designated sector, usually to a depth of forty feet or so, and connecting them up by what was known as a gallery. From this gallery a number of tunnels would be driven out in the direction of the German lines, and at the end of each tunnel crouched two or three men whose task it was to listen for enemy tunnelling. At first the Mark I ear, pressed against the face of the tunnel, was used as the detection instrument, and later a tinful of water in which was placed a stick, the latter gripped between the teeth. Eventually a variation of the doctor's stethoscope was used. If enemy tunnelling was detected then a team would tunnel out as fast and as silently as possible towards the German tunnel, with the aim of either blowing it in or breaking into it and killing the enemy miners in hand-to-hand combat. Initially the British too used black powder, but this swiftly gave way to ammonal, a much safer and more reliable explosive, which came in tins and could be more easily manhandled.

Offensive mining involved tunnelling beneath the enemy trenches and placing explosives at the end of the tunnel, to be set off by electrical detonators at the opportune moment, usually in conjunction with an attack above ground. In Flanders the surface layer was of water-bearing clay, and any tunnelling through this was difficult, dangerous and slow, as pumps had to be used to remove the water and the tunnel had to be shored up to prevent it collapsing. Underneath this water-bearing layer, however, was a layer of blue clay, which still had to be shored up but which did not hold water, and most tunnelling was done through this. Further south, when the British line at last extended well out of Flanders, the chalk downs of the Somme were relatively easy to tunnel through as the chalk drained well and shoring did not have to be used along the entire length of a tunnel.

Blowing increasingly larger mines under the enemy positions had three main aims: firstly to collapse dugouts and bunkers and kill the infantry in them; secondly to cause confusion and dislocation of command and control systems; and thirdly to blow a crater in the enemy lines which, if seized by friendly infantry, could form a strongpoint within the enemy defences. It has to be said that while the British were much better at producing the craters, the Germans were much better at seizing them.

On 1 July 1916 eighteen mines were blown by the British at 0728 hours, two minutes before zero hour (a nineteenth was, controversially, blown earlier). One of the largest, on the high ground overlooking the village of La Boisselle, actually consisted of a Y-shaped tunnel, with the two mines sixty feet apart. The tunnel took three months to dig and the two mines contained no less than 60,000 pounds of ammonal between them. The explosion, when it came, was spectacular. It was said that the roar was clearly heard in Whitehall (unlikely – the mandarins of Whitehall rarely arrived in their offices before 0900). In any event, a great mountain of debris rose up into the air, crashing down again for hundreds of yards around. A crater 450 feet across was created, 100 yards of German trench ceased to exist, and it is estimated that nine German dugouts were destroyed, causing several hundred casualties. Despite the devastation around them, the Germans reacted more quickly than did the British. The crater was not seized, and the area not captured until two days later.

At Messines Ridge in June 1917 the British planted twenty-one mines, with a total of over one million pounds of explosive between them, under the German lines. The largest, near Spanbroekmolen, was eighty-eight feet underground and contained 91,000 pounds of ammonal. All these mines had been completed a year earlier, since when the firing circuits had been regularly checked by Royal Engineer officers to ensure that they would still function. At 0310 hours on 7 June 1917 the mines were blown. Nineteen went off, and again it was said that Prime Minister Lloyd George could feel the shock waves in his office in Downing Street. Again, this is unlikely. Energetic fellow though he was, Lloyd George would have been fast asleep at three o'clock in the morning, and that not in his office. The attack itself was a great success, but given that it was preceded by a seventeen-day artillery bombardment, in which two and a half million shells were fired during the last seven days alone; that it was supported by seventy-two Mark IV tanks; that the British had complete control of the skies thus preventing any German reconnaissance; and that the British were attacking with nine divisions against the Germans' six, of which only two were on the ridge itself, it would have been a success anyway. Nevertheless the mines did cause confusion amongst the Germans – in Lille the tremors were thought to be an earthquake – and they certainly cheered the British attackers.[12]

After the initial shock of the German tunnelling successes in 1914, the British quickly established superiority underground, a lead that they never lost. While defensive mining certainly did make a contribution to victory, offensive mining was perhaps not as cost-effective given the number of men employed in it. Withal, it was a lonely, dark, frightening, claustrophobic sort of war, working in a space rarely more than two feet wide and four feet high, with little chance of rescue if a tunnel collapsed or was blown in, as often happened. That view was not shared by all those who took part, however. As one old soldier told this author in 1973: 'We had a kushi number. We were out of the rain, we didn't do fatigues, the sergeant major never saw us, nobody worried about our dress, we didn't have to get our hair cut, and we didn't have to do sentry. Great it was!' When one recalls that most of these men had come from the coal mines or from tunnelling for the underground railway or the London sewers, when health and safety at work was not a priority and where accidents were common, this underground warrior's opinion becomes explicable. Army tunnellers were better fed, and at least as well paid and housed, as their civilian counterparts; safety was a major consideration of their officers; and the risk of being blown up by the Germans was probably only marginally greater than the chances of roof collapse, flooding or gas explosion in their civilian occupations.

It was not only in the invention of new – and unsporting – weapons of war that the Germans were and are accused of beastliness. During the initial phase of the war, when the Germans were advancing through Belgium, British and French newspapers reported such atrocities as the mass rape of nuns, the cutting-off of women's breasts, babies being bounced on German bayonets, and even the roasting of small children alive. As the Germans were not, at this stage of the war, short of food, this latter activity was presumably engaged in for the amusement of the troops.

The *Daily Mail* of 12 April 1915 carried an extract from *The Official Book of German Atrocities*, and included brief case histories of the violation of women and young girls by German soldiers in Belgium. Miss Y was reported as having been ordered to undress by a German NCO prior to being violated on a mattress; at Corbeck-Loo a sixteen-year-old girl was raped by a succession of German soldiers and then bayoneted in the breast; a mother and daughter aged forty-five and eighty-nine were said to have been raped, the older woman dying a week later as a result; seven Germans raped a woman and then killed her at Wakerzeel. Additionally it was alleged that the German army were forcing Belgian women and children into the vanguard of their advance. The report ends with a rallying call: 'British Men, Do you want Your women violated? Enlist today!'

It is probably unnecessary to say that there is not the slightest shred of evidence to substantiate any of these increasingly lurid tales of individual nastiness, although it has to be said that rapes occasionally do occur in all armies. There is, however, ample evidence of officially condoned acts of terror during the initial invasion of Belgium, acts which, if committed in a later war, would have led to trials for war crimes. In 1870 the Prussian army had defeated the French regular forces and had accepted the surrender of the Emperor Napoleon III at Sedan. The war was over, but a French 'Government of National Defence' had refused to bow to the inevitable and declared that the struggle would go on, prosecuted by irregulars. These *francs-tireurs*, some in uniform and some in civilian clothes, forced the Prussians to devote almost one-third of their strength to guarding their lines of communication, and a great many Prussians were killed in ambush and by snipers. The Prussians, with some legal justification, regarded this as murder and took severe reprisals against the resistance movements.

The lessons of 1871 had not been lost on the German commanders of 1914, and resistance by Belgian irregulars was punished by the shooting of hostages and the razing of particularly troublesome villages. Here the Germans were on much shakier legal ground. The laws of war, embodied in the Hague Convention of 1907, stated that belligerents were not allowed to move troops and war material across neutral territory. This portion of the convention went even further: neutral countries were forbidden to permit such movement, and there was a clear legal duty on the Belgians to resist. German protestations that 'acts of terror' committed against them by Belgian civilians, and the subsequent German reprisals, were the 'fault of the Belgian government' (which in any case denied civilian involvement) carry no weight: the Germans had no right to be in Belgium in the first place.[13]

In the east the German treatment of the Poles was brutal, and included deportation for forced labour – but then in their brief periods of independence the Poles have always showed a rather unwise propensity to be rude to both the Russians and the Germans at the same time. Once the initial war of movement was over German occupation in the west was severe; but while strict it was by and large legal. Race memory and myth persist, however, and this author was assured by a local battlefield guide in Saint-Mihiel in 1999 that on one occasion (variously 1914, 1916 and 1918) the occupying Germans lined up all the postmen and shot them! The truth is less dramatic. The French and the British ran intelligence networks behind German lines. As movement was restricted by the occupying power, the obvious people to recruit as intelligence-gatherers were those whose occupations allowed them to move around the countryside, and this included postmen, priests, doctors and itinerant tradesmen. Some agents were, inevitably, caught by the Germans; they were then tried for spying and, in accordance with the laws of war, suffered the death penalty. Some postmen in the employ of the Allied intelligence services were caught and shot, but this is far from wholesale elimination of the mail-delivery system.

In many cases the Germans acted legally but with little regard for the effects of their actions on neutral opinion. The case of Edith Cavell is a classic case in point. Cavell was the daughter of the Rector of Swardeston in Norfolk, and took up a post as governess in Brussels in 1890. Later she trained as a nurse, and in 1907 was appointed supervisor in a training school for nurses, also in Brussels. In 1914 she was visiting her mother in Norwich when war broke out. She immediately returned to Brussels where her nursing school was now a Red Cross hospital. She nursed Belgian and Allied soldiers, and when the Germans occupied the city she remained. At this stage of the war there were many British and Allied stragglers who found themselves behind the German lines, and Nurse Cavell became involved in hiding many in the hospital and then passing them along an escape route to neutral Holland, from where most of them managed to return to England or France.

About 200 soldiers had been helped to escape when in July 1915 the Germans arrested two members of the underground network, and in early August they arrested Nurse Cavell. She was brought to trial in October 1915, accused of helping Allied soldiers to escape, and admitted that she had indeed done so. She was sentenced to death and shot by firing squad at a rifle range outside Brussels at dawn on 12 October 1915.[14] Contrary to the impression given even today, Edith Cavell was not a naive young girl, but was fifty years old at the time of her death and presumably knew exactly what she was doing. The laws of war accepted that a civilian in occupied territory, regardless of nationality, who aided the enemy could be prosecuted, and, if found guilty, could be put to death. In law the Germans were perfectly entitled to execute her, as the Allies did with German agents found in French territory. Whether it was wise to have done so, however, is another matter. Her supposed last words – the oft-quoted 'Patriotism is not enough…' – rang round the world; 'Remember Edith Cavell' became a rallying cry of recruiters and a great boost to the postcard industry. She was given a memorial service in St Paul's Cathedral on 29 October 1915. After the war her body was repatriated and given a funeral service in Westminster Abbey and a grave in a prominent position just outside the east end of Norwich Cathedral. She has two statues, one in Norwich and one in St Martin's Lane in London. Brave and patriotic Edith Cavell certainly was: murdered she was not. Her execution was a public-relations disaster for Germany, but it was not unlawful.

Apart from its submarines the German navy was largely confined to port for most of the war, but the occasional ship did slip out and shell English coastal towns, to the great embarrassment of the Royal Navy. The only other way for Germany to hit the British mainland was from the air. On 10 January 1915 sixteen German aircraft were seen over the Channel. Bad weather prevented them from making an attack, but on the 19th two German Zeppelins dropped bombs on Yarmouth and King's Lynn, killing four civilians and damaging property. After the by now standard British remonstrations against uncivilised behaviour, forty aircraft of the Royal Naval Air Service bombed Ostend, Middelkerke, Ghistelles and Zeebrugge on 19 February, causing a panic but little damage. The Germans responded on 21 February by sending one aircraft to bomb Colchester, Braintree and Coggeshall, to no effect. On 14 April Zeppelins were over the Tyne, causing minor damage, and on the 15th a Zeppelin bombed Lowestoft and Southwold, while an aircraft attacked Faversham and Sittingbourne. The British gleefully reported this last effort as causing the death of one blackbird.

On 10 May Zeppelins dropped 100 bombs on Southend, killing a woman and causing £20,000-worth of damage, and on 13 May the King ordered the German Kaiser, the German Crown Prince, the King of Württemberg and the German princes struck off the roll of Knights of the Garter. Bombing continued throughout May, and Ramsgate, Southend and London were all attacked, the score being four civilian deaths (including a child), four civilians injured and some, mainly slight, damage.

The British had airships too, largely in the hands of the Royal Navy and very effective when used as convoy escorts in an anti-submarine role, but no dirigibles of the size and range of the Zeppelin. As the Zeppelins could fly at a greater height and for longer than could most aircraft, they were very difficult to deal with. At last, on 7 June 1915, Flight Sub Lieutenant R. A. J. Warneford, RN, piloting a Royal Navy aircraft, shot down a Zeppelin at 6,000 feet over German-occupied Belgium. He was awarded the Victoria Cross, but was himself killed ten days later when his aircraft crashed near Paris.

German bombing now improved, and between 7 June and mid-September 1915, when the air offensive against the British mainland ceased for the year, bombs from German Zeppelins and aircraft killed sixty civilians and injured 140. [15]

Throughout the war there were twelve shellings of the British coast by German ships, resulting in the deaths of 143 civilians and fourteen soldiers and sailors, and injury to 604 civilians and thirty servicemen. Zeppelin raids on the British mainland killed 498 civilians and fifty-eight servicemen, and injured 1,236 civilians and twelve servicemen. Ten Zeppelins were shot down or crashed on British territory or just off the coast. German aircraft raids on the United Kingdom accounted for 619 civilian and 238 military deaths, and injuries to 1,650 civilians and 400 servicemen. Full details of casualties inflicted by Allied air raids on German territory are not available, but in 1922 the War Office quoted a German estimate of 720 killed and 1,754 injured. [16]

While 1,570 deaths from coastal shelling and air raids was minuscule compared with casualties in the war zones, it was the first time for well over a century that an enemy had been able to visit death and destruction on civilians in the British homeland. Bombing of civilians from the air was regarded as a terror tactic, and it had a profound effect on British government and military thinking. It gave rise to the post-war theory that 'the bomber will always get through' and led to the (erroneous) belief, in Germany and in England, that bombing of cities would so disrupt industry and reduce civilian morale that a future war could be won from the air. It did, however, have the benefit that by 1939 about the only field of warfare in which Britain was reasonably well prepared was the air defence of the United Kingdom.

On 18 February 1915 the Germans, increasingly concerned with the effects of the Royal Navy blockade, declared that British territorial waters would henceforth be considered a war zone, in which all shipping, including neutral shipping, would be sunk on sight without warning. As the German surface fleet was penned up in port by the Royal Navy, this meant unrestricted submarine warfare. The German logic was sound: Britain could not be invaded, and defeat of her army in Flanders seemed unlikely. Britain did, however, import a large proportion of her food and raw materials, and if the flow of food and goods could be cut off, then Britain could be starved out of the war.

Such a declaration was undoubtedly a departure from the laws of war, which did allow the sinking of enemy – but not neutral – merchant shipping by submarines, but only if the submarine surfaced first and gave the enemy crew the opportunity of taking to their lifeboats. The Germans had observed this restriction in the very early days of the war, but British Q ships – merchant ships with disguised weaponry, or Royal Navy vessels disguised as merchant ships – made the practice hazardous, and increasingly German submarines would remain submerged and sink without warning. Logical it was, but the affect on neutral opinion, particularly on the only neutral of any importance, the United States, was catastrophic. On 1 May a German submarine attacked the US tanker *Gulflight*. Only two of her crew were lost, but the incident led to a formal protest by the US government. On 7 May a far greater public outcry was caused by the sinking of the *Lusitania*. The *Lusitania* was a British-registered passenger liner and was carrying war materials as part of her hold cargo. She was therefore a legitimate target, and the German embassy in Washington had actually warned US citizens not to sail on her. The only legal argument that there can possibly be is whether the submarine was entitled to sink without warning.[17] One thousand one hundred and fifty-four lives were lost on the *Lusitania*, and 114 of these were US citizens. American opinion, hitherto not actually anti-British but certainly annoyed by the British blockade, now began to swing towards irritation with Germany. Other sinkings followed, including that of the British liner *Arabic* on 19 August 1915 with the loss of four American lives. Vehement American protests persuaded Germany to abandon unrestricted submarine warfare, for the time being at least, on 1 September 1915 – quite possibly to Germany's serious detriment, for by then she had sunk almost one million tons of Allied shipping. Unrestricted submarine warfare was tried again in 1916, and again American protests persuaded Germany to call it off. By the time Germany was prepared to have another go at strangling Britain from beneath the seas, in 1917, it was too late, for now this was one of the major factors precipitating America's entry into the war on the Allied side.

On balance, then, Germany was first to use 'weapons of terror' – gas, flame and tunnelling – but it was the British, and by extension the French, who developed these same weapons and became far better at using them than their originators. The Germans got the blame for their introduction, while the British reaped what military benefit there was to be had. The shooting of Belgian hostages and the burning of villages in reprisal turned much neutral opinion against Germany, while unrestricted submarine warfare, the one piece of frightfulness that might have won them the war – or at least led to a negotiated peace – was abandoned in 1915 just when it was becoming effective.

NOTES

1 There are some indications that the Germans had experimented with lachrymatory (tear-gas) shells during the winter of 1914, but the cold weather inhibited the diffusion of the gas and the effects were almost unnoticeable.

2 Major-General Sir Henry Thuillier, *Gas in the Next War*, Geoffrey Bles, London, 1939.

3 L. F. Haber, *The Poisonous Cloud*, Oxford, 1986.

4 Papers of Generalleutnant Nachlass Freiherr von Hügel, Commander German XXVI Corps, quoted by Ulrich Trumpener, 'The Road toYpres: the Beginnings of Gas Warfare in World War I', in *Journal of Modern History*, September 1975, quoted in Simon Jones, 'Under a Green Sea, the British Responses to Gas Warfare', in *The Great War*, Vol. 1, No. 4, August 1986, pp. 126–32, and Vol. 2, No. 1, November 1989, pp. 14–21.

5 Haber, op. cit.

6 I am grateful to Mr Simon Jones, Curator of the King's Regiment Museum, Liverpool, for permitting me to use the results of his research in arriving at this conclusion.

7 Brigadier General J. E. Edmonds, *Military Operations France and Belgium 1915, Winter 1914–15*, pp. 162 et seq., Macmillan, London, 1927.

8 In legal terms the 'Tu Quoque' defence, specifically ruled inadmissible as a defence at the Nuremberg International War Crimes Tribunal after World War II.

9 Simon Jones, op. cit.

10 The number is probably understated, as some would have been returned as 'killed in action'; but even so, the proportion is tiny.

11 The PPCLI had been raised as a private finance initiative by the owner of Eaton's Stores in Canada. Named after the daughter of the Duke of Connaught, brother of King George V and Governor General of Canada, it was open only to ex-regular soldiers of the British army, and to Canadians who had served in the South African War. It was able to move to Europe much earlier than the units of the Canadian Corps and was, so far as is known, the only battalion to take its colours into the line.

12 Of the two that failed to go off, one went up in 1955 as a result of a lightning strike and the other, just to the north of Ploegsteert Wood, is in the process of being removed at the time of writing.

13 It is true that the uniform of the Belgian Civil Guards – an overcoat of civilian pattern and a hat looking very much like a truncated topper – did make them look like civilians from a distance.

14 It was stated – with great indignation – that the trial was held 'in secret'. No military trial in wartime, German, French or British – then or now – is open to the public or press.

15 Details of air raids from *The Annual Register 1915*, Longmans, London, 1916.

16 *Statistics of the Military Effort of the British Empire during the Great War*, War Office, London, 1922.

17 It might be argued that as the British reaction to the German declaration that British waters were a war zone was to repudiate the provisions of the 1909 agreement in regard to restrictions on blockades, then the Germans were only doing to the British what the British were doing to them – applying starvation tactics. The difference was that the British stopped neutral shipping bound for Germany and impounded – or bought – the cargoes; they did not sink the ships and drown the crews.

7

THE DONKEYS

Alan Clark wrote a book about the British generals, *The Donkeys*, in which he quotes General Hoffman, one of the more tactically astute German First War generals, as describing the British Army of 1914–18 as being composed of 'lions led by donkeys'. Clark is scathing as to the abilities of British generals during the war; John Laffin describes them as 'butchers and bunglers'; Basil Liddell Hart says that most were incompetent; and Lloyd George, in his 2,108-page, two-volume *My War Memoirs* rarely has a good word to say about them. The public perception of British generals of the Great War is of men obsessed with mass frontal attacks, who refused to learn from the slaughter, were blind to technological advances and whose war plans were no more sophisticated than a desire to kill Germans regardless of the losses to our own side. The typical British general of the time is thought to be old, grey-haired, overweight and sporting a large moustache, a cavalryman dressed in boots and breeches and carrying a swagger cane. Comfortably ensconced in their chateaux well behind the lines, oblivious to the trials and tribulations of the men in the trenches, the 'donkeys' continued to send men in parade-ground formation across machine-gun-swept open ground onto impenetrable barbed wire, which their own artillery had failed to destroy. The awkward fact that the Allies did actually win the war is variously ascribed to German exhaustion and social unrest, the Americans, the French or the

Royal Navy blockade. That the British army was the only major army on the Western Front which did not suffer a major collapse of morale is explained by British stolidity in the face of incompetent leadership.

Armies are hierarchical institutions. The organisation of British armies had been arrived at by trial and error and 250 years of experience.[1] By 1914 the pyramid structure of section, platoon, company, battalion, brigade and division was well understood and had worked satisfactorily in wars, major and minor, all over the world. The creation of higher formations – corps and armies – followed naturally as the army expanded.

The pre-war British army was tiny by European standards. Employed mainly as an imperial garrison, only the Expeditionary Force in Aldershot was trained or equipped to take the field against a first-class enemy. Few senior commanders had any experience of handling anything larger than a brigade in the field. Sir John French, the BEF's first commander, had impeccable qualifications for his post. Aged sixty-two when war broke out, he had started his career as a fourteen-year-old midshipman in the Royal Navy, which he left after four years to join first the Militia and then the regular army in the 8th and later the 19th Hussars. He was clearly considered to be able as he was appointed adjutant of the 19th Hussars (the regimental staff officer and the commanding officer's right-hand man) the year he joined, and was promoted to captain in 1880. After a period away from the regiment as adjutant of a Yeomanry regiment he saw active service with the Hussars in the Egyptian campaign of 1884, being promoted major at the early age of thirty-one and brevet lieutenant colonel at thirty-three. He commanded his regiment, a cavalry brigade and then a cavalry division in the South African War, by the end of which he was a lieutenant general. He had ample experience of active service, had served on the staff in the War Office as a colonel, and was well decorated. He became successively Commander-in-Chief Aldershot (the major peacetime command at home), Inspector General of Cavalry and, in 1912, Chief of the Imperial General Staff, or professional head of the British army. A field marshal by March 1914, French had little choice but to resign when the government felt unable to honour certain guarantees that he had given during the so-called Curragh Mutiny.[2] As field marshals do not retire, he was the obvious choice as Commander-in-Chief of the

BEF when it deployed in 1914. The only other possible candidate was Field Marshal Kitchener, but he was wanted at home as Minister for War.

It has to be said that Sir John French had certain temperamental weaknesses that militated against him in a coalition war. He distrusted his French allies and did not speak their language. He had a mistress, Mrs Winifred Bennet, and this liaison offended his more censorious colleagues, quite apart from the fact that she was considerably taller than he, so that the pair cut a faintly ridiculous figure. He had a quite unnecessary disagreement with one of his two corps commanders, Lieutenant General Sir Horace Smith-Dorrien, which he allowed to drag on long after the initial cause – the Battle of Le Cateau – was over. Certainly by late 1915 he had lost the confidence of one of his (by now) two army commanders, Sir Douglas Haig, who would eventually replace him. Nevertheless French was not incompetent, and his removal in late 1915 was due more to his failure to win the war that year than to any perceived military failings. That no one else could have won the war in 1915 was irrelevant – politicians require scapegoats and French had to go.

French's place in British military history would be a lot more secure than it is had he kept his pen in his pocket, but on removal to England and appointment as Commander-in-Chief Home Forces he wrote *1914*, severely criticising the political direction of the war. Politicians inevitably felt bound to rebut; much censure of French ensued, which was not mollified by a subsequent and somewhat carping book by his son that denigrated Haig.[3] French also behaved quite disgracefully in his manipulation of the press. Frustrated (understandably) by the failure of British industry to supply him with the quantity and quality of shells that he needed, he used his personal friendship with the journalist Charles Repington to plant stories in *The Times* attacking the government and its direction of the war. Repington had a personal axe to grind. He had been a lieutenant colonel in the army, but in 1902 had been forced to resign for failing to keep his willy in his trousers.[4] He had an antipathy to the War Office, disliked Haig, distrusted Kitchener and was delighted to act as French's stooge. His reports precipitated the 'Shells Scandal' of May 1915, led to the appointment of Lloyd George as Minister of Munitions, and eventually helped to bring about the fall of Asquith's government.

There can be no excuse for French's behaviour in using the press to pursue his ends, right though those ends were. Serving officers in the British army are the servants of the state, and while they may lobby, protest, complain and badger in private, and ultimately resign if need be, they should not carry a professional disagreement with their masters into the public arena, and certainly not in time of war.

Of the corps commanders of 1914, Haig (I Corps) and Pulteney (III Corps, formed on 31 August) were fifty-three years old, and Smith-Dorrien (II Corps) was fifty-six. Grierson, who was originally appointed to commanded II Corps but who died of a heart attack on 17 August, was fifty-five. Rawlinson, who commanded IV Corps from its inception on 10 October, was fifty while Allenby, the cavalry commander, was fifty-three. Of the six divisional commanders on the Western Front in 1914, Lomax (1 Division) was fifty-nine, Keir (6 Division) fifty-eight, Snow (4 Division) fifty-six, Monro (2 Division) fifty-four, and Hamilton (3 Division) fifty-three. The boy of the bunch was Fergusson (5 Division) at a mere forty-eight. Apart from Fergusson, the senior generals would now be considered to be old – but not excessively so – for a field command.[5] A small army in peacetime, particularly a small professional army, cannot offer the speedy promotion that is found today in, for example, Israel, where the bulk of the army is made up of conscripts or part-timers, there is only one (third-class) threat, and generals retire at forty to take up a lucrative career in politics or business. Professional armies have to offer a full career, and this inevitably means that in peacetime promotion is slow. All the senior officers of 1914 were vastly experienced. All had seen active service, nearly all had commanded a battalion or its equivalent and all had commanded at least a brigade. Contrary to popular received opinion, of all the commanders down to and including divisions, only French, Haig and the cavalry commander Allenby were cavalrymen. Keir was an officer of the Royal Artillery and all the rest were infantrymen.

By the end of 1914 there were eighteen infantry brigades in the BEF, each commanded by a brigadier general. All were from the infantry except for Hunter-Weston who was a Royal Engineer. The youngest (Count Gleichen, commanding 15 Infantry Brigade in 5 Division of II Corps) was fifty-one, and the three oldest (Landon, McCracken and Wilson) were fifty-five, again all getting on a bit by modern standards. The four cavalry brigade commanders ranged from Bingham at fifty-three to Gough who was a stripling of forty-four. Of the infantry brigade commanders of 1914, six would become major-generals and no fewer than eight lieutenant generals and corps commanders. Three became corps commanders within a year, Hunter-Weston having the fastest rise, taking over VIII Corps in May 1915. All four cavalry brigadiers became corps commanders, and one – Gough – an army commander.

There is a huge difference between commanding a brigade of around 4,000 men, which might hold 1,000 yards of front, and a corps with up to 100,000 men, responsible for perhaps ten miles. Command of a brigade, with its four battalions, was personal. The commander would know all the officers and a good number of the men in his brigade. Command of a corps required a far wider perspective and a completely different style of command. The command of a brigade in operations was detailed; the command of a corps could only be by directive to the divisional commanders. In peace an officer might command a brigade for four years and a division for another four before being entrusted with the command of a corps (not that the tiny British army had many corps). In August 1914 the BEF consisted of four divisions of infantry and one of cavalry – a total of eighteen infantry and four cavalry brigades – organised into two corps. By 1918, with the enormous expansion necessitated by all-out war, this had grown to nineteen corps – sixteen British, one Australian, one Canadian and one Portuguese – organised into five armies. There were fifty-one British, five Australian, four Canadian, one New Zealand and two Portuguese infantry divisions and three cavalry divisions – a total of 188 brigades. This is to say nothing of commands like the Tank Corps and the Machine Gun Corps, unthought of in 1914, and a hugely expanded air force. Progress up the ladder of command during the war was thus very rapid indeed. If the junior officers and the soldiers were learning on the job, far more so were the generals. This was not anybody's fault, but an inevitable consequence of having a small professional army in peace that had to be converted into a mass continental army in war. The wonder is not that mistakes were made – and there were plenty – but that they were relatively few and rarely repeated.

There was no need for the army level of command in the first few months of the war, but at Christmas 1914 the BEF was reorganised into two armies – First and Second. In 1918 the five army commanders (generals) were aged from sixty-one (Plumer, Second Army) to fifty-three (Birdwood, Fifth Army), and the average age of the sixteen British corps commanders was fifty-four, ranging from Watts (XXX Corps) at sixty to Butler (III Corps) who was forty-eight. Three of these (Fergusson, Godley and Morland) had entered the war in 1914 as major-generals, twelve were brigadier generals in 1914 and one (Butler) had been but a lieutenant colonel when the war started, so that his span of command increased by a factor of fifty in four years.

At divisional level in 1918 few of the major-generals were over fifty, most were in their late forties and Jackson (50 Division) was thirty-nine. Most had started the war as lieutenant colonels, although Jackson was a captain in 1914 while Gorringe (47 Division) seems to have made no progress at all, entering and leaving the war as a major-general.

At brigade level there was a wide range: most brigadiers were in their late forties, and hardly any were over fifty in 1918. Jack (28 Brigade, 9 Division) and Brand (25 Brigade, 8 Division) were thirty-eight and had started the war as captains in 1914, as had Grogan (aged forty-three and commanding 23 Brigade, 8 Division in 1918). Most had started the war as majors.

Further down the chain of command, lieutenant colonels commanding battalions were often in their thirties – or even twenties – by 1918; in peace such an appointment would rarely be held by an officer under the age of forty-five.

Altogether four British lieutenant generals, twelve major-generals and eighty-one brigadier generals died or were killed between 1914 and 1918. A further 146 were wounded or taken prisoner.[6] Whatever else the generals were doing, they were certainly not sitting in comfortable chateaux.

The war was only six weeks old when it claimed its first British general. Brigadier General N. D. Findlay was Commander Royal Artillery of 1 Division during the advance from the Marne to the Aisne in September 1914. On 10 September Findlay was selecting a gun position when he was killed by German shelling.

In some cases the attrition rate amongst senior officers was very high indeed. The Battle of Loos, which began on 21 September 1915 and went on until 8 October, involved nine British divisions, six in the initial attack and three in reserve. Each division was commanded by a major-general, and three of the nine were killed in action during the course of the battle, or died of wounds received in it.

Major-General Sir Thompson Capper was fifty-one in 1915 and commanded 7 Division at Loos. He had already been injured by flying grenade fragments during a demonstration of the jam-tin bomb in April 1915. On 26 September, five days into the Loos battle, the division was held up in its attempt to capture German-occupied quarries near Hulluch. Capper left his headquarters and went up to get the attack going again. He left his horse in the rear and went on foot to the forward positions of the 2nd Battalion the Worcestershire Regiment, the lead battalion of the division. While (successfully) encouraging the men to attack once more, Capper was shot through the lungs and died the next day. It was said that he even took part in the charge, waving his parade cane.

The commander of 9 Division at Loos was the forty-seven-year-old Major-General G. H. Thesiger. He had been a major-general for four months and in command of the division for two weeks. On 27 September he went forward to find out why his lead brigade was held up near the Hohenzollern Redoubt. Thesiger, one of his staff officers and his aide-de-camp (ADC) were all killed. Thesiger's body was never found, or if found was never identified, and he had no known grave.

Major-General F. D. V. Wing, aged fifty-five in 1915, recovered from a German shrapnel bullet in his leg in September 1914, and at Loos commanded 12 Division. On 2 October 1915 he was on his way back from visiting the front-line positions of his division when he and his ADC were killed by German shelling.

It can be argued that generals should not be anywhere near the front line. It is not the business of a general to kill the enemy, but to control the battle so that units under his command can do the killing. Here was one of the great quandaries of the war. The general had to be close enough to the fighting to know what was going on, but far enough from it to be able to exercise control. Exercising control meant being able to communicate: with the artillery, with his own subordinate formations, with flanking units and with his own superiors. Today a general, at whatever level of command, can operate from a relatively small and mobile headquarters, using radio and satellite communications. None of this was available to a commander of 1914–18, and while static headquarters (corps level and above) did have some primitive radio communication, it would be a very long time before a radio that was sufficiently reliable and portable to be used in battle was available. Communication in the Great War was by telephone, flares, runner and galloper, with even pigeons and the heliograph being used on occasion. In defence the brigade and divisional headquarters was usually set up in the cellar of a French or Belgian house, where telephone lines could be installed and run up to the units manning the firing line. These lines could be dug in and were generally secure. Once units started to move, however, communication became difficult: while advancing troops would run out a telephone line behind them as they proceeded, these lines were susceptible to shellfire and were often severed. Runners got lost, got shot, or took time to bring their information back, by which time the situation had changed and the information was out of date.

A commander with no reserve cannot influence the battle. In order to deploy reserves to exploit a local advantage the commander must have information, and must be able to communicate with his reserve. In this war reserves could not be held too far forward, or they would be caught up in the enemy's defensive fire and pinned down; if, on the other hand, they were held far enough back to be safe during the opening phases, they would arrive too late when needed. It was a problem that would not be solved until the advent of battlefield radio during the next war.

Generals who went too far forward could not be in touch with their own headquarters, with its communications and access to reserves, and were thus not suitably placed to exercise control of the battle. At the same time, these were men who had been brought up in a professional army where personal bravery was highly prized. They had themselves been junior officers in a firing line and they naturally felt the need to get forward and see for themselves, quite apart from the morale factor of the general being seen to share the dangers of his men. One of the criticisms that can be directed against Sir John French is that he was too often away from his headquarters, visiting the troops at the front, when he should have been

with his communications and his staff, and thus in a position to apply some
direction to the course of the battle.

After a hit rate of one-third of the divisional commanders at Loos, it
was realised that the British army simply could not afford the loss of such
highly trained men. You can train an infantry private soldier in a few weeks,
but you have to grow leaders, particularly senior commanders, and that
takes time. Warning memoranda came from General Headquarters,
advising senior officers not to become personally involved in the fighting;
but it was a difficult order to enforce, and even more difficult to obey.

Whether or not generals should have visited the front lines, the fact is
that they did, regularly and frequently, as a glance at any unit war diary
shows. Battalions in the line would see their brigade commander at least
once a week, usually more often, with rather rarer visits from divisional,
corps and army commanders. As a divisional commander would have
under him twelve infantry battalions (from 1917, nine) – to say nothing of
his artillery, engineer, machine-gun, medical, signals, transport, pioneer,
cavalry and supply units – it would be difficult for the major-general to see
every unit more often than once a fortnight, even if he made one visit a
day. Corps commanders would be even rarer – hardly surprising with up to
sixty battalions to worry about – and an army commander could not
possibly visit a battalion more than once or twice in a year, even if he spent
all his time on the road, which he clearly could not. Much so-called anecdotal history complains that the generals were rarely seen. Rarely seen by
the writer perhaps, but most brigade and divisional commanders were
somewhere in the front lines at least once a day, even if an individual in
the visited unit might not personally meet him. The purpose of a visit by
the general is not only to pat backs and hand out praise and encouragement. Visiting senior officers went to the front to check, supervise, brief,
cajole, inspect and evaluate, and not everyone wanted their superior to
visit too often, any more than they do today. It was a matter of getting the
balance right, and by and large British generals did.

Most generals slept in a bed with a roof over them – they could not
possibly have done their job in a dugout in the firing line – but they were
very busy men. A typical divisional commander's day might begin at
0700 hours with reports of the previous night's activities and returns of

casualties and ammunition states. After breakfast there would be a conference with the artillery, engineer and supply and transport commanders, followed by visits to units, usually on horseback until close up to the front, but increasingly by car as the war went on. Lunch would be taken on the hoof or with the unit being visited, and the afternoon would be devoted to paperwork, the inevitable reports and returns associated with modern warfare. There would be a further staff conference in the evening and after dinner the general would be working in his office until well into the night. Many of the senior commanders of 1918 had been at the front since 1914, with very little leave or time off, and the strain was considerable. Some – a few – could not take the pace and were removed or sent home sick, but they were a robust breed and the vast majority discharged their awesome responsibilities to the best of their considerable abilities.

Generals, and indeed officers of any rank, may seem uncaring to the civilian mind. A commander cannot allow the death of one, or a hundred, or a thousand of the men placed under him to affect his performance. If it does, that commander cannot properly discharge his responsibilities to the others who are still alive. Life has to go on, and while any commander will miss a fallen comrade, and regret his passing, he must move on: there is little time to mourn. Any general will make his plans with the possibility of casualties well to the forefront of his thinking, but war is a nasty business, and killing and being killed is a part of it. British generals were not uncaring – as the number of British troops was finite, they could not afford to be – but they accepted, as they had to, that the very nature of this war, particularly on the Western Front, would lead to many deaths however hard they tried to avoid them.

Many British generals are known to history only by a sobriquet attached to them at some time. 'Hunter Bunter' was Lieutenant General Sir Aylmer Hunter-Weston. Born in 1864, he attended the Royal Military Academy Woolwich and was commissioned into the Royal Engineers. He had extensive active-service experience on the North-West Frontier of India, attended the Staff College and was on Kitchener's staff for the Nile Expedition of 1896. He served as a staff officer and as a mounted-column commander in South Africa, where his activities as a raider behind the Boer lines led to him being described as having 'reckless courage combined with technical skill and great coolness in emergency…'[7] Prior to the outbreak of war he was Assistant Director of Military Training at the War Office. He commanded 11 Brigade in 4 Division in 1914, and handled it well at Le Cateau and during the advance from the Marne to the Aisne, where he travelled around the battlefield on the back of a motorbike, often appearing in the most surprising places. As a result of his skilful handling of 11 Brigade he was promoted to major-general in the field, and took 29 Division to Gallipoli.

It is not the intention in this book to examine the Gallipoli campaign. Suffice it to say that the concept was sound and offered a realistic chance of keeping Russia in the war and knocking Turkey out of it. It has to be said, however, that the execution was flawed, and that when the Royal Navy failed to force the narrows and destroy the Turkish forts, the caper should have been abandoned. That it was not, cannot be laid at the door of the generals in the field at the time.

Hunter-Weston's handling of his division at Helles Beach on 25 April 1915 was one of the more competent aspects of the bloody landings, although he did fail to switch the point of landing to a far safer alternative which was available. That he did not do so was due to poor communications. For all sorts of reasons the operation began to go sour shortly afterwards, but Hunter-Weston's handling of his division, once ashore, was thoroughly competent. Although severe sunstroke led to his having to be invalided out in July, Hunter-Weston's performance brought him another field promotion, to lieutenant general, and command of a corps.

For the Somme battle in 1916 Hunter-Weston was in command of VIII Corps, which was responsible on 1 July, the opening day of the offensive, for attacking the German lines between Serre and the River Ancre. In the centre of the corps area was a huge mine – known as Hawthorn Redoubt mine – one of the nineteen mines placed under the German positions by the tunnelling companies Royal Engineers. The plan was for these mines to be blown just before zero hour, the start of the attack. The mines would disorientate the German defenders and kill quite a few of them. The British infantry would then seize the craters before the Germans could react, thus obtaining strongpoints right on the German front line. Hawthorn was the only mine north of the Ancre, and Hunter-Weston wanted to blow the 40,000 pounds of ammonal under the Hawthorn Redoubt at half-past three in the morning, four hours before zero hour. The redoubt was a particularly formidable German defence work dominating the intended line of the British advance. Hunter-Weston's intention was not only to destroy the redoubt but to have the resultant crater seized and held by the infantry. If this were done four hours before zero hour, any stand-to or heightening of alert states ordered by the Germans would have time to die down before the attack proper began.

Hunter-Weston put his suggestion to the army commander, Rawlinson, who passed it on to General Headquarters of the BEF. There it was vetoed. The Inspector of Mines pointed out (not unreasonably) that the British had a poor record of seizing craters, and that blowing the mine early would probably mean the Germans' being found in occupation of the crater at zero hour. As a compromise Hunter-Weston was allowed to blow ten minutes before zero, which he thought would still give him an advantage if the crater could be seized.

The order to blow at 0720 hours meant that the British heavy artillery would have to stop firing on the German front-line positions ten minutes before zero – to continue firing would endanger the troops attempting to seize the crater – but there would be some fire support from Stokes mortars. The Hawthorn mine was duly blown, and two platoons of the 2nd Battalion Royal Fusiliers, with four Lewis guns and four mortars, set off to take the crater. Unfortunately the Germans got there first. When the Fusiliers got to the lip of the crater they found the far rim and the flanks already occupied. The lifting of the heavy artillery and the mine explosion had warned the Germans that an attack was due and their machine guns, no longer suppressed by artillery, were able to fire on the troops forming up in no man's land, causing very heavy casualties. Hawthorn crater was not captured until 13 November.

In hindsight Hunter-Weston was wrong, and the premature blowing of the Hawthorn mine did give the Germans warning of the coming attack. The lifting of the artillery barrage, ten minutes before it would otherwise have become necessary, allowed the Germans to man their defences and catch the attacking infantry in open ground. That said, Hunter-Weston's logic was not necessarily at fault. He was wrong in thinking that the seven-day artillery bombardment would so disrupt the German defences that

Stokes mortars would be adequate when the British heavy artillery lifted, but in this he was at one with nearly every other commander on 1 July. He had more faith in the ability of the infantry to reach the crater first than had the Inspector of Mines, but then most of the large mines blown on 1 July were occupied by the Germans before the British could get there. Whether the casualties would have been much fewer had the mine been blown just before zero is debatable: they probably would have been, but it is still unlikely that the British could have taken the crater first.

Hunter-Weston was a competent commander acting in good faith and with the best of motives. At a distance of eighty-five years one can see that he got it wrong on 1 July 1916. He continued as a corps commander and does not deserve the vilification thrust upon him for one mistake, costly though it may have been, that has obliterated all the good things he did and all the good service he rendered before, during and after the Somme.

Lieutenant General Sir Richard Haking was the son of a vicar and was commissioned into the infantry from Sandhurst in 1881. Pre-1914 he had seen active service in Burma and the South African War. He was both a graduate of the Staff College and an instructor there, and produced a series of training pamphlets that were considered to be first-class. Even today his work on company training has a freshness about it and an insight into human characteristics that would not be out of place in a modern military work.[8] In 1914 he commanded 5 Brigade in 2 Division, one of the few brigades to fight its way onto the escarpment of the Chemin des Dames after the crossing of the River Aisne on 14 September. He was wounded next day but his skilful handling of his brigade earned him promotion to major-general and command of 1 Division. Further promotion came in September 1915 when he assumed command of XI Corps, and although this corps was engaged in the Battle of Loos, Haking had little to do as his divisions were taken under command of GHQ. After Loos, Haking's corps took over the left of the First Army front, from Vermelles to Laventie, and so was only peripherally involved with the two great British battles of 1916 and 1917, the Somme and Third Ypres. For a time Haking and his corps were in Italy assisting the stiffening of the Italian front after the drubbing of Caporetto. Back in France, XI Corps under Haking did well in resisting the 'Kaiser's offensive' of 1918 and earned a high reputation in the subsequent British offensive that ended the war. His post-war career was distinguished and he retired in 1925 as a full general.

Why should this intelligent and capable man be remembered only as 'Butcher' Haking? It appears that the name was bestowed upon him by the Australians, who disliked his penchant for ordering trench raids. It is not even known how pejorative the appellation really was – after all, to Australians 'bastard' is almost a term of affection.

A cardinal principle of military doctrine, at least in the British army, is that defence must be aggressive, and that in defence one must endeavour to dominate no man's land. By doing so the defender has the initiative: the enemy is prevented from close reconnaissance and from interfering with the defenders' obstacles (at that time, barbed wire). Aggressive defence for the infantry means patrolling, sniping and ambushing in no mans' land, and trench raiding. A trench raid is exactly that: a local attack on a portion of the enemy line, carried out by anything from a section of ten men to a battalion of 800. It has no strategic object but its intention may be to kill the enemy, to destroy his defence works, to gain intelligence by capturing documents or prisoners, or a combination of all three. Trench raiding is one way of ensuring that one's own troops do not become defensive-minded, but think aggressively and have a sense of hitting at the enemy rather than just holding a line of trenches. As XI Corps had less to do during 1916 and 1917 than many other formations, Haking rightly encouraged trench raids. These were not senseless forays in pursuit of self-aggrandisement, but serious, useful, and necessary operations of war. Some were successful, others were not, but it was a perfectly proper way of conducting a defence, and had XI Corps not adopted a policy of raiding when they were not otherwise engaged, Haking would have been rightly condemned.

Haking also presided over the attack on Fromelles, on Aubers Ridge, in July 1916. The capture of Aubers Ridge had long been an aspiration of the British as it would have removed the Germans' ability to overlook British positions north of La Bassée, and it had been a phase two objective of the Battle of Neuve-Chapelle in March 1915. The 1916 attack, by one Australian and one British division, failed with heavy casualties, but it did prevent the Germans from shifting reserves south to the Somme battlefield, and cannot be said to have been without point.

The life and work of Sir Douglas Haig, commander of the BEF from December 1915 and a field marshal from January 1917, has probably been the subject of more contradictory analysis than any other general in British military history. To some he was a butcher and a bungler, to others the man who won the war. Born in 1861 he passed out top in the order of merit from Sandhurst having, unusually for the time, attended Oxford University first. A cavalry officer, he experienced active service as both a commander in the field and as a staff officer in the campaign against the Mahdi (he was at Omdurman in 1898) and in the South African War, before being appointed Inspector General of Cavalry in India, where he undertook a thorough and much-needed reform of that arm. As Director of Staff Duties in the War Office from 1907 to 1909 Haig was responsible, along with Haldane (Secretary of State for War from 1905), for the transformation of the British army's haphazard reserve system by welding Militia, Volunteers and Yeomanry, all with different terms of service and varying standards of training and administration, into one Territorial Force; this was to become an essential element of the army's expansion from 1914. Pre-war he commanded Aldershot District, the nerve centre of the British combatant army, and was appointed to command I Corps of the BEF in August 1914.

By any standard of military competence Haig was fully qualified to command a corps, and then the First Army from Christmas 1915. On the removal of Sir John French there was really no choice but I Iaig as a replacement for the Commander-in-Chief. The only other possible contenders were ruled out by political or military considerations, or by character traits that made them unsuitable in a coalition war. Ian Hamilton, later to command at Gallipoli, although younger than French was, at sixty-one, probably too old for the Western Front, and he had been away from the European theatre for five years. Smith-Dorrien, commander of II Corps in 1914 and of the Second Army from Christmas 1915, was a man of considerable intellect but fiery temper, and had in any case been sacked in May 1915 (for advocating a withdrawal around Ypres to more favourable ground – militarily sensible but unacceptable politically). James Willcocks had been senior to Haig as a corps commander in the BEF, but his experience was mainly with the Indian army; he was a respected and popular commander of the Indian Corps but insufficiently flexible to merit further promotion, as well as being too old. Robertson was needed as CIGS back at home, and few in the army trusted Wilson, who was in any case better employed using his talents in liaison with the French.

Haig was not a social person: he was abstemious, disliked having to explain himself and could best be described as dour. Nice men, however, do not necessarily win wars and the fact was that the obvious and best-qualified candidate for overall command – by training, experience and performance in the BEF to date – was Haig. When Haig assumed command of the BEF in December of 1915 it consisted of thirty-seven British and two Canadian infantry divisions and five cavalry divisions, or about 600,000 men all told: a mix of regulars, reservists and Territorials, with the New Armies only just beginning to appear. By 1918 this army had expanded threefold and had absorbed the New Armies and the conscripts. In December 1915 the BEF held thirty miles of front; in February 1918 it held 123 miles. It was Haig who had to manage that expansion; and train, equip, deploy and fight the largest army that Britain has ever had, an army set down in another country and, until 1917 at least, the junior partner in a coalition war with difficult allies. Alone amongst the original warring powers, the morale of the British army never cracked, and it was the British army that in 1918 was the only Allied army capable of mounting a massive and sustained offensive. During the 'Hundred Days' of 1918 Haig's army decisively defeated the German army on the Western Front. When criticism of him began at home in the 1930s, General Pershing, Commander-in-Chief of the American army on the Western Front and not a man naturally inclined towards the British, said, 'How can they do this to the man who won the war?'

There can be no doubt that Haig was a superb military manager. Unlike his nearest equivalent in the Second World War, Montgomery, Haig was not only in supreme command of the BEF but also had to deal directly with his own and Allied governments and with the Allied military commanders. Montgomery always had an Alexander or an Eisenhower to fly top cover for him, and to allow him to concentrate on commanding the troops. Haig's nearest comparison might be Wellington, who was sole commander in theatre and sole conduit to government and ally; but

Wellington's army in the Peninsula was never more than 100,000 men, and communications with home were such that he was allowed far more latitude than the British government would permit to Haig.

It is not Haig's management that is faulted by his critics, but his supposed stubbornness in persisting with attacks when they were, it is said, obviously going to fail. This is to look at the Western Front from an Anglo-centric viewpoint and to neglect what was happening elsewhere. The Somme, as we shall see, had to be persisted with because of what was happening 100 miles away at Verdun, and the prolongation of Third Ypres bought time for the French army, almost destroyed by mutiny, to be reconstituted. Haig wanted a breakthrough; he never wanted to engage the British army in battles of attrition. Until 1918 that breakthrough was never achieved, but nor could anybody else on either side achieve it. Haig was neither hidebound nor resistant to technology; indeed it was Haig who, on taking over command of the BEF, first heard of the experiments with tanks and insisted that development should be given a high priority. That tanks when first used were not the hoped-for war-winning weapon was nothing to do with Haig, but rather with problems inherent in the development of any new method of waging war. Haig encouraged the development of air power, and it was the BEF who by 1918 had the only strategic bomber force capable of any meaningful contribution to the war.

Haig is pictured as uncaring, and his failure to visit the wounded in hospital is often cited as an example of his unfeeling attitude to deaths that resulted from his plans. Haig did visit the wounded regularly in the early days. It was his staff officers, noting the effect it had on him, who advised him to stop. A commander who is psychologically damaged by the sight of so many wounded and maimed soldiers – his own soldiers – cannot be at his best, and the advice, while perhaps not meeting the requirements of a modern public-image consultant, was sensible and right. Contrary to common belief Haig still visited the wounded, but not as often as hitherto. On balance Haig was the best commander that the British army could produce at the time, and had there been any other general capable of stepping into his shoes, Prime Minister Lloyd George would have found him. Anyone who examines Haig's relations with his own government is driven to the conclusion (as Haig was at times) that no commander-in-chief should be so treated in the midst of a war on foreign soil.[9] Historical opinion is shifting, and shifting in favour of Haig. Public opinion has yet to follow, but much of the received wisdom about Haig is founded on tainted evidence, or on no evidence at all. This author, at least, can only conclude that Haig has been grievously wronged.

It is said that all the generals were cavalrymen, as if this should in some way disqualify them from command of what was mainly an infantry and artillery war. The British army has always insisted (and still does) that commanders of field formations (brigades, divisions, corps and armies) must be from the combat arms – cavalry, artillery, engineers and infantry – rather than from the supporting arms or services, and this is reinforced by the fact that one of the qualifications for high command is success with a formation at the level below. As an aside, the insistence that only officers from the combat arms could command field formations was probably an unnecessary constraint, and one that did not apply in the German army. Command at corps level and above was and is largely a matter of planning, management and administration; and a good general can discharge these functions perfectly capably whatever his arm of the service. French and Haig were both cavalrymen, but command in 1914 was heavily weighted towards the infantry as we have seen. In 1918, of the five army commanders, one was from the cavalry, one was a Royal Engineer and three were infantrymen. Of the corps commanders, two were Royal Engineers, one was an artilleryman and only one (Kavanagh, commander of the Cavalry Corps) came from a cavalry regiment. Two were colonials: Currie and Monash, commanding the Canadian and Australian Corps. All the others (twelve) were from the infantry. If the high command of the army suffered from anything, it was not from an excess of cavalrymen, but from a paucity of gunners!

In the BEF of 1918, three of the five army commanders and seven of the sixteen British corps commanders were graduates of the pre-war Staff College, an unusually high proportion when one considers that entry into Staff College as a captain was then by no means necessary to advancement, and was even frowned upon by some senior officers in the 1880s. Haig himself was a graduate of the Staff College, and it is often claimed that he had failed to gain entry in 1893 and was then admitted without taking the entrance examination in 1895, owing somehow to improper influence. In fact entrance to the Staff College was either by competition or by nomination. All candidates had to take an examination, and those scoring more than fifty per cent of the available marks were described as having 'passed' and automatically secured places, regardless of their arm of the service. Vacancies remaining on each two-year course were then filled by nomination by the Commander-in-Chief (later by the Army Council), who presided over a selection board that looked at all officers who had 'qualified' by scoring between thirty-seven and a half and fifty per cent in the exam. The number of students nominated varied from two to twenty a year, and Haig, having 'qualified' in 1893, was nominated in 1895, the year that the Duke of Cambridge finally retired as Commander-in-Chief of the Army. Haig passed out in 1897, the year that 'Wully' Robertson (who had only just failed to 'pass') was nominated and became the first officer commissioned from the ranks to go to Staff College. There was nothing underhand about Haig's attendance at Staff College, and given that the majority of the officers who 'passed' and secured automatic places were of the infantry, it was perfectly normal for Haig as a cavalry officer to be nominated. In the years before his entry to Staff College Haig had been employed observing European cavalry and in translating German and French training manuals. His good work in this employment, coupled with reports as to his previous career, made him an eminently suitable student for the college, and he did well there [10]

No commander in modern war can possibly direct all the multifarious activities of his command by himself. Even at the lowest level, the corporal commanding a section of ten men had and has a lance corporal to assist. As the technology available to commanders grew, so did the number of people needed to help a commander carry out his function. A divisional staff in Wellington's army had up to six staff officers; in the intervening century this had trebled, and even so was barely sufficient. The general's job is to direct and plan, and the task of the staff is to provide the general with the information he needs, and then to turn his ideas and plans into reality. To the staff is delegated responsibility for the details of operations of war, the administration, discipline and movement of the troops, provision of equipment, ammunition and stores, and health, welfare and career management

– all this in addition to keeping the commander informed of what is going on. A good staff officer will take as much of the detail as possible onto himself, thus allowing the commander to get on with what that officer is trained and paid to do: command the troops. Unlike the German system, where the commander and the chief of staff shared joint responsibility, British staffs were subservient to their commander. A German chief of staff who disagreed with his commander's decision had the right of appeal to the chief of staff of the next higher formation; in the British army a chief of staff owed his allegiance to his commander alone. There were good reasons for this. The German army was large enough to accommodate a specialist stream of staff officers, a luxury that the British army could not afford, and British officers were expected to be able to fill command and staff appointments, often alternating between the two. There had been a British staff college since the Napoleonic Wars, but it was not highly regarded before the late 1880s; then staff training began to be seen as important, largely because the lessons of the Franco-Prussian War had been absorbed. Even so, in 1914 there were only around 700 staff-trained officers in the whole of the British army. They were spread around the world and many were at a stage in their careers where they were not available for employment on the staff. Despite this, the majority of the key staff posts in the BEF of 1914 were filled either by staff-trained officers or by officers who, while not graduates of the college, had already satisfactorily filled staff appointments.

As has been explained, the staff was divided into three branches, G, A and Q. At divisional level, G Branch had a General Staff Officer Grade I, or GSO1, a lieutenant colonel who was in fact if not in name the chief of staff. Under him were a GSO2, a major, and a GSO3, a captain. A and Q Branches were headed by the Assistant Adjutant and Quartermaster General, or AAQMG, a lieutenant colonel, with a major as Deputy Assistant Adjutant and Quartermaster General (DAAQMG) and a captain as Deputy Assistant Quartermaster General (DAQMG). There was a Deputy Assistant Director of Ordnance Services, (DADOS), usually a captain but sometimes a major, a colonel of the Royal Army Medical Corps as Assistant Director of Medical Services (ADMS), with a major as his deputy (DADMS). A captain or major Deputy Assistant Director of Veterinary

Services (DADVS) was responsible for the division's animals, and a Deputy Assistant Provost Marshal (DAPM) looked after discipline, route signing and traffic control. Not technically a staff officer, but very much part of the headquarters, was the general's aide-de-camp or ADC, in peacetime not much more than a social ornament and dog-walker, but in war an essential adjunct to command. The ADC looked after the general's personal welfare, compiled his daily programme and often acted as his eyes and ears. With the divisional headquarters and responsible to it were the artillery and engineer staffs. The Brigadier General Royal Artillery (BGRA) with his Brigade Major Royal Artillery (BMRA) and Staff Captain Royal Artillery (SCRA) commanded the divisional artillery and coordinated the fire planning, while the Commanding Royal Engineer (a lieutenant colonel but often in practice a major) and the Adjutant Royal Engineers coordinated all engineering activity in support of the division.[11] At corps level the staff system was duplicated, with rather more staff officers, while the Brigade Commander had but a Brigade Major and a Staff Captain to assist him.

In war and in peace, regimental officers and soldiers have always blamed everything not to their liking on the staff: the anonymous 'they', who are seen as the architects of all that is uncomfortable and unnecessary, and who are completely out of touch with what is happening on the ground.[12] As an anonymous poet of the trenches warbled:

Good Gracious, Uncle, what is that?
With red and gold upon his hat?
Such lofty brow and haughty face,
Such easy condescending grace
Surely belong to no one save
The very, very, very brave!

They drive about in handsome cars,
And sit for simply hours and hours
In chateaux round by Saint-Omer
Evolving little *ruses de guerre*.

Now and again, if things are slack,
They organise a large attack,

And watch the battle from a hill
Some miles away, or farther still;
They see what fighting there has been,
Quite clearly – on the tape machine.

When a staff officer visited the forward trenches – and they did visit, frequently, as indeed they had to – he might on occasion be looked upon as a dilettante from some other world, with his clean boots, brassard and red collar patches. In general, however, the perfectly normal irritation vented on the visitor from a headquarters was rarely directed at brigade or divisional staffs. The composition of brigades did not change very much in the four and a quarter years of war, and brigades rarely moved to another division. Regimental officers got to know the brigade and divisional staff officers, and with personal knowledge antipathy – often artificial anyway – disappeared. It was much easier to be rude about the corps staff, as divisions did move around from corps to corps, or about the army or GHQ staff, whom regimental officers did not know at a personal level. While the BEF began the war with well-trained staff officers, the enormous expansion of the army that had to be undertaken meant that many staff officers had not been formally trained for the posts they had to fill. Like everyone else, generals to private soldiers, staff officers learned by doing it, and the great majority did a pretty good job under conditions for which they had not been trained and which they had not expected. As the war went on most officers appointed to the staff had already experienced life in the trenches, and knew perfectly well what the troops had to put up with.

The Staff College itself was closed on the outbreak of what many thought would be a short war. In hindsight this was a mistake, and officers with the coveted '*psc*' (Passed Staff College) after their names were soon snapped up. The continuing need for more and more staff officers led to suitable regimental officers being attached to a headquarters as 'staff learners', and very soon it became necessary for GHQ and armies to set up their own staff schools in France to train potential staff officers. As uniformity in teaching was vital, a central staff school was set up at Hesdin in France, and by early 1916 there were staff schools in the UK as well, training officers for both junior and senior staff posts.

In April 1916 Army Council Instruction 786 laid down the criteria for staff employment, which were either to hold the qualification *psc*, or to have already held a staff appointment, or to have completed a staff course with an army in the field, or to have been recommended as a result of a staff-school course. These courses lasted for six weeks, and had to be preceded by an attachment of one month as a staff learner.[13] As the shortage continued, Army Council Instruction 1128 of June 1916 exempted officers intended to fill staff posts at home from attending any courses, but retained the requirement to serve one month as a staff learner. By September 1917 a further instruction laid down that the qualification for a Grade 3 post was a satisfactory attachment to a headquarters as a learner, while for Grades 2 and 1 an officer had to have completed a junior or senior staff course.[14] The Staff College premises at Camberley, when not being used as accommodation for officers of the New Armies undergoing their one-month commissioning course at Sandhurst, were used to run a tactics course for senior officers, and courses to prepare officers who had held Grade 2 staff appointments to fill posts at Grade 1.[15]

It was probably a mistake to take away some of the officers filling key posts in the War Office and in other commands in the United Kingdom to staff the headquarters of the BEF in August 1914, for this led to muddle and confusion at home just when steady and practised hands were needed. Wilson, Director of Military Operations at the War Office, left to become Major-General, General Staff BEF; Macready vacated the War Office post of Director of Personnel Services to take up that of Adjutant General of the BEF; Robertson had been Director of Military Training at the War Office when he was moved to France as Quartermaster General; Horne was Inspector of Horse and Field Artillery and now found himself as BGRA I Corps; while Forestier-Walker moved from being Brigadier General, General Staff Ireland, to the equivalent post in II Corps. All these men made good staff officers, and served the BEF well. Operational needs must take priority, but the removal of all these officers at once did leave holes that were not easy to fill, just as the army was gearing itself up for high-intensity warfare. That the gaps left at the War Office were initially largely filled by officers brought back from retirement meant that the War Office, which should have been directing the activities of the army, was greatly reduced in influence: the power was with GHQ in France and the Cabinet in Whitehall.

The Chief of the Imperial General Staff was the professional head of the army, and even with the appointment of a soldier – Field Marshal Lord Kitchener – as Secretary of State for War in August 1914, the army needed a steady and resolute figure to represent it and safeguard its interests, preferably one who had been in post long enough to have got to know and understand how power in Whitehall worked. Sir John French had felt it necessary to vacate the post in April 1914, and was replaced by Sir Charles Douglas who died in October of the same year. Douglas's replacement was Sir James Wolfe Murray, whose long experience in intelligence and administration made him a master of detail, but also made it difficult for him to stand back and look at the war overall. He was far too inclined to defer to Kitchener and the politicians, and too soft-hearted to sack those around him who were not up to the job (not many, but there were some).

Wolfe Murray lasted for less than a year, and left the post in September 1915, probably to his own immense relief. The new CIGS was Sir Archibald Murray, who had been Wolfe Murray's deputy, responsible for the training of the New Armies, since February 1915, and who had previously commanded 2 Division of the BEF. Murray too was not equal to the challenge of directing the army and dealing with the two sources of pressure – from GHQ in France and from Kitchener at home. Political scheming for the reduction of Kitchener's powers at last led to a satisfactory appointment: Sir William 'Wully' Robertson, hitherto Quartermaster General and then Chief of the General Staff of the BEF. Robertson had a remarkable career, one that would not be possible today and was extraordinary then.[16] Born in humble circumstances in 1860 he enlisted as a private in the ranks of the 16th Lancers at the age of seventeen.[17] Eight years later he was a troop sergeant major (equivalent to a staff sergeant of today) when his commanding officer suggested that, as a bright young lad, he should try for a commission. He was coached for the entrance examination by regimental officers and passed through Sandhurst, being commissioned as a second lieutenant in the 3rd Dragoon Guards. His career thereafter was rapid and marked by dedication and professionalism. He narrowly failed to get a competitive vacancy for the Staff College and attended as a nominee. He later became its commandant. Robertson was shrewd, blunt, highly skilful at his profession and nobody's poodle. He stood up to Kitchener and forged a strong bond of mutual respect and even friendship with him. After Kitchener's death in HMS *Hampshire* in 1916, Robertson was able to resist all the blandishments and politicking of members of the government, and acted as a stout defender of the army and as an invaluable buffer between Haig and the manipulations of Lloyd George, until the latter eventually sacked him early in 1918.

Years after the war, when disillusionment set in and people saw that England had not been transformed into a 'land fit for heroes', the hunt for someone to blame began. It was exacerbated by authors with an axe to grind (like Basil Liddell Hart) and poets who wrote for money.[18] 'British generals did the best they could with what they had, and were by and large successful in a war that no one had expected or trained for' makes a dull headline. 'Butchers and bunglers' sells books and newspapers, particularly when the objects of attack are dead or retired. Alan Clark was an amusing writer, a brilliant storyteller and a bon viveur. British political life is the poorer for his passing, but he cannot be described as a historian. When pressed to say just when and where General Hoffman described the British army as 'lions led by donkeys', Clark admitted that he had made it up![19]

NOTES

1 The modern British army can be said to date from Cromwell's New Model Army, the first British army to be recognisably regular and professional.

2 There was a possibility that the army might be asked to put down 'loyalist' unrest if Irish home rule was granted. Many officers were unhappy about the prospect of military action against those whom they saw as their own people, and there were threats of mass resignations should action be ordered. See Ian F. W. Beckett (ed.), *The Army and the Curragh Incident*, Bodley Head, London, 1986, for a detailed explanation of this affair.

3 Major the Hon. Gerald French, DSO, *French Replies to Haig*, Hutchinson & Co., London, 1936.

4 He was a known philanderer and, when cited as co-respondent in a divorce case, was alleged to have broken his previously given written word not to see the lady again.

5 In today's British army major-generals retire at fifty-four in peacetime. Age is no bar to field success, however: Blücher was seventy-two when he (very successfully) commanded the Prussian army at Waterloo in 1815, and Sir Charles Napier was sixty-one when, musket in hand, he led the decisive infantry charge at Meanee in 1843.

6 For an exposition of general-officer casualties in the Great War see Frank Davies and Graham Maddocks, *Bloody Red Tabs*, London, 1995. While concentrating on dead, wounded

and captured generals this book also does much to dispel the popular myth of uncaring and ignorant generals. It is meticulously sourced and should be compulsory reading for all those who question the competence of senior officers in the Great War.

7 *Dictionary of National Biography*.

8 Brigadier General R. C. B. Haking, CB, *Company Training*, Hugh Rees Ltd, London, 1914.

9 See Keith Grieves, 'Haig and the Government 1916–1918', in Brian Bond and Nigel Cave (eds.), *Haig, a Reappraisal 70 Years On*, Barnsley, 1999.

10 Variations of this system continued until 1969, since when there has been one pass-mark in the exam and students are all selected from those who pass.

11 All these titles had been in use for well over a century, and had the great advantage of indicating immediately the rank of the holder. They remained in use until the 1980s when the British army converted to the NATO system of staff nomenclature (effectively the American system). Thus the senior administrative staff officer is now the Chief G1/G4 and could be a major, lieutenant colonel, brigadier or major-general depending upon the level of the headquarters. This makes it very difficult for a regimental officer to know how rude he can be to a staff officer on the telephone.

12 Having been both, this author as a regimental officer frequently (and usually wrongly) considered that the staff had no grasp of reality, while as a staff officer he frequently (and usually wrongly) considered that the battalions had no idea of the imperatives of the big picture.

13 Pre-war courses at the Staff College lasted two years.

14 Since 1969 all officers, on reaching the rank of captain, are required to be trained for junior staff appointments. The Junior Command and Staff Course was first run at the School of Infantry Warminster, then at the Royal Military Academy Sandhurst, and now at the Joint Services Command and Staff College Shrivenham.

15 For a description of how the Staff College worked and how entry was achieved prior to 1914, see Major A. R. Godwin-Austen, OBE, MC, *The Staff and the Staff College*, Constable & Co. Ltd, London, 1927.

16 Impossible today because combatant commissions are not awarded over the age of twenty-five; any later and it is not possible for the young officer to gain all the qualifications needed, including serving the requisite periods at regimental duty, to have a full career. Late entry commissions (the old quartermaster commissions) are still, of course, awarded to deserving warrant officers and senior NCOs.

17 He is often described as having been a trooper. Without undue pedantry, it was only the Household Cavalry that had troopers until the end of the First War; prior to that, the junior rank in the cavalry of the line was private.

18 Many of those whom we now know as 'War Poets' had been published commercially before the war. Few publishers will invest in work that will not sell, and from about the early thirties onwards, anti-establishment doom and gloom was always a winner.

19 He may have been quoting a Russian general in the Crimea, when the description might have had a measure of truth, although pots and kettles come to mind.

8

KANGAROO COURTS AND FIRING SQUADS

Military discipline is rather different from the code of conduct found in any other workplace. It has to be. A worker who decides not to bother reporting to the factory on a Monday morning might lose a day's pay; the army would call it absence without leave and lock him up. A nightwatchman who falls asleep might get the sack; a sentry who does the same on active service risked, until very recently, the death penalty. It has long been recognised, in all armies, that a legal code designed to regulate civilian society is impractical for the business of waging war. When an occupation requires participants to engage in activities that human nature and common sense militate against, it requires its own rules. The natural reaction of any normal person faced with a risk of death or injury is to avoid it. If an army is composed of soldiers whose major driving force is to avoid risk, it loses battles. Armies are often accused of brainwashing their soldiers during training. The British army does not, and did not, brainwash its men, but it does seek to instil into them an automatic reaction to warlike situations so that they react instinctively to them, particularly if they occur when there is no one around to tell the soldier what to do. Training, leadership, inspiration and motivation all contribute to the soldier's performing his duty as desired by the army, and to back these up there is a set of rules by which the soldier is expected to conduct himself. Most people like to know where they stand. The army says, 'Do this, and do not do that, and you will have a secure place in the family, honour, promotion and a fair wage; contravene these rules and you will be punished.' Military law draws a sharp line between what is acceptable and what is not. The man knows that if he stands within the law he is safe; if he goes outside it, he is in trouble. The whole purpose of military law is to maintain the discipline of the army, and acts and omissions that in civil law may be mere breaches of contract (such as desertion or disobedience to orders) must, by the very nature of what the army is for, be made offences that attract penalties; and these penalties must be more severe in wartime, when the effects of transgression are more serious. The army wishes to ensure that men work as a team, obey the orders of their superiors, and use all their talents in the achievement of the team aims. The only difference between an army and an armed rabble is discipline: military law is the bedrock of that discipline.

Military law, as it applied in the army of 1914, was embodied in the Army Act 1881, an amalgam of various acts (including the Mutiny Acts and the Articles of War), orders in council and royal warrants existing before that time. The Army Act, with regular amendments to keep it up to date and relevant to contemporary military requirements, was brought into effect each year by the Army Annual Act. This had to be passed by Parliament, for if it was not, the army ceased to have any legal existence (today the Act must be passed every five years). The Army Act 1881 was part of the statute law of England, from which it was distinct only in that it was administered by military officers and military courts rather than by civilian judges. There was a similar act, the Naval Discipline Act, to regulate the Royal Navy.

Unlike the situation in many other countries, the British soldier, while subject to the Army Act, was not exempt from the provisions of civilian law. If a soldier in the United Kingdom committed a major offence such as murder, manslaughter or rape, whether or not it was committed on military property or against soldiers or civilians, he was liable for trial in a civilian court. Less serious offences (theft or assault) committed by a soldier against soldiers would, for convenience, usually be tried under military law, but the civil authority had the right to demand jurisdiction. As English criminal law did not apply outside the King's domains, Section 41 of the Army Act specifically made it a military offence to commit an act that would be a criminal offence in England: soldiers could be, and were, brought to trial abroad under the provisions of that section.

The Army Act and its various applications were contained in a book, the *Manual of Military Law*, which all officers were expected to know and study, and which was issued to every unit and sub-unit. It explained the law, gave practical examples of how a charge under each section should be framed, and laid down the procedures to be followed by those enforcing the law.[1]

The Army Act dealt with all manner of subjects that regulated the way the army did its business, from terms of enlistment to the number of guns to be fired at a funeral, but the portion of the Act that most impinged on the soldier was that which spelled out offences and punishments. Punishments that could be imposed on other ranks under the Army Act were death, penal servitude for a term of not less than three years, imprisonment (with or without hard labour) for a period not exceeding two years, detention for a period not exceeding two years, discharge with ignominy from His Majesty's Service, loss of seniority or reduction in rank (if an NCO), fines, forfeitures and stoppages of pay. Originally penal servitude was awarded for a felony while a misdemeanour attracted imprisonment, but by 1914 there was no practical difference between the two. Both penal servitude and imprisonment could be served in a civilian prison (albeit only where British law held sway, that is, in the United Kingdom or in a colony), but the man was nearly always returned to the UK to serve his sentence, which carried with it automatic discharge from the service. A period of detention was served in a military prison and was looked upon as having an improving as well as a punitive function, and the soldier continued in the service on completion of his sentence. A monetary fine had the same effect as a fine by a civilian court; forfeiture of pay was where a man was ordered not to be paid for a period of absence or where he had by neglect rendered himself unfit for duty, or was in detention; stoppages of pay were awarded where a man was to repay the cost of public property that he had lost or damaged. For officers, cashiering or dismissal from the service were substituted for dismissal with ignominy; an officer could also have seniority removed, but could not be reduced in substantive rank. Additionally, an officer could be sentenced to a severe reprimand or a reprimand.

Some sections of the Army Act prescribed one level of punishment for an offence committed in peacetime, with a higher level applicable on active service. A soldier who contravened Section 6 of the Army Act by 'breaking into a house in search of plunder', in peace, anywhere other than in the United Kingdom (where he would be dealt with by the civilian courts for burglary), could be sentenced to imprisonment for up to two years. The same offence on active service carried the death penalty. The reason is obvious: ill-treatment of civilians in a war zone was liable to turn the local inhabitants against the occupying force. This could lead to partisan warfare with all its attendant horrors, as the French found to their cost in Spain during the Peninsular War, and the Germans in Russia in the Second World War. By 1914 British soldiers were not inveterate looters, but in the previous century they had been, and the law reflected this.

As the Act applied during the Great War, offences were divided into groups. Section 4 dealt with offences in relation to the enemy, and included shamefully abandoning a post, giving up a post, casting away arms in the face of the enemy, giving intelligence to the enemy, giving arms or ammunition to the enemy, voluntarily taking service with the enemy, misbehaving in front of the enemy in such a way as to show cowardice, and knowingly assisting the enemy. Encouraging others to commit any of the offences listed was treated as severely as was the offence itself. On active service, death, or 'such lesser punishment as is in this Act mentioned', could be the penalty.

Section 6 covered looting, leaving a post, striking a sentry, assaulting a person bringing supplies or provision to the forces (who might be a civilian), intentionally causing false alarms, giving away the password to a person not entitled to receive it, being drunk while on sentry, sleeping while on sentry, and leaving a post while on sentry. All these offences carried the death penalty if committed on active service. It is sometimes asked why a soldier, who may be exhausted, wet and hungry, should be executed for falling asleep on sentry, however hard he tries to keep awake. Soldiers who are resting, sleeping, or working in an exposed position rely entirely on the sentry to warn them of an enemy approach. The life of everyone depends upon the sentry remaining awake and alert, and failure to do so is rightly regarded as a most serious offence. In practice the army did its best to ensure that sentries did not go to sleep. A lone sentry was rarely posted; normally there would be two, each man doing a two-hour shift with one being relieved every hour. Inevitably men did go to sleep, but it was difficult to prove and most officers and NCOs did their best to avoid having to charge a man with the offence. Although 449 men were sentenced to death for sleeping at their post between 1914 and 1918, in only two cases were the sentences actually carried out, and in both cases the circumstances were very grave.

Section 7 dealt with mutiny, perhaps the most serious offence in the military glossary. Mutiny is resistance to lawful military authority, and it is a collective offence – that is, it cannot be committed by one man alone but requires two or more acting in concert. As mutiny strikes at the very heart of military discipline it could result in the death penalty in peace as well as war.

Section 8 made it an offence punishable by death to strike, or threaten to strike, a superior in the execution of his office. Section 9 laid down the death penalty for disobedience of a lawful command, provided such disobedience showed wilful defiance of authority. Disobedience without wilful defiance rendered the offender liable to penal servitude. The *Manual of Military Law* made it very clear what was a lawful command and what was not, explaining that an order which was clearly in contravention of the laws and usages of war (the example given is of an order to open fire on an unarmed civilian bystander) must not be obeyed, and that an order unrelated to military duty and given for the attainment of a private end need not be obeyed; the rather quaint example of the latter being an order to a soldier to deliver a letter dealing with private theatricals. At the same time, in a long chapter dealing with the laws and usages of war on land, and listing offences proscribed by international law, the *Manual* said: 'It is important, however, to note that members of the Armed Forces who commit such violations of the recognised rules of warfare as are ordered by their government or by their commander are not war criminals and cannot therefore be punished by the enemy.'[2] In other words, 'superior orders' was an absolute defence to prosecution for acts committed in contravention of international law. This paragraph was not deleted from the *Manual* until April 1944, when it dawned belatedly on the British governments' legal advisers that such a clause would scupper their plans to try German and Japanese officers and soldiers for war crimes.[3]

Section 12 prescribed the death penalty for desertion while on, or warned for, active service, attempted desertion, or the encouragement of others to desert. Desertion was the leaving of the service with the intention never to return, as opposed to the lesser offence of absence without leave. Normally the prosecution had to show that the offender did not intend to return, and unless he had burned or thrown away his uniform or assumed a false identity, this was very difficult to prove. On active service, however, there was a presumption of desertion if the offender absented himself without reasonable excuse.

Section 41 made it legal to try, under military law, an officer or soldier serving abroad for an offence which, if committed in England, would be an offence under criminal law. Murder was punishable by death, with no other sentence open, and treason could be punished by death. In both cases these were the same punishments as were laid down by the civilian law of the time.

With the exception of murder, for which, as in civilian law, no sentence other than death could be handed down, offences carrying the death penalty could also be punished by any lesser punishment allowed by the Act. Accepting that imprisonment and detention were not always practical under the conditions of active service, and that confinement to barracks was pointless, the Act allowed the imposition of 'field punishment'. There were two grades of field punishment, both of which allowed the offender to be manacled and to carry out fatigues. In the case of Field Punishment Number One he was also tied to a fixed object (often a gun carriage) for up to two hours a day. Otherwise the soldier undergoing punishment could be made to bear arms and carry out all the normal duties of a soldier. It was a degrading punishment, effectively the successor to flogging, but could be imposed swiftly and in any conditions.

Military law originates from a different source than does English civilian law, and its procedures reflect that. Civilian law is adversarial: that is, it is the duty of the court to hear the prosecution and the defence and to decide which has made its case. It is not the task of the court itself to extract evidence, or to call witnesses, or to question witnesses except to clarify what they have said. Military law, on the other hand, descends from Roman law and the process is inquisitorial: it is the duty of the court to discover what actually happened. There is a prosecution and a defence, but the court is perfectly entitled – indeed required if need be – to summon and to question witnesses. As the person or persons trying the case are themselves soldiers, they have full knowledge of the circumstances under which the offence may have been committed. Modern critics say that this means that the army is judge and jury in its own case; but this is to miss the point that it is soldiers, and only soldiers, who fully understand the significance of an act or an omission in the military context. To hand the administration of military justice over to civilian courts or to magistrates would not only be impractical and time-consuming, it would negate the very purpose of military law, which is to maintain good order and military discipline and allow an army to operate as it should. A soldier joining the army surrenders some of his civil rights, and in an army, particularly an army at war, individual rights must be subservient to the rights and duties of the force as a whole.

This is not to say that military justice in 1914–18 was oppressive or unfair. Sections of the Army Act were regularly read out to soldiers on parade: there was no excuse for not knowing the law, or for not being fully aware of the punishments that might be inflicted for contravening it. The rules of evidence in military law were exactly the same as those in civilian law, and the rights of the accused were laid down in detail in all the rules of procedure.

The sentence that could be passed depended not only on the available penalties for the offence, but also on the level of the court trying it. At the bottom of the scale was the commanding officer, the officer in command of the offender's unit. His powers were very limited, much more so than those of a commanding officer today. Under the 1914 Act a commanding officer could investigate any offence but could only deal with minor offences (drunkenness and absence without leave being the most common). The maximum punishments the commanding officer could impose were twenty-eight days' detention, a fine of ten shillings (for drunkenness), stoppages of pay (for lost or damaged equipment), confinement to barracks, or extra guards and piquets. He could reduce a lance corporal to the rank of private, or any other NCO from his acting to his substantive rank. Other than lance corporals and NCOs with acting rank, the commanding officer could not punish an NCO at all, except by admonishment or reprimand. Even for a man holding the acting rank of colour sergeant or above, the commanding officer had to have the agreement of his own superior before he could proceed. On active service the commanding officer could award field punishment to a private soldier, but not to an NCO.

A commanding officer could, and usually did, delegate to company and equivalent commanders the power to investigate and try most minor offences, but their powers of sentencing were limited to seven days' confinement to barracks. If, after trying the case, the commanding officer felt minded to impose a punishment that would affect the man's pay – a fine, stoppages, and also detention (during which a man was not paid) – the soldier had to be given the option of either accepting the commanding officer's award or being tried by court martial. The vast majority accepted the commanding officer's decision.[4]

For an offence that the commanding officer was not permitted to try, or where the commanding officer considered that a punishment greater than that which he could impose was called for, a soldier was tried by court martial. There were four types of court martial: Regimental, District, General and Field General. The lowest court was the Regimental Court Martial, composed of a minimum of three officers, normally of the accused's regiment, each member to have held a commission for at least a year. The president of the court had to be of at least captain's rank. By 1914 Regimental Courts Martial were hardly ever convened, as commanding officers' powers had recently been increased to allow them to award up to twenty-eight days' detention.

A District Court Martial consisted of a minimum of three officers, of different regiments, each having held a commission for at least two years. The president had to be a field officer (major or above). The court could not try an officer, neither could it impose the death penalty or penal servitude.

A General Court Martial had at least nine members if held in the UK, India, Malta or Gibraltar, and a minimum of five if held elsewhere. The president had to be a lieutenant colonel or above (he was usually a brigadier general) and each member had to have held a commission for at least three years. This court could try an officer, and could impose the death penalty or any other sentence prescribed by military law. If the court passed a death sentence, at least two-thirds of the members had to agree. In all other cases a majority verdict sufficed, arrived at by asking members for their opinion individually and in ascending order of seniority. If the court was equally divided (possible where its numbers were more than the legal minimum), the accused had to be acquitted.

District and General Courts Martial were well suited to the administration of justice in peacetime, but were not always practical on active service, where it was often impossible to assemble the required number of officers of the prescribed rank. Military justice had to be swift, and to cater for this there was the Field General Court Martial, only convened in time of war and in the field, where it was not possible for the normal rules to be followed. A Field General Court Martial had to consist of three officers with a field officer as president. It could try any case and award the same punishments as could a General Court Martial, but if it imposed the death penalty then all the members had to agree. In very special circumstances the membership of a Field General Court Martial could be reduced to two officers, but in this case the court could not impose the death penalty and was limited to sentences of two years' imprisonment or three months' field punishment.

In all cases there were strict rules to prevent anyone having a personal interest in the case, or anyone involved with the prosecution of the accused, from sitting on the court. All members of the court swore an oath on the Bible:

> I do swear that I will well and truly try the accused person before the court according to the evidence, and that I will duly administer justice according to the Army Act now in force, without partiality, favour or affection, and I do further swear that I will not divulge the sentence of the court until it is duly confirmed, and I do further swear that I will not, on any account, at any time whatsoever, disclose or discover the vote or opinion of any particular member of this court martial, unless thereunto required in due course of law. So help me God.[5]

There was no appeal from the finding or sentence of a court martial, but there were checks and balances to ensure against a perverse verdict. No sentence of a court martial could be carried out until it had been confirmed. The confirming officer was usually the divisional commander, but for death sentences was the Commander-in-Chief (French and then Haig for the BEF). The confirming officer was required to review the sentence and could send it back to the court for reconsideration, but only a downward revision was allowed – the court could not increase the sentence, whatever the confirming officer thought. In the case of a death sentence the court could make a recommendation for mercy, as could all levels of command – brigade, division, corps and army – on the way to the Commander-in-Chief. The members of the court were themselves liable to sanctions under both military and civilian law if they behaved unlawfully in the trial of an accused.

In a serious case a court martial often had a civilian judge – the Judge Advocate – sitting not as a member but to advise the members as to the law. On active service this was not always possible, but military law is deliberately uncomplicated, and the lack of legal qualifications did not impede a fair hearing. As long as the court followed the established rules of procedure, and likewise the rules of evidence – and if they did not, the confirming officer would quash the finding – then the trial would proceed fairly. Members had to weigh the evidence that was presented, and decide what weight to give to each portion, before arriving at a decision.

The procedure at trial was straightforward. The accused was informed of the charges he faced and was then asked if he objected to any member of the court. If the objection was reasonable (such as the accused having had a run-in with one of the officers in the past), then that member would be replaced. The prosecution then presented its case, calling witnesses on oath, who could be questioned by the accused or by his defending officer or, if necessary, by the court itself. Defending officers were not required to be legally qualified, although if such an officer was available he might well defend. The accused had the right to ask for any officer he wished as his defender, and if that officer was available and not disbarred (by, for example, being the accused's commanding officer and thus involved in the prosecution), then he had to undertake the defence.

LEFT The village war memorial, Knowlton, Kent. Most memorials commemorate those who died: this one commemorates those who survived. By the end of the first six months of the war the entire male population of military age (twelve of them) was in the army. As there was no local Pals battalion, nor any affiliation to a particular Territorial Force unit, they joined a variety of regiments, and all came back. Statistically, one of them should have been killed. (*Author*)

BELOW New Army recruits being paid in Trafalgar Square, London, in August 1914. For many of these men the attractions of a reasonable wage and three good meals a day were a significant boost to patriotism. While military clothing has not yet been issued, the men are in uniform of a sort and some elementary drill has been absorbed. (*IWM Q53219*)

RIGHT A British trench (probably the Firing Line) at Thiepval, September 1916. The soldier asleep on the fire step has a bolt cover fitted to his rifle to prevent it becoming clogged by mud, and is wearing standard web equipment with a box respirator in the bag resting on his waist belt. The dixies covered by an empty sandbag no doubt contain the men's lunch (typically tea and tinned meat sandwiches). (*IWM Q1071*)

ABOVE A field kitchen in a man-made cave under the city of Arras in March 1918. The cook is using a Soyer Stove, invented during the Crimean War by Alexis Soyer, one time Head Chef of the Savoy Hotel London, and author of *Shilling Cooking for the People*, which sold 100,000 copies. The Soyer Stove is still in use in some locations by the British Army today, and the pattern of the food containers on the floor has not changed. (*IWM Q10713*)

LEFT Men of the Scots Guards in October 1915 during the Battle of Loos. This is probably a bombing party as the two men squatting are priming grenades by inserting the detonators. Grenades of this type were in very short supply at this stage of the war and generally reserved for bombers. Others had to make do with a variety of expedients, often ignited with a match or cigarette end. (*IWM Q17390*)

BELOW A British hospital train about nine miles behind the front in September 1916. Although nurses – military, Red Cross or volunteer – were supposed to be kept well away from the fighting, they were not infrequently caught in air raids or long-distance shelling. At this stage no women other than nurses were directly involved in military operations, but later on some were employed as drivers behind the lines (in an age when driving was not a universal skill, one source of drivers was tradesmen's daughters). (*IWM Q1319*)

ABOVE Lightly wounded British soldiers. Complete with souvenirs, they are waiting by a Casualty Clearing Station at Heilly during the Somme offensive. The two Grenadier Guardsmen are lance corporals, despite their wearing two chevrons (corporals in the Guards wear three chevrons, rather than two), and are regular soldiers – the Guards had no Territorial Force units and raised no New Army battalions. (*IWM Q1256*)

BELOW A British eighteen-pounder field gun in a prepared emplacement. Most positions for field artillery were temporary as, if they stayed in the same place for too long, they risked interdiction by the Germans. In long periods of defence, however, increasingly sophisticated emplacements, such as this one, could be built. In this, obviously posed, photograph, the gun crew are wearing box respirators. (*IWM Q49083*)

TOP A British eight-inch howitzer in action at Longueval during the Somme offensive. This weapon had a range of six miles and was used mainly to break up German fortified positions and to bombard likely supply routes, ammunition dumps and forming-up places with high explosive shells. As the gun's counter-bombardment protection is scanty, it will not be intended to remain in this position for long. (*IWM Q1257*)

ABOVE The Lewis Light Machine Gun. Invented by an American and initially turned down by everybody except the British, the Lewis was the best gun of its type in the War and provided the infantry with its own intimate fire support after the withdrawal of Vickers guns to the Machine Gun Corps in late 1915. Gas-operated, air-cooled, with an effective range of 800 yards and weighing 27 lbs, the infantry version had a 47-round drum magazine. Eventually adopted by several major armies it remained in service until well into the Second World War. The British version was of .303 calibre, thus firing the same ammunition as the rifle and the Vickers. (*Cassell*)

ABOVE Despatch riders of 9th Hodson's Horse at Flers during the Somme offensive. One brigade of Indian cavalry arrived on the Western Front in September 1914, and by 1916 had expanded to two divisions. While the breakout to allow cavalry to realise its full potential was never achieved, cavalry were invaluable as despatch riders, for reconnaissance, outpost duties and as escorts. The horse was still the fastest way to get a man across country, and British and Indian cavalry were trained as mounted infantry. Note the extra bandolier of rifle ammunition round the horse's neck. (*IWM Q1226*)

BELOW A farrier shoeing transport horses. All armies relied on horse-drawn transport for most movement of artillery and stores. Under war conditions a set of shoes on a cavalry horse would last around three weeks provided a shoe was not pulled off in muddy ground. Transport horses did much of their work on roads, often cobbled, and would need shoes replacing about every two weeks. Note the picket ropes, used to hobble horses when stabling was not available. The British had docked their horses' tails since at least the late eighteenth century, which made grooming easier but deprived the horse of his natural flywhisk. (*IWM Q17354*)

LEFT Men of the 2nd Battalion Argyll and Sutherland Highlanders (a regular battalion) in early May 1915. The first use of gas by the Germans was at Second Ypres on 22 April 1915, and the mask shown was the British first response. It was manufactured and issued remarkably quickly (this battalion got theirs on 3 May) and, combined with goggles, afforded good protection against chlorine gas launched from cylinders, albeit awkward to wear. It was replaced by the smoke helmet and finally by the box respirator. The men are wearing canvas covers over their kilts, partly as camouflage and partly to keep the mud off. (IWM Q48951)

RIGHT An artilleryman wearing a smoke helmet with mouthpiece fitting gas masks to his horses. Perhaps surprisingly, given that they have no ability to vomit, horses were relatively unaffected by gas discharged from cylinders, possibly because by the time the gas reached them it had sunk to below horse-head height. On the move the man will steer by riding one of the horses, and the metal plate strapped to his right leg is to protect it from being crushed by the other horse in the pair. (IWM Q10739)

'Some Generals of the Great War'. British and Empire generals of the Great War, painted in 1922 by John Singer Sergeant (1856–1925). The painting, described by one Director of the National Portrait Gallery as 'Still Life with Boots', could not be painted from life – it is unlikely that all the generals were ever together in one place, and in any case two were dead by the time the painting was begun. Left to right are: Birdwood (Commander ANZAC Corps at Gallipoli, later Commander Fifth Army and Administrative Controller Australian Imperial Force); Smuts (South African Commander Imperial Forces in East Africa, member of the War Cabinet, later Prime Minister of South Africa during the Second World War); Botha (South African Prime Minister); Byng (GOC Canadian Corps May 1916 to June 1917, then Commander Third Army, and, after the war, Governor General of Canada by Canadian request); Rawlinson (Commander Fourth Army on the Somme); Lukin (Inspector General South African Army, Commander South African Brigade and later 9th (Scottish) Division on the Western Front); Monash (Commander Australian Corps from June 1918); Horne (Commander First Army); Milne (Commander British Forces Salonika); Wilson (British representative at Versailles and CIGS from February

1918); Russell (Commander New Zealand Division); Plumer (Commander Second Army);
Cowans (Quartermaster General); Haig (Commander-in-Chief BEF from December 1915);
French (Commander-in-Chief BEF August 1914 to December 1915); Robertson (CIGS from
December 1915 to February 1918); Maude (Commander-in-Chief Mesopotamia from 1916
until his death from cholera in 1917); Allenby (Commander Third Army and Commander-
in-Chief Egyptian Expeditionary Force from June 1917); Marshall (Commander-in-Chief
Mesopotamia from 1917); Currie (Commander Canadian Corps from June 1917); Cavan
(Commander British Forces Italy); Dobell (Commander Allied forces Cameroon, later
Commander Eastern force in the Egyptian Expeditionary Force until relieved and sent to
India as a divisional commander in 1917 – it is unclear why he is in this painting!). Absent
is General Sir Ian Hamilton (Commander of the Gallipoli expedition), presumably because
he was considered to have failed, and Trenchard (Commander Royal Flying Corps), presumably because he was an officer of the Royal Air Force from April 1918. The painting
was commissioned by Sir Abraham Bailey to commemorate the generals who had won the
war. (*National Portrait Gallery*)

RIGHT A statue in Norwich to Nurse Edith Cavell, shot by German firing squad in Belgium on 12 October 1915 for helping Allied soldiers to escape. Her grave is by the cathedral walls, and she has at least one other statue, in London, opposite the National Portrait Gallery. Brave and patriotic she certainly was: murdered she was not. The Germans were fully entitled to shoot her, but it was a public relations disaster for them. (*Author*)

BELOW A German flamethrower detachment taking on a tank. The round vessel on the back of the man on the right is the fuel container with the pressure pump in the middle. This photograph was obviously taken in training as the tank appears to be the German A7V, of which only a few were manufactured and which was liable to turn turtle over obstacles or on sloping ground. Flamethrowers had little effect in this war, mainly due to a limited range and the obvious target posed by the crew. (*IWM Q55426*)

LEFT Field Marshal Lord Kitchener (1850–1916). The 'First Soldier of the Empire', Kitchener's appointment as Secretary of State for War in August 1914 was an imaginative act by Prime Minister Asquith. Historians have not been kind to Kitchener, but it is doubtful if anyone else could have galvanised the country behind total war, and his raising of the New Armies was a major contribution to victory. He restored Sir John French's will to fight in 1914, and had the courage to call off the Dardanelles campaign in 1915. His distrust of politicians and his political naivety led to friction with the government, and by the time of his drowning in HMS *Hampshire* in 1916 his authority had largely been eclipsed. (*Author*)

LEFT The grave of Rifleman Arthur Allsop KRRC. Allsop was conscripted in June 1916, was punished summarily for Absence without Leave in August of the same year; brought before a District Court Martial and sentenced to detention for Desertion in November 1916; went to France with the 12th Battalion of his regiment and again deserted in February 1917. This time he was sentenced to death, later commuted to imprisonment and the sentence suspended. Again he deserted, on 24 April 1917, just before an attack, and after being arrested twenty-four miles behind the lines, once more appeared before a court martial. Found guilty of Desertion and sentenced to death, he was shot by firing squad on 15 June. One could not say that he had not been given every chance. Executed criminals were buried in the same way as any other soldier, and there is no indication on the graves that they died other than in the normal course of duty. (*Author*)

RIGHT German prisoners near Fricourt during the Somme offensive in September 1916. Webbing, weapons and helmets have been removed (many of the latter no doubt becoming souvenirs) and the men are wearing the soft fatigue cap. Many are very young and few appear to be unduly dismayed at having been captured. *(IWM Q1229)*

LEFT Men of 1/7 Worcesters, a Territorial Force battalion, resting during the Somme offensive in September 1916. The officer's Sam Browne belt and soft cap, and the absence of web equipment and Lewis guns, indicate that the men are a fatigue party, or on training, rather than waiting to go into action. The war marked the shift from pipe to cigarette smoking amongst soldiers (the latter were more convenient in operational conditions and were easier to issue), but seven smokers out of the seventeen men shown is a higher proportion than would be found in a similar group today. (*IWM Q1081*)

ABOVE The village of Le Sars at the furthest point of the British advance of the Somme offensive. Once a small rural French village it was reduced to matchwood and rubble by the combined efforts of both sides' artillery. Ruins like this were easy to defend and very difficult to attack. (*IWM Q4903*)

RIGHT David Lloyd George (1863–1945). British Chancellor of the Exchequer, Minister for Munitions, and Prime Minister from 1916. The 'Welsh Wizard' or the 'Welsh Goat', ambitious, brilliant, kick-starter of the British armaments industry, self-seeking and self-promoting, conspiratorial, opportunist, the personification of Britain's will to win; it all depends upon the viewpoint. There is no doubting George's determination to win the war, but by his mistrust of the military, his constant interference in matters he did not understand and his search for the 'quick fix' he made it very difficult for his generals to do so. (*Author*)

LEFT General (later Marshal) 'Papa' Joffre (1852–1931), Chief of the French General Staff from 1911 and Commander-in-Chief 1914–1916 until replaced by Nivelle. An engineer of humble origins, he owed his promotion more to a lack of any strong political or religious views than to outstanding merit. A man of great resilience, his refusal to panic in 1914 when things were not going well provided a steadying influence for generals and politicians alike.

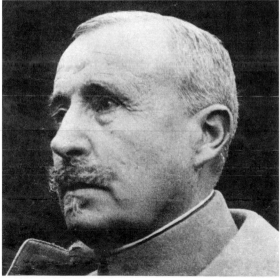

LEFT General Robert Nivelle (1856–1924). An energetic and articulate artillery officer who rose from regimental commander in 1914 to Commander-in-Chief of the French armies in December 1916, largely as a result of his recapture of Forts Vaux and Douaumont at Verdun. Fluent in English, he convinced the French and British politicians (but not the French and British generals) that he had the secret of winning the war in a matter of days. He was the architect of the disastrous offensive of April and May 1917, which led to the mutinies in the French army and his own dismissal. (*Author*)

LEFT General (later Marshal) Philippe Pétain (1856–1951). The son of a peasant, he was a regimental commander in the rank of colonel at the outbreak of war; by June 1915 he was commanding the French Second Army. The 'Saviour of Verdun', he succeeded Nivelle as Commander-in-Chief of the French armies in May 1917 and resolved the mutinies. His reluctance to take the offensive in 1918, in order to preserve the fragile morale of the French army, led to disagreements with Haig and the appointment of Foch as Allied co-ordinator. His contempt for politicians in the disastrous Battle of France in 1940 led to his leadership of the Vichy regime and imprisonment for treason at the end of the Second War. (*Mary Evans Picture Library*)

LEFT General (later Marshal) Ferdinand Foch (1851–1929). A fighting general and an intellectual, he commanded the French Ninth Army in 1914 and the Group of Armies of the North in 1915 and 1916, until falling out of favour along with Joffre. Recalled as Chief of Staff when Pétain became Commander-in-Chief in May 1917, he was appointed allied 'Generalissimo' – in effect co-ordinator of all military effort on the Western Front – in 1918, largely on the insistence of Haig who wanted a 'General who will fight' during the dark days of the Kaiser's offensive. He was probably the greatest French general of the twentieth century. (*IWM Q66052*)

LEFT General (later General of the Armies) 'Black Jack' Pershing, Commander-in-Chief of the American Expeditionary Force. The junior of the seven major generals in the pre-war American army in 1917, Pershing walked a difficult line between his professional under-standing of the imperatives of war and the political restraints imposed by Washington. The US had not come to France to fight the Allies' war for them, but to make its own contribution to peace, an attitude that often infuriated the French and British generals. Pershing presided over the massive and rapid build-up from a tiny peacetime army to two million men in France by 1918. He got on well with Haig on a personal level, and found the British way of waging war more to his liking than that of the French. On a number of occasions he relaxed his insistence (laid down by President Wilson) that American troops would not engage in combat until they could do so as part of an American army. The Meuse Argonne offensive was the American Somme, and the war ended before Pershing could show his true abilities as a Commander-in-Chief.

After the prosecution case the defence called its witnesses, if any, and made its own case. Then the two sides summed up, the accused or his defending officer having the last word. The court adjourned to consider its finding, and when it had arrived at a decision, this was announced. If the finding was 'not guilty', that was the end of the matter. If the finding was 'guilty', the court heard the accused's record read out, and any plea in mitigation of punishment, and any statement that the accused wished to make. The court adjourned again and decided upon sentence, which was duly announced in open court.[6]

Something open to the confirming officer, which was not to be available in civilian trials for many years to come, was the power to suspend a sentence 'for such period that seems expedient'. This was a useful instrument which meant that the sentence was not put into effect provided the man behaved, and it was often used.

The public perception of military justice in the Great War is of an oppressive and cruel system hauling young men before hastily set-up courts which sentenced them to death without thought or sympathy for the reasons for their behaviour. Much of the criticism comes from those who simply fail to understand how an army works and what the military imperatives are and were; some is simply founded in ignorance of the facts. Altogether, throughout all the theatres of war, there were 286,185 courts martial of all types and for all offences in the British and Indian armies, and in Dominion and Colonial forces under British command, between 4 August 1914 and 11 November 1918. This means that, in an average year, about one man in every 200 was brought before a court martial of some sort. As a number of men were tried more than once, the impingement of military justice on the average soldier is less than this, but compares favourably with the averages brought before civilian magistrates and courts in the United Kingdom in peacetime. Of these courts martial eighty-nine per cent resulted in guilty verdicts, the rest being either acquittals or cases where the finding was quashed by superior authority.

In the theatres of war a total of 2,229 officers were brought to trial by General Court Martial during the same period. Of these trials seventy-five per cent resulted in a conviction. Offences varied from drunkenness (thirty-seven per cent, and by far the most prevalent) to absence without leave (thirteen per cent) and cowardice (nine cases, or 0.3 per cent), and included quitting a post, ill-treating a civilian, fraud, desertion (eighteen cases), neglect, lying, disobedience, insubordination, indecency and escaping from confinement. Twenty-three per cent of trials were for 'miscellaneous military offences', which covered everything from conduct unbecoming an officer and a gentleman to driving without a licence. The most common sentence handed out after conviction of officers by General Court Martial was a reprimand, a rather more serious punishment in the military than in the civilian context, as it was nearly always a bar to further promotion. Of the 2,347 convictions of officers by General Court Martial 1,437, or sixty per cent, resulted in a reprimand. Five sentences of death were awarded, of which three were carried out. Thirty per cent of convictions resulted in cashiering or dismissal from the service, while twenty-one per cent involved loss of seniority. The difference between cashiering and dismissal is that the former not only carries a greater stigma, being the equivalent of discharge with ignominy for other ranks, but also forfeiture of pension and a bar on any further employment under the Crown (with one exception), including employment by a local authority. Thirty convictions resulted in imprisonment, which automatically included cashiering. Lest it be thought that cashiering or dismissal allowed the offender to escape the horrors of war, once out of the service the ex-officer immediately became liable, after February 1916, to conscription as a private soldier.

There were 252 officers brought before Field General Courts Martial. Seventy-six per cent resulted in convictions, and once again the most common offence was drunkenness (fifty-two per cent). Other charges included cowardice (one case) and most of the offences enumerated above. Sentences included 192 reprimands, forty-four forfeitures of seniority, ninety cashierings or dismissals, and two sentences of imprisonment.

As only a General or Field General Court Martial could deal with an officer, offences which, if committed by a private, would be dealt with at company or battalion level theoretically led to an officer's appearing before a court martial. To balance this, however, was the reluctance to wash regimental dirty linen in public, and there was (and still is) a well-established – and totally illegal – system of punishing officers for relatively minor offences without their having to appear in public. These long-accepted penalties included stoppage of leave, extra tours as orderly officer, and invitations to contribute financially to battalion welfare funds.

District Courts Martial in war theatres saw 4,132 other ranks appear before them, with an eighty-two-per-cent conviction rate. The major single offence was drunkenness, at seventeen per cent of all charges, followed by absence without leave at fifteen per cent. The three offences of disobedience, insubordination and using violence to a superior together accounted for twenty-seven per cent of cases, quitting a post for five per cent, and desertion for three per cent. The most common sentence awarded (fifty-seven per cent) was one of imprisonment or detention, usually for three months, followed by reduction in rank, fines or stoppages of pay (twenty-two per cent). Other punishments included field punishment and discharge with ignominy, but the latter was used sparingly (fewer than one per cent of sentences) as the man was then no longer liable for conscription.

General Courts Martial dealt with 144 other ranks, usually offenders in base areas where such a court could be convened, and charges were obviously more serious than those dealt with by District courts. Forty-seven per cent of trials were for mutiny, sixteen per cent for offences involving violence or disobedience, and twenty-one per cent for miscellaneous military and civilian offences. Drunkenness was alleged in only three cases, each of which must have been the result of a monumental beano, or very serious and persistent offending, as most cases of inebriation were perfectly capable of being handled by the company or battalion commander, or at worst by a District court. Sentences handed down to soldiers by General Courts Martial ranged from death to penal servitude, imprisonment or detention (fifty-eight per cent of all sentences), one third of them for a period of two years, field punishment (seventeen per cent), discharge with ignominy (seven per cent), and fines, stoppages of pay or reduction in rank (seven per cent).

The Field General Court Martial was the main judicial instrument that dealt with other ranks facing serious charges. There were 123,383 of these courts and twenty-three per cent concerned absence, closely followed by our old friend drunkenness at twenty-one per cent, violence, disobedience and insubordination at eighteen per cent, desertion at five per cent, and one per cent each for ill-treatment of civilians (around 1,200 cases) and mutiny. Cowardice was alleged in 0.4 per cent of cases.

Sentences handed down by Field General Courts Martial to other ranks and actually implemented included the death penalty in 337 cases. Sixty-four per cent of sentences took the form of field punishment, twenty-eight per cent of penal servitude, imprisonment or detention, and twenty-two per cent of fines, stoppages or reduction in rank.

Despite the popular belief that most soldiers who were shot had been found guilty of cowardice, this charge was only levied at 551 trials, or 0.2 per cent of cases. Cowardice was dealt with under Section 4 of the Army Act, which stated:

> Every person subject to Military Law who commits any of the following offences, that is to say...
>
> (7) Misbehaves or induces others to misbehave before the enemy in such a manner as to show cowardice, ...
>
> shall on conviction by court-martial be liable to suffer death, or such less punishment as is in this Act mentioned.[7]

'Misbehaves' was defined in the Act as meaning that the accused 'from an unsoldierlike regard for his personal safety in the presence of the enemy, failed in respect of some distinct and feasible duty imposed upon him by a specified order or regulation, or by the well understood custom of the service, or by the requirements of the case, as applicable to the position in which he was placed at the time'.[8] Key words in this section are 'in the presence of the enemy', which did not mean that the enemy had to be actually within touching distance, but had to be in the vicinity. Thus a man who, on a route march from a billet ten miles behind the lines, ran away when he heard a lorry backfiring could not be charged with cowardice, whereas a man who did the same when he was ordered to leave his trench and advance across no man's land clearly could be. Despite the Act's attempt to make the offence unambiguous, what did and what did not constitute cowardice were inevitably subjective, and very difficult to prove. The charge was therefore only preferred in cases where there could be no doubt whatsoever that the man had behaved in what the average soldier would consider to be a cowardly fashion. Cowardice was undoubtedly present on other occasions, but the offences of desertion, quitting a post or casting away arms were much more clear-cut and more likely to be cited.

The figures given above refer to sentences actually carried out. In many cases courts handed down heavier sentences, which were reduced or suspended on their way up the chain of command. Altogether 3,080 death sentences were passed by courts martial on British, Dominion and Colonial officers and soldiers, and to members of native labour corps subject to military law, between the outbreak of war and 31 March 1920 when active service officially ceased. Of these the great majority were passed in France and Belgium, where the bulk of the British and Empire armies were. Death sentences had to be confirmed by the commander-in-chief of the theatre, who held a royal warrant authorising him to do so, and of the 3,080 men sentenced to death only 346 were actually executed: 322 in France and Belgium, five in East Africa, four in Mesopotamia, four in Constantinople, three in Gallipoli, three in Salonika, two in Egypt, one in Italy, one in Palestine and one in Serbia. Nearly ninety per cent of those ordered to be executed had their sentences commuted to penal servitude, imprisonment or field punishment, or suspended. Of the 346 men actually put to death, 291 were of the British army, twenty-five were members of the Canadian forces, five were New Zealanders, four were in the British West Indies Regiment, employed mainly on labouring duties on the Western Front, and the remaining twenty-one were civilians subject to military law, including the Chinese Labour Corps, who exhibited a remarkable tendency to murder one another.

Indian army disciplinary records were kept separately, and no fully accurate breakdown now exists; but discipline in the Indian army, which remained an all-regular volunteer force throughout the war, was generally very good. Indian army courts martial also had a let-out denied to the British, which was the power to substitute flogging for a sentence of death or imprisonment. From battalion war diaries and personal accounts, there appear to have been very few soldiers of the Indian army executed, and only one definite case on the Western Front (a cavalryman convicted of murder).

It will be noted that no Australians were executed, despite their having five divisions on the Western Front from 1916 onwards, and two cavalry divisions in Palestine. It is often alleged that 'Australians could not be shot'. In fact Australian military law was virtually identical to that of the British, and 113 Australian soldiers were sentenced to death, three for cowardice, two for striking a superior, two for disobedience and the rest for desertion. No sentence of death on an Australian was ever carried out as, alone amongst the Dominion forces, the Australian government had reserved the power to confirm a death sentence not to the commander-in-chief of the theatre but to the Governor General of Australia; this was Sir Ronald Munro Ferguson (who was himself British and not Australian), and he invariably commuted the sentence to imprisonment. There were occasions when the Australian generals would have dearly liked to shoot a few of their men, whose superb fighting record was counterbalanced by appalling discipline. With seven per cent of the strength of the BEF, the Australians provided twenty-five per cent of its deserters, and when they were out of the line drunkenness, fighting and theft were rife. Statistically an Australian soldier was nine times more liable to serve a term of imprisonment than was his British counterpart, and these were sentences handed down by Australian courts martial, composed of Australian officers. In March 1918 nine out of every thousand Australians on the Western Front were in prison, compared with one in every thousand British.[9] In December 1918 there were 811 Australian soldiers serving sentences in military prisons, compared with 1,330 British and a combined total of 314 Canadians, New Zealanders and South Africans. Outwardly Australians laughed all this off, attributing it to the independent, happy-go-lucky attitudes of the freeborn Australian jackaroo (despite most Australian recruits coming from cities), but inwardly the Australian army absorbed the lessons, and discipline in the Second World War was much better.

Men actually executed had been found guilty of the following offences:

Mutiny	3
Cowardice	18
Desertion	266
Murder	37
Striking or using violence to a superior	6
Disobedience to a lawful command	5
Sleeping at post	2
Quitting a post without authority	7
Casting away arms	2

Criticism of British military executions in the Great War has grown more vociferous over the years. It emanates from those who are opposed to the death penalty under any circumstances, and from those who believe that trials were conducted hastily, without legally qualified supervision and without the accused being given an opportunity to defend himself. It is also alleged that many of those executed were suffering from medical or mental conditions which were ignored, and which, if taken into consideration, would have led to a commutation of sentence.

To those who oppose the death penalty *per se*, one can only reply that it was allowed by the law as it stood at the time. The thirty-seven murderers executed by the military would have suffered death by hanging had they been brought before a civilian court in England. While the death penalty is no longer on the statute books of most western democracies, there is an argument for its retention in war. In the future it may never have to be applied, but should the British army ever again have to expand far beyond its peacetime strength by the addition of conscripts and men to whom the military life does not come naturally, then an ultimate sanction to ensure good behaviour may be needed. The army asks a man to risk life and limb in the furtherance of operational tasks. If he refuses to carry out those tasks, or runs away, then he will be punished. 'Go forward and there is a risk of death; run away and there is a certainty of death' is persuasive. If, on the other hand, the punishment for failing to go forward is a term in prison with a good chance of an amnesty when the war is over, the imperative is somewhat lessened.

Although 337 of the 346 executions carried out were ordered by Field General Courts Martial, this is not to say that the proceedings were in any way summary or that justice was skimped. Justice in the middle of a war has to be swift, but it does not have to be unfair. In each and every case the accused was offered the services of a defending officer (known to the military as a 'prisoner's friend'), usually of the accused's choice. A criticism often levelled is that some of the accused were 'not defended', when in fact they had elected to defend themselves, as they were fully entitled to do, rather than speak through a representative. It is said that a lawyer who defends himself has a fool as a client, and that may be true in civilian law where cases are decided on the small print of strict legality; but it was not the case in a military court, where the men trying the case were well aware of the circumstances prevailing, and could, and did, themselves question witnesses should the accused miss a vital point. A sentence of death had to be unanimous, with the junior member tendering his opinion first, and there was thorough, albeit speedy, review all the way up the chain of command. By the time a death sentence arrived on the desk of Sir John French or Sir Douglas Haig, or their counterparts in other theatres, unit, brigade, division, corps and army commanders had all commented in writing on the appropriateness of the sentence. The Commander-in-Chief had to take into account not only the views of the accused's superiors but also the prevailing conditions. He was entitled – indeed he was required – to consider the unit's state of discipline at the time and whether or not the offence was prevalent.

Military justice is not only punitive, it is exemplary. All death sentences for sleeping on sentry – 393 of them in all theatres – were quashed, commuted or reduced to terms of imprisonment or field punishment, until two men, private soldiers of the 6th Battalion the South Lancashire Regiment, were executed in February 1917 in Mesopotamia. These were the only executions during the war for this offence. Privates Burton and Downing were a pair of sentries, and were required to remain standing up on the fire-step so that they could watch over the top of the parapet of their trench for enemy approach. What probably did for them was that they were found asleep together and sitting down in the bottom of the trench, so that they were presumed to have made a deliberate decision to chance their luck and go to sleep.[10] No doubt the Commander-in-Chief in Mesopotamia, Lieutenant General Sir Frederick Maude, felt that there had been far too much sleeping on sentry and that an example had to be made. The show of force may have worked, as up to that date eighteen death sentences for sleeping on sentry had been handed down in Mesopotamia, none of which were carried out, whereas after it (with a much larger army in theatre) only six were passed, again none of them being carried out.[11]

In most cases the officers sitting on a Field General Court Martial had to make a simple decision of fact, based on the evidence. A man was either at his post or he was not; a man had either run away or he had not. If it was felt that there could be any argument over legal niceties then a legally qualified officer was appointed to sit on the court, and in any case the Judge Advocate General at GHQ examined all the papers when they arrived for the Commander-in-Chief's decision. As the war went on, more and more legally qualified officers became involved, and a Courts Martial Officer was established at the headquarters of each corps to oversee procedures. From early 1915 onwards accused persons were not permitted to plead guilty to a charge that could attract the death penalty – the case had to be heard in full and proved.

'Shell shock' is frequently cited today in exculpation of many of those who were executed. Medical men had known for many years that the stress of battle could induce neuroses in soldiers, although the British had paid less attention to psychiatric medicine than had some European armies, perhaps because battle-induced trauma was more likely, or at least more numerous, in large conscript armies than in small professional ones. There were cases of psychological breakdown in the British army during the South African War, and these were generally classified as 'insanes' and evacuated like any other casualty. By and large, very little was done to examine the causes of such trauma, or to cure it, and cases which did not recover by themselves were generally discharged. In 1914 the term 'shell shock', coined by Dr Charles Myers, one of the first neurologists to work with military casualties, came into use to describe battle-induced psychological trauma. On first encountering trauma cases in 1914, when working in a British hospital in France, Myers thought that they were caused by the explosion of a shell in close proximity to the man, damaging the membranes of the brain. Hence the observed symptoms could be explained by a physical cause. Officers of the Royal Army Medical Corps, and medical men generally, objected to this term very early on and frequently thereafter, on the grounds that the symptoms of hypersensitivity to stimuli, startle reactions, irritability, tiredness, lack of concentration, exaggerated fear (phobias), disorientation, disassociation, sleeping disorders and incoherence were psychological rather than physical in origin. Myers himself changed his view as more and more cases appeared where a shell was not a contributory factor, but by 1915 the term had passed into the language.

'Shell shock' – nearly always placed in inverted commas by medical men to indicate their disapproval of the term as misleading – is simply stress induced by combat, and 'combat stress' is a far more accurate description than 'battle fatigue' or the modern 'post-traumatic stress disorder'.[12] It is not an illness confined to those exposed to battle, but was and is found in civilian practice, though the content of the phobias (in soldiers the fear of being buried alive was common) may be different.

It is now accepted by many medical authorities that even witnessing a traumatic event – such as a natural or man-made disaster, or a violent death – can induce psychological stress in suggestible people, something that the compensation industry has not been slow in grasping. Things were rather different in the early years of the last century, and the idea that the headmaster of a school should have to be sent on sick leave and given psychiatric counselling because one of his pupils was drowned in an accident hundreds of miles away, as happened in England in July 2001, would have appeared ridiculous to soldiers of 1914–18, who might have asked questions about the responsibility of the headmaster to the children who had not been drowned.

Persons suffering from psychological stress are not always responsible for their actions. The British army in the First War recognised this, and accepted that battle casualties included what they termed 'neurasthenic' cases. The difficulty, as with gas injuries, was that 'shell shock' was easier to fake than a physical wound, and was a defence often seized upon by offenders with no other excuse for their behaviour. A War Office inquiry after the war pointed out that 'To the relatives of a soldier who had broken down mentally, or who by reason of an inherently timorous disposition could not face the military life, or where natural tendencies had led to his getting into trouble; the use of the term "shell shock" came as a great relief'. It is unfortunate that some campaigners have managed to convince the public that anyone punished for a military offence in time of war must have been suffering from 'shell shock', and was therefore not responsible for his actions, when this is palpably untrue.

A diagnosis of 'shell shock' was not a disgrace, but a war injury like any other.[13] The history of a New Army Royal Engineers company being raised in Nuneaton in 1915 describes its NCOs as being a company sergeant major who was a recalled reservist, and a Corporal Seymour, 'stout and amiable' and 'a bit of lad', who had 'been in France in 1914 but was sent home with "shell shock'". There is no inkling of disapproval or criticism.[14] Erratic or even unlawful behaviour that was diagnosed as being due to 'shell shock' was dealt with by sending the man to a rear area where he could recover, or in really bad cases to training or administrative units at home, or to a hospital where he could be treated. If 'shell shock' was cited as a defence at a court martial the doctors were asked to pronounce, and in no case was a soldier whom the medical staff certified as suffering from 'shell shock' executed. On occasions when 'shell shock' was alleged but not supported by the doctors it was not, of course, accepted as a defence. That said, there appear to have been very few cases where men who alleged 'shell shock', but whose claim was denied, were actually executed.

In 1920 the government set up the 'Southborough Committee', or more properly 'The War Office Committee of Enquiry into the Causation and Prevention of Shell Shock'.[15] The Chairman was Lord Southborough and the members were eleven medical practitioners with experience of wartime casualties, two MPs and the ex-Deputy Judge Advocate General of the BEF in France. The committee heard evidence from historians, from combatant officers, including at least one who had himself suffered from 'shell shock', from lawyers and from civilian and military doctors. The committee's report began by demanding that the term 'shell shock' should be expunged from the language as a 'gross misnomer' (sadly, it has not been). The report accepted that 'shell shock' was a genuine affliction, but felt that it should be regarded as a sickness rather than as a battle casualty, and concluded that battle-induced traumas were no different in medical terms from those encountered in civilian life. The report explained that there appeared to be certain indicators of susceptibility to 'shell shock', and these included a family history of mental illness, low intelligence and high suggestibility. Recruits should be screened for these factors which, said the report, should be grounds for rejection. The report emphasised that in a unit where morale was high – one that was well motivated, well led, and well disciplined – cases of 'shell shock' had been considerably fewer than in units where these happy circumstances did not apply.

The committee also examined court-martial procedure, and were satisfied that from as early as autumn 1914 military legal and medical authorities examined very carefully any allegations that 'shell shock' had been a contributory factor to the offence alleged. In such cases the committee was satisfied 'that the best possible medical advice was called for'. Members devoted considerable time to a definition of cowardice, and found that while all men might feel, or even show, fear, this only developed into cowardice when the man was capable of controlling his fear but did not do so. It is hard to disagree.

The committee found that any type of individual could suffer from nervous disorders if exposed to battle conditions for long enough, and one witness (a Royal Air Force medical officer) likened it to a 'run on the bank'. He felt that everybody had reserves of courage and self-control, and that if a man was not given sufficient time to restock, his 'current account' would run out and he would eventually break down. This point is generally accepted in today's army. Colonel J. F. C. Fuller, then Deputy Director of Staff Duties (Training) at the War Office and a man who had seen much action during the war, felt that 'shell shock' could be contagious, and cited an instance where mass panic had set in on the Ancre in 1916 when British troops had fled en masse, and another (unique) case where numbers of soldiers had deserted to the Germans in November 1917. The Director General of Army Medical Services, Lieutenant General Sir James Goodwin, accepted the difficulty of identifying potential cases during the enlistment process, but felt that 'gradual, sympathetic, efficient and thorough training' could lessen or prevent incidences of 'shell shock'. Men who had experienced but a short and rushed period of training were, Goodwin believed, more likely to break down. Many witnesses were adamant that regular changes of environment, regular periods of rest and recreation and not being left in the same sector of front for too long would all contribute to a good state of mental health. It was generally agreed that nobody liked the Ypres salient, where instances of 'shell shock' were greater than elsewhere, and that 'lonely' jobs (manning an observation post in a sap going out into no man's land or patrolling in very small groups) increased the risks. On the matter of officers who had suffered from 'shell shock', a number of witnesses, including Sir Frederick Horne, who had started the war as a brigade commander and finished it as a full general commanding an army, told the committee that having responsibility generally protected officers from mental trauma, but that when that responsibility was removed (during periods of rest or while in billets), or if they were promoted beyond their capabilities, then officers were vulnerable.

The committee found, *inter alia*, that anyone could suffer from 'shell shock' in time, and that certain individuals were unlikely ever to become efficient fighting soldiers. The committee recognised the importance of training being gradual, and found that in many cases warning signs were indulgence in too much alcohol, drugs or sex. They also found that a previous incidence of concussion – not necessarily experienced in the war – could be a contributory factor. The committee did not agree with one witness who said that men from an outdoor civilian occupation were less susceptible than 'artisans and clerks' – the statistics showed that previous employment was no pointer to resistance to trauma. The report made a number of recommendations for reducing the incidence of 'shell shock', and for its treatment. These included regular rotation of troops through the front lines (which had been the norm throughout the war), and transfers to different sectors of the front. All soldiers should be given instruction in fear, which all would encounter on active service, and officers should be trained in character assessment. The importance of welfare, good food and comfort was stressed, and men showing signs of 'shell shock' should be removed from the front lines at the earliest opportunity and treated behind the lines. There were many examples where timely action had ensured that men could continue to perform useful service if treatment was carried out promptly. The committee recognised the difficulty of identifying, at the moment of enlistment, those susceptible to mental trauma, but felt that if they could in some way be detected they could still be employed in a military capacity behind the lines and away from the fighting.

Modern psychiatrists would agree with most of what the Southborough Committee said, although Brigadier Douglas Wickenden, Consultant Psychiatrist to the British Army, has pointed out to this author that the feeling of helplessness, of inability to control what is going on, is a major factor in breakdown under stress, and that it can occur even when the patient is no more than a witness of a traumatic event that may not affect him or her physically. This would support the finding that officers and NCOs, who had at least some sense of being in control, were less likely to suffer from 'shell shock' than private soldiers who simply obeyed orders and went where they were led. Combat stress is now accepted as a combination of acute and chronic or repeated stresses, from which there is no acceptable voluntary escape except through some form of breakdown. In a mass army of millions of men, that so few did in fact break down during the Great War says much for the inherent resilience of the men, for the leadership and training they were given and for the progress made during the war towards a proper understanding of mental illness.

It is clear from the voluminous evidence gathered by the Southborough Committee that, even in the state of psychological knowledge and psychiatric medicine at the time, men who succumbed to 'shell shock' were recognised and treated as medical cases and not as criminals. Some of the treatment was, of course, experimental, and some was barbaric by modern standards, but by the latter stages of the war the importance of speedy removal from the battle area and sympathetic treatment behind the lines was recognised. Today 'shell shock' has not gone away but, in the modern British army at least, it is recognised, and training and medical practice takes its existence into account. A soldier in the Falklands War who deserted in the face of the enemy, and whose actions could have led to a court martial for what was still a capital offence in military law, was on medical examination found to be suffering from battle-induced trauma and treated as a casualty rather than as an offender. In the last few years soldiers have committed suicide in Northern Ireland and in the Balkans, almost certainly as a result of what used to be called 'shell shock'. The problems are still with us, and there are too few psychiatrists and it is too expensive to screen every potential recruit; but careful and thorough training, as recommended by Southborough, has ensured that cases are few. Suggestions that 'shell shock' victims were executed during the Great War are not supported by the evidence.

Sentences of death were carried out by firing squad. The firing squad was commanded by an officer and normally consisted of twelve men armed with rifles. Occasionally the firing squad was drawn from the prisoner's own regiment, but this was unusual. The firing squad was paraded and then ordered to load. The men then grounded arms, turned about and marched ten or so paces away from their weapons. While there was nothing in the rules to enforce it, it seems to have been usual for the officer of the firing squad then to unload one or more of the rifles; the idea was presumably that any member of the firing squad could, in later years, say that his was the rifle that was empty. In some cases the officer even mixed up the rifles, which, by causing soldiers to fire rifles that were not zeroed to them, was actually more likely to result in a botched shooting. The men were then turned about, marched back onto their rifles and made to pick them up. The condemned man was brought out and tied either to a chair or to a post, blindfolded, and had a square of paper pinned to his heart. The squad was then ordered to aim and fire. It was the job of the officer commanding the firing squad to administer the *coup de grâce* with his pistol if the man was not killed outright by the firing squad. Executions were usually carried out at dawn, not for any legal reason but because it was a quiet time – casual bystanders were not welcome.

Two cases that arouse controversy even today are those of Sub Lieutenant Dyett of the Royal Navy, and Lance Sergeant (equivalent to acting sergeant) Stones of the 19th Battalion the Durham Light Infantry. Even after eighty-five years relatives of both these men, supported by various interest groups, regularly raise their cases in the press, usually in the lead-up to Remembrance Sunday.

Edwin Leopold Arthur Dyett was the son of a Merchant Navy captain, and after five years as an apprentice in the Merchant Navy he volunteered for the Royal Navy in June 1915, four months before his twentieth birthday. By education and background he was officer material, and after training was commissioned as a sub lieutenant. He had hoped to serve at sea, but the navy had all the sea officers it needed at this time, and Dyett was posted to the 63rd Royal Naval Division. He went to France with the division in May 1916, in the Nelson Battalion of 189 Brigade, and took part in the training for the Somme offensive, which was to begin in July 1916. The Royal Naval Division's first taste of action since leaving Gallipoli was on 13 November 1916, towards the end of the Somme battles, when the division was ordered to attack along the northern bank of the River Ancre towards the village of Beaucourt. The division was to attack with two brigades up and one in support, with 189 Brigade on the right next to the river. The Hood and Hawke Battalions of 189 Brigade were to lead, with the

Drake and Nelson Battalions following up. Zero hour was first light, or about 0700 hours British Double Summer Time.

It was normal in this war for each battalion to nominate a small number of officers and men to be 'left out of battle', or LOB, who did not take part in the attack but were available to reinforce if necessary, or to act as a cadre upon which the battalion could be reformed if mass casualties occurred. The LOB party normally consisted of the battalion second-in-command, all company seconds-in-command, one platoon commander from each company and about ten per cent of the other ranks. On 13 November 1916 Dyett was one of those nominated to remain behind. It is alleged today that the inclusion of Dyett in the group not taking part indicated that the commanding officer knew he was not up to the rigours of war. In fact junior officers and soldiers joined the LOB group strictly in rotation. To leave the same man behind more than once was not only insulting to him, but would have caused resentment amongst others who had to take part.

By about noon the attack had achieved much but had become bogged down, and the Nelson Battalion had suffered heavy casualties. Dyett and another officer, Sub Lieutenant Truscott, were ordered forward to rejoin. The two officers were taken by car from the divisional headquarters to the brigade tactical headquarters, and were eventually told to make their way up to the Nelson Battalion on foot. It was getting dark, there was fog, the ground was badly churned up and there were occasional German artillery shells falling around. The two men parted company. Although all he had to do was follow the river bank, Dyett floundered about and then found another sub lieutenant, who was organising the move of stragglers up to the front line. This officer, Sub Lieutenant Fernie, told Dyett to join the column, and to remain at the rear to ensure that no one fell out. Dyett declined to play, saying that he was returning to brigade headquarters for further orders. This was an odd way to behave. Even if, as alleged later, the sub lieutenant organising the move to the front was junior to Dyett and could not therefore give him a lawful command, the fact is that Dyett had been told to rejoin his battalion and here was a way for him to do so. Dyett eventually took refuge in a dugout, and was subsequently reported by Fernie as having refused to go up to the front and to have walked in the opposite direction. Dyett was eventually found and arrested in the battalion billeting area in the village of Englebelmer, three and a half miles behind the lines, two days later on 15 November. He was charged with desertion under Section 12 of the Army Act, in that he absented himself from his battalion, and, as an alternative charge, with conduct to the prejudice of good order and military discipline in that he did not go up to the front line when ordered to do so. Alternative charges were common in military trials, and if the more serious charge was not proven then the lesser alternative could be considered.

Dyett was brought before a General Court Martial at Le Champ Neuf on 26 December 1916.[16] The president of the court was Brigadier General S. F. Metcalfe of the Royal Artillery, and the members were Major (Temporary Lieutenant Colonel) C. J. Martin, commanding 2nd Battalion the Highland Light Infantry, Major F. R. Day and Major H. P. M. Bernay-Fickling of the 8th Battalion the Norfolk Regiment, Major L. W. Miller of the Royal Marines and Captain (Acting Lieutenant Colonel) J. S. Collings-Wells, commanding 4th Battalion the Bedfordshire Regiment. The fifth member should have been a Captain (Temporary Major) B. A. Winter of the 23rd Battalion Royal Fusiliers, but when it was found that he had not held a commission for the requisite time he was replaced by Collings-Wells. All were combatant officers with considerable experience of life in the trenches. Captain T. S. Griffith-Jones, 10th Battalion South Wales Borderers, who was a qualified barrister, sat as judge advocate; the prosecutor was Sub Lieutenant H. S. Strickland of the Nelson Battalion (presumably the adjutant, as was normal), and Dyett was defended by Sub Lieutenant C. S. Trevanion of the Hawke Battalion, a qualified solicitor.

Dyett pleaded not guilty – a not guilty plea was, of course, mandatory where the death penalty was possible. In evidence the facts adduced by the prosecution were not disputed, but the defending officer maintained that Dyett had merely got lost, not absented himself. In cross-examination the Commanding Officer of the Nelson Battalion, the aptly named Lieutenant Commander Nelson, said that Dyett was a very poor officer, whose authority in command of men was not good. He explained that the accused had asked for a transfer to the sea service, and had 'told me that he was of a very nervous temperament and that he was not fitted for the Front Line'. Nelson said that he had felt some apprehension in sending Dyett forward that day, but 'I had to send two officers and these were the only ones.' Sub Lieutenant Truscott told the court that on arrival at brigade headquarters, between Mesnil and Hamel, he and Dyett were ordered by the brigade commander to join their battalion on the 'green line' in a trench on the Beaucourt side of Station Road. On arrival at Beaucourt the two met Lieutenant Herring, of another battalion, with a large number of men, presumably stragglers. Truscott said that he found twenty-five men of the Nelson Battalion and at about 1745 hours set off towards the battalion position, leaving Dyett arguing with Herring.

Lieutenant Herring, of the Drake Battalion, said in evidence that he was the brigade administrative officer whose duty it was to resupply the forward troops from dumps in the rear. At between 1630 and 1700 hours he saw Truscott and Dyett and about 200 men. He ordered an about-turn and told Dyett to follow on in rear towards the front lines. Dyett told him: 'I am not the senior officer, and I find such chaos here. I think I had better go back and report to the brigade'. Herring followed Dyett as far as his dump in Hamel, and did not see him again. Later he reported Dyett for not having gone up to the line. Cross-examined by the defence, Herring denied that there was bad blood between Dyett and himself.

Able Seaman (Acting Petty Officer) Cunes of the Drake Battalion said that he heard Herring tell Dyett, 'Give Lieutenant Truscott a hand with some of these men,' to which Dyett answered, 'I cannot take charge amongst all this chaos and disorder. I will return to brigade for orders.' Cunes gave it as his opinion that Dyett did not seem to grasp the situation when Herring told him to go with Truscott. Dyett, said Cunes, did not look afraid or as if he was 'in a funk', but 'he looked as if he wanted to get out of it'. Evidence was given that Dyett eventually appeared at the battalion billets at Englebelmer and that when he was asked by an officer of the Royal Naval Division whether he wanted to go up to his brigade at the front, Dyett said no, he would wait for the battalion.

This concluded the case for the prosecution, and the president now asked Dyett three questions: 'Do you apply to give evidence yourself as a witness?' 'No.' 'Do you intend to call any other witnesses in your defence?' 'No.' 'Have you anything to say in your defence?' 'I do not wish to say anything at all.'

Dyett had opted not to make any defence to the charge. Whether this indicated tremendous confidence that he was innocent, or a guilty knowledge that he was not, we shall never know.

It was now for the prosecution and the defence to make their closing addresses. Recognising that cross-examination had exposed doubt as to exactly what orders Dyett had been given, and argument as to the relative seniority of Dyett, Truscott and Herring, the prosecutor made the simple point that no matter what orders were received, it was Dyett's duty to rejoin his battalion, and he had not done so.

The defending officer, given little or no ammunition by his client, nevertheless did his best. He told the court that Dyett had made four separate applications for transfer to the sea service and that the accused was 'of a highly neurotic disposition and has for a long time felt himself unfit to occupy the position of an officer over troops in the field'. He said that the accused was confused and astounded by the state of chaos prevailing, and that he had gone to brigade headquarters for orders. Desertion, said the defending officer, was not proved by the evidence and while Dyett had shown a lack of initiative, he had only gone to brigade headquarters for further enlightenment.

The judge advocate now summed up. He told the court that it had to decide what orders, if any, had been given to Dyett. If the court thought that the accused's neurotic and nervous condition was such as to make it impossible for him to perform his duty – if such duty existed – it would find justification for his conduct and acquit. On the other hand, no medical evidence had been called, and the accused did not report to brigade head-quarters. The court, went on the judge advocate, must be satisfied as to intent. It must be satisfied that there was an intention to avoid some particular duty before it could find the accused guilty of desertion. Finally, he reminded the court that a mistake, or an error of judgement, did not amount to desertion.

The court then retired and considered its finding. It reassembled and announced that it found Dyett guilty of desertion. The assistant adjutant of the battalion then read Dyett's service record to the court and the presi-dent asked Dyett, 'Do you wish to address the court?' Dyett replied, 'I have nothing to say.' The court then retired to consider sentence, which was announced in open court as 'death by being shot'. The court, as it was entitled to do, nevertheless recommended mercy: 'He is very young and has no experience of active operations of this nature. The circumstances, namely growing darkness, heavy shelling and the fact that the men were retiring in considerable numbers were likely to affect seriously a youth, unless he had a strong character.'

The papers now began their journey up the chain of command, for comment and confirmation or otherwise. On 31 December the Divisional Commander, Major-General Shute, the man detested by A. P. Herbert, wrote: 'The Division did very well on the Ancre and behaved most gallantly. Added to this Sub Lieutenant Dyett is very young and inexperienced. Beyond the above, I know of no reason why the extreme penalty should not be exacted. I recommend mercy.'

Lieutenant General Claud Jacob, commanding II Corps, disagreed: 'I see no reason why sentence should not be carried out'; so did General Hubert Gough commanding Fifth Army: 'I recommend that the sentence be carried out. If a Private had behaved as he did in such circumstances, it is highly probable that he would be shot.'

The Commander-in-Chief of the BEF confirmed the sentence on 2 January 1917. Dyett was told of the decision at 1900 hours on 4 January, and was shot by firing squad at 0730 hours on 5 January 1917. Lieutenant H. J. Davidson of the Royal Army Medical Corps certified that death was instantaneous.

There can be no doubt that the composition of the court, and the presence of a judge advocate and a legally qualified defending officer, made the trial as fair as it was possible to be. There can also be no doubt that Dyett was young, inexperienced, inadequate, nervous, fearful and quite unsuited to life in an infantry battalion in war. The selection system had got it wrong, and by the Second War he would never have been commissioned. There can also be little doubt, regardless of General Gough's comments, that had Dyett been a private soldier he probably would not have been shot. The fact remains, however, that, whether he should have been one or not, Dyett was an officer. He had been entrusted with the lives of the King's soldiers and it was incumbent upon him to set an example. He did not want to be on the Western Front, but then neither did several million others, who did not run away. Dyett had to be shot: to excuse an officer would have made it impossible ever to execute an other rank for the same offence. If Dyett was facing a serious charge in a civilian court today, his personal weaknesses and character defects would be taken into account and might reduce his punishment; but the exigencies of war made it imperative that he should be executed. He had failed the test, and it was right that he paid the price. One can feel great sympathy for the man and for his family, but it would be difficult to argue that the execution should not have been carried out.

Later it was alleged – and it is still being alleged – that A. P. Herbert's novel *The Secret Battle,* in which the narrator refers to an officer shot by firing squad as 'the bravest man I ever knew', actually referred to Dyett. As 13 November 1916 was Dyett's first battle, he had not had an opportunity to show whether he was brave or not, so any contention that the novel is fact disguised as fiction must itself be fiction.

Another case that regularly surfaces in the British press is that of Lance Sergeant Stones. Stones was aged twenty-five in 1916 and was a coal miner in civilian life. He had enlisted in the 19th Battalion the Durham Light Infantry in March 1915. This was a 'bantam battalion', made up of men who failed to meet the army's minimum-height requirement of 5ft 3ins., and was part of 35 Division, an all-bantam formation. The bantam experiment was one that failed: while the original recruits, despite being short in stature, were fit and tough, far too many of the reinforcements were not only below the height requirement, but were also found to be physically incapable of infantry soldiering. Bantam formations were broken up in 1917.

On the night of 26/27 November 1916 Stones's battalion was holding a sector of the front line in the Arras sector. Stones was the 'NCO of the watch' (senior NCO of the sentry group) and with the officer of the watch was patrolling the firing line when there was a German raid. The officer was wounded and some soldiers in the line panicked and ran. Stones left the firing line and was stopped at a checkpoint some 750 yards along a communication trench behind the line. He was without his rifle. On Christmas Eve 1916 Stones was brought before a Field General Court Martial charged under Section 4 of the Army Act with 'shamefully casting away his arms', in that he had thrown away his rifle and run away from the front line. The president of the court was a lieutenant colonel, the commanding officer of an infantry battalion; and the members were three captains, including a legally qualified Courts Martial Officer. Stones was defended by a captain of his battalion who was a qualified solicitor.

During the hearing there was dispute as to whether Stones had run away and left his wounded officer. The prosecution said he had, the defence said that the officer had told Stones to raise the alarm. The men at the checkpoint said that Stones had told them that he had dropped his rifle and bayonet across the trench on his way down to give the alarm. In evidence in his own defence Stones said that he had placed his rifle across the trench to stop the Germans getting at him: his intention was to create a barrier to stop enemy progress. Evidence was also given as to Stones's state of health, and there was argument as to whether there was or was not anything wrong with his legs. Stones was found guilty, and the subsequent character reference was favourable to him. The court sentenced Stones to death, and while both battalion and brigade commanders recommended mercy, the divisional, corps and army commanders did not. The sentence was duly confirmed by the Commander-in-Chief and Stones was executed on 18 January 1917.

It is not, of course, possible at this distance to know how the court arrived at its finding; but reading the surviving record of the trial, one cannot help doubting whether the 'running away' was proved in law.[17] Protagonists of Stones today aver that, far from casting away his arms and running, Stones was actually acting in a heroic fashion because he built a barrier to the enemy before going to give the alarm. To the military eye this simply does not stand up to scrutiny. A rifle placed, or even wedged, across a trench does not constitute a barrier. Even the puniest German could jump over it, duck under it or simply brush it aside. It would be a ridiculous claim from a private, never mind from a senior NCO. A far more practical method of stopping them would have been to open fire! Stones admitted that his rifle was loaded, although the breech cover (a canvas cover over the breech and bolt to prevent clogging by mud) was on. Removal of a breech cover takes less than one second.

Again, if Stones had been a private soldier he might well have had the benefit of any doubt there may have been; but he was an NCO, and more importantly the NCO in charge of the men in that sector. He should not have acted in the way that he did, he should not have dumped his rifle, and given that discipline in that battalion was bad, and that a number of men had panicked, Stones had to be shot, as much to make the point as in punishment for his behaviour.

Of the 346 men executed during the war, no fewer than ninety-one were already under suspended sentences for serious offences, and nine were under two suspended sentences. Of these, forty were under suspended sentences of death, and one man had already been sentenced to death twice. It cannot be said that the army did not offer a man a second chance.

There will always be a proportion of men in any society who are psychologically unsuited for the business of war. In a small regular army they would be weeded out, but when a mass army has to be raised and deployed quickly, some, through no fault of their own, will slip through the net. Nevertheless, in the exigencies of all-out war these men had been enlisted; they had taken an oath to do their duty, and they had to endure like everyone else. That some were incapable of so enduring may make them victims of the war, but there can be no room for sentimentality when the very existence of the state is in danger.

Regardless of what the present campaign for pardons for all men executed may claim, the men executed by the British army in the war were fairly tried and sentenced under the law as it then stood. Far from being blunt and bloody instruments, courts martial went to great lengths to be fair, and avoided the maximum punishment whenever they could. Even then, nearly ninety per cent of the sentences of death were not carried out, and it is difficult for a soldier reading the records today to find a single case where it is obvious that an injustice has been done. That there is a memorial to those 'shot at dawn' in the commemorative arboretum near Lichfield is an insult to the millions of men who did their duty, frightened and inexperienced as most of them must have been. Those who were shot had let their comrades down. They had failed. They are not martyrs to injustice, and those who demand pardons for them (and presumably, by extension, for any soldier ever punished in any way by military law) show a complete lack of understanding of conditions and requirements in a mass army at war. It may have been hard justice, but it was justice, and this was a hard war.

NOTES

1 *Manual of Military Law, War Office, 1914*, HMSO, London, 1914.

2 Ibid., p. 302.

3 For the legal arguments see J. R. Morgan, KC, *The Great Assize*, John Murray, London, 1948.

4 This author recalls one of his Gurkhas being tried before the commanding officer for a minor traffic offence. When asked whether he wished to accept the commanding officer's award or be tried by court martial, he opted for the latter. As this had never happened before there was consternation, until questioning revealed that the young rifleman thought he was being given the option of being tried by the quartermaster, who was generally believed to be a soft touch!

5 *Manual of Military Law, War Office, 1914*, HMSO, London, 1914, p. 633.

6 This author has sat as a member, prosecuted or defended at over a hundred courts martial of British soldiers over a period of thirty-five years, ranging from murder to fraud. He has not infrequently known the guilty to be acquitted, but never an innocent man convicted.

7 Ibid., pp. 378–9.

8 Ibid., p. 379.

9 Robert Blake (ed.), *The Private Papers of Douglas Haig*, Eyre and Spottiswoode, London, 1952, p. 291.

10 Public Record Office, Kew, WO 90/7.

11 Gerard Oram, *Death Sentences Passed by Military Courts of the British Army 1914–1924*, Francis Boutle, London, 1998.

12 A charity founded in 1919 to care for psychological casualties of the war was called 'Combat Stress'.

13 Although there were attempts to divide these cases into ones that were classified as 'wounds', thus attracting a wound stripe, and those that were 'sick', which did not.

14 James Sambrook, *With the Rank and Pay of a Sapper*, Paddy Griffith Associates, Nuneaton, 1998.

15 Public Record Office, Kew, WO32/47/48, *Report of the War Office Committee into the Causation and Prevention of Shell Shock*, HMSO, London, 1922.

16 Public Record Office, Kew, ADM 156/24, Record of Trial Sub-Lt Dyett.

17 Public Record Office, Kew, PRO WO71/535, Record of Trial L/Sgt Stones.

9

A NEEDLESS SLAUGHTER

The Battle of the Somme, as the series of attacks either side of that river came to be known, is probably more deeply ingrained in British folk memory than any other episode of the Great War; indeed the first day of the Somme is about all that much of the British public remembers about the Great War. The Somme is often cited as an example of naïve bravery pitted against hopeless odds, coupled with stubborn pursuit of goals that were quickly obvious as being incapable of achievement. To many, perhaps most, the Somme epitomises all that was wrong about the conduct and leadership of the war. Sixty thousand British casualties on 1 July 1916 says it all.

The French had always favoured the offensive: a great swathe of their country was occupied by the enemy and they wanted him out. The British, traditionally wary of involvement in mass engagements with no discernible aim save the wearing-down of the enemy, would have preferred to wait until their army was ready, and then strike a swift blow that might end the war, or that would at least lead to some clear advantage for the Allies. As the junior partner in a coalition, however, the British had little choice but to accede to French strategic priorities.

Plans for Allied operations in 1916 began to be formulated at a conference at Chantilly on 6 December 1915. Representatives of the French,

British, Russian and Italian governments, with their military advisers, met to review the war situation and to take decisions as to future action. It was pointed out that with the virtual elimination of Serbia from the war, the evacuation of the Serbian government to Corfu and the retreat of the Serbian army into Macedonia, the Germans could now add ten divisions from the Serbian front to their existing twelve-division reserve on the Western Front, giving them a total of 110 divisions there. This meant that if the Germans stood on the defensive in the east, they could mount a serious offensive in the west. The conference concluded that, to forestall German attacks in the west, the Allies should mount simultaneous offensives on every front, and that until the Allies were ready to do so, those nations with reserves of manpower (Great Britain, Italy and Russia) should mount local attacks with a view to wearing down German resistance. It was also agreed that there should be no further attempts in the Dardanelles and that the Gallipoli adventure should be closed down completely. The British troops from Gallipoli should be redeployed east of the Suez Canal, to defend only, and on the Salonika front the French and the British, reinforced by the redeployed Serbian army, should likewise remain on the defensive, the aim being simply to prevent further German expansion. The western Allies should step up their assistance to Russia, to allow that country to mount an offensive when the time came, and there was discussion concerning the supply of Italian labourers for French factories to manufacture the heavy artillery that Russia badly needed.

The general staffs now withdrew to work out their ideas as to how the conclusions of the conference could be implemented. The British General Staff paper, signed by the CIGS, Murray, on 16 December 1915 and submitted to the British government, began by putting up a number of military skittles to ensure that they were knocked over. Although the results of the Gallipoli campaign removed one prominent 'easterner' – Churchill – from the government in the short term, there were still many British politicians who yearned for a cheaper way to defeat Germany than by facing her full strength on the Western Front, and who searched for soft underbellies and props that might be knocked away. The General Staff pointed out that shortage of shipping prevented any new fronts from being considered, and emphasised that should the full weight of British military strength not be deployed on the Western Front, then the garrison of the UK would have to be considerably increased to counter invasion. The defence of Britain, they said, was best done in France. Any ideas that the politicians might have about a landing in the Adriatic, cooperation with Russia in Asia Minor or a renewed attempt on Constantinople via the Dardanelles were dismissed. What was more, said the paper, if the French and British adopted nothing more than a defensive posture on the Western Front, then there was still an invasion threat because the Germans might launch their own offensive and capture the Channel ports. The General Staff's conclusion was that there should be concerted, coordinated offensives on the Eastern, Western and Italian Fronts. 'The ruling principle must be to place every possible [British] division – fully manned and equipped in all respects – in France next Spring.'[1] The paper explained that there was now (December 1915) stalemate on the Western Front, but that the enemy could be defeated there if the Allies went about it the right way. There was no point in simply standing on the defensive – what had been taken could not be regained in that way.

The British generals had now accepted that any ideas of waiting until they had a massive army, trained and equipped, and then delivering the decisive blow and dictating the future shape of Europe, must be abandoned; but the government had not entirely given up hope that that it need not yet launch the British army into a mass offensive. On 23 December 1915 the new CIGS, Sir William Robertson, wrote to the War Committee of the Cabinet asking them if they accepted that France and Flanders were the main theatre of war, and whether they would confirm that there should be offensive operations there in 1916.[2] The reply, dated 13 January 1916, gave authority for preparations for offensive action to take place, but added that the actions themselves would not necessarily be agreed to.[3] At a further conference at Chantilly on 12 March 1916 the Allied commanders-in-chief agreed their military strategy, but it was not until another somewhat testy memorandum from Robertson to the War Committee on 31 March, effectively saying, 'Come on, government, can we attack or can't we?', that the government approved British participation.[4]

After the Chantilly conference of December 1915 the British high command, as the junior partner on land, accepted that there would be offensive action in 1916; the question was, where should it be? From the perspective of General Sir Douglas Haig, commanding the BEF since December 1915, the major effort should be in Flanders. Britain was the protector of Belgium, and an attack out of the Ypres salient could sever German railway communications and allow the BEF, even if it failed to break through the German defences and restore mobility, at least to improve its position from the flat, wet and enemy-overlooked localities that they had held since late 1914. Here there was a clear British strategic interest, which diminished as the front ran south.

True, the ground was less favourable to the attacker in Flanders than it was around Arras, or even as far as the Somme, but capturing ground for its own sake was not part of the British way of making war. Even as late as January 1916 there were Anglo-French discussions about an offensive in the area of Arras, and the impression gained by many in the British GHQ was that Joffre, commanding the French armies, would favour – or at least consent to – a British effort in Flanders provided that it was coordinated with whatever the French might do to the south. A number of possible plans were under preparation, including one for a joint effort astride the Somme, but as time went on it became increasingly clear that it was a Somme offensive that Joffre wanted. In August 1915 the British had been persuaded to extend their front by taking over a fifteen-mile sector north of the Somme, previously held by the French, and with the French Tenth Army initially sandwiched between the north of the new British sector and the south of the rest of the BEF at Loos. By June 1916 the BEF had also taken over the French Tenth-Army stretch, and now joined with the French on the river Somme. The French were never entirely convinced that the British were making full use of their available manpower, and British ripostes that they had two million men in the Royal Navy who ensured freedom of the seas for all the Allies fell on deaf ears. There is some evidence that French insistence on the Somme area for the major effort of 1916 was to make sure that the British took part – certainly the British Official Historian thought so – and planning was now concentrated on that area.[5]

Reluctantly the British acceded to French demands. There was, however, a major difference in the purpose of the Somme offensive as viewed by the two commanders-in-chief. Joffre saw it as a battle of attrition – the aim was to kill Germans. Haig hoped for penetration of the German defence lines and a subsequent breakout. The British did not engage in battles of attrition: winning by one wicket was not a procedure favoured by a nation with a small volunteer army, even though it was now placing more men in the field than ever before in its history.

Originally the Somme offensive was to be over a front of sixty miles, with the French providing the major share of the troops, and preparations proceeded along those lines. Then, on 21 February 1916, the entire plan was thrown into confusion. The Germans at last launched an offensive of their own, and attacked the French at Verdun. Verdun had an almost mystical significance for France. It was there that in 843 the heirs of Charlemagne had divided up Europe between them, and although it became German in 923 it was French again by 1552, and was besieged in the Thirty Years War. In 1792 French revolutionary armies held out against German attackers until the commander, General Beaurepaire, committed suicide (or was murdered by less patriotic inhabitants). Verdun's resistance became a rallying cry of the revolutionary Danton, and in 1870 it was the last French fortress to fall to the Prussians. In 1914 it was the strongest fortified town in the world (or seemed to be), and was the key to the French frontier defences. By 1916, however, the French had accepted that forts were no longer an effective means of defence and had largely disarmed them. It would have made military sense for the French to give up Verdun in 1914 and to hold a shorter line further back; but the symbolic importance of Verdun remained, and it formed the base of a salient that jutted out into German-occupied territory.

The Chief of the German General Staff, Falkenhayn, who had taken over from the younger Moltke in November 1914, saw an attack on Verdun as a way to remove the British from the war. He saw Britain as being the bar to a German victory, not because of its little army, but because of the Royal Navy and British money. A direct attack on the British in Flanders would be difficult – the ground was as bad for an attacker moving west as it was for the British who wanted to move east – and as England could not be invaded, the solution was to grind the French army down and eliminate its capacity to make war. A resounding defeat of the French, and a collapse of French political and military will, would force British withdrawal from the continent and, so Falkenhayn reasoned, from the war. It was not Falkenhayn's intention to capture Verdun – or at least not swiftly – for to do so would negate the very purpose of the attack. The French would defend Verdun to the last man; more and more French divisions would be drawn in, and the Germans would 'bleed the French army white'. The Germans wanted the Verdun battle to last long enough for that to happen.

Falkenhayn ordered the German Fifth Army to attack 'in the direction of Verdun'. The Commander of the Fifth Army, Crown Prince William of Prussia ('Little Willy'), no doubt realising the difficulty of persuading soldiers to attack but not to succeed too quickly, modified the aim in his orders to the army and instructed it to 'capture Verdun'. Although a figure of fun to the British public, the Kaiser's son was by no means incompetent as a general, and he had the highly capable General Schmitt von Knobelsdorf as his chief of staff. The German Fifth Army had nine divisions, or 140,000 men, available, and they were to be supported by 3,406 field guns, 542 heavy guns, 152 trench mortars, 168 aircraft, fourteen balloons (for artillery-spotting) and four Zeppelin dirigibles. There was a massive deception plan to hide the forthcoming attack from French intelligence, which included hiding the assault troops in massive underground bunkers or *Stollen*. The German Fifth Army was initially to attack over a front of eight miles on the east bank of the River Meuse (there were insufficient troops to attack on both banks simultaneously), and each corps of two divisions would have 6,000 wire-cutters, 17,000 spades, 125,000 hand grenades, one million sandbags and eighty-eight tons' weight of barbed wire.

As it was, the attack was delayed by snow, and British naval intelligence discovered, almost at the last moment, that the expected German assault would in fact fall upon Verdun. Although the French army was able to begin to reinforce before the German attack began, at first all went according to Falkenhayn's hopes, and French troops were hastily removed from other parts of the front to defend the sacred soil of Verdun.

The Somme offensive would still take place – indeed it was imperative that it did, if only to take the pressure off Verdun – but there would now be fewer French troops available. The planned French contribution of forty-two divisions and 356 heavy guns on a front of twenty-eight miles was reduced at the end of April 1916 to thirty divisions and 312 heavy guns over sixteen miles. As more and more French divisions were sucked into the meat-grinder of Verdun, on 22 May there was a further reduction to twenty-two divisions over seven and a half miles.[6] The British would now assault over fourteen miles to the north of the River Somme, with eleven divisions jumping off on the first day. In the event the French could provide only twelve divisions with two more in reserve, but over a front of twelve miles, astride and to the south of the Somme (where the ground was more favourable to the attacker).

There was, of course, an immense amount of preparatory work to be done. Ammunition for the artillery was only one of the myriad problems facing the British staffs. Each field battery of eighteen-pounder guns carried with it, or in its own ammunition columns, 354 rounds per gun. This would be nothing like enough for the forthcoming attack, and it was decided that the requirement would be 1,000 rounds to be dumped beside each gun, with a further 250 rounds per gun in divisional dumps. The figures for the six-inch howitzers were 650 rounds by the gun and another 200 in the corps dump, with 500 rounds dumped beside each eight-inch howitzer. To move all this would take between seven and ten trainloads per day from 8 June onwards in the British sector alone, to say nothing of the effort required to manufacture and deliver so much ammunition. Roads in France were not good, even by the standards of the time. Most main roads had only three inches of tarmac above a chalk base and were not designed for military traffic, particularly the weight of traffic involved in supporting a major offensive. Side roads were little more than tracks. In a traffic census carried out at Fricourt, three weeks into the Somme offensive, it was found that in one twenty-four-hour period, 26,536 men on foot, seventy-six guns and gun carriages, 1,806 motor vehicles, 617 motor cycles, ten tracked vehicles, 3,756 horse-drawn vehicles, 5,404 men on horseback and 1,043 bicycles had passed along one narrow road.[7] Admittedly this was during the battle, but traffic during the preparatory period cannot have been much less. If the mass of material needed to permit an attack on the scale intended was to be delivered to the front, and resupplied throughout the offensive, then new roads had to be constructed and existing ones improved, repaired and widened, and passing places built. There was a shortage of gravel and of steamrollers, and roads already damaged by shelling could in many cases only be 'darned' – as the expression was – and have their potholes filled in. Nevertheless, the Royal Engineers and the infantry labour and pioneer battalions worked wonders. Working day and night, often under desultory shelling, they improved the roads and built new ones, many of 'corduroy' (tree trunks) or planks laid on level ground.

One of the great problems facing all armies of the time was communications. Divisions would have a wireless station to communicate with corps headquarters and with aircraft, but these were not mobile, and most communication behind the firing line would be by telephone. As a heavy howitzer shell could penetrate to a depth of five feet, telephone line was ordered to be buried to a depth of six feet. Signals staffs arranged for the burying of 7,000 miles of cable, and for the installation of 43,000 miles of cable above ground in rear areas where the risk of cutting by artillery was less.

Five days' rations were delivered to the front-line units, with another three days' held in brigade and divisional stores; gun positions had six days'-worth of rations dumped by the gun, and copious supplies of water were pre-positioned in metal tanks, barrels and used petrol tins. Medical units set up extra casualty clearing stations and medical stores; small-arms and mortar ammunition was dumped as close to the front line as possible, and the soldiers' personal effects and greatcoats were stored well behind the battle area in the charge of one man per battalion.

While the fact that a major offensive was in the offing could not be hidden entirely from the Germans, prodigious – and largely successful – efforts were made to conceal the exact place and time. Dumps of shells and ammunition so close to the firing line were dangerous, and they were skilfully camouflaged. The Royal Flying Corps and the Royal Naval Air Service flew throughout the day – and increasingly by night – to prevent German aviators from seeing or interfering with preparations. During the entire preparatory phase hardly a single German aircraft got anywhere near the area, and the only interference was from a bomb dropped by mistake from a Royal Navy aircraft.

Besides the administrative effort, the troops had to be briefed, trained, equipped and moved ready for the attack, now agreed as starting on 29 June 1916. It was a huge task, and it all had to be organised and supervised by the staff – those chinless wonders in shiny boots so beloved of those who criticise the conduct of the war. Between August 1914 and June 1916 the BEF had expanded from four infantry divisions to fifty-eight, to say nothing of all those units and formations that did not even exist in 1914. The staff had not expanded commensurately. In 1914 there were twenty-two general staff officers at GHQ of the BEF. Now there were thirty. The Engineer-in-Chief's staff at GHQ had admittedly increased ninefold, but as there was only one staff officer in 1914, nine in 1916 was hardly excessive. In 1914 the headquarters of the various administrative services had forty-five staff officers, whereas now they had 129; and a corps headquarters had grown from nineteen staff officers to twenty-four. Staff officers at division and brigade headquarters had not increased at all. It was an immense operation, carried out pretty well as planned, by officers who got little sleep for months and had in many cases been only hastily trained. It would have been an impressive achievement in peacetime; in war it was nothing short of miraculous. The staff earned their dry beds, not that they spent much time in them.

After much discussion amongst and between the various GHQ, Fourth Army and corps staffs as to exactly how the agreed Franco-British (or now perhaps, more properly, Anglo-French) attack along the Somme should take place, General Sir Douglas Haig issued an order to the Commander Fourth Army. Dated 16 June 1916, it laid down the aim of the offensive: 'The Third and Fourth Armies will undertake offensive operations on the front Maricourt to Gommecourt in conjunction with the French Sixth Army astride the Somme, *with the object of relieving the pressure on the French at Verdun and inflicting losses on the enemy...*' (author's italics).[8]

There is no mention now of a breakout. The British have, *faute de mieux*, accepted that the aim of the attack has changed: the pressure must be taken off the French, and Joffre's battle of attrition is, at least officially, accepted. It is clear, however, that Haig had not altogether abandoned hope of being able to break out of the German defence lines and restore movement to the war. The Fourth Army is instructed that in the first phase of the operation they are to seize and consolidate positions along Pozières Ridge, between Montauban and the River Ancre, with good observation to the east, and also positions between Serre and the Ancre in order to cover subsequent operations south of that river. The implication here is that once the initial positions had been taken, thus getting the British on to the high ground, subsequent operations would probably be mounted between the Ancre and Montauban.

The Commander-in-Chief explained that the second phase of the offensive would depend upon the situation. Should German resistance collapse, the cavalry would be passed through with a view to their swinging north and rolling up the German flanks in rear; alternatively, should the German resistance continue to be fierce, it might be better to shift the weight of the attack away from the Somme area altogether, to some other portion of the British front. If all this seems a little vague, in fact it makes good sense. The Commander-in-Chief was giving direction to the Fourth Army, not telling it how to do its job. No tactical plan survives the first contact with the enemy, and while the execution of the first phase – the initial attack – was spelled out in great detail, subsequent operations could only be expressed in very general terms at this stage: it all depended on the enemy.

The main British attacking force would be the Fourth Army, of sixteen divisions and nearly half a million men. The Third Army (Allenby), to the north, would assist with diversionary attacks, and the Reserve Army (Gough) would stand by to reinforce and to roll up the German flanks if breakthrough was achieved. Hunter-Weston's VIII Corps would be responsible for the area between Serre and the River Ancre, while X (Morland), III (Pulteney), XV (Horne) and XIII (Congreve) Corps would attack between the Ancre and Maricourt, just north of the Somme.

To the right (south) of the Fourth Army was the French Sixth Army, commanded by the sixty-two-year-old General Émile Fayolle.[9] This army would be astride the Somme, with XX Corps, nicknamed the 'Iron Corps' from its performance at Verdun, of four divisions, to the north of the river, and I Colonial Corps, with three colonial divisions and one territorial, and XXXV Corps of four divisions to the south of it. In reserve would be II Corps. In addition to their field artillery, XX Corps would have thirty-two batteries of heavy artillery, I Colonial Corps sixty-five heavy batteries, and XXXV Corps thirty-two. In contrast the British XIII Corps had eighteen heavy batteries.

Of the eleven British divisions of General Sir Henry Rawlinson's Fourth Army which would attack on the first day of the Somme offensive – now agreed as 30 June 1916 – three (4, 8 and 29 Divisions) were composed of regular battalions, five (18, 31, 32, 34 and 36) were New Army formations and three (7, 21 and 30) were a mix of regular, Territorial Force and New Army battalions. The Territorial Force battalions had little experience, the New Army ones virtually none and even the regulars had been brought up to strength by recruits recently out of training, and with officers and NCOs two or three ranks higher than they had been in 1914. It was a very inexperienced and undertrained army. Few of the New Army (or 'pals') battalions had seen a shot fired in anger, and when two New Army divisions – 21 and 25 – were employed in the Loos battle of September 1915 they had collapsed in disorder.[10] The men of these battalions had, of course, been in the army for at least a year, many of them since August 1914, but it is one thing to train private soldiers and quite another to furnish the officers and NCOs to lead them. If all the peripherals are cut out, it was and is possible to train a man to a standard where he can take his place in a rifle section in a few weeks. In the Great War he needed to be able to march, to shoot and to perform tactical manoeuvres directed by his officers and NCOs. To produce those officers and NCOs takes far longer. They cannot be made; they must be grown, and growing takes time. With only two or three officers and perhaps half a dozen NCOs with any experience in a battalion of 1,000 men, only the simplest of tactics could be employed – the battalions were just too inexperienced for anything more complex. The Territorial Force was little better, and even the regulars were not the men of Mons and Le Cateau, the Marne and the Aisne, or even of First Ypres. While pre-war soldiers – regular and Territorial Force – were expected to be able to fire fifteen aimed shots a minute when rapid fire was ordered, and some could manage twenty, a rapid-fire shooting competition in the BEF prior to the Somme produced a winner who could fire only twelve.

General Haig and his army, corps and divisional commanders knew

all this only too well, but the lack of experience and consequent inflexi-
bility of the troops could be compensated for. If the German defences
were subjected to sustained and intense artillery bombardment prior to
the attack, then they would be so disorganised and their defensive positions so damaged that the British infantry would be able to close with them
before any serious resistance could be mounted. The engineers and the
gunners did their sums, and calculated that four days of bombardment all
along the front of the projected attack would collapse German dugouts,
knock out machine-gun positions and blast holes in the German wire.
Some naïve junior officers told their men that when the whistles blew it
would be little more than a stroll in the park. General Haig was concerned
when told by the Fourth Army that a four-day bombardment was needed.
He pointed out that ammunition was short and that guns firing for that
length of time could become so worn that their ability to provide fire
support thereafter would be jeopardised. Finally, however, after the calcu-
lations had been revised, he agreed to five, not four, days, and the staff got
to work to provide the necessary guns and ammunition. It was this decision
to concentrate all available artillery and ammunition in the Somme area
that made it less likely that Haig's earlier idea of a move to another part
of the British front could actually be realised.

For the artillery bombardment the Field Artillery would provide 808
eighteen-pounders and 202 4.5-inch howitzers. There would be a total of
182 heavy guns of various types and 245 heavy howitzers. In addition there
were available twenty-eight heavy and 288 medium trench mortars. The
French would lend sixteen 220-mm howitzers, twenty-four 120-mm guns
and sixty 75-mm field guns converted to fire gas shells. All along the British
front of attack there would be one field gun for every twenty-one yards
and one heavy gun per fifty-seven yards. On the French front it was one
heavy for every thirty-six yards. The bombardment plan was carefully laid
down and agreed between Headquarters Fourth Army and GHQ BEF.
Tasks were allocated to the various artillery units and included cutting
gaps in the German wire, destruction of German defence works and
machine-gun posts, shelling of German ammunition and stores dumps,
bombardment of crossroads and communications behind the German
lines, counter-battery work and deception.

The German lines were protected by belts of barbed wire, up to forty feet deep in places, in which gaps had to be blown to enable the attacking infantry to close with the enemy. This task was to be achieved by the Field Artillery eighteen-pounders. The heavy guns and howitzers would take on redoubts and machine-gun nests, stores and communications and billets, and would also engage in counter-battery work (the engagement of German artillery positions). Each day, at a different time, there would be one particularly intense period of firing, lasting eighty minutes. This was intended to lull the Germans into thinking that eighty minutes was the standard time for a 'hate', during which they would evacuate their forward positions and take cover in underground shelters, emerging when the eighty minutes was up. On the last day, just before zero hour, the maximum-intensity bombardment would begin as usual but would cease after sixty-five minutes, when the infantry would advance and, it was hoped, take the German forward positions before they could be reoccupied by the defenders.

Included in the bombardment programme was registration, the process of establishing the exact range and elevation required to be set on a particular gun to hit a particular target. As well as keeping German aircraft away, the Royal Flying Corps and the Royal Naval Air Service would over fly German-held territory, spot for the Allied artillery and bring back air photographs to indicate how the artillery were doing. There would be a lull in the firing to avoid hitting our own aircraft. British aircraft would also take on German observation balloons.

The bombardment began at 0600 hours on 24 June. As air photographs came in, targeting was adjusted to ensure that all targets laid down were shelled, and to include any new ones found by aircraft. As the 24th was cloudy and aircraft could not observe all the results of counter-battery work, and as the 27th and 28th were cloudy and misty, Haig and Joffre agreed on a forty-eight-hour postponement. Zero hour would now be at 0730 hours on 1 July, and the bombardment would now last seven days rather than five. First light in France in July is at around 0345 hours GMT, or 0545 hours British Double Summer Time (or French Summer Time), to which the Allies were working. Some commanders would have preferred to make their assault then, but the artillery commanders advised that daylight was needed for the artillery observation officers to make their final adjustments, and when Foch, commanding the French Northern Group of Armies, insisted on a daylight attack, this was accepted. The French XX Corps, on the British right and north of the Somme, would attack at the same time as the British; but for the French troops south of the river, zero hour would be two hours later – 0930 hours – in order to lull the Germans into thinking that there was no offensive planned south of the river and thus catch them unawares.

Altogether, from 0600 hours 24 June until 0600 hours on 1 July, the British artillery fired a total of 1,508,652 shells, seventy-one for every yard of front. Guns fired in a roster to give time for crews to be relieved and barrels to cool, and artillery observation officers were changed over every two hours, day and night. While the artillery thundered, the infantry was being brought into position within marching distance of the jump-off line and final briefings were taking place.

In order to find out what effect the British bombardment was having on the German lines, trench raids were mounted nightly, with the bombardment being lifted from that portion of the opposing trench to be raided. Reports were mixed. In some areas the raiders reported the wire to be blown away, in others to be 'passable', in yet others to have gaps in it. In some cases reports were conflicting, but these reports, coupled with the evidence of air photographs, seemed to indicate that the wire was being cut. Haig was sceptical of the value of reports coming in from VIII Corps, north of the Ancre. He said that the staff of that corps had little experience of the Western Front (true – they had been in Gallipoli) and he had doubts as to whether their trench raids and patrols were reporting accurately. Nevertheless, fires were seen to be raging in the areas of German stores dumps and all in all the signs were good.

At British-soldier level, the plan for the first phase – the assault on the German forward defences – was straightforward. Prior to the assault, the troops would cross no man's land and get as close as they could to the trenches they were to attack, while the British artillery bombardment gave them cover and pounded the German firing line to prevent it being manned. There was discussion as to how close the safety distance should be: that is, how close to their own artillery fire could the men be without being themselves in danger. Some thought forty yards would be safe, but the general consensus was 100 yards, and that was the order given. The safest way to approach the bombardment across no man's land would be to dig communication trenches out towards the German lines, but there were objections that this would tell the Germans exactly where an attack was coming. This drawback could, of course, be obviated by digging out all along the front, and by making preparations for feint attacks elsewhere. Eventually it was left up to corps commanders to decide whether or not they would dig out across the intervening space. Some did, others did not.

However the troops got into position, as near as they could to their objective, they would lie down until the signal to advance was given. In general there would be four assault waves. A battalion would have two companies forward in the first wave, and two behind in the second. The third and fourth waves would be provided by another battalion. At company level there would be two platoons up and two back. The purpose was to ensure that the attack had depth: in other words, should a battalion, company or platoon – or even an individual – be held up for whatever reason (which included being killed), there would be troops following on to press home the attack. Each wave was to follow the one in front at a distance of 100 yards.

At zero hour the artillery bombardment would have to lift, and would switch to the next line of German trenches. The infantry should then only have to cross 100 yards of open ground before reaching a German trench that had been subjected to seven days of constant bombardment. Dugouts and bunkers would have collapsed, defenders would be disorientated and demoralised and the first waves would be able to establish themselves in the German firing line before going on to take the next lines. The casualties would be heavy. Whatever some of the inexperienced optimists may have said, senior officers knew that fighting would be hard until the British got through the forward positions, and they were well aware that the Germans had had eighteen months in which to strengthen and fortify their lines.

During the night of 30 June the troops who were to carry out the assault moved into the forward British trenches. Because of the two-day postponement some had been waiting close up behind their own lines in temporary bivouacs for up to three days, and rain during the last night did

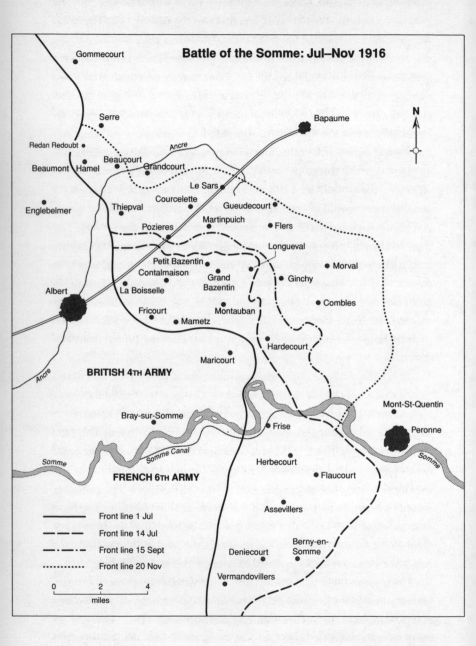

Battle of the Somme: Jul–Nov 1916

N

Gommecourt

Serre

Bapaume

Redan Redoubt

Ancre

Beaucourt

Grandcourt

Beaumont Hamel

Le Sars

Englebelmer

Thiepval

Courcelette

Gueudecourt

Pozieres

Martinpuich

Flers

Longueval

Petit Bazentin

Contalmaison

Grand Bazentin

Ginchy

Morval

Albert

La Boisselle

Combles

Fricourt

Montauban

Mametz

Hardecourt

Maricourt

BRITISH 4TH ARMY

Ancre

Mont-St-Quentin

Bray-sur-Somme

Frise

Peronne

Somme Canal

Somme

Herbecourt

Somme

FRENCH 6TH ARMY

Flaucourt

Assevillers

Berny-en-Somme

Deniecourt

Vermandovillers

	Front line 1 Jul
	Front line 14 Jul
	Front line 15 Sept
	Front line 20 Nov

0   2   4
miles

not help. Despite this, all received a hot meal before going into the firing line, and in most battalions each man was issued with the British army's great morale-booster – a tablespoonful of rum.

From 0630 hours onwards on 1 July the British troops filed out of their trenches, moved through the gaps in their own wire and out into no man's land to their allotted positions, where they lay down. There was no interference with this. The German trenches were still being bombarded and there was no one on the German fire-step.

Shortly before 0730 hours the mines were blown, and at zero hour precisely the whistles blew and the soldiers stood up and began to move forward. The artillery now switched off the German firing line and began to bombard the support line.

The extreme left of the British attack was the responsibility of 31 Division (Major-General Wanless O'Gowan), of three brigades made up entirely of 'pals' battalions. This division was to attack and capture the village of Serre, on a ridge overlooking the British line, and then wheel to their left and form a flank guard to prevent a German counter-attack coming in behind the advancing British. To their north Allenby's Third Army mounted a two-division diversionary attack against the village of Gommecourt, in order to prevent German reserves from interfering with the main attack.

The division attacked with 94 Brigade on the left and 93 Brigade on the right, with 92 Brigade in reserve. The troops lay on the ground 100 yards forward of their own trenches until the whistles blew, when they got up and advanced up a gentle incline towards the German lines along the ridge, 150 yards to their front. They moved through a smokescreen, which was quickly blown away by the breeze. The British artillery had to lift, and once it did so the Germans, far less mauled than had been thought or hoped, began to man their trenches. Machine guns were brought up from underground bunkers on wooden sleds, and before the British had advanced more than fifty yards or so, the killing began. It was sudden and horrific. Men who got as far as the German wire found that it was uncut, and moved along it to find a gap. Since the wire was so laid as to channel attackers into killing areas, men crowding together in an attempt to get through were easy targets for the German machine guns and trench mortars, now free from the attentions of the British artillery. There were two regiments (six battalions in German terms) defending Serre, and at least ten machine guns that had escaped the bombardment. The first attacking wave was all but wiped out, while the second, third and fourth waves hardly got off the ground.

By 1200 hours the attack had petered out. To the right of 31 Division some Territorials of the Royal Warwicks, in 4 Division, did get into the village, but they could not be supported and were soon ejected. All the British could do now was to try and retrieve their wounded from no man's land, while the Germans did the same on their ridge. There was mutual tolerance until someone on the British side shot a German stretcher-bearer, and then the gloves were off. By nightfall the British were back in their front-line trenches and nothing had been achieved.

The left-hand brigade of the 31 Division attack, 94 Brigade, had two battalions, 12th Battalion the York and Lancaster Regiment (Sheffield City Pals) and 11th Battalion the East Lancashire Regiment (Accrington Pals), in the first wave. The 12th York and Lancs had seven officers and 241 other ranks killed on that morning, and the 11th East Lancs five officers and 113 men. On the right the leading battalions of 93 Brigade, 15th and 16th Battalions the West Yorkshire Regiment (Leeds Pals and 1st Bradford Pals), had, respectively, fourteen officers and 156 men and nine officers and 140 men killed. Battalions in the succeeding waves suffered less, but a butcher's bill of seven officers and ninety-three men in the 18th West Yorks (2nd Bradford Pals) and a combined total of nine officers and 164 men killed in the 13th and 14th York and Lancs (1st and 2nd Barnsley Pals), and sixty-seven men killed in the 18th Battalion the Durham Light Infantry, was bad enough. The reserve, 92 Brigade, which consisted entirely of 'pals' battalions recruited from Hull and was never even able to leave the forward trenches, got off with five other ranks killed all told. Figures like these seem to bear out the notion of the Somme being a callous slaughter, with inexperienced troops thrown against impregnable obstacles.

On the extreme right of the British attack, in the area of Maricourt, was another 'pals' division, the 30th, commanded by Major-General Shea. The division was to capture the eastern half of the village of Montauban and the German trenches running to the Maricourt road, at the end of which was a strongpoint, known to the British as the Dublin Redoubt. The redoubt itself was to be taken by the French. The German forward positions were 1,000 yards from the British front lines, and although here saps had been dug out into no man's land, there was still an advance of 700 yards or so across open ground. On the division's right was 89 Brigade whose objective was the line of trenches between Montauban and the Dublin Redoubt. The brigade consisted of the 17th, 19th and 20th Battalions the King's (Liverpool) Regiment, all 'pals' battalions, and a Territorial Force battalion, 2nd Bedfords. At 0730 hours on 1 July 1916 the men from Liverpool and Bedford got up and advanced towards the German lines. The attack against strongly held positions was a complete success. At the end of the day 89 Brigade had captured all their objectives. In 17th King's two men were killed, in 19th King's thirteen men, in 20th King's one officer and twenty-two men, and in the 2nd Bedfords six men. Forty-five deaths in 89 Brigade at Maricourt; 539 in 94 Brigade at Serre.

In between the results were mixed. North of the River Ancre there was hardly any advance at all, and the Newfoundland Regiment south of Auchonvillers had 200 men killed in three-quarters of an hour to no result. The British did have some good fortune when the Germans blew up their own redoubt on the northern end of Redan Ridge by mistake, killing the crew of machine-gunners. South of the Ancre things were slightly better. The 36th (Ulster) Division initially made amazing progress.

The old adage that nothing in Ireland is ever simple is well illustrated by the example of 36 Division. Prior to the outbreak of war there had been four armed and uniformed bodies in Ireland. Two, the British army garrison and the Royal Irish Constabulary, were legal and under the control of the British government. The two others, the Ulster Volunteer Force and the Irish Volunteers, were illegal but the government could do little about them.

By late 1914 the Irish Home Rule Bill had completed its tortuous progress through Parliament in England, and awaited only the Royal Assent to become law. It offered the Irish rather less devolution than Scotland has now, but it aroused powerful emotions. The Ulster Protestants, who feared domination by a largely Roman Catholic south, declared their determination to 'use all means' to resist the bill. Urged on by Sir Edward Carson, a Unionist MP, they raised the Ulster Volunteers who were uniformed, commanded by ex-British army officers and equipped with a mixture of British and German arms (Germany being always willing to stir up trouble for the British). In the south of Ireland, as a response, the Irish Volunteers were formed under the aegis of John Redmond, MP, leader of the Irish Nationalist Party at Westminster. They vowed to impose Home Rule, also by force if need be, and were uniformed, commanded by rather fewer ex-British army officers, and likewise armed by the Germans. On the outbreak of war, Carson and Redmond agreed that the German threat was rather more serious than their own differences, and agreed to put the question of Home Rule aside until the war was over. The Ulster Volunteers were absorbed into the British army as the 36th (Ulster) Division, while the Redmondites became the 16th (Irish) Division. Both divisions were given British army officers to command them. The 36th got Major-General Oliver Nugent, a regular officer who until August 1914 had been on half pay, whiling away the idle hours as commander of the Cavan branch of the Ulster Volunteers, and to the 16th went Major-General William Hickie, also a regular officer and a southern Irish Catholic.[11]

On 1 July 1916 36 Division was to push half a brigade (two battalions) up the north bank of the Ancre, while the rest were to assault and capture the Schwaben Redoubt, a strongpoint to the south of and overlooking the River Ancre; the redoubt supported and was supported by the German-held village of Thiepval. The division would attack from a jump-off line at the edge of Thiepval Wood, and had about 250 yards to go before reaching the first German defence line. Being Irish, the units of 36 Division blew bugles rather than whistles, and at 0730 hours they bounded from their jump-off line up the slope towards the German lines. They bounded because Nugent considered that speed was of the essence. If his men could get onto the Schwaben Redoubt before the Germans surfaced from their underground bunkers, then the day would be his. At first all went as planned. On the right the men of the 11th Royal Irish Rifles and the 9th and 10th Battalions Royal Inniskilling Fusiliers found the German wire cut and reached the redoubt. Speed was a factor, but the Ulster Division was also helped by the fact that most of the German machine guns that would have targeted them were busy firing across in the direction of Thiepval

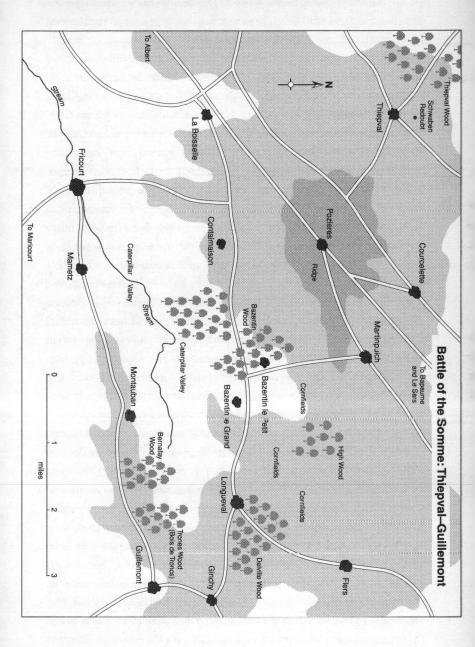

Battle of the Somme: Thiepval—Guillemont

village, which was being assaulted by 32 Division; a further advantage was provided by a farm road (now gone) that ran diagonally across the German positions and offered some dead ground for the attackers.

The first of July was the anniversary, in the old-style calendar, of the Battle of the Boyne in 1690. Not a battle which is instantly recalled by most British students of military history, it has enormous significance in Ulster, for it was on the Boyne river that the army of William of Orange (later William III, co-ruler with his wife Mary) defeated the forces of the Catholic James II and sealed the success of the 'Glorious Revolution', one of the seedier political machinations in the annals of the British constitution. Many of the Ulstermen of 36 Division on 1 July wore the brightly coloured sashes of the Orange Order, an organisation originally founded to press for religious toleration, but by now an exclusively Protestant body much opposed to Catholicism. The Orangemen caused some consternation among their English comrades when they went up the hill shouting, 'No surrender!' – this was an attack, and surrender had not been contemplated – until it was explained that this was a traditional Ulster cry indicating resistance to the forces of popery.[12] It was understandable but unfortunate that the officers in command of the leading troops did not stop at their designated objective – the Schwaben Redoubt – but, seeing an opportunity, plunged on into German territory. By late morning they had penetrated one and a half miles, and had the troops on either side been able to make similar progress, this would have been a great day for Ulster. Sadly, it all now began to go wrong. On the Ulstermen's right 32 Division could make no progress against Thiepval village, and on the left 29 Division were unable to progress much beyond their own jump-off line. The men of the 36th found themselves occupying a long thin salient with Germans to right and left and ahead of them. In the eagerness to press on, the Schwaben Redoubt had not been properly cleared of Germans, and now the Ulstermen began to be attacked in flank and in rear. Carrying parties with extra ammunition, grenades, wire and digging implements could not get forward, and the lead battalions had no choice but to start retracing their steps. By last light what remained of 36 Division was back in Thiepval Wood. One officer and 133 men of the 11th Royal Irish Rifles were dead, and between them the 9th and 10th Inniskillings lost thirteen officers and 333 other ranks killed. Churchill's 'dreary steeples of Fermanagh and Tyrone' had paid a high price.

Five and a half miles south-east of the Schwaben Redoubt was the village of Montauban. On 1 July 1916 the left half of Montauban and the German trench systems to the west of the village were the objectives of 18 Division, a New Army division commanded by Major-General 'Ivor' Maxse, who would cooperate with 30 Division to the right. Maxse's Division did dig out into no man's land, mainly by means of Russian saps, and by zero hour the attacking infantry were well forward of their own trenches, but still with around 500 yards to cover before closing on the German defences.[13] By 1600 hours all objectives had been taken, despite German machine guns and a stout defence. Nine British battalions took part in the fighting, and those on the right of the attack, heading for the village, had severe casualties. The 10th Essex had one officer and 208 men killed, the 7th Queen's six officers and 153 men, the 8th East Surreys five officers and 133 men, and the 8th Norfolks three officers and 105 men. Of the other five battalions involved, the dead varied from eighty-seven other ranks in the 7th Bedfords to one officer and twenty-eight men in the 7th Royal West Kents.

The attack of 18 Division was a complete success, and the size of the butcher's bill depended upon whether or not a particular battalion found itself in a killing zone where the German machine guns and trench mortars had not been eliminated. The right-hand company of 18 Division was B Company, 8th Battalion the East Surrey Regiment, and was commanded by Captain Wilfred Percy Nevill, known as 'Billy'. Nevill had been captain of cricket at his public school, and then went up to Cambridge where he distinguished himself at cricket, hockey and rugby. Contrary to received opinion he was not a professional footballer, and had probably never played soccer in his life. Nevill was six feet tall and regarded as a battalion joker, largely because his dentures fitted loosely and he was a master of funny faces.

Nevill did not approve of alcohol, and refused to issue the men of his company with a rum ration before the attack on 1 July. Instead he gave each platoon a football, painted with 'East Surreys versus Barbarians, kick-off 1 July 1916'. This was to take the men's minds off what was to come, and a prize was offered for the first platoon to get its football into the German lines. The men would probably have preferred the rum. Nevill himself kicked off at zero hour; but the prize was never won, because Nevill was killed a few hundred yards beyond the jump-off line. Much was made of the incident in the English newspapers, where it was seen as an outstanding example of British pluck. The German newspapers too picked it up, interpreting it an outstanding example of British stupidity.

On the British right the French XX Corps took all its objectives. The commander of the left-hand French battalion even left the jump-off line arm in arm with the commanding officer of the right-hand British battalion. Both survived and they shook hands in the German trenches. South of the Somme too the French achieved all their goals. As dusk fell on 1 July, to the southern end of the combined offensive most objectives, British and French, had been attained.

Overall, however, it had been an appalling day for the BEF. Commanders realised that there would be casualties, but none had thought that there would be so many, and none had thought that German resistance would amount to very much after seven days of constant artillery bombardment. That none of the objectives north of the river Ancre had been taken, and few between the Ancre and the Albert–Bapaume road, came as a shock.

There were around 60,000 British casualties on the first day of the Somme offensive, and nearly 20,000 of these were dead. In Bradford 361 black telegrams brought the news of those who were killed on 1 July or who died of wounds in the two days afterwards; for Leeds the figure was 493, for Barnsley 213, for Belfast 839. It is no wonder that the first day of the Somme is engraved in the national memory. In France, however, commanders were trying to piece together what had happened and asking why. Why had the extreme left-hand battalion suffered 248 deaths and the extreme right-hand battalion only two? Why had the New Army 31 Division failed to take Serre, a few hundred yards away, whereas the New Army 18 Division had taken Montauban West, 800 yards away? Why had the French seized all their objectives while the British had only managed to capture a few?

The reasons for 1 July 1916 being as it was are many. Firstly, despite the best efforts of the gunners the bombardment did not achieve what was hoped. It did cause great destruction to the German positions, but it did not reach all the underground bunkers and dugouts, some up to forty feet deep, that the Germans had been constructing since late 1914. Not only were the infantry new to the job, but so were the artillerymen. Some of the heavy guns were obsolete and the barrels worn from use in the South African War. There was too much reliance on 4.7-inch howitzers manufactured in 1895, and on the six-inch version dating from 1896. The six-inch guns dating from 1898 fired shells weighing 100 pounds each to a range of 17,700 yards, but there were not enough of them. Many of the shells failed to explode or, in the case of some of the heavies, exploded prematurely, killing or injuring the gunners. This was nobody's fault – British industry simply could not go from supplying a small regular army fighting colonial campaigns to equipping a mass army for intensive war in Europe in less than two years, and the hasty recruitment of workers to manufacture shells led to failures in filling the shells and errors in the tolerances allowed. There was almost a scandal over ammunition made in America as a result of contracts that had been let by the British government after it became apparent that British industry could not yet cope. Anecdotal evidence claimed that some American shells had been filled with sand, and there were stories of machine-gunners going through their ammunition stocks and throwing away bullets made in the USA. Conspiracy theorists saw this as an anti-British plot or the work of Irish sympathisers, although the real reason is almost certainly that American manufacturers were as raw to the business as were the British. Whatever the truth, the claims about dud US ammunition were hushed up: America was a vital source of supply for the Allies and it would have been foolhardy to upset her. By the battles of Arras the following year workforces in both England and America were far more experienced, and these problems did not recur.

Nobody, on either side, had ever attacked after such a long and sustained bombardment. Everyone thought it would work, and that it did not is one of the risks inherent in trying something for the first time.

To the south, in the area of Fricourt, Mametz and Montauban, the British positions overlooked those of the Germans, which was not the case anywhere else. This meant that artillery observation officers could see the fall of shot and adjust accordingly, rather than having to wait for air photographs up to twenty-four hours later. In many places the artillery did not cut the German wire; but in many places it did, as evidenced by the patrol reports and trench raids. However, the British underestimated the German ability to repair breaches in the wire at night when, although still being shelled, they were subjected to a less intense, and unobserved, bombardment.

The critical time for the infantry was between the British artillery's lifting from the German front line and the British infantry's closing on that objective. Had more use been made of Russian saps and digging out across no man's land, the attacking infantry might have been able to start their attack much closer to the German lines than they actually did. Perhaps this advantage was not considered worth the effort and the loss of surprise involved. A distance of 100 yards between waves of assaulting infantry was probably too short, because when the first wave was held up the second wave was already in no man's land and vulnerable to German fire. The move of the infantry and the artillery had to be carried out in accordance with a set timetable – fire-control methods of 1916 were not yet sophisticated enough to have 'on call' fire plans – and the timings allowed little flexibility.

The French, to the south of the Somme, had to attack over ground which offered more cover, in the shape of small woods and folds in the ground; they were helped by a river mist, and they had a lot more artillery. It was this superiority in artillery that allowed the French to assist the bombardment of the extreme right end of the British sector and thus allow the 17th King's to take its objectives with only two men killed. There was more to it than just ground and artillery, however. The French army consisted of men who had at least the rudiments of military training when they were mobilised in 1914. By 1916 the French army, unlike the British, had considerable experience of major offensive operations. When the French jumped off on 1 July they used fire and movement to cover open ground: that is, one group would fire on the German trenches while another group would move forward, before stopping and providing covering fire themselves. In this way French infantry leapfrogged forward and there was always at least some fire coming down on the enemy. The British knew about fire and movement perfectly well. It had been drilled into the regular army and used to great effect in 1914. But this was not the regular army; it was an inexperienced force fighting its first major battle, and it was simply not capable of using fire and movement. If it had tried to do so, control would have been lost and more casualties inflicted on its own men than on the enemy. Afterwards it was suggested that the British soldiers were unable to think for themselves, unlike the French infantry who disobeyed orders when it suited them and used their initiative. The British as a race are no less innovative than the French, but the use of initiative requires experience on which to base it, and the British army of 1916 – at all levels – lacked that experience. Fire and movement would become a standard tactic of the British infantry again, but not yet.

Critics of the Somme make much of what they see as insistence on parade-ground precision, with men being ordered to walk and keep in line. This had nothing to do with ceremonial parades, but was a perfectly sensible rule to ensure that control was not lost, that men were not shot by their own side, and that they all arrived on the objective together and in a fit state to engage the enemy. Scorn is also poured on the need for the attacking infantry to carry packs weighing sixty pounds. This is one of the enduring myths of the First World War, and derives from an imperfect reading of Field Service Regulations. In fact, it was everything that the man carried and wore that weighed sixty pounds: the uniform he stood up in, the boots on his feet, his weapon and its ammunition. In the attack large packs were left behind, and the small pack contained only the essentials for the operation. That said, each man still had to carry his entrenching tool, extra rations, two gas helmets, wire-cutters, 220 rounds of ammunition, two grenades and two sandbags, while ten picks and fifty shovels were taken by each leading company.[14] This was no light burden, and the follow-up troops, coming immediately after those who carried out the actual assault, carried a great deal more. It is one thing to capture ground, quite another to hold it. Once into a German position the objective had to be consolidated and held against the inevitable counter-attack. This meant that the existing defence works had to be turned round to face the other way, wire obstacles had to be constructed and communications had to be established. Ammunition, grenades and digging implements had to be there, to say nothing of signals cable, water and food, and there was no other way of making all this immediately available to the infantry than by having them carry it with them.

The British had been reluctant to accept an offensive on the Somme, rather than in Flanders, and would have been even more reluctant if they had known that events would force them to shoulder the greater share of the burden. For sound strategic reasons, however, there had to be an Allied offensive somewhere on the Western Front in 1916; and once the Germans began throwing their armies at Verdun, the Somme had to be persisted with at least until they gave up.

Planning was exact and the staff work preparatory to 1 July was superb. The troops were brought into position, the bombardment went as planned, even if the results were not as hoped, and it is difficult to see what else could have been done to minimise casualties. The reason that 1 July 1916 saw more British deaths than any other day in British military history is a combination of there never before or since having been a British offensive of such ferocity, against the main enemy in the main theatre of war, and the lack of experience of the troops and their leaders at battalion level. While to the British 1 July 1916 is the first day of the Somme, it was also the 121st day of the Battle of Verdun, and by then the French had already taken half a million casualties. Playing in the major league has its price: the British would learn from 1 July, and it was, after all, only the first day.

NOTES
1 Paper by the General Staff on the Future Conduct of the War, 16 December 1915 (amended 17 December), quoted in J. E. Edmonds, *Official History, Military Operations France and Belgium 1915*, Appendix 2, HMSO, London, 1932.

2 Edmonds, *Military Operations France and Belgium 1916*, Vol. I, HMSO, London, 1932, p. 10.

3 Ibid., p. 12.

4 Ibid., p. 13.

5 Ibid., p. 30.

6 Jean-Baptiste Duroselle, *La Grande Guerre des Français 1914–18*, Perrin, Paris, 1994.

7 Edmonds, *Military Operations France and Belgium 1916*, Vol. I, HMSO, London, 1932, p. 283.

8 Edmonds, *Military Operations France and Belgium 1916*, Appendix 13, HMSO, London, 1932.

9 The French army had only two general ranks: *général de brigade* and *général de division*. Thereafter rank was equivalent to the appointment held. Thus Fayolle, commanding the Sixth Army, was a *général de division*, with the same rank as, but senior to, his corps and

divisional commanders; he in turn was junior to Foch, also a *général de division* but senior by his appointment as Commander of the Northern Group of Armies. The rank of marshal was by now usually honorary, although in Napoleon I's time corps commanders were often marshals.

10 Although 15 (Scottish) Division, also a New Army formation, had done well.

11 By joining the UVF Nugent was breaking the law: despite being on half pay he was still a serving officer. His view was that had he not accepted the post, a local Cavan hothead would have. Hickie became a senator (member of the upper house of Parliament) in the Irish Free State after the war.

12 Most German soldiers were Protestants, but never mind...

13 A Russian sap was a tunnel dug just below the surface (so shoring up was not needed) and through which the troops could break out when the moment came.

14 Edmonds, *Military Operations France and Belgium 1916*, Vol. I, HMSO, London, 1932, p. 313.

10

MORE NEEDLESS SLAUGHTER

During the evening and night of 1 July 1916 reports were coming in to the headquarters of the Fourth Army and information was being collated and passed on to GHQ. At first it was thought that around 8,000 British soldiers had been killed on the first day of the Somme, but as many of the missing were found to be dead, that total mounted. North of the Albert–Bapaume road very little had been achieved. On the credit side, however, on over half of the attacking front – the whole of the French sector and from Fricourt to Maricourt for the British – there had been considerable success. In the air the Allies had established complete air superiority; 110 British aircraft had been in action, and forty bombers each carrying two 112-pound bombs had attacked Bapaume and numerous German-held villages, as well as railway trains and stores dumps. The German infantry had not escaped lightly: the 109th Bavarian Reserve Regiment, with a strength of around 2,500 all ranks, suffered 2,147 casualties (around 700 of them killed) where they faced the Anglo-French junction point at Maricourt, and many of the Germans along the front of the attack had received no rations for several days owing to the attentions of the Allied artillery.

The question now was what to do next. The obvious move was to reinforce success and switch all resources down to the Fricourt–Mametz–Maricourt sector and, in conjunction with the French, push on next day.

That was what Generals Haig, Rawlinson and Fayolle would have liked to do, but it simply could not be achieved. There was complete gridlock behind the Allied junction point. Roads were incapable of supporting the necessary move of artillery and resupply columns; fresh divisions could not be moved up in time. Traffic control on this scale was still a new art for the British. At 2000 hours on the night of 1 July General Rawlinson ordered the attack to be continued all along the front the next day, and while he was now beginning to regard the offensive as being in the nature of a siege operation, both he and Haig still had their eyes on the south of the British front. Three fresh divisions (17, 19 and 12) were fed in during the night, and while there were some German counter-attacks, nearly all beaten off by artillery firing shrapnel before they could close on the British-held positions, it was a relatively quiet night. Next day only six British divisions did anything very much, and these were mainly tidying-up operations in which Fricourt and Mametz were cleared of Germans and the village of La Boisselle was captured. A new chapter of beastliness was opened when the British artillery carried out its first test of incendiary shells, containing thermite, in an attempt to set Bernafray Wood, east of Montauban, on fire. Five hundred shells failed to ignite the wood, but roasted a large number of German soldiers.

There was another opportunity that might have led to a real strategic gain had it been seized. On the morning of 2 July the French were only four miles from Péronne. General Fayolle wrote in his diary: 'All the front positions of the Boche have been taken with great élan, and 4,500 prisoners captured. Saw Joffre. He is radiant.'[1] By 3 July the French had taken Frise, Herbécourt and Assevillers and were poised on the plain of Flaucourt. They had achieved complete surprise south of the Somme and Falkenhayn ordered the evacuation of the German second line. For two days there was but a very thin crust of defenders covering the southern approaches to Péronne, and Fayolle wanted to smash through it. Had he been able to do so, the German forces to the north of the Somme would have had their left flank exposed, and would have had little choice but to withdraw. Joffre and Foch considered the position, and demurred. It was too risky an operation to undertake without massive artillery support, and the artillery would take days to move into position. By noon on 4 July

German reserves brought down from the Arras front had filled the gap and the opportunity was lost.[2]

On 3 July came the first major disagreement between the British and the French. According to the French accounts Joffre and Foch arrived at the British GHQ, demanding that the British alter their plans for further assault to conform with those of the French. Joffre was furious that whereas the French axis was from west to east, towards Péronne, an important centre of road and rail communication for the Germans, the British intended to attack to the north-east towards Bapaume, also an important junction. Joffre said that if this went ahead, it would be impossible for the Allies to attack 'shoulder to shoulder'.[3] The British account says the opposite, and claims that Haig wanted to reinforce success in the area of Montauban, whereas the French wanted him to renew the failed attack on the Thiepval–Pozières sector.[4] Whatever the truth of these conflicting accounts, Haig determined to make his next major effort in the Mametz–Montauban sector; but from now on, while the Allies would cooperate where they could, the offensive would often be two separate battles.

There were disagreements within the French ranks too. General Fayolle considered that his superior, Foch, had no conception of a war of manoeuvre. Foch had already made it clear that in his view the Somme was 'a battle of wearing down, yes; a battle of rupture, no'. He thought that Fayolle 'is an excellent man, but he is afraid of grinding'.[5]

The next phase of the battle began on 14 July. The British had learned much from 1 July, and from 2 July onwards memos, reports and notes of advice trickled up and down between army, corps, division, brigade, battalion and company. Rawlinson now determined to capitalise on the successes gained around Montauban and wished to mount an attack out of the salient gained there, but using a rather different approach from that employed at the beginning of the battle. The suggestion put up to Haig by Rawlinson was for a dawn attack on the villages of Bazentin-le-Grand, Bazentin-le-Petit and Longueval, and the woods around and between those locations. Haig was fully in favour of the objectives suggested, but was firmly against the attack being made at dawn, as he did not consider the troops to be up to it. A dawn attack confers great advantages on the attacker: surprise, cover of darkness for the move of the troops to the assembly areas, little visibility for enemy machine-gunners once the jump-off line has been crossed, and the whole of the day to consolidate positions taken. It also has disadvantages. Control and navigation are difficult; movement is slow, and if the enemy do find out what is up then the troops are very vulnerable if caught by artillery in open ground in the dark. Haig did not consider that the staff was capable of moving four divisions half a mile in the dark, and of getting them into their attack formations and facing the right way before dawn broke.

Haig's views were reinforced by an unsuccessful night attack at 0200 hours on 7 July, when 52 Brigade had attempted to capture German positions lying between Contalmaison and Mametz Wood in order to obtain a better jump-off line for 14 July. The 9th Battalion the Northumberland Fusiliers lost five officers and sixty soldiers killed, the 10th Lancashire Fusiliers six and seventy nine, and the 10th Sherwood Foresters, in support, two and thirty-five. The attack failed less because it was done at night than because the objective was well supported by German positions on its flanks, and because the defenders were well equipped with flares and other forms of illumination. Initially this cut no ice with Haig, but eventually, on 12 July, he bowed to Rawlinson's insistence that his men were capable of a dawn attack.

The objectives were bombarded from 11 July, but there was a severe shortage of heavy artillery ammunition: the fifteen-inch guns were restricted to twenty-five rounds per day, the 9.2-inch to fifty and the eight-inch to 110, while the six-inch guns had a more generous 250 rounds per day. For the bombardment and the battle itself, two thousand rounds were available for each eighteen-pounder gun in the field artillery. Instead of the standard thirty-minute intense bombardment before zero hour, there would only be five minutes. This was not to save ammunition – Haig had made it clear to Rawlinson that all reserves of artillery ammunition could be expended if necessary – but as a surprise measure, the Germans having become accustomed to a thirty-minute 'hate' prior to an assault. Haig and Rawlinson had hoped that this would be a joint Anglo-French attack, but the French declined to play. They did not consider the artillery bombardment to be sufficiently intense, and in any case they thought a dawn attack had no chance of success.

The troops were brought into position after dark on 13 July and lay down along taped-out jump-off lines, or in specially prepared advance trenches. In order to secure the right flank of the attack 18 Division was ordered to complete the capture of the Bois des Troncs, known to the British as Trones Wood, in which fighting had gone on since the first phase of the attack on 1 July. The battalions involved in the Trones Wood attack in the small hours of 14 July had not been in action since 1 July, when they had got off relatively lightly. The fighting inside the wood was severe, but by 0930 hours it was in British hands. This was well after the dawn attack had started, but the German defenders of Trones Wood were far too busy in the defence of their own position to be able to interfere with the advance on their right. The casualties of the six battalions of 18 Division engaged in the Trones Wood battle on 14 July included seven officers and seventy-four other ranks killed, ranging from one private soldier in the 7th Bedfords to five officers and thirty-six men killed in the 6th Northamptonshires. Given the importance of securing the British right flank, this was not an exorbitant price.

At 0320 hours the artillery ranged all its guns on the main German positions and at 0325, as the first glimmer of light showed on the horizon, the troops moved off. They moved behind a creeping barrage, but this time the barrage was exclusively of high explosive rather than of a mix containing shrapnel. Experience gained on 1 July showed that shrapnel did not cut wire, and from now on it would be used less and less by the British. On the right the 9th Scottish Division deployed two of its brigades. There were four battalions in the assault, two in support and one in reserve. A third brigade, the South African Brigade, was also in reserve. The division had not been engaged on 1 July, and this was its first major action on the Somme. The plan worked, and the men had crossed 800 yards and reached the outskirts of Longueval village and the edge of Delville Wood before the Germans fired a shot. Total deaths were 287, ranging from sixty other ranks of the 7th Seaforth Highlanders to nine men of the 5th Cameron Highlanders.

In the centre, 3 Division, in its first action on the Somme, was to attack in the direction of Bazentin-le-Grand. On moving into the line this division had established an outpost line 1,000 yards out into no man's land, from which active patrolling and raiding allowed them to dominate the ground between the opposing trenches. On the night of 13/14 July they dug communication trenches even further out, making a jump-off line about 250 yards from the German positions. Within two hours of zero the division had captured Bazentin-le-Grand. At one stage 8 Brigade was briefly held up by uncut wire until the brigade major, with a machine gun and a company of 2 Royal Scots, led an attack on a flanking trench and bombed his way along it, allowing the rest of the brigade to get through. The brigade major may well have been brushing the crumbs of a good dinner from his immaculate service dress jacket; what he was not doing was skulking back at the base. The five battalions chiefly involved had a total of thirteen officers and 352 other ranks killed, most of them in the 8th East Yorks and the 7th Shropshire Light Infantry, the first to assault. It was a serious bill, but far less than some battalions suffered on 1 July, and for more gain.

The 7th and 21st Divisions were to cooperate in the capture of Bazentin Wood and the village of Bazentin-le-Petit. For 21 Division this was their first attack of the battle, but 7 Division had only been out of the line for five days and were still absorbing reinforcements, some of whom only joined their battalions on the way up to the line. No man's land was 1200 yards from the British trenches, so the battalions moved out under cover of darkness until they were around 300 yards away from the Germans. The wood was taken by 0430 hours and the village by 0700. Casualties were light: 164 deaths all told in the seven battalions involved, with the heaviest losses being in 2nd Battalion the Royal Irish Regiment which had fifty-nine other ranks killed, and the smallest in the 2nd Gordon Highlanders who lost three.

All in all the new methods, learned the hard way from the experiences of 1 July, had worked. The troops had shown that they could move into position at night, jump-off lines were established close to the German positions, the staff officers were able to arrange all the preliminaries and the creeping barrage of HE had done most of what it was supposed to do. Casualties had been moderate and a real advance had been achieved. Such an operation would not have been possible a fortnight earlier but everybody, from corps and divisional commanders down to corporals commanding sections, was learning.

The British experience in the First War is often referred to in the modern idiom as a 'learning curve'. In fact the process of gaining experience, learning from it and improving methods and equipment was not a curve at all, but more of a staircase. Lessons were learned and implemented, and then followed by consolidation before the next intellectual leap forward. After the initial success of the dawn attack there followed a period of hard slogging. The Germans held on grimly to Delville Wood, and once 9 Division had captured the village of Longueval, its third brigade, the South African Brigade, was ordered to take the wood.

South Africa was the one part of the Empire where British entry into the war was not greeted with near-universal approval. As the law stood in 1914, once Britain declared war the whole of the Empire was automatically at war. In South Africa there was a revolt, led by two former Boer generals, Christiaan de Wet and Salomon Maritz, which was promptly put down by two other former Boer generals, Jan Smuts and Louis Botha. South Africa had a tiny regular army and her defence was based on the militia, which all males of European descent had to join. While South Africa's main war effort was concentrated on German South West Africa (now Namibia), and German East Africa (Tanganyika, now Tanzania), she sent an infantry brigade and supporting arms to Egypt and then to the Western Front.

The South African Brigade attacked Delville Wood at dawn on 15 July. For six days they fought in appalling conditions, finally managing to force the Germans into the north-west corner of the wood. By this time the brigade's casualties were such that they could do no more, and they were relieved by 26 Brigade on the night of 20/21 July. It might be wondered why on the earth the Germans should fight so hard for an insignificant clump of trees. Delville Wood itself appears to have no importance, but it supports and is supported by other woods on the ridge line that the British wanted to establish themselves on. Mametz Wood, Bazentin Wood, High Wood, Delville Wood and Trones Wood formed strongpoints in the German defences that had been hastily cobbled together after the capture of Montauban on 1 July. If they could be held then the British could not advance over the open ground between, and German observers in one wood could see, and support, their comrades in another. Mametz, Bazentin and Trones Woods had gone, but if the Germans could keep Delville Wood and High Wood then they could hold the British up for a long time – as happened. The north-west corner of Delville Wood was not finally cleared of Germans until 25 August, and even then one small party hung on at the extreme eastern edge until 15 September.

Having taken the two Bazentin villages and the wood of the same name, the British were poised on the northern edge of what was known as Caterpillar Valley, looking across at High Wood about 1,200 yards away and across open fields of grass. The valley was in dead ground to Delville and High Woods, and Bazentin Wood, whence fire could have been directed into the valley, had been taken. Into the valley came medical units, artillery guns and ammunition columns, brigade and battalion advanced headquarters, and the Secunderabad Cavalry Brigade. All was now ready to push on and take the next ridge.

If High Wood and its supporting strongpoint of Delville Wood could be taken, then the way to Flers, Gueudecourt and the German third line of defences was open. It was not to be. The cavalry was sent in and succeeded in driving in the German outposts, but successive attacks by infantry could not get across the open ground and into the wood. In the following weeks, attack after attack was launched against High Wood using infantry, gas, flame-throwers and machine-gun barrages. All was to no avail, and the wood would not be taken until the next phase of the battle, by infantry of 47 Division, with tanks in support.

The success of 14 July was followed by more hard grinding, the British trying to get onto the Pozières Ridge, the French hammering at Péronne. For a few days the offensive became a series of isolated battles. On 20 July General Fayolle noted in his diary: 'Visited the 1st Colonial Corps. They strike me as having a great desire to do nothing…The English mean to do nothing!'[6] The British army did, at this stage of the war, take longer to deploy and prepare than did the French, but on 26 July the 1st Australian Division took Pozières village, with around 1,000 men killed in so doing, and the 2nd Australian Division got onto the ridge on 4 August. There was now a pause and a period of tidying-up, as the British prepared for the next phase of the offensive.

The Australians defended Pozières village and the ridge to the east of it, and at first light on 6 August the Germans launched a counter-attack on the village, astride the road running from Courcelette south-west to Pozières. The Australian platoon dug in either side of the road was commanded by Second Lieutenant Albert Jacka, one of the great characters of Australian military history. As a lance corporal in Gallipoli in May 1915 he had earned the Victoria Cross, the first to an Australian during the war, and had risen to the rank of sergeant before being commissioned in the 14th Battalion, Australian Imperial Force.

In the morning of 6 August the Germans rolled over Jacka's position and into the village. The first Jacka knew about what was happening was when a grenade came tumbling down the steps of his dugout (originally constructed by the Germans and now taken into use by the British). Emerging from the dugout, Jacka saw that a party of Australian prisoners was being hustled along the road by German soldiers. Grabbing what men of his own he could, Jacka led a very gallant counter-attack using boots, fists, rifle butts and bayonets, with the result that the prisoners were freed and the Germans sent scurrying back to their own lines. Jacka himself was wounded in the affair, and there can be no doubt that it was his swift action that prevented a local counter-attack from developing into the recapture of Pozières Ridge.

Jacka was awarded the Military Cross, but he felt he had been harshly treated and should have been given a bar to his Victoria Cross. Many Australians, at the time and since, agreed, and felt that Jacka did not receive the recognition that he deserved. This became something of a cause célèbre after the war, and there were suggestions that it was the stuffy British who would not sanction a second VC to a working-class colonial. It was not, of course, for the British to recommend or reject Jacka for anything, but the responsibility of his own, Australian, officers. Jacka was outspoken, no respecter of rank and certainly seen by some as a disruptive influence, despite his undoubted gallantry. This may have had something to do with the non-recommendation – assuming of course that the action was worthy of a VC, and we only have Jacka's and some of his colleagues' word for that.

One has to ask, however, how it was that the Germans were able to mount an attack across 1,200 yards of open ground in daylight, with at least 100 yards to cover when the artillery lifted, without the alarm being given. The suspicion must be that the sentries were asleep, or below ground in their dugouts. Fair enough while the bombardment was going on, but they should have been up on the fire-step as soon as the shelling stopped. As Jacka was in command of that sector he must take the blame for the defenders being caught by surprise, and despite his recovering a potentially very nasty situation, perhaps he was lucky to get an MC rather than a court martial.

The Australians were relieved on Pozières Ridge by the Canadian Corps on 2 and 3 September. Like those of the other Dominions, Canada's army was tiny before the war, with only around 3,000 regulars stationed in important garrisons or employed as training teams, and Canada's defence was based on the Militia, equivalent to the British Territorial Force. Unlike Australia, where the vast majority of the population was of British origin and only half of one per cent of Australians were of German or Austrian descent, in Canada seven per cent of the population was of enemy extraction. Canada nevertheless very quickly began to raise an army, and the first Canadian division arrived on the Western Front in February 1915, another in September of the same year, and two more in 1916. The Canadian government had hoped that the raising of a mass army for the war would be a form of nation-building exercise, and would help weld the French-speaking and English-speaking communities together. Although French Canadian battalions did join the BEF and a French Canadian won a Victoria Cross, in general the French Canadians did not join. In Quebec a French-speaking population of 1,700,000 produced only 7,000 recruits, whereas the 400,000 English-speakers of the same province provided 22,000. Initially this was a puzzle. This was a French war, so why would the French Canadians not join? The answer lay in the history of Canada. When General Wolfe scaled the Heights of Abraham on 12 September 1759 and resolved once and for all that it should be the British and not the French who would rule North America, the French aristocracy, the officers, the wealthy and the educated returned to France; left behind were the fur-trappers and the peasant farmers, who saw themselves abandoned by those to whom they looked for leadership. Their descendants saw themselves not as Frenchmen, but as Canadians who spoke French. They had no loyalty to France nor any to England, and the bulk were not interested in involving themselves in a European war. Despite this, Canada sent 400,000 men to the Western Front. They were well led and highly motivated, and by 1918 they were almost the shock troops of the BEF.

By late August 1916 the Somme offensive, combined with a gradual turning of the tide at Verdun – itself precipitated by what was happening on the Somme – was beginning to have its effect on the German army. On 25 August Falkenhayn was dismissed as Chief of the General Staff and sent off to the Romanian front. His successor was the sixty-nine-year-old Paul Ludwig von Beneckendorff und von Hindenburg, known as von Hindenburg for short, and a field marshal since November 1914, supported by his *éminence grise* General Erich von Ludendorff (the 'von' was a recent acquisition) as First Quartermaster General.

The next major phase of the Somme offensive began on 3 September, with the French attacking in the direction of Maurepas. The French infantry had recovered from what their commander considered to be an outbreak of idleness and, incredibly, French regiments carried their colours into the attack, sounded trumpets, and sang the 'Marseillaise' as they advanced. In five hours they had captured Leforest and Cléry, only two miles north-west of Péronne. Once again, according to General Fayolle, 'Father Joffre is radiant.' By 12 September the French had taken Bouchavesnes, five miles behind the German lines, and were astride the vital north–south road from Béthune to Péronne. Meanwhile the British took Guillemont between 3 and 8 September, and on 9 September the 16th (Irish) Division captured Ginchy. The seven Irish battalions chiefly involved in the fighting for Ginchy lost eight officers and 220 soldiers killed on 9 September, ranging from none in the 6th Battalion Royal Irish Rifles to six officers and sixty-one men in the 9th Battalion the Royal Dublin Fusiliers.

It is sad that the actions of 16 Division, formed from Redmond's Irish Volunteers, have been all but forgotten in British and Irish history. When the division's demobilised soldiers returned to Ireland after the war the political situation had changed, and many Irish people considered that these men had supported the oppressor. Some were even assassinated. Although all Ireland was part of the United Kingdom until 1921, conscription was never applied there, and its status as a traditional source of recruits for the

British army had been declining for many years. The so-called Easter Rising of 1916 in Dublin, a petty failure in military terms, was opposed by the great majority of the Irish people; but the British reaction to it, with eighty-eight of the ringleaders being tried for rebellion and sentenced to death by military courts, and fifteen actually being executed, turned Irish opinion from merely wishing for Dominion status to demanding complete sever-ance from Britain. It also horrified neutral opinion, particularly in the United States, and was a rare – and seized-upon – opportunity for German propaganda. The trials were fair and the sentences legal. The British view at the time was that the actions of the rising's organisers amounted to a stab in the back and a betrayal of all that their countrymen were doing in France. While it is difficult to conceive of a more serious offence than rebellion in the middle of a war, in hindsight it might have been wiser to lock the rebels up rather than execute them. The morale of the 16th Division seems to have been largely unaffected, but the outcome of the affair had major repercussions on recruiting in Ireland.

When most of Ireland left the United Kingdom on the formation of the Irish Free State in 1921, the six old Irish regiments that had marched with Marlborough and Wellington, and that had shed so much blood in the Great War, were disbanded, and forgotten except by those who had served in them. Today, while there is an imposing monument to the 36th (Ulster) Division at Thiepval, there are but two little Celtic crosses to commemorate the 16th Division at the Somme.[7]

The next phase of the Somme offensive was to inaugurate a seminal change in the shape of battle, although it would take another war for the innovation to reach full fruition. On 15 September the British attacked High Wood, Mouquet Farm, Courcelette and Flers while the French went on in the direction of Combles. It was the first day on which tanks were ever used in battle.

Winston Churchill was a man whose true character may never be truly fathomed. On the one hand he was a charismatic, inspirational leader, and on the other a man whose mind could never be focussed on any one thing for very long. He constantly sought what would later be known as the indirect approach to warfare. Out of every hundred of his great ideas and schemes, ninety-nine were hopelessly impracticable while one would be breathtakingly brilliant. The trick for those around him was to recognise the brilliant one. Since at least 1910 Churchill had been interested in some sort of machine that could roam the battlefield and provide support to the infantry, and if the original concept was not his, it was he who was the driving force behind its development as long as he was at the Admiralty. Initially experiments were conducted with steam propulsion, and by 1914 thought was being given to a caterpillar-tracked vehicle to serve as a 'machine-gun destroyer'. In January 1915 the Admiralty, under Churchill, set up the Admiralty Landships Committee and by Christmas 1915 the prototype vehicle was given the code name of 'tank', the cover being that it was a self-propelled water-carrier. When Sir Douglas Haig took over as Commander-in-Chief of the BEF in December 1915, he heard of this com-mittee and immediately sent a staff officer off to England to find out all about it. Contrary to his popular image as a hidebound cavalryman who distrusted technology, Haig was anxious to seize any development that might save lives, and he became an ardent supporter of the tank. After discussions between the BEF and the developers, it was agreed that the tank must be able to cross trenches, go through barbed-wire obstacles, travel over any ground, and be able to provide intimate fire support to the infantry. It was to be protected by armour and capable of moving at the same speed as the infantry walked.

In August 1916 Haig was informed that the first batch of tanks was now ready. There was debate as to whether these first tanks were suffi-ciently reliable to be used, and whether there were enough of them to make a difference. There were those, including Lloyd George, now Secretary of State for War after the death of Kitchener, and Robertson the CIGS, as well as many of the tank officers themselves, who would have preferred not to expose the new weapon yet, but to wait until mechanical teething problems had all been ironed out, and until there were sufficient tanks available to strike a decisive blow. As it was, Haig decided to use what was to hand. On 29 July he wrote to Robertson:

> I am fully alive to the disadvantage of using the tanks before the full number
> on order [150] are available...if the enemy is not forced from his entrenched
> positions – as there is good hope that he will be – before the autumn, it is

unlikely to prove possible to arrange for another simultaneous effort on such a large scale before next spring. In these circumstances, if opportunity should offer to gain valuable results in the present struggle by the use of even a few tanks, I should have no hesitation in taking advantage of it, and I consider it of very great importance that such number of tanks as can be made available should be sent to France with the least possible delay...[8]

In hindsight Haig may have been wrong, but in a battle that was killing an average of 500 British soldiers every day, anything that might help was better than nothing.

Forty-nine tanks, stencilled 'With care – Petrograd' (the cover story now was that these were water-carriers destined for the Russians) went by rail and boat to Le Havre and then by rail again to Bray-sur-Somme, a railhead about eight miles behind the British lines. There were two types, male and female. The male weighed twenty-eight tons and was twenty-six feet long, fourteen feet wide and eight feet high. It carried two six-pounder guns mounted on spontoons either side of the tank, with 324 rounds of ammunition, and three Hotchkiss machine guns mounted (plus a spare) with 6,000 rounds. The female version weighed slightly less and had no six-pounders, but was instead armed with four Vickers machine guns mounted and 31,000 rounds of ammunition. Both types were powered by a six-cylinder petrol engine. There were eight crewmen in each tank: a commander, usually at this stage an officer, a driver, two gearsmen (the tank was steered by varying the engine power transmitted to each track), and a number one and a number two for each six-pounder gun. Each man could, at least in theory, fill in for any of the others should they be wounded or killed. For communications each tank carried carrier pigeons, flags and flares, and a method of communicating with aircraft had been worked out. During the attack, lanes would be left in the artillery barrage to allow the tanks to advance ahead of the infantry without molestation from friendly fire.

The main attack on 15 September was to begin at 0620 hours, but before that the right flank for the advance on Flers had to be secured by the removal of a stubborn party of Germans still holding out in the southeast corner of Delville Wood. This was to be the first-ever appearance of the tank on a battlefield. It was originally intended to use two tanks; but one broke down on the way, and the tank that made history was number D1, commanded by Captain H. W. Mortimore. The tank started from about 300 yards behind the British lines and clanked its way at one mile per hour up to the British trench line, itself about 100 yards from the German position. The tank followed a line of white tape, and an aircraft of the Royal Flying Corps circled overhead to drown the noise of the tank engine. At 0515 hours tank D1 crossed the British line, trundled up to the German trench, turned right and drove along the trench peppering it with machine-gun fire. Two companies of the King's Own Yorkshire Light Infantry charged across the intervening ground and leaped into the German trench, and in a few minutes the defenders were dead or had surrendered. It was a promising beginning to armoured warfare, although Mortimore now decided to carry on towards the main German position, where his tank was hit by an artillery shell, lost one of its tracks, and played no further part in the battle.

On the British left, High Wood was attacked by infantry supported by four tanks, and the wood was taken by mid-afternoon. In the centre the Canadians attacked from Pozières Ridge, where they had taken over from the Australians in early September, towards Courcelette. Here too zero hour was 0620, and the attack was to be supported by six tanks. All six broke down or ditched or were knocked out except one, christened by its crew *Crème de Menthe*. When the infantry were held up by fierce resistance at a sugar factory just short of Courcelette village, *Crème de Menthe* obligingly fired one of its six-pounders through an embrasure in the factory wall; the fifty occupants surrendered and the position was taken.

On the right good progress was made, with the New Zealand Division and 41 Division being supported by tanks, two of which got into Flers village by 0820 hours. It was D17, *Dinnaken*, commanded by Lieutenant S. H. Hastie, that gave rise to the reports in the English newspapers that 'a tank is walking up the High Street of Flers with the British Army cheering behind it'.[9] *Dinnaken* achieved another first by shooting down a German observation balloon with its six-pounder on the way into Flers. Two tanks got even further, into Gueudecourt village. They were both knocked out by German artillery; the infantry were unable to follow and it was not until 26 September that Gueudecourt was finally taken.

The attack was an undoubted success, capturing more than six miles of German trenches to a depth of a mile and a half. The performance of the tanks was less clear. Initially their appearance caused panic in some German units, and whole platoons surrendered to these lumbering beasts They were useful in providing covering fire for the infantry at High Wood, but the Canadians would probably have taken Courcelette without them, though it would have taken longer. Of the forty-nine tanks sent to France, only two were unscathed at the close of business on 15 September. Thirty-two got as far as their start point; of these fourteen broke down or ditched before or just after crossing the jump-off line, and of the eighteen that took part in the battle six ditched, five were hit by artillery and knocked out, three were hit by artillery and went on fire, and two caught fire unaided by the Germans. In many cases the tanks could not keep up with the infantry. It was not very impressive, and the existence of these new weapons was now exposed. That said, the tank had proved that it could cross trenches, force a passage through wire and provide the infantry with mobile fire support. Only nine members of the Heavy Branch of the Machine Gun Corps (as the Tank Corps was then called) had been killed all day, so despite the tank's vulnerability to aimed shellfire, it gave its crew at least a modicum of protection. There was nothing wrong with the idea; the trick was to make the machine reliable, work out how to use it to best effect in cooperation with infantry, artillery and the air, and improve its communications. Valuable lessons were learned, modifications were incorporated into the design and production was stepped up. The tank was an undoubted boost to the morale of the troops on the ground and to the public at home. The tank was not the wonder weapon that the newspapers claimed, but it was something that the British had and the Germans did not, and that it appeared at all is a tribute to the designers and engineers who produced it in such a short space of time.

From now on in this war tanks would be used more and more, and they would get better and better. The Germans, for once well behind the British in things technical, did try to compete by producing a tank of their own, the A7V, in spring 1917. It was an ungainly twenty-four-foot-long monster weighing thirty tons, with a crew of eighteen. It was top-heavy and had a distressing tendency to turn turtle on sloping ground. The

Germans produced only twelve of them, and much preferred to use captured British tanks. In the meantime the German reaction was to issue elephant guns, originally intended for German South West Africa, which could penetrate the armour of the British Mark 1 tank; later they adapted artillery pieces to the anti-tank role. The Germans took note of the lessons, however, and while the British had invented the tank, it was their enemy that would become the chief proponent of armoured warfare in the next conflict.

Between 15 and 17 September the French took Berny, Deniécourt and Vermandovillers, and on the 26th, with some help from the British, they took Combles. The British were now outstripping the French, however, and were in danger of having their right flank exposed. The main British thrust would now shift to Morval and Thiepval Ridge, still unconquered since 1 July.

September 1916 was not a good month for Germany. Forced to shift thirteen new divisions to the Somme, she had gone onto the defensive at Verdun on 2 September. In that month alone the Germans had expended nearly six million rounds of field-artillery ammunition and one and a quarter million heavy artillery rounds, and still they lost ground on the Somme and gained none at Verdun. On 15 September the new Chief of the General Staff, Hindenburg, ordered the construction of the Siegfried Line (known to the Allies as the Hindenburg Line) further back, thereby creating positions to which his troops could withdraw in order to shorten their front. At home the German government lowered the minimum age for compulsory military service from nineteen to sixteen, and raised the upper limit from thirty-nine to sixty. By the end of the year they would make all males between seventeen and sixty, unless already in the armed forces, liable to conscription for the war industries.

A foothold on the Schwaben Redoubt on Thiepval Ridge, which had first fallen to and then defeated the Ulstermen on 1 July, was eventually gained by Major-General Maxse's 18 Division on 28 September, and fighting to the north of it continued into October. While the British casualties now were nothing like as severe as they had been in the first phase of the offensive, there were still personal tragedies. The Fifty-fifth Brigade of 18 Division was in reserve for the attack on the Schwaben Redoubt on

28 September, and during that night took over the front line. This brigade had been in action on 1 July (when Billy Nevill had led the right-hand company of the 8th East Surreys with his football), again on 14 July in Trones Wood and in the subsequent operations in Delville Wood. Maxse ordered 55 Brigade, augmented by a fifth battalion, 6th Royal Berkshires, to clear the remnants of the Schwaben Redoubt and to occupy the high ground to its north. There was confused fighting from 30 September to 5 October, with little progress and with fourteen officers and 227 other ranks of the brigade killed. On 6 October the brigade commander, Sir Thomas Jackson, was removed from command. Major-General Maxse said, 'In my opinion the 55th Brigade was not handled with firmness and the attacks were too partial. The situation should have been grasped more firmly by the brigade commander concerned and he was so informed.'[10]

Jackson was a regular officer who had earned the Distinguished Service Order in the South African War.[11] By 1914 he was a company commander in the 1st Battalion the King's Own (Royal Lancaster) Regiment, and went to France with his battalion on 23 August 1914. In July 1915 he was promoted to command the battalion, and in October 1915, at the age of forty, he became a brigadier general and took over command of 55 Brigade. By October 1916 Jackson had been on the Western Front for over two years, and for all of that time he was in an operational infantry unit. He had argued with Maxse before, nearly always to oppose what he saw as pointless attacks, and his continuing to disagree with his divisional commander was what got him the sack. It is a measure of the man that, despite losing his brigade and reverting to his substantive rank of lieutenant colonel, Jackson asked to remain on the Western Front. There must have been some sympathy for Jackson in the higher echelons of the army, for instead of being sent home in an administrative or training capacity, as usually happened to commanders who failed, he was allowed to stay and was appointed commanding officer of 11th Battalion the Manchester Regiment, in another division. He collapsed while on a route march in September 1917, was invalided back to England, spent seven months in hospital, and then commanded a holding unit until the end of the war.

Maxse was probably unfair to Jackson. Very early on, the British had learned the importance of alternating men between the front lines and billets well back, but little attention was paid to commanders. During the Somme offensive battalions rarely spent more than one day in the firing line before being relieved, but there was no relief for a brigade commander as long as any of his four battalions was forward. It would not be surprising if Jackson was completely burnt out, and the award of a bar to his DSO in January 1918 is evidence that little stigma was considered to attach to his dismissal. The importance of rest for commanders was another lesson that the British would learn the hard way.

In October the tide, already turning in favour of the Allies, began to flow more strongly. On 24 October French troops of General Mangin, and under the direction of General Robert Nivelle, now commanding at Verdun, recaptured Fort Douaumont, and the Germans began to lose more men than the French. On the night of 2/3 November the Germans evacuated Fort Vaux.

By now, however, the French were very tired. They had fed forty-four divisions into the Somme battle, thirty of which had already been through the meat-grinder of Verdun. Fayolle was becoming disillusioned: 'Joffre and Foch want Bapaume,' he wrote in his diary on 21 October, 'but if 60,000 are lost to get there, where is the benefit?'[12]

The British battled their way up the Bapaume road and along the banks of the Ancre, but the weather had turned against them and movement became more and more difficult. Le Sars was captured on 7 October, the Schwaben Redoubt was finally cleared of Germans on the 14th, and Beaumont-Hamel was taken on 14 November. The French reached Mont Saint-Quentin, overlooking Péronne, but there they stuck.

Joffre and Foch would have liked to go on. Fayolle noted on 3 November: 'Foch says the Germans are done with. He has been saying that since the start of the battle…for him the troops are always ready to attack indefinitely.'[13] In truth, the Germans were very nearly done with. They had mounted few counter-attacks on the Somme since September, and those that were put in lacked the verve and aggression of the old German army of 1914 and 1915. A combination of weather, Allied exhaustion, and the lack of a large force of fresh British or French divisions to feed in forced the closure of the Somme offensive on 18 November, the day the first winter snow appeared. On 15 December the Germans finally accepted defeat at Verdun when the French pushed them back nearly two miles. The policy of bleeding the French white had failed, but only just.

The Somme had relieved the pressure on Verdun. The Somme sector was originally held by six German divisions. Had the Allies not attacked there, at least half of the sixty-nine German divisions eventually engaged on the Somme would have been available for Verdun; the Germans could have attacked on both banks of the River Meuse simultaneously, and there can be little doubt that the French army would have been defeated. Such a defeat could well have led to a complete collapse of French military will, and to a German victory in the west.

The Somme offensive had recovered seventy square miles of occupied French territory and fifty-one French towns and villages. The villages were now little more than piles of rubble, but at least their owners could return and reconstruction could start. The Germans had been forced back between five and seven miles along ten miles of front, and knocked off their forward defensive positions over another twelve miles on the flanks. Of the sixty-nine German divisions engaged on the Somme, many were so badly mauled that they were useless until rebuilt with recruits from Germany. They had suffered half a million casualties, of whom around 150,000 were killed. These figures, added to about 143,000 German deaths at Verdun and those inflicted by the Brusilov offensive on the Eastern Front, made 1916 a black year for the German army.

Joffre, the French Commander-in-Chief, had been quite clear what the Somme was to be: a battle to relieve the pressure on Verdun and to kill Germans. Haig, albeit reluctantly, had accepted that aim, though he always hoped for a return to a war of manoeuvre, far more in keeping with British military doctrine. Those who aver that Haig had somehow failed because a breakthrough was not achieved are wrong – as Haig's directive to the Fourth Army plainly shows.

Verdun had been relieved and a lot of Germans had been killed. The Somme offensive had achieved its aim. What made, and makes, the Somme a source of controversy to the British even today is the price paid for that achievement. Total British and Empire deaths on the Somme amounted to around 95,000, and the overall casualty list totalled 400,000 killed, wounded, missing and taken prisoner. Of the dead, nearly 20,000 were killed on the first day, and British ignorance of the scale of continental warfare, combined with the way in which the British had expanded their army by the use of 'pals' and Territorial battalions, made the battle seem a terrible slaughter. In fact the death rate on the Somme was less severe than it was in Normandy, when twenty-eight years later another undertrained and inexperienced British army would be loosed against the Germans. The table below shows a comparison of British Empire dead in the two campaigns:

Table 12

	Number of weeks	British divisions engaged	Total dead	Dead per division per week
The Somme 1.7-18.11.1916	20½	53	95,000	89
Normandy 6.6-25.8.1944	11½	19*	22,000	100

* There were a number of independent brigades engaged in Normandy. In order to provide a proper comparison I have combined them into divisions

Normandy is not engraved on the British national consciousness as a slaughter. Partly this is because in Normandy there was not much doubt that the British were winning, but more importantly we did not recruit our infantry battalions from small geographical areas. The 6th Battalion the Green Howards, a Territorial battalion supposedly raised from the Middlesbrough area, lost thirty-one men killed and took 250 casualties overall in one day, at Cristot on 11 June 1944. In the First War they would all have come from the same town or village, and their relatives would all have known one another. It would have been a significant loss, and the entire toll would have been engraved on one war memorial and remembered down the generations. As it was, two of the dead were American-born, two were from Liverpool, two from Sheffield, two from Birmingham, two from Derby and two from Middlesbrough. The homes of the other nineteen ranged from Edinburgh to Glamorgan, no two coming from the same place. The bill went unnoticed except by those most closely involved.

The Somme is often thought of as five and a half months of staggering about in mud and attacking in blinding rain. In fact, for the whole months of July and August the temperature never dropped below a comfortable 60° Fahrenheit. In September it dropped below 60° on three days, and for roughly half of October the temperature fluctuated between 50° and 58°, with four days being described as 'very cold'. In November it stayed between 54° and 57° until the last four days of the battle, when it fell to 37° on 17 November. In July 1.3 inches of rain were recorded over four days, in August two inches over twelve days and in September 2.8 inches over nine days; in October there were two inches of rain in sixteen days, and just under one inch over ten days before 18 November, the last day of the offensive. On that day also the first snow of the winter fell. On two days (16 October and 9 November) frost was recorded.[14] The wettest period was the last two days of October and the first week of November, when 1.3 inches of rain fell in eight days. There is no doubt that towards the close of the battle the weather did have an effect on operations, not so much because the infantry could not fight in the mud as because movement of vehicles and artillery was hampered. On 10 November it was recorded that no movement at all was possible owing to the state of the ground. That said, the picture of a constant sea of mud is clearly false.

Why did Haig not stop the battle when he saw that the casualties were so great? This oft-posed question assumes firstly that the casualty list was somehow disproportionate, and secondly that Haig could have stopped the battle. Of all the British soldiers involved in the Somme offensive, seventy-four per cent emerged at the end of it without a scratch. Given that one of the primary aims was to relieve the pressure on Verdun and thus prevent the Germans winning the war, a twenty-six per cent toll of killed, wounded and taken prisoner is not excessive, although I accept that to be a subjective opinion. Haig could not have stopped the battle because the British were not alone. This was a coalition war and this was an Allied offensive. Given their involvement at Verdun, which absorbed seventy-three French divisions, one could not have blamed the French had they declined to take part at all.[15] As it was, their part in the Somme, while considerably smaller to begin with, was eventually not much less significant than that of the British – forty-four divisions compared to fifty-three – and they had around 90,000 men killed there.[16] There were 160,000 French deaths at Verdun, and the total for the year of 1916 came to 270,000 dead

French soldiers. The British Empire lost 115,389 dead in 1916: 109,411 on the Western Front, 3,871 in Mesopotamia, 579 in East Africa, 857 in Salonika, 471 in Palestine, 180 in Gallipoli and twenty in minor theatres elsewhere. The British had come through 1916 much less scathed than their principal ally or main enemy.[17]

Haig did not want to attack on the Somme at all, but since the politics of a coalition war meant that he had to, the preparation and planning were as good as they could be. That more was not achieved was due to an underestimation of the strength of German defences, a shortage of artillery ammunition and, more than anything else, the lack of experience of the New Armies. Once the Germans had attacked towards Verdun, waiting another year before launching a major offensive was simply not an option for the British. The Somme had to happen, and it had to continue until German reserves were used up, and until the Germans could not win the war in 1916. The tactics were simple because it was all that the New Armies, in their first blooding, were capable of at the time. Had Haig been left to follow his own counsel and attack out of Flanders, or anywhere else for that matter, he could not have lowered the ante for putting a civilian army into the field, in its first battle, against an enemy that had had universal male conscription since 1870, had prepared for European war for twenty years and had spent eighteen months preparing his positions for defence. Even so, the damage inflicted on the Germans by these New Armies was far more than might have been expected. Ludendorff, effectively Chief of Staff of the German army, admitted that his troops had suffered very heavy losses, first at Verdun and then on the Somme, and that morale was at a low ebb. Before the end of the year both he and Hindenburg would be demanding the use of child labour in Germany to release men for the front.[18] It was far from being a needless slaughter.

The British learned much from the Somme, and this was reflected in new methods and structures implemented during the winter. The infantry platoon – the basic building block of that arm of the service on which the bulk of the fighting fell – underwent a radical change. Instead of a headquarters and four sections, each section with the same weapons mix and with the same tasks, the platoon was now reorganised on a functional basis. The new infantry platoon still had a headquarters consisting of a subaltern officer, a sergeant and two private soldiers, and each section had an NCO commander and a minimum of eight men, but each section would now have its own specific role: bombers, Lewis gun, riflemen and rifle bombers.

The Bomber Section had two teams, each of two bombers and two bayonet men. Their task was to bomb along an enemy trench, the throwers protected by the bayonet men. Each thrower carried five grenades, and the rest at least ten each. The Lewis Gun Section provided the platoon's fire support. Two men operated the gun itself, the remainder carried ammunition for it (a total of thirty forty-seven-round drums) and protected the gunners. The Rifle Section had the platoon's picked shots and bayonet-fighting experts, and also provided scouts when the platoon was moving across country. The Rifle Bombers were armed with rifles and a cup discharger for firing grenades into an enemy trench or behind cover. They were described in the training pamphlet issued in February 1917 as 'the howitzer of the infantry'.[19] In addition to his specialist role every man had to be able to fulfil any other of the platoon's roles, and throughout the winter training was carried out to accustom the troops to the methods learned at great cost on the Somme.

A suggested format for platoon training programmes was laid down, with the first period devoted to individual and section training and the second to platoon training, after which the men would move on to battalion and company training, then to training by brigades and divisions. A typical training programme laid down for the first phase for platoons out of the line was:

Before Breakfast
Section drill

After Breakfast
One hour each section in its own weapon, the rifle sections being allotted half to the Lewis Gun Section and half to the Rifle Bomb Section.

One hour the whole platoon bomb throwing. [As there were insufficient grenades for this always to be done 'live', trainers improvised. In one brigade turnips were used, with nails stuck in them to represent the pin.]

One hour physical training and bayonet fighting.

Finish the morning with ceremonial, that is to say, form up and march past the Platoon or Company Commander on the way to dinners.[20]

After Dinners
Communicating drill and control of fire drill. Musketry on the range alternately by sections.[21]

Recreation at 4 p.m.

NCOs refreshed in the next day's work at 6.30 p.m.[22]

For the second phase of training men were also to be practised in wiring and digging, map-reading, message-writing, communications, mopping-up and 'simple tactical schemes'.

By the spring of 1917 the British army was no longer a collection of enthusiastic amateurs but a hardened, skilled and trained force, which got better and better as the war went on.

NOTES

1 André Laurent, *La Bataille de la Somme 1916*, Martelle, Amiens, 1998.

2 Laurent, *La Bataille de la Somme 1916*, Martelle, Amiens, 1998.

3 Jean-Baptiste Duroselle, *La Grande Guerre des Français 1914–18*, Perrin, Paris, 1994.

4 Miles, *Military Operations in France and Belgium, 1916*, Vol. II, Macmillan, London, 1938.

5 Jean Autin, *Foch*, Perrin, Paris, 1987.

6 Laurent, *La Bataille de la Somme 1916*, Martelle, Amiens, 1998.

7 Times are changing for the better, however. In 1998 a joint Anglo-Irish initiative erected a memorial at Messines to the 16th and 36th Divisions, and the annual Remembrance Day parade in Dublin is at last recognised by the government of Ireland. One might ask why, if the two traditions could work together so well in war, they cannot do so in peace?

8 Quoted in Trevor Pidgeon, *With the Tanks at Flers*, Vol. I, Fairmile Books, Cobham, 1995.

9 Hastie was an officer of the Highland Light Infantry. 'Dinnaken' is Scots for 'I do not know'. I am grateful to Lt Col. Ian Tedford, of the Scottish persuasion, for his assistance in translation.

10 John Baynes, *Far from a Donkey: the Life of General Sir Ivor Maxse*, Brasseys, London, 1995.

11 The DSO was then a decoration for junior officers, with their seniors getting the CB (Companion of the Order of the Bath). In 1915 the MC (Military Cross) was instituted and the DSO became a leadership award for more senior officers.

12 Duroselle, *La Grande Guerre des Français 1914–18*, Perrin, Paris, 1994.

13 Autin, *Foch*, Perrin, Paris, 1987.

14 Chris McCarthy, *The Somme: The Day-by-Day Account*, Arms and Armour Press, London, 1993.

15 Forty-three French divisions served one tour at Verdun, another twenty-three spent two tours there, and a further seven divisions served there three times or more. A tour was until the division was considered to be 'used up', which averaged fifteen days. William Serman and Jean-Paul Bertaud, *Nouvelle Histoire Militaire de la France*, Fayard, Paris, 1998.

16 Most French sources say 140,000 killed, but when looked at in conjunction with official French returns of the total killed for 1916 and the number killed at Verdun, this is an over-estimate.

17 The death total for the British army alone for the whole of the Second World War was 171,000.

18 Major-General Sir John Davidson, *Haig, Master of the Field*, Peter Nevill, London, 1953, and General Erich von Ludendorff, *The General Staff and Its Problems*, Hutchinson, London, 1920.

19 *Instructions for the Training of Platoons for Offensive Action 1917*, General Staff, February 1917.

20 In the British army the midday meal for other ranks is always known as 'dinner'. The evening meal is 'tea'. Just to confuse, officers eat lunch at midday and dinner in the evening.

21 Although the musket disappeared in the mid-nineteenth century, the British army continued to refer to rifle shooting as musketry until the late 1960s.

22 Ibid.

11

THE FROCKS AND
THE BRASS HATS

It has become a cliché that 'war is too important to be left to generals'. Why so? One might as well say that flying an aeroplane is too important to be left to the pilot or a heart transplant too important to be left to the surgeons; that architecture cannot be left to architects, or making shoes to cobblers. The origin of the saying is lost, but one can be pretty sure that a politician coined it. Most democratic politicians, whose authority derives from an election every five years or so, are suspicious of an institution that is patently non-democratic and which, in the way that it carries on its business, is even anti-democratic. Governments are reluctant to embark on a venture whose course they cannot predict, like a war, but when they do embark on it they want to control it. Ever since the Restoration of 1660 the British constitution has incorporated checks and balances to guard against an over-mighty monarch, and by extension to keep the army under firm civilian control. The memory of Cromwell's major-generals may have faded, but until very recently the legal life of the army was for only one year at a time, and if the Annual Army Act was not passed by Parliament the army ceased to have a lawful existence.

In Imperial Germany the constitution gave the army almost unfettered discretion once war started; the British army, however, operated under a system of control designed to make a military coup impossible, and which actually made operations of war very difficult. For centuries Britain's defence had been the Royal Navy, and the voters were interested in the Naval Estimates. The army, on the other hand, was seen an imperial police force, was not highly regarded by the public in peacetime, and was rarely an electoral issue. It was usually neglected and underfunded, and was always far smaller than that of any potential European enemy, relying as it did on voluntary enlistment. As the first decade of twentieth century wore on and it became more likely that there would be a European war, some thought was given to Britain's likely role, and this thinking was accelerated with the establishment of the Expeditionary Force. Even then, the Expeditionary Force was not intended solely for Europe, but was available for deployment wherever Imperial interests might be threatened. Some soldiers who were advocates of the 'WF' or 'With the French' policy pointed out that the British could never, by voluntary enlistment, recruit an army of the size that might be needed for European war; but when in 1912 Field Marshal Lord Roberts, in a scaremongering speech warning of a German invasion, expressed support for the National Service League – which advocated conscription – a motion to reduce his half-pay was tabled in the House of Commons.

Of course war cannot be waged in a political vacuum, and of course it is right that the British army should be subordinate to government control. It is for the government to decide whether to go to war, when to go to war, who to go to war with and who to go to war against. Having taken the nation into war, the politicians then expect the soldiers to win it, and the soldiers would much prefer the government to allow them to get on with plying their trade, which they have trained for and prepared for all their lives. This did not happen in the Great War, and the history of political–military relations between 1914 and 1918 is one of the generals trying to prevent what they saw as meddling by ignorant amateurs, and the politicians trying to restrain what they thought was a coterie of bloodthirsty generals who had no conception of the political imperatives.

Soldiers and politicians rarely understand each other, for they have different aims. Politics is about consensus, whether nationally or within the Cabinet, and it is about power – the winning of the next election, and the patronage and opportunities that flow therefrom. Soldiers have a much simpler aim: the destruction of the enemy's armed forces. Politicians are accustomed to discussion, with everyone having their say; soldiers make a decision, issue the necessary orders and get on with it. Politicians accommodate; soldiers reject anything that does not contribute directly to the fulfilment of the operational requirement.

The British army had a long tradition of remaining aloof from politics, but this did not mean that generals of the early twentieth century did not intrigue. Senior officers and senior politicians were, in the main, drawn from the same social class, and if they did not often meet professionally, they did socially, and generals did lobby those whom they thought sympathetic to their cause. The army had very nearly become politicised over the issue of Irish Home Rule in 1914, when many in the military sympathised with Protestant opposition to a dilution of the British connection with Ireland, but politicians and soldiers withdrew from the brink just in time. Even though many of their fellow officers privately shared their views, those who had been too vociferous in the Unionist interest, like Major-Generals Wilson and Hugh Gough, were regarded with some suspicion by their colleagues. Sir John French, who would command the BEF on the outbreak of war, had to resign along with the Secretary of State for War, J. E. B. Seeley, when their written guarantees to officers that the army would not be called upon to put down Ulster Protestant resistance to Home Rule were publicly repudiated by the Prime Minister, Herbert Asquith.[1]

As the war went on, confrontation and disagreement between British politicians and soldiers proliferated. Inevitably perhaps, the politicians have won the historiographical battle, for it was they who had access to the press and who could have their speeches recorded in Hansard. The public perception now is of decent elected representatives of the people trying to curb pig-headed generals from wasting the lives of yet more young British men, and of the government being prevented from applying an intelligent eye to the war by generals fixated upon a Western-Front strategy. For many years that viewpoint was reinforced by writers such as Basil Liddell Hart, whose doctrine of the indirect approach was not far short of a mantra for critics of the conduct of the First World War.[2]

Constitutionally, in 1914, the army and the navy owed their loyalty to the King, to whose orders they were subject. In practice the government controlled the army through the Secretary of State for War, a Cabinet minister, who chaired the Army Council, which in turn gave instructions to the Chief of the Imperial General Staff (CIGS), the professional head of the army. Another Cabinet minister, the First Lord of the Admiralty, controlled the Royal Navy in a similar fashion.

When Britain declared war against Germany on 4 August 1914, the post of Secretary of State for War had been taken on temporarily by the Prime Minister since the resignation of Seeley over the Home Rule imbroglio. Asquith's Liberal government invited Field Marshal Lord Kitchener of Khartoum to fill the vacancy.

Kitchener had been the British Agent in Egypt – effectively the Governor General – since 1911. He arrived in England on inter-tour leave in June 1914, and as the First Soldier of the Empire was consulted by both soldiers and politicians during that trying summer. Asquith was impressed by Kitchener's grasp of world affairs and of strategy, particularly when he was asked for his opinion on the defence of the Mediterranean in the event of a war. Kitchener had long believed that there would be a European war and was a supporter of the 'With the French' group, which considered that if hostilities broke out Britain should intervene on the side of France. When war was declared Kitchener immediately prepared to return to his post, as the government had ordered all heads of mission to do. He was summoned from the Boulogne ferry at Dover by a telephone call from the Prime Minister, and on 5 August it was announced that he was to be appointed Secretary of State for War.

Kitchener had no wish to become involved in political affairs. Like most soldiers of the day he distrusted politicians and thought they were 'meddlers', constantly interfering in matters about which they knew nothing. He had hoped to return to Egypt, finish his tour there, and then to be appointed Viceroy of India. Reluctantly he responded to appeals to his patriotism and agreed to serve, provided that he was excused parliamentary duties. He was to be a minister without party, and would have his field marshal's salary augmented by £5,000 per annum as a minister, and by a special allowance of £1,150. Grey, the Foreign Secretary, was dubious about the appointment, and Haldane, standing in for the Prime Minister at the War Office, was against, but the public and the press were jubilant. As *The Times* of 6 August exclaimed,

> We need hardly say with what profound satisfaction and relief we hear of Lord Kitchener's appointment as Secretary of State for War...there has been abundant testimony to the confidence which his name inspires in the public at this tremendous crisis...we heartily congratulate the Government on the promptitude with which they have confirmed the popular choice. In the huge task of equipping and dispatching our land forces, as well as perfecting the measures for protecting these shores, Lord Kitchener's services will be invaluable.[3]

It was said, then and later, that Kitchener was the first soldier to sit in the Cabinet since General Monck in 1660. This is false, as the Master General of the Ordnance, a serving general, was an ex officio member of the Cabinet and its principal military adviser until 1854, but it is true that no soldier had been entrusted with so much political power for centuries. The fact was that Kitchener's enormous prestige at home, in the Empire and in Europe was a much-needed boost for a weak government, and a reassurance to the public that the war would be conducted by someone who knew how to do it, and whom they could trust.

On 25 August Kitchener made his first speech in the House of Lords, having been tactfully dissuaded from sitting on the first available bench, which was reserved for bishops. He was listened to in respectful silence, although his assertion that Britain would need a mass army of thirty divisions horrified some (they would be even more horrified later, when he recommended seventy). Kitchener was well aware, long before any politician came to accept it, that this would be a long war and that Britain would have to field an army far larger than any in her history. He was sympathetic to the National Service League, which had campaigned for conscription since 1905, but he was astute enough not to press these views too publicly. Kitchener probably could have got Parliament to accept conscription in the first flush of bellicosity in 1914, but he was unwilling to create political waves, and deferred to Asquith's advice that the time was not yet ripe. In any case, he thought that the whole process of getting the measure through both Houses, and setting up the machinery to register those eligible, would take too long.

There can be no doubt that Kitchener's greatest service to the nation's war effort was the raising of the New Armies, which were colloquially known as the 'Kitchener armies'. Here he began to upset politicians. Kitchener had little time for the Territorial Force – unlike Haig who had helped to set it up – and considered it to be largely a drinking club which played at soldiers at weekends. He also disliked the fact that the Territorial Force was not under the direct control of the War Office but was managed by County Associations, with all sorts of local interests to placate.[4] Kitchener was perhaps too direct in his comments about the Territorial Force, which upset Liberal politicians who liked the idea of a citizen army.

Kitchener was accustomed to absolute power, and had always managed to avoid serving at the War Office. As Commander-in-Chief of the army in India from 1902 to 1909, he had seen off no less a personage than the Viceroy, Lord Curzon, and in Egypt his power was almost unfettered. He saw no reason now to take politicians into his confidence on matters which they could not understand, and considered most of them to be a security risk: 'If I tell them anything, they tell their wives, except for Lloyd George who tells somebody else's wife,' he is reputed to have said. Lloyd George was a consummate Welsh politician, pure but by no means simple. He was witty, he could be charming, he was a master of the quick riposte and had much Celtic romanticism in his veins. He was also inconsistent and was seen by many as an opportunist lacking principle. A political chameleon, he was a master of the spoken word and an expert at grubbing about in the political weeds. His real surname was George. He had tacked on the Lloyd, presumably to add a bit of class, and was annoyed if he was referred to as Mr George. Apart from parliamentary reports he was said to read nothing but sermons written in Welsh, and although his military experience was limited to brief service in the old, pre-Haldane, militia, he was given to monumental flights of strategy, usually based on little knowledge of the true situation and often on none at all. He began the war as Chancellor of the Exchequer and would, via the Ministry of Munitions and the War Ministry, become Prime Minister in December 1916. Major-General

Sir Frederick Maurice (whose career came to an abrupt end when he accused Lloyd George of lying to the House of Commons) said, 'Lloyd George's strengths as a war minister were his faith in victory and his power of keeping the confidence of the public. His weaknesses were his belief in his military judgement, his power of deceiving himself, his failure to understand that opportunism, sometimes successful in peace, is highly dangerous in war.'[5]

Lloyd George had little time for Kitchener's methods, but Kitchener did not help matters by inviting unnecessary conflict with ministers. He should never, for example, have got himself involved in the row over chaplains. Prior to 1914 recognised religions in the British army were Church of England, Church of Scotland, Roman Catholic, Jewish (there were hardly any) and 'OD' or other denominations. Chaplains were appointed in proportion to the numbers of soldiers professing those religions. Only those ODs listed in King's Regulations were recognised. Lloyd George, then Chancellor of the Exchequer, raised in Cabinet the spiritual welfare of Welsh recruits to the New Armies who might belong to one of the multifarious Nonconformist sects existing in Wales, which included Congregationalists, Welsh Baptists, Primitive Methodists and more. Kitchener flatly refused to appoint any chaplains from those faiths. The row escalated until Kitchener threatened to resign if the matter was pressed, after which he gave way 'gracefully'.[6] The War Minister should never have taken a stand on an issue such as this. The provision of chaplains was a matter for the Adjutant General, and should have been dealt with through the normal administrative machinery of the army. Lloyd George should not have raised it in Cabinet, and probably did so to cause mischief; Kitchener should have refused to be drawn.

Kitchener and Lloyd George also disagreed over the raising of a New Army Welsh division. The long martial tradition of the Scots was well understood in the army, and there were Scottish divisions. There were also three Irish divisions, one regular (10 Division) and two New Army (16th (Irish) and 36th (Ulster) Divisions). Wales was a slightly different matter, however. There was little love for the army in the industrial and mining areas where troops had been used to break strikes; pre-war recruiting from Wales had long been difficult, and Nonconformist preachers tended to expound a doctrine of anti-militarism. Lloyd George won the day: a Welsh division was raised, and Kitchener's view of Lloyd George as a meddler was confirmed. Again, it would have been better for Kitchener to give way and reserve his firepower for more important issues. In the event the Welsh joined with almost the same enthusiasm as did the English (twenty-two per cent of the adult male population of Wales against twenty-four per cent in England) and the Welsh Division was as least as good as any other New Army formation.

The eventual marginalisation of Kitchener was due as much to the army as to political distaste for his methods, his reluctance to take politicians into his confidence and his abrupt attitude towards them. With the removal of many of the senior officers in the War Office to man the BEF in France, and a weak CIGS, Kitchener found himself not only Minister for War but also sole military adviser to the Cabinet. Kitchener and French, Commander-in-Chief BEF, had disagreed as to the likely duration of the war. French resented Kitchener's coming to France in full field marshal's uniform to exhort the Commander-in-Chief on no account to withdraw the BEF to the Channel ports when the Allies were in full retreat in 1914; he was no happier when Kitchener insisted that the BEF should fall in with French plans for the Loos battle in 1915. Withdrawal of officers and NCOs from the BEF to train the New Armies was another source of friction. When Colonel Reppington exposed the 'Shells Scandal' in *The Times* in May 1915 much of the fallout landed on Kitchener, who was responsible for military policy, manpower and the provision of weapons, equipment and ammunition. That the BEF was severely deficient in ammunition was not the fault of Kitchener, but of the pre-war policy of stockpiling for an army of six divisions fighting a war of the intensity of the South African War, red tape in the procurement system, and the refusal of the government to put the country and its industry on a full war footing. The scandal did eventually allow the politicians to take the provision of munitions away from Kitchener, and while a great deal of fuss and feathers looked good to the public, it is highly questionable whether Lloyd George and his Ministry of Munitions achieved much more than Kitchener would have done with full government backing.

Even if the army did not entirely blame Kitchener for the shortage of munitions, senior commanders felt that Kitchener's military experience was out of date. By taking everything on himself, Kitchener had reduced the CIGS to little more than an office manager, and improvements in the military direction of the war were stalled until the reshuffle precipitated by the removal of French from command of the BEF and the appointment of Robertson as CIGS in December 1915.

The ill-fated Dardanelles campaign was an example of the primacy of political over military concerns. In January 1915 the Tsar had asked the Allies to mount an operation against Turkey to draw pressure off the Russians in the Caucasus. The British and French governments were concerned that Russia might be tempted to make a separate peace, and agreed to do something to help. The War Council – effectively a subcommittee of the Cabinet – considered what might be done. Kitchener realised that Russia did need some assistance but emphasised that Britain's reserves of manpower were still small, and would be needed in Flanders. Anything to help the Russians must not involve large numbers of soldiers. Lloyd George floated a grandiose scheme that involved shifting a large proportion of the British army to the Balkans where, in concert with Serbia, Romania and Greece, it might be used to knock both Turkey and Austria-Hungary out of the war. As Serbia was all but defeated and neither Greece nor Romania was a belligerent (and would not be until June and August 1917 respectively), and as the cooperation of Italy would be essential but was not yet assured (Italy would join in May 1915), this was a highly speculative plan, and Kitchener was fortunately able to quash it.

Churchill, First Lord of the Admiralty, and like Lloyd George always seeking a clever way to outflank the Western Front, suggested that the navy should land a British force at Zeebrugge and Antwerp. This too was rejected by Kitchener – the navy could certainly land a force there, but it would be far too small to achieve anything. Having pointed out that any action on another front would need a minimum of 150,000 men – who could not be spared – Kitchener reluctantly agreed at least to consider an operation in the Dardanelles. This horrified Sir John French, who saw that the only way to make troops available for an adventure away from the Western Front would be to reduce the number of divisions available to him. Then Churchill struck again. He now proposed a purely naval assault on the Dardanelles. The navy could force the narrows, knock out the Turkish forts, sail into the Sea of Marmara and bombard Constantinople. Turkey would leave the war and the Allies could attack the Central Powers through the Balkans. It seemed the answer to everybody's problems. It would help Russia, it would not need any troops, and it would preserve the Western Front as the main theatre on land.

The Royal Navy failed to knock out the Turkish forts, thus confirming what most sailors knew already, if only they had stopped to think about it. The Admiralty now announced that the campaign could still be won if the army took a hand. Kitchener was unhappy, but his Middle-Eastern experience inclined him to the view that a campaign once started had to be seen through to victory, otherwise British prestige would suffer a blow from which it might not recover. Churchill was optimistic and Kitchener reluctant, but British troops were sent, and as France was suspicious about British long-term intentions in the Dardanelles, French troops went too. Gallipoli was a bloody failure, sucked in more and more British, Indian, French, Australian and New Zealand troops, and had to be abandoned in December 1915.

The Gallipoli campaign did much to destroy Kitchener's position with the politicians. While it was they who had initiated the scheme, Kitchener had gone along with them and they could blame him for its supposed mismanagement. They could also blame him for the failure of Loos in 1915, although it was the politicians who had insisted that the BEF should conform to French wishes against the advice of the soldiers, who knew that resources were insufficient to support two major campaigns 1,000 miles apart. Matters were not helped by the Cabinet's seeing a letter written by Keith Murdoch, an Australian war correspondent (and father of the twentieth-century press baron Rupert Murdoch), which accused everybody in the Dardanelles except the Australians of incompetence and mismanagement; nor was Kitchener's standing enhanced by the appointment of his old adversary Lord Curzon to the government as Lord Privy Seal. Increasingly Kitchener was being forced on the defensive in Cabinet by the well-honed rhetoric of Lloyd Gorge and the legal precision of Carson (Attorney General in Asquith's government from May to October 1915). Many politicians who were in favour of conscription were turned against

Kitchener by the field marshal's insistence, contrary to his own private view, on staying loyal to Asquith, who was against it.

While Kitchener was away in the Gallipoli Peninsula in November 1915, making a personal inspection in order to decide what to do next, his enemies struck. Led by Lloyd George, Curzon and Carson (now temporarily out of office, but still with considerable influence), and with the support of others in the Cabinet, the government was prevailed upon to reduce the powers of the Secretary of State for War. All control over munitions was removed from him, and henceforth the Master General of the Ordnance, the responsible military officer, would report to the Ministry of Munitions. Sir John French was removed from command of the BEF and replaced by Sir Douglas Haig (a move of which Kitchener approved), and Sir William Robertson was appointed CIGS.

Robertson would only accept the job if he was allowed to fulfil what he – and many senior officers – saw as being the proper function of the CIGS, which was to manage the conduct of the war as a whole and be the sole professional military adviser to the Cabinet. This was a severe truncation of Kitchener's powers, but it placed responsibility for the military direction of the war where it always should have lain: with the professional head of the army rather than with one man who, for all his greatness, could not possibly fill a Cabinet post and be de facto head of the army at the same time.

As it happened Robertson and Kitchener got on well together, and both men arrived at an acceptable modus vivendi. Robertson's difficulties were to increase greatly when Kitchener was drowned on HMS *Hampshire* on his way to Russia in June 1916, and Lloyd George became Secretary of State for War.

Robertson was brusque to the point of rudeness; like Kitchener he had no time for armchair strategists or enthusiastic amateurs, and he had little time for party politics. On one thing, however, he was quite clear: the war would be won or lost on the Western Front because that was where the bulk of the German army was, and it was there, and only there, that it could be defeated. Any dilution of Allied effort on the Western Front was to be resisted to the utmost.

What now needed resisting was another bright idea dreamed up by politicians. Opposed to any major effort on the Western Front in 1916, Lloyd George, supported by Balfour (who had succeeded Churchill as First Lord of the Admiralty), again urged action in the Balkans. The British had already been sucked into that theatre when Bulgaria joined the war on the side of the Central Powers, and the pro-Allied Prime Minister of Greece, Venizelos, asked for Allied assistance. On 9 October 1915 French and British troops landed in Salonika, at the head of the Aegean Sea, hoping that they might be able to do something to help Serbia. Unfortunately for the Allies King Constantine of Greece was not at all in agreement with his prime minister, for despite having an English wife he was strongly pro-German. He dismissed Venizelos and declared Greek neutrality. The position of the Allied forces in Salonika was not improved when the Serbs were soundly trounced; indeed the very presence of the British and French was now pointless. When Robertson took over as CIGS he advocated the withdrawal of troops from Salonika. They could do little, and every man sent there diminished Allied strength in the main theatre – the Western Front. Despite military advice the government would not accede to withdrawal from Salonika, and even insisted on reinforcing it. At one stage Lloyd George even wanted to go to war against Greece (he was dissuaded), and by 1917 the Allies had half a million men in Salonika, many of them incapable of doing anything because of the ravages of malaria.

Lloyd George persisted throughout the war in seeing opportunities in the Balkans. On 4 July 1917 Robertson wrote to Lord Curzon:

It would be valuable if you would kindly explain to the Prime Minister [Lloyd George since December 1916] during the discussion on the Salonika question what the nature of the Balkan country is. He seems quite unable to envisage it and to understand the difficulty of getting heavy artillery forward in an advance and in supplying an army. No one can explain the matter to him as well as yourself. Amongst other things he seems to think that there is a single range of hills between the Salonika forces and Sofia [the Bulgarian capital], whereas the whole country is a mass of mountains. The country is, in short, one in which a small army would be murdered and a large army would starve, and it is of a highly defensible nature. No amount of argument and no amount of heavy artillery will alter it.[7]

Initially operating as two separate forces, the French and the British in Salonika were eventually brought under a unified (French) command that included the Serbian army, which arrived via Macedonia and Crete, and the Greek army once Greece had sent King Constantine packing and replaced him with King Alexander, who reinstated Venizelos as prime minister and joined the war on the Allied side. Eventually, after the arrival of the competent French General Louis Franchet d'Esperey (known as Desperate Frankie to the British) in 1918, the Allied army managed to force Bulgaria out of the war on 29 September 1918, and by the time of the Armistice Desperate Frankie's soldiers were approaching the Danube.

Bulgaria would have collapsed anyway once German support was withdrawn, and the soldiers tied down in Salonika would have been of far more use on the Western Front. It was an unnecessary campaign, forced on the army by the politicians who refused to heed military advice, and who claimed (spuriously) that it had to be persisted with as an example of Allied solidarity. Although Robertson did not succeed in having the Salonika caper closed down completely, he did at least manage to prevent Lloyd George from making it the major focus of British efforts. This, by fatally weakening the Western Front, would have been disastrous.

Robertson barely concealed his contempt for Lloyd George's military opinions. At Cabinet meetings Lloyd George would lean back, fix Robertson with a steely glare and say, 'CIGS, I have heard…' before going on to expound his latest flight of strategic fancy. Robertson would listen in silence and then reply bluntly, 'I've 'eard different,' and slap his ruler on the table to end the discussion. However, there were occasions – a few – when political interference was helpful. The BEF had taken some limited expertise in the management of railways with it to France in 1914, but nobody had realised then how the transport infrastructure needed to supply the war would grow. As Minister of Munitions Lloyd George was instrumental in setting up a commission to examine transport problems on the Western Front; he thought (rightly) that these were causing bottlenecks in the provision and distribution of ammunition. While some generals were opposed to civilians examining military problems, Haig was happy to accept any expert help he could get. The commission, which visited the Western Front in August 1916, was led by Sir Eric Geddes, then in the Ministry of

Munitions but up to 1914 the Deputy General Manager of the North Eastern Railway, one of the largest British railway companies. Geddes already had some experience of army transport problems as he had advised on the restructuring of Indian railways in 1904, when there was a (largely unfounded) fear of a Russian invasion via Afghanistan. Geddes' commission looked at military transport as an entity, rather than dividing it into road, rail and canal as the army did. He found that it was lack of organisation rather than of rolling stock that was the main problem, and produced a number of far-reaching and sensible recommendations. Nearly all of these were accepted by Haig, who began to implement them. Lloyd George now invited Geddes to fill the newly created post of Director General of Military Railways at the War Office, insisting that the army make him a major-general to kill military objections to a civilian giving orders to people in uniform. A day later, on 22 September 1916, came a request from Haig that Geddes should join GHQ of the BEF as Director General of Transport. Lloyd George agreed. Geddes' position in France was not an easy one to begin with; no doubt there were embarrassing moments when the new general wondered which hand to salute with, and got to grips with the differences between a lance corporal and a colonel, but Haig granted him direct access to himself and gave him his full support. The appointment was a huge success. By 1917 the army was going to have to move 2,200 tons for each mile of front, and Geddes' reorganisation of the transport system, including the establishment of a light rail network to deliver stores from the standard-gauge railheads to just behind the lines, was to revolutionise the military supply system. Other civilian experts followed.

Despite some grumbling by soldiers, Haig had no doubts. In his diary for 26 October 1916 he wrote:

> There is a good deal of criticism apparently being made at the appointment of a civilian like Geddes to an important post on the Headquarters of an Army in the field. These critics seem to fail to realise the size of this Army, and the amount of work which the army requires of a civilian nature. The working of the railways, the upkeep of the roads, even the baking of bread, and a thousand other industries go on in peace as well as in war. So with the whole nation at war, our object should be to employ men on the same

work in war as they are accustomed to do in peace. Acting on this principle, I have got Geddes at the head of all the railways and transportation,
with the best practical and civil engineers under him. At the head of the
road directorate is Mr Maybury, head of the Road Board in England. The
docks, canals and inland water transport are being managed in the same
way, i.e. by men of practical experience. To put soldiers who have no practical experience of these matters into such positions, merely because they
are generals and colonels, must result in utter failure.[8]

Would that the civilian/military interface always worked so smoothly.[9]

After the first experience of using tanks on the Somme in 1916, Haig
determined to use the new weapon to fight a decisive battle. On 20
November 1917 nineteen British divisions supported by 378 tanks attacked
in the direction of Cambrai over a six-mile front. They advanced nearly
three miles, and church bells rang in England. The attack petered out at
the end of November, largely because there were no fresh divisions to
follow through, and when the Germans counter-attacked the exhausted
troops on 1 December, they regained much of the ground they had lost.

That there were no fresh divisions to reinforce success at the Battle of
Cambrai was partly due to the Third Battle of Ypres which had only just
been closed down in Flanders, but partly also to another politicians' wheeze:
the removal of five British and six French divisions from the Western Front
to prevent an Italian collapse. Italy had been a member of the Triple Alliance
with Germany and Austria before the war, but had always made it clear
that she would not go to war against the British (which, given that Britain
controlled the Mediterranean, would have been foolish in the extreme);
in any case, the alliance with Austria was unpopular with the Italian public.
Once war started in 1914, Italy held out to see what she could extract from
the two opposing camps. What she really wanted was Trieste, Italian-
speaking but still held by Austria after the wars of Italian liberation between
1866 and 1870. Austria was prepared to grant Italy neither Trieste nor any
other territory; but Britain and France were happy to offer concessions at
Austria's expense, and Italy joined the war on the Allied side in May 1915.
Italy made some progress against the Austrians, who appealed for German
help. Initially this was not forthcoming, but after the Somme offensive

and the German withdrawal to the Hindenburg Line in February 1917, Ludendorff relented. Germany sent seven divisions[10] to the Italian front, the logic being that if Italy was threatened the French and British would reinforce her, thus weakening the Allied strength on the Western Front. Additionally, if the Italian front could be shortened, this would release some Austrian divisions for the Western Front; and if all went really well, Italy could be knocked out of the war and Germany could occupy northern Italy and threaten the Allies from a new Alpine front. All these prospects except the first were delusions. Austria was already seeking a way out of the war and would have been most reluctant to send anybody to the Western Front; and a glance at the map shows that any meaningful threat to France through the Alps would have taken up far more resources than could justify any potential gain.

In October and November 1917 the Battle of Caporetto and the subsequent Austrian advance, spearheaded by German troops, pushed the Italians back to the River Piave; requests for British and French help were renewed with urgency. Up to now Robertson had usually managed to resist such pleas, pointing out that the Italians had ample manpower to defend their own frontiers, and he supported Haig's protests when Lloyd George suggested sending some heavy guns that were sorely wanted on the Western Front.[11] On that occasion Lloyd George had his way, and in the spring of 1917 seventy six-inch howitzers were despatched to the Italians, thus reducing the number available to Haig for Third Ypres. It was not the first time that Lloyd George had attempted to be profligate with equipment badly needed by the British: in March 1916, as Minister of Munitions, he had urged the sending of machine guns to Romania. Robertson said that he would certainly send some as soon as there were enough to equip the British army, and the matter was dropped.

In September 1917 Robertson again managed to dissuade Lloyd George from sending men and guns to Italy; but now, in October, Lloyd George insisted and they went. They spent November trundling to Italy at a stately pace on French railways, and were available neither for Third Ypres nor for Cambrai. In early 1918 the German troops were withdrawn back to the Western Front. The French and British defended successfully against an Austrian attack in the Asiago in June 1918, and participated in the final advance across the River Piave and on to Trento in October and November 1918; but by then the Austrians were near collapse. This again was an unnecessary campaign, initiated by politicians who thought they knew more about waging war than did the professionals. It held down Allied troops who would have been far better employed in France and Flanders. Italy could well have been left on the defensive, but was insistent on taking the offensive in order to capture Trieste, her sole reason for coming into the war in the first place. An offensive could only take place if the Italian armies were stiffened by French and British divisions. As it happened Trieste was captured not by the Italian army, but by a landing by the Allied navies on 3 November 1918.

Divide and rule has ever been a popular political ploy. While Robertson as CIGS did not always agree with Haig's ideas about the Western Front, he took care never to let any difference of opinion show. Lloyd George was increasingly distrustful of Haig, but as long as the CIGS supported him there was little that Lloyd George, as Minister of Munitions, War Minister (from July 1916) or Prime Minister (from December 1916), could do. This did not stop him trying, and when Robertson was away from London visiting Haig and the French GHQ in June 1916, Lloyd George was instrumental in setting up a 'War Policy Committee' with a brief to investigate the naval, military and political situation and present a full report to the War Cabinet. The members were Curzon, Milner, Smuts and Lloyd George. Curzon and Milner were not on good terms with each other. Smuts had undergone a Pauline conversion to the cause of British imperialism, but his military experience had been gained as the leader of a people's militia in a very different war. This left Lloyd George to control the committee and to decide from whom to take evidence.

Lloyd George simply did not accept that the Western Front was the only theatre where the Germans could be beaten. He spoke loftily of 'knocking away the props', by which he meant Turkey, Bulgaria and Austria-Hungary, while failing to understand that it was Germany that was the prop: defeat her, and all else would crumble. In some ways the removal of Germany's allies would help the German war effort, for it was German money, German equipment and German advisers that kept them in the war. If Lloyd George could not persuade the generals and the rest of the government to divert attention from the Western Front, he had to find a way of obstructing the Commander-in-Chief of the BEF, Haig, and Haig's supporter and protector, Robertson. So occurred the most dishonourable and underhand attempts ever by a British politician to stab his own commander-in-chief in the back.

After the Somme offensive of 1916 Joffre and Haig had agreed to mount another joint offensive in 1917, the tentative date being February. Then there was a major change in the French high command. French politicians and the French public were weary of the seemingly endless casualty lists with no victory in sight. They felt that a change at the top was needed, and so Joffre was made a Marshal of France and hustled off to a non-job at Versailles, where he had a telephone that never rang and an in-tray into which no papers ever came. In his place the French government chose General Robert Nivelle. It was Nivelle who had been responsible for the one ray of sunshine amid the gloom of Verdun, the recapture of Fort Douaumont. Nivelle declared that he had the secret: he had devised methods that could break through the German defences in forty-eight hours. The French government seized on this energetic, articulate general who seemed the one man who could break the stalemate and end the war. As a Protestant he was attractive politically; for although France was a Roman Catholic country there was traditional suspicion, going back to the Revolution, of clerical influence – indeed it was said that Joffre had only been appointed Commander-in-Chief because he was known to be a good republican. Nivelle was promoted over the heads of Foch, Pétain and de Castelnau, all considerably senior to him. His first decision was to delay the opening of the 1917 offensive until his own plans were ready.

Nivelle had an English mother and spoke excellent English, which enabled him to impress Lloyd George and seduce the British Prime Minister, briefly, from his antagonism to the Western Front. Nivelle, thought Lloyd George, could be the saviour of the Allied cause, and the way to rein in Haig and the BEF would be to subject them to Nivelle's control. The plot was hatched between Lloyd George and the French Prime Minister, Briand, with Nivelle's full knowledge, and announced in guarded terms at a Cabinet meeting in London on 24 February – a meeting to which neither the Secretary of State for War (now Lord Derby) nor the CIGS, Robertson, were invited to attend. As it was known that the King would never agree to what was being planned, the copy of the minutes normally sent to the palace immediately after Cabinet meetings was delayed, and not sent to the King until 28 February.

The Calais Conference of 26 and 27 February 1917 was ostensibly called to discuss transportation problems on the Western Front. The French railway system was having difficulties in supplying the trains needed for the build-up of the French and British armies for the forthcoming offensive, and it does look as if the British were asking rather too much (almost twice as many trains as the French, for about half the troops). Present at the conference were Prime Minister Briand, General Lyautey (the Minister for War) and General Nivelle representing the French, and Lloyd George, Field Marshal Haig and General Robertson for the British. Both delegations were attended by technical advisers. After some discussion about transport, Lloyd George pitched his bombshell into the middle of the table. On the pretext of achieving unity of command for the 1917 offensive, he proposed that the BEF should become subservient to Nivelle. A unified command was of course sensible, and had the suggestion been for an overall Commander-in-Chief (who would have had to be French) to whom both Nivelle and Haig would be subordinate, then no one – least of all Haig and Robertson – could have disagreed. What was not acceptable was Lloyd George's plan for the five British armies to become armies in Nivelle's command, to be employed by him like any of his French armies. Orders to the British would be transmitted through a British chief of staff (Nivelle had asked for the very dubious Wilson), and Haig would be responsible only for administration and discipline. Not only was this completely unacceptable to Haig and Robertson, it had not even been discussed with them beforehand. This was not an attempt to achieve unified direction, but an effort to undermine the British chain of command and reduce Robertson and Haig to mere lackeys of the French. Perhaps Lloyd George was hoping that the CIGS and the Commander-in-Chief BEF would resign on the spot, but in the event hard negotiation diluted the proposal – which even the French generals cannot have believed would be accepted. The outcome was that the BEF would remain a distinct entity, with Haig still in command, but would be under Nivelle for the duration of the 1917 offensive only.

On his return to London Robertson wrote to Haig on 28 February:

> He [Lloyd George] is an awful liar. His story at the War Cabinet gave quite
> the wrong impression this morning. He accused the French of putting
> forward a monstrous proposal, and yet you and I know that he was at the
> bottom of it. I believe he equally misled the Cabinet last Saturday [the
> meeting at which Lord Derby and Robertson were not present]. Derby [War
> Minister] is telling Balfour [Foreign Secretary] the whole truth. The former
> talked of resigning last night. He was furious and disgusted. He spoke up
> like a man for you this morning and insisted on a letter of confidence and
> appreciation being sent to you. This will come in a day or two. Meanwhile
> I pray you and Nivelle may hit it off. These things always happen in war.
> But they are worse now than ever. Still, I cannot believe that a man such as
> he can for long remain head of any Government.[12] Surely some honesty and
> truth are required.[13]

As it happened not too much harm was done, except in the relations
between Lloyd George and Haig: the latter never trusted the Prime Minister
again. Nivelle moved the focus of the 1917 campaign south, to the River
Aisne, requiring the BEF to mount only subsidiary attacks around Arras.
The Arras battles were successful, showing that the British army had indeed
learned from the Somme; the main offensive was a total disaster, and Nivelle
ceased to trouble historians thereafter.

Lloyd George had failed to reduce Haig's powers by placing the BEF
under the French, but he had not given up hope of defeating the Western
Front advocates. He now turned to his War Policy Committee. As might
have been expected, the committee was able to place other theatres back on
the agenda. Russia, the Balkans, Palestine and Italy all raised their heads
again. Robertson was able to head off a proposal to make Palestine the
major focus of British offensive operations in 1917 and 1918 only by telling
Allenby, commanding in that theatre, to ask for another thirteen divisions
in order to strike the decisive blow. As this was manifestly impossible, the
plan was not proceeded with.

Lloyd George now decided to seek alternative military advice. While
constitutionally the military adviser to the Cabinet was the CIGS, a committee could seek advice from whom it liked. Claiming that a terminally

ill patient is entitled to seek a second opinion, Lloyd George and the War Policy Committee heard evidence from elsewhere. The evidence was selective, to say the least, for two of the principal witnesses were Sir John French, still smarting over his supersession as Commander-in-Chief of the BEF, and Sir Henry Wilson, clever, sociable, and regarded with great suspicion by most soldiers as an inveterate intriguer.

Lloyd George could not persuade these two to recommend a diversion from the Western Front – as professional soldiers they knew only too well that it was there that the Germans must be defeated – but they did recommend moves towards much closer coordination of the war effort. Thus arose the Inter-Allied Supreme War Council. On the face of it this was a sound proposal, agreed at the Rapallo Conference on 7 November 1917. A body made up of senior Allied politicians and soldiers would sit at Versailles to oversee Allied strategy. They would advise Allied governments directly and would be able to take a joint decision with greater speed than could be achieved by discussions between the various capitals. The devil was in the Supreme War Council's direct access to governments, or more properly in the senior British military representative's being in direct contact with Lloyd George without going through the CIGS. Again, this was not unity of command, but division of direction: the old politicians' ploy of playing one off against the other. Robertson saw it for what it was: an attempt to sideline his increasingly unpalatable but realistic opinions in favour of advice from a more congenial source. If Lloyd George could direct British strategy through the Supreme War Council rather than through the CIGS, Robertson could find himself implementing plans with which he disagreed, and which he had had no part in formulating. He was in an impossible position.

This disagreement between Lloyd George and Robertson very nearly caused an open breach between the Cabinet and the army. Little was hidden from the press, and newspapers took sides for or against Robertson. Robertson's reply to the proposal for a Supreme War Council was to suggest that he (or anyone else appointed as CIGS in his stead) should also be the British Military Representative on the council, thus avoiding conflicting advice. If this was not acceptable then the council representative should be a deputy to the CIGS, thus preserving the chain of command. Lloyd George would have none of it and Robertson submitted his resignation, being persuaded to stay on while the politicians wheeled and dealed to find a successor. The original suggestion had been for Henry Wilson to sit on the council, and when Robertson demurred Lloyd George offered Robertson the post on the council while Wilson became CIGS. Again Robertson refused: the principle had not altered, whoever was CIGS and whoever went to the council. Plumer was invited to become CIGS, and he (probably wisely) turned the offer down. Inevitably the politician won. Robertson left the War Office and replaced French as Commander-in-Chief Home Forces; Wilson became CIGS, and Rawlinson went to Versailles. Fortunately for the conduct of the war, Haig was persuaded not to add his resignation to that of Robertson, and Haig had a good working relationship with Rawlinson, the erstwhile commander of the Fourth Army.

While the manoeuvrings to set up the Supreme War Council were going on, Lloyd George saw another way to hobble Haig. The casualties of the Third Ypres battles (about which more later) had horrified the Prime Minister, who told Haig that he was considering telling the soldiers that 'the attacks in Flanders were a useless loss of life and all the sufferings and hardship they had endured were unnecessary'.[14] Lloyd George was convinced that the failure to capitalise on the initial successes of the Cambrai battle was not due to the lack of the five divisions and the heavy guns sent to Italy on his orders, but that 'this action was grossly bungled and the tank success was thrown away by the ineptitude of the high command'. He particularly blamed Brigadier General Charteris, Haig's Chief of Intelligence, for failing to predict the German counter-attack of 1 December 1917 that recaptured much of the ground taken at Cambrai. He made a speech critical of the generals at a lunch in Paris during the negotiations for the Supreme War Council, and when he agreed to executive powers for the military representatives on the council (Wilson and Foch), this was the last straw for Robertson. Lloyd George still believed that the men who fought the Third Ypres battles should have been transferred for use against the Turks; one shudders at the consequences had his thinking prevailed.

While Lloyd George did not feel sufficiently confident to sack Haig – the press was already running articles headed 'Hands off the Generals' – he decided that the way to stop Haig wasting yet more lives was not to give him any more lives to waste. The year 1917 had cost the BEF around 160,000 men killed up to the end of November, and another 400,000 or so wounded in various degrees. Reinforcements were badly needed to bring battalions and divisions back up to war establishment. There were men available in garrisons in England, and industry had not been combed out for those men medically fit and of military age who were not essential to the war effort. Some drafts were sent, but they were nothing like sufficient to fill the gaps. If Lloyd George could not get rid of Haig, he would make it impossible for him to launch another offensive. In fact, by the end of 1917 Haig had come to the conclusion that what mattered now was to keep the French army in the war, and that it would be the Germans who would do the attacking in 1918. Pétain, now commanding the French army in place of Nivelle, thought that his army would not be ready to go onto the offensive until 1919. Haig regarded the German logic as based on the following premises: that although the Americans were now in the war, it would be some time before they were capable of doing very much; that Russia was all but out of the war, which would allow German divisions to be transferred from the Eastern Front; that Germany's allies were showing strong signs of war-weariness; and that the Allied blockade was biting as never before. All this being so, the Germans had no option but to try to win the war, or at least put themselves in a position for a favourable peace, by an offensive in 1918 before American troops were ready to take the field. It would be a gamble of Napoleonic proportions, but it was Germany's only hope. While the BEF could go on the offensive if enough reinforcements were forthcoming (but Lloyd George was ensuring that there would not be), the French most certainly could not. This, thought Haig, led inevitably to an Allied defensive posture for the beginning of 1918, and on 19 December 1917 Charteris predicted that the German onslaught would fall in March 1918.[15] Lloyd George refused to believe in a German offensive. He tried to persuade Haig that his fears were groundless and that 'the German army was done – there would be no German offensive'.[16] Haig was unmoved.

If the politicians could not replace Haig – there was no one else willing and able to assume the mantle, and such a step would have led to an almighty row in Parliament and in the press – they could chip away at some of the lesser lights. Lieutenant General Sir Launcelot Kiggell had been Chief of the General Staff of the BEF since Haig assumed command in December 1915. He was a highly experienced staff officer, a graduate of the Staff College and its commandant prior to the outbreak of war. He tended to be over-optimistic and was somewhat of a plodder, but Haig had tremendous confidence in him. Now Lloyd George and his henchmen wanted rid of him. As the doctors had reported that Kiggell was suffering from nervous exhaustion, Haig was prepared to let him go and wanted to appoint his deputy, the forty-seven-year-old Major-General Richard Butler.[17] The government refused to accept Butler, and the job went to Herbert Lawrence. Butler was given command of a corps, which he probably very much preferred. Charteris, the head of intelligence, was forced out in favour of Brigadier General Edward Cox from Intelligence Branch in the War Office, and even the Quartermaster General, Maxwell, had to go, replaced by Lieutenant General Travers Clarke, previously Deputy Adjutant General. All of these new brooms were competent staff officers; they did a good job and Haig was happy with them. But for the politicians to attack the chief by axing his closest colleagues was pure spite, and to refuse him the man whom he knew, whom he had groomed and whom he had requested as Chief of the General Staff, was petty interference on a grand scale.

Haig did not get his reinforcements. Even Churchill, another opponent of the Western Front strategy, thought this was inexcusable, but the government continued to search for other less expensive ways to win the war. The Head of the Air Board, Lord Rothermere, demanded that Major-General Trenchard, commanding Haig's air forces in France, be sent back to London to become Chief of Air Staff. Rothermere knew a great deal about newspapers, very little about aircraft and nothing at all about fighting a war. Trenchard thought that Rothermere and others who thought that the war could be won from the air were 'off their heads'.

With insufficient reinforcements to keep the BEF up to strength, and with Lloyd George agreeing to take over more and more sectors of the front from the French, the only options open to Haig were to disband divisions or restructure the existing ones. Haig elected to follow the German practice, and by February 1918 each brigade had been reduced from four infantry battalions to three, giving each division nine battalions in place of twelve. Divisional artillery was also reduced. Although the deficiencies were to some extent compensated for by an increase in machine-gun support and by the augmentation of corps and army artillery, divisions had to cover the same – and in some cases an increased – length of front with a reduction of one-third in the men available to man the trenches. Only the Canadians opted out, and to the end they continued to man four divisions, each with three four-battalion brigades.

As the generals had predicted and as Lloyd George stubbornly refused to believe, the Germans did launch a massive offensive in March 1918. The strength of the German army on the Western Front had increased by a quarter since November 1917, mainly through transfers from the Eastern Front following the Treaty of Brest-Litovsk, while that of the British had decreased by the same percentage thanks to Lloyd George. Operation 'Michael' fell on the British Third and Fifth Armies in the Somme area from 21 March to 5 April 1918, while 'Georgette' hit the Second Army in Flanders from 9 to 11 April. 'Blücher' and 'Yorck' went for the French Sixth Army from the Chemin des Dames on 27 May; 'Gneisenau' attacked the British Fifth Army again on 9 June; and 'Marne' and 'Reims' took on the French Sixth Army and the junction of the French Second and Fourth Armies between Dormans and Reims from 15 to 17 July. Paris was bombarded by long-range German artillery, which achieved little militarily, but the killing of eighty-eight worshipers, including three children, in the church of Saint-Gervais on Easter Sunday handed Allied propagandists another example of German beastliness.

The aim of the German offensive was to split the British from the French and drive to the Channel ports. The French army had largely recovered from its experiences of 1917, but there was still little enthusiasm for a fight. The British were short of men and their divisions were spread far too thinly. The Allies had no choice but to retreat. The German storm troopers came on, and the Allies went back. The Franco-British elastic stretched and stretched but never broke, and the German offensive ran out of steam and ground to a halt. The Royal Navy can take some credit for this, as the Germans, very short of rubber owing to the blockade, were running their motor transport on wheels without tyres, and could not resupply their forward troops along the French roads. For a brief period the Germans occupied Albert, headquarters of the British Fourth Army during the Somme offensive of 1916. Having been told that the British were starving and that one more push would win the war, the German infantry were astounded to uncover dumps of British rations containing delights that the Germans had not seen for two years. The appropriation of stocks of British rum did not assist German officers in their efforts to prevent looting and persuade the troops to keep going. The 'Kaiser's offensive' failed. The German army had shot its bolt and there would not be another to fire, but it was a close-run thing. Lloyd George's attempt to save lives had actually had the opposite effect, for if the British divisions had been up to strength the offensive would have been stopped long before it actually was.

Politicians, like most of us, do not like to admit having been wrong, but a prime minister with an ounce of grace might have confessed to error in his misappreciation of German plans for spring 1918. Far from doing so, Lloyd George tried to fudge the issue and put the blame back onto the generals. In a speech in the House of Commons on 9 April 1918 he announced that the British army in France was 'considerably stronger' on 1 January 1918 than it had been on 1 January 1917, and that when the 'Kaiser's offensive' began the combat strength of the German army on the Western Front was less than that of the Allies. Lloyd George's extraordinary contention was that a numerically greater force, in defensive positions, had been beaten by a smaller force attacking it.

Not only did the Prime Minister fail to emphasise that the Allies had in fact brought the German army to a complete standstill, he was making positive assertions that were nonsense. On 1 January 1917 the total strength of the BEF was 1,532,919 and on 1 January 1918 it was 1,750,892, on the face of it an increase of almost 218,000 men. What Lloyd George knew perfectly well, however, but did not tell the House, was that of the 1918 figure 335,454 men were not soldiers at all but in the Labour Corps, which had not existed before June 1917 and whose ranks were filled largely by coloured labour from South Africa, China and India. A Chinese coolie, for all his admirable qualities, is not the equivalent of an infantry soldier with a rifle or a Lewis gun, and the fighting strength of the army was thus

117,481 men smaller on 1 January 1918 than it had been a year before. Worse still, the infantry, the arm most needed for a successful defence in the event of a German offensive, had diminished from fifty-nine per cent of the BEF, or 904,422 men, on 1 January 1917 to thirty-six per cent, or 630,321 men, on the same date in 1918, leaving nearly a third fewer infantrymen to cover a longer sector of front.[18] All this because the government would not send out the reinforcements needed and available in England (where there were 92,000 infantry alone), or agree to withdraw divisions from Palestine to bolster the Western Front (which could have been done without detriment to operations in that theatre). On 21 March 1918, when the German offensive began, there were 191 German divisions on the Western Front compared with an Allied total of 165, with many of the British divisions severely under strength.

This announcement by the Prime Minister appalled Major-General Sir Frederick Maurice, who had until recently been Director of Military Operations at the War Office and knew exactly what the true picture was. Maurice had visited the BEF in France and found that the speech had caused a great deal of annoyance amongst officers and soldiers, who saw that Lloyd George was blaming them for something they had warned the Prime Minister about, but which he had ignored. Maurice had now finished his tour in the War Office and was on leave pending a new appointment (probably to Chief of Staff of one of the armies in France). When on 23 April Andrew Bonar Law, now Chancellor of the Exchequer and Leader of the House of Commons, gave misleading answers to questions in the House arising from the Prime Minister's speech of the 9th, it was too much. On 6 May 1918 General Maurice sent a letter to *The Times*, the *Morning Post*, the *Daily News*, the *Daily Chronicle*, and the *Daily Telegraph*. All except the *Telegraph* published it. The letter described Bonar Law's answers to questions, and the original facts as given by the Prime Minister, as containing 'mis-statements' which were 'misleading' and 'incorrect'. Maurice concluded his letter by saying that his reason for wishing it published was the hope that Parliament might order an investigation into its allegations.

'Communicating with the press', as the army calls it, was and is a serious offence for a serving officer. The army is rightly seen as the servant of government, and soldiers are forbidden from public expression of any opinion with a political connotation. Maurice did not get his investigation, and was forced to resign. Only many years later did Lloyd George admit that he had misinformed the House, but the letter did raise enough eyebrows to help prevent Haig being dismissed.[19]

No commander-in-chief in the field should have been subjected to the sort of interference, distrust and undermining that Haig had to suffer at the hands of his own government. A democratic government is fully entitled to reject the military advice it is given and to replace the advisers. What is not acceptable is for a government to send its generals off to war and then make it as difficult as possible for them to win it. No one suggests that Lloyd George, Churchill, Derby, Rothermere, Curzon, Carson, Balfour, Bonar Law and the other frocks did not want to win the war; but by refusing to accept the price of winning that war, and by constant obstruction and interference in matters which they did not understand, and by their constant search for a strategy that fudged the issue of the Western Front, they in fact prolonged the slaughter.

Lloyd George said, 'There is no greater fatuity than a political judgement dressed in a military uniform.'[20] One might well riposte that an equal fatuity is a military judgement dressed in a frock coat.

NOTES

1 Ian F. W. Beckett (ed.), *The Army and the Curragh Incident 1914*, Bodley Head, London, 1986.

2 See Brian Bond, 'Liddell-Hart and the First World War', in Brian Bond et al., *Look to Your Front*, Spellmount Publishers, Staplehurst, 1999, for an exposition of Liddell Hart's views on the war and how he came to form them.

3 Quoted in Trevor Royle, *Kitchener the Enigma*, Michael Joseph, London, 1985.

4 Not a great deal has changed then, but in the absence of conscription the Territorial Army, the present successor to the Territorial Force, is probably the best sort of reserve we are likely to get. Today, professional military opinion is increasingly of the view that any idea of deploying the TA as formed combatant units should be abandoned, and that the TA should be converted into specialist units of people not needed in peacetime but essential in war, and a pool of individual reinforcements. Progress is slow owing to entrenched local interests – one TA infantry battalion, with around 500 men on its books, has no fewer than four honorary colonels, all influential civilians. Current concern (2002) about the terrorist threat may cause part of the TA to be used as a guard force.

5 Nancy Maurice (ed.), *The Maurice Case*, Leo Cooper, London, 1972.

6 David Lloyd George, *My War Memoirs*, Vol. I, Odhams Press, London, 1938, p. 451.

7 David R. Woodward (ed.), *The Military Correspondence of Field Marshal Sir William Robertson*, Army Records Society, 1989, p. 199.

8 Robert Blake (ed.), *The Private Papers of Douglas Haig*, Eyre and Spottiswoode, London, 1952, pp. 173–4.

9 For a full account of Geddes' work with the BEF see Keith Grieves, 'The Transportation Mission to GHQ, 1916', in Brian Bond et al., *Look to Your Front*, Spellmount Publishers, Staplehurst, 1999.

10 Five ordinary divisions, one *Jäger* division and the Alpenkorps, which was equivalent to a division.

11 Woodward (ed.), *The Military Correspondence of Field Marshal Sir William Robertson*, Army Records Society, 1989, pp. 168 and 171.

12 Robertson was wrong. Lloyd George remained as Prime Minister until 1922.

13 Ibid., p. 155.

14 Edward Roberts (ed.), *The Private Papers of Douglas Haig*, Eyre and Spottiswoode, London, 1952, p. 265.

15 Ibid., p. 274.

16 Ibid., p. 278.

17 Haig had wanted Butler as his Chief of the General Staff on taking command of the BEF in December 1915, but Butler was considered too junior, and Haig got Kiggell instead.

18 *Statistics of the Military Effort of the British Empire in the Great War*, War Office, London, 1922.

19 For a full account of the Maurice affair see Nancy Maurice (ed.), *The Maurice Case*, Leo Cooper, London, 1972.

20 Lloyd George, *My War Memoirs*, Vol. I, Odhams Press, London, 1938, p. 451.

12

EVEN MORE
NEEDLESS SLAUGHTER

If most of the British public know only of the Somme when thinking about the Great War, then that portion that knows a little more will have heard of Passchendaele, where Butcher Haig, having learned nothing from the slaughter of the Somme in 1916, spent 1917 in again throwing the flower of British manhood against impregnable German wire and machine guns, through waist-deep mud, to no avail.

There was indeed a major British offensive in 1917, and it did kill a great many British and Empire soldiers, but the reasons for it have been forgotten or expunged. It is seen as a pointless battering against a brick wall, and even the name Passchendaele is misleading, for the attack and eventual capture of that village was but a part of the great offensive more properly known as the Third Battle of Ypres.

Haig had always considered that the British interest lay in Flanders, and he had been planning an offensive there since 1915. This was, however, still a coalition war, with the French as the leading Allied player. Although the British Prime Minister Lloyd George was in principle opposed to large-scale British attacks on the Western Front, he had been convinced by the loquacity of the new French Commander-in-Chief General Robert Nivelle, and both governments agreed to an Allied offensive in 1917 with the French army taking the lead. Nivelle, as we have seen, was relatively junior in the French military hierarchy. Born in 1856 and commissioned from the École Polytechnique into the artillery in 1878, he was a colonel commanding an artillery regiment in August 1914. In October 1914 he was promoted to *général de brigade*, and in February 1915 he was appointed to command a division. Further swift promotion followed: III Corps Commander at the end of 1915, Commander of the Second Army from April 1916 and finally Commander-in-Chief, succeeding Joffre in December 1916. His rise was nothing short of meteoric, but he was a very convincing fellow: the troops liked him and believed in him; he was politically astute, got on well with his own and Allied politicians, and was careful not to antagonise those generals over whose heads he had been elevated. Bullshit does not often baffle brains, but in Nivelle's case, sadly, it did.

Had Nivelle launched an attack in February 1917, the originally agreed date, he might have had some success against the German salient that stuck out into Allied territory between Péronne and Soissons. As it was, Nivelle delayed the offensive until his new plans were ready; and when the Germans withdrew to the Hindenburg Line in February 1917, destroying the villages and poisoning the wells on the way, the salient was no more. Nivelle shifted the focus of his assault to the area of the River Aisne, and he now proposed to attack over a forty-mile front between Soissons and Reims. The main strike would be carried out by the Reserve Army Group (GAR) commanded by General Micheler and comprising the French Fifth Army (General Mazel), Sixth Army (General Mangin) and Tenth Army (General Duchêne). The Central Army Group (GAC – General Pétain), the Eastern Army Group (GAE – General de Castelnau) and the Northern Army Group (GAN – Desperate Frankie) would assist, and elements would also support a diversionary attack by the British in Artois and Picardy. Altogether sixty-eight French divisions would be involved, and on the main Aisne front forty-nine divisions of infantry, five cavalry divisions and 128 French tanks would cross the jump-off line at 0600 hours on 12 April 1917. They would be supported by 5,300 artillery pieces, 1,900 of them heavy guns, which would bombard the German lines from 2 April. The French would be attacking twenty-one German divisions in the line with another seventeen in reserve, and, Nivelle assured all who would listen, would break through and out within forty-eight hours.

There were a number of factors that, in the view of the British generals, militated against success. For a start the ground on which the German positions lay was very well suited for defence, and very difficult to attack. Much of the River Aisne is overlooked from the north by an escarpment, known as the Chemin des Dames after a road built along its edge to allow the daughters of the pre-Revolutionary French kings to ride from Soissons to Berry-au-Bac. Nivelle considered rightly that surprise was essential, but there was precious little of it. The movement of thousands of troops, the stockpiling of ammunition, the building of roads and light railways and the construction of jump-off trenches could hardly be concealed, and to cap it all a copy of the complete French plan for the attack was captured by the Germans in early April. The loss was only reported to Nivelle on the 7th, but he decided to go ahead anyway. Despite Haig's doubts about the soundness of Nivelle's plan, and especially about the French general's optimism with regard to a speedy victory, the British had little choice but to go along with their allies. The role of the BEF would be subsidiary to begin with, involving a series of attacks from Arras designed to tie up German reserves. Once the Nivelle offensive had succeeded in breaking through the German defences, the French army would pursue while the British would break out of the Ypres salient, the Belgians would attack from Diksmuide, and a French corps would drive along the Belgian coast and take Ostend. It would be a great victory to end the war.

It was not only the British generals who had reservations, but the French ones too. Of the three army groups that would be involved in the main attack, the main burden was to be assumed by General Micheler's GAR. He was so worried that he wrote a number of letters to his political contacts expressing his anxieties, and these were eventually shown to the Minister for War, Paul Painlevé. Painlevé called a council of war to resolve the matter. A council of war was a medieval concept with little place in modern soldiering, and none had previously been convened in this conflict. Nevertheless it was allowed for in French regulations, and so Nivelle and the army group commanders, Franchet d'Esperey, Micheler and Pétain, were summoned to give their views to the War Minister on 8 April. The subordinate generals were careful as to what they said to a politician in front of their Commander-in-Chief. Pétain thought that it would be better to do nothing and wait for the Americans (the USA had declared war on Germany two days before), while all three army commanders thought that while the German first and second lines might be captured, the chances of a breakthrough – *rupture* as the French had it – were slight. Nivelle promptly threatened to resign, thus frightening the council and the minister into agreeing to the offensive's taking place as planned, with the proviso that it would be called off if not successful. President Poincaré and Prime Minister Ribot also agreed that the attack should go ahead.

According to Nivelle's plan the British were to move off on 8 April, while for the French *Jour J* would be 12 April.[1] Weather and problems with the artillery bombardment necessitated delays, and the British eventually went into action on 9 April when the Canadian Corps stormed and took Vimy Ridge. The French GAR crossed their jump-off line at 0600 on 16 April. It was misty and overcast, and German machine guns sited on reverse slopes soon began to cut down the advancing French infantry, while counter-attacks drove them off many of the positions initially gained. Despite the fourteen-day artillery bombardment much of the German wire was uncut. North of the Aisne some progress was made, but on the right of the attack the troops were stopped on the Aisne–Marne Canal. The French tanks were of little help. They were too lightly armoured and could not cross major obstacles; and when they did score a success, the infantrymen were too exhausted to keep up with them. Of the 128 tanks involved, sixty-two were put out of action by enemy fire and eighteen broke down. By last light on 16 April no Frenchman was forward of a line that should have been taken by 0930 hours. Next day the French Sixth Army did manage to push the Germans out of the Braye-Condé-Laffaux triangle, back as far as the Hindenburg Line. On the same day a subsidiary attack by the French Fourth Army in Champagne, mounted at 0445 hours in driving rain and snow, made appreciable gains. By 20 April the French had taken 20,000 prisoners and captured 147 guns; they had cut the main Soissons–Reims railway line, taken the German second line south of Juvincourt, and were on some of the fortified hills in Champagne. But still there was no breakthrough, and no sign of one, and casualties were far higher than expected. The Germans were able to leapfrog their artillery guns back, and their reliance on reverse-slope defence made Nivelle's much vaunted creeping-barrage tactics a hit-or-miss (too often miss) affair. The French medical system was totally unequal to the task it had been given, and lines of wounded lying out in the open waiting for treatment that came too late, or sometimes not at all, did not help morale.

By 25 April the attack had virtually stalled. Measured against the build-up it had been given, with Nivelle's exaggerated promises of a quick breakthrough followed by a pursuit into Germany, it had been a disaster. French dead in those nine days numbered 15,589 with a further 20,000 reported missing, many of whom were in fact dead; total casualties, including those of two Russian brigades taking part under French command, were nearly 100,000. The offensive went on, but only limited attacks were sanctioned. Even so, things would get worse.

On 27 April the French government set up a *Commission de l'Armée* to investigate what had gone wrong. Nivelle blamed his subordinates, claiming that they had failed to understand his requirements for the artillery, and tried to sack General Mazel, commanding the Fifth Army. The Minister for War refused to allow it. Nivelle now turned his ire on Mangin, one of the better army commanders, and he was dismissed on 29 April. This was not enough to save Nivelle, and a change in the higher management of the war was demanded. Pétain was appointed Chief of the General Staff, a new post modelled on the British CIGS, the aim being for him to rein in Nivelle and provide the French government with an alternative source of military advice. Pétain was replaced as Commander of the GAC by General Fayolle, who had commanded the French troops during the Somme offensive of 1916. The Major General of the Army (equivalent to Chief of Staff of the field army) was also sacked. Nivelle could not, however, escape responsibility: he was the Commander-in-Chief, he had promised a lightning victory and he had to pay. He was eventually asked to resign on 10 May, but refused. He insisted that he had done nothing wrong; if the government wanted rid of him they could dismiss him, but he would not resign. On 15 May he relented and offered his resignation – by which date French casualties had risen to 271,000. Nivelle was rusticated to French North Africa, a military backwater, for the rest of the war and a court of inquiry later absolved him from culpability. He was replaced as Commander-in-Chief by General Pétain.

For many French soldiers in the ranks it was the final straw. Not only had the great offensive failed, but now the generals who had ordered and directed it were falling out amongst themselves. It was not so much the casualty rate, or the simple lack of success, that caused morale to tumble, but the dashing of great expectations. Almost immediately mutiny, the nightmare of generals in all armies everywhere, began to break out. The French commanders had long been concerned about anti-war propaganda amongst the troops. Men going on leave were waylaid at Paris railway stations and harangued by pacifists, who were reasonably restrained, and Communists and anarchists who were not. There were well-organised underground agencies that existed to help soldiers who wanted to desert. Tracts condemning the war circulated in the ranks, and the Interior Minister, Malvy, seemed powerless to prevent this subversion or to close down anti-war newspapers like the Communist *Bonnet Rouge*. It was a common article of belief that munitions workers at home were earning far more than the men in the trenches, and Annamese troops from Indo-China were widely believed to be stalking French cities and towns, coupling furiously with women whose husbands were away at the front. Many French soldiers readily believed such propaganda. As conscripts their pay was derisory, their rations bad and their welfare facilities almost non-existent. In some units there had been no leave for twelve months, and for those fortunate few who did manage to obtain leave, arrangements to get them home were regarded by the French staff as a very low priority. The French army was far more egalitarian than the British, and was (almost) a meritocracy; but many British officers commented with surprise that while French officers led their men in action most gallantly, once the battle was over the officers decamped and left the men to their own devices. British officers had it drummed into them that the welfare of their men was one of their major responsibilities; they organised football matches, set up canteens, administered leave, laid on band concerts, ran theatricals, held gymkhanas and inspected the men's billets and meals regularly. It has been suggested that it was the social difference between officer and soldier in the British army that allowed officers to be in close touch with their men's off-duty activities without the risk of undue familiarity; a contrasting situation to that of the French, whose officers were far better educated professionally than were the British, but who came from the same social class as many of their men. Whatever the reasons, the French army was ripe for what happened.

In many ways it was rather a peculiar mutiny, and the French never used the word, preferring instead '*mouvements collectifs d'indiscipline*' – but collective indiscipline is mutiny nonetheless. It began with refusals to parade, and disobeying orders to move from billets into the line. It was a sullen, hangdog sort of affair, a far cry from the enthusiasm of the French Revolution: there was little cheering, no bands playing, precious few caps of liberty. Not many officers were ill-treated; a handful were shot, some were jeered at and stoned, and one general was tied up and forced into the firing line. It started in a small way, the first recorded instance being on 17 April when seventeen men deserted from the firing line. In the main, however, it began not at the front but behind the lines. On 29 April a battalion of the 20th Regiment of Infantry refused to parade, but there was no violence.[2] Rumour abounded and refusals to go back to the firing line spread.

The 18th Regiment of Infantry had been relieved in the line on 8 May. This regiment had been badly knocked about in the fighting between 4 and 8 May and had lost twenty officers and 824 men killed, wounded and missing out of a strength of around 2,500. The regiment had just received 1,000 recruits to bring it up to strength, but there had not yet been time for them to settle in and become part of the team. The regiment's major grievance was that there had not been enough leave. French soldiers were supposed to get seven days' home leave every four months, but this was often cancelled owing to the exigencies of war or the inability of the staff to organise transport. On 27 May the 18th Infantry was warned for a return to the trenches. Already disgruntled about the lack of leave, poor billets and bad food, the men refused to parade. They milled about, firing their rifles in the air, singing the 'Internationale' and waving red flags. Some slashed the tyres of the lorries intended to take them back to the front. Officers who knew the men and who had shared their hardships tried to reason with the mutinous troops. By 2230 hours the 3rd Battalion had thought better of what they were doing and agreed to embus for the front. The 1st Battalion followed and only the 2nd Battalion refused to move. Next day, at 0500 hours, a contingent of gendarmes arrived at the camp.[3] Twenty soldiers of the 2nd Battalion gave themselves up immediately, sixty refused absolutely while the remainder were confused and unsure what to do. The battalion agreed to move to La Fère-en-Tardenois, the nearest town, and set off surrounded by gendarmes, but still with their weapons and still firing them in the air. By 0730 hours fervour had evaporated and the battalion agreed to go up to the lines. The whole regiment, now reunited, fought well in the ensuing battles. Twelve ringleaders of the 18th Infantry were subsequently brought before courts martial. Five were sentenced to death, of whom three were actually shot; one was pardoned and one escaped from custody and was never seen again.

The 41st Division of Infantry had been in the line continuously from 28 January to 12 May 1917. They had taken a large number of casualties and were brought out of the line into billets for a rest. The billets were overcrowded and unheated, and when the men were warned for a return to operations on 1 June, revolt flared. The trouble started in the 23rd Regiment of Infantry, billeted near Ville-en-Tardenois, and spread to the other regiment of the 1st Brigade, the 133rd Regiment of Infantry in nearby Chambrecy. A noisy column formed, red flags were produced and the men left camp to march to Ville-en-Tardenois singing the 'Internationale'. General Bulot, the Brigade Commander, and a colonel tried to reason with them. The general was stoned and the stars of his rank torn off his uniform. The mutineers were reported to have shouted, 'Murderer – drinker of blood – death to you – up the revolution – peace at any price – we are fed up with the war!'[4] If this sounds rather dramatic – comical even – to English ears, it is a lot more bloodthirsty in French. Those men who would talk to the officers said that the blacks (*les noirs*) at Firminy and the *Annamites* at Saint-Denis were violating French women and then shooting them. Revolution had broken out in Paris, said the mutineers, and the Louvre was ablaze. This was, of course, largely nonsense, but there was considerable resentment against colonial troops who had taken over duties in rear areas to free up French troops for the front. At last the divisional commander, General Mignot, arrived. He promised the men that they would not be sent back to the trenches, and things quietened down. A hundred of the ringleaders were locked up in the *mairie* while transport was arranged for the rest. Next day, 2 June, there was another demonstration when at 1800 hours around 1,000 men marched round the town with red flags, but that was the end of it for the 1st Brigade. On 3 June both regiments were taken away, and after the subsequent courts martial nine soldiers were sentenced to death, of whom five were actually executed. There was no trouble at all in the division's 2nd Brigade.

These two incidents were fairly typical. In all there were outbreaks of mutiny in sixty-five divisions on the Western Front, or in about two-thirds of the army. In most cases divisions in the trenches remained in position, with the exception of a battalion of the 66th Regiment of Infantry which abandoned its sector, chased away its officers and camped in the woods behind the lines. Anecdotal evidence says that the Commander Tenth Army, General Duchêne, surrounded them with cavalry and gendarmes and then ordered one of the battalions to be decimated – one in every ten men to be shot summarily without trial.[5] This salutary tale was widely believed, and is still believed, in France and in England; but a recent study by the French academic G. Pedroncini, who had access to military archives not previously released, produces convincing evidence that it was never ordered and never happened, although a number of men of the battalion were sentenced to terms of imprisonment. Other regiments at the front assured their officers that while they would not advance, or agree to any attacks, neither would they allow the Germans to advance. That the most serious mutinies occurred in units out of the line may be partly accounted for by that catalyst for indiscipline in all armies: drink. The French army paid its men in arrears, usually when they came out of the line, and there were always purveyors ready to exchange large quantities of cheap red wine for wads of francs. Many of the mutinies broke out in the evening, after the soldiery had spent the day imbibing the local *pinard*, and ended early in the morning when hangovers had reduced revolutionary ardour.

The two Russian brigades under French command – part of a 'troops for arms' swap agreed in 1915 – had also mutinied, but this was due to events at home and was unrelated, except chronologically, to what was happening in the French army. The movement was put down by firm French action, assisted by loyalist Russians.[6]

Over the next few months the mutinies spread, as did desertion by individuals. The 38th Infantry Division had seventy-three cases of desertion to the interior (i.e. not to the enemy) between 1 January and 16 April 1917. In the month of May alone there were forty-six desertions and for June the number rose to eighty-eight, and the 38th was a relatively well-behaved division. For the whole French army on the Western Front, desertions to the interior dealt with by military courts had been running at an average of 370 a month in 1916. The incidence dropped slightly in early 1917 when from 1 January to 15 April there was a total of 775 desertions. In the second half of April, that is from the start of the Nivelle offensive to the end of the month, there were 618 desertions to the interior; in May there were 1,291, in June 1,619, in July 1,147 and in August 784, before settling down again in September to 410. Those were the deserters who were apprehended and dealt with; there would have been many more who were never caught. Desertions to the enemy also rose. Prior to the attack on 16 April these were averaging sixty a fortnight; in the second fortnight in April there were 289 desertions to the Germans.[7] If even the 'normal' rate of desertion to the enemy seems very high to British eyes, it must be remembered that many of the French soldiers came from areas occupied by the Germans, and were no doubt trying to get back to their families rather than seeking to aid the enemy.

It was noted that trains carrying those who had managed to get some leave were packed with soldiers chanting anti-war slogans, expressing approval of the Russian Bolsheviks. (After the Tsar's abdication in March 1917, Russia was, until October of that year, under the control of the Menshevik provisional government which was trying to stay in the war, whereas the Bolsheviks wanted out.) Soldiers on leave were chanting that named politicians and generals should be 'done away with' (à bas and even à la lanterne). Some units dissolved into bands of brigands, others began to march on Paris to present their grievances, others went home, some stayed at their posts but elected their own officers, and a sizeable minority remained steadfastly loyal and untroubled. Although there were calls for peace and for revolution, the mutineers' most often repeated demands concerned not the direction of the war but pay, rations and – above all – leave. The mutinies would rumble on until August, and for France, and indeed for the alliance, it was the crisis point of the war. If the Germans knew what was happening, they would launch an offensive augmented by divisions released from the Eastern Front – an offensive that the French army was in no state to resist, and against which the British army was too small to defend along the whole front. On 4 June the French government was informed that between Soissons and Paris there were only two divisions that could be relied upon.

The first priority was security. Strict censorship was imposed and very little leaked out. The Minister of War was not told until the mutinies were well under way and the French government was never told the full extent of the trouble until it was over. The British Cabinet knew almost nothing and even Haig, commanding the BEF, was only made aware of the true extent of the collapse on 2 June when the new Chief of Staff of the French Field Army, General Dubeny, briefed him and explained that General Pétain was frightfully sorry, but the French army could no longer assist with the next phase of the offensive due to start on 10 June – in fact, said Dubeny, (no doubt crossing his fingers behind his back as he delivered what he must have known to be a whopper), they could do nothing at all for at least a month.

The French government, stung by the report of the *Commission de l'Armée*, which not only castigated the generals but also the saboteurs behind the scenes, began to act. The *Bonnet Rouge* was closed down and its editor, Duval, put on trial charged with treason for trading with the enemy (the *Bonnet Rouge* was found to be subsidised by German money). He was found guilty and later executed. The Minister of the Interior, Louis Malvy, who had inexplicably been unable to curb the activities of anti-war agitators and the Communist and anarchist press, was also arrested, as was Director Leymarie of the Sûreté (the French internal secret service), who, it was discovered, had covered up for Duval. Both were lucky. Malvy, who had undoubtedly encouraged unrest in the army and tolerated the existence of desertion agencies, got away with five years' banishment, and Leymarie was sent to prison. Perhaps they knew too much. Ribot could not remain as Prime Minister (President of the Council in French terms) and was replaced on 12 September by Painlevé, who in turn gave way to Clemenceau on 16 November.

It seems that the Germans never did discover the extent of the mutinies. They certainly received fragmentary reports of what was going on, from agents in place and from escaped German prisoners, but they do not seem to have believed them. The French security blackout worked.

It was now for the British to distract the attention of the Germans while Pétain tried to restore the French army to something like a fighting force. It would take until the winter of 1917, and even after that the French army was never the same again. Pétain was a very different man from his predecessor, Nivelle. The latter was an aggressive, energetic, articulate proponent of the offensive; Pétain was of peasant origin, stolid, secretive, a thinker and a specialist in the art of defence, as he had shown at Verdun. He firmly believed that the de Castelnau school of offence à l'outrance was wrong, and that what mattered was guns. Although a Catholic, he was politically acceptable as he was reputed not to have been to mass for forty years. A fifty-eight-year-old colonel in 1914, he had done well at the First Battle of the Marne and was promoted to général de brigade in the field. When Joffre, as Commander-in-Chief, sacked two out of five army commanders, ten of the twenty corps commanders and forty-two of the seventy-four divisional commanders as a result of the First Battle of the Marne in 1914, Pétain's rise was rapid. By late 1916 he had commanded in turn a division, a corps and an army, before commanding the GAC in Nivelle's offensive and then replacing him.

Pétain's policy for the restoration of the army to its allegiance was one of severe punishment for ringleaders, forgiveness and better conditions for the rest. His first acts were to send nearly half of the whole army on leave, and then to institute measures to improve pay and rations. He made frequent visits to units and talked to the men. As he was untainted by the debacle of the April attacks, the soldiers trusted Pétain, and gradually matters began to improve. Courts martial were quickly set up and the trials began. The French code of military justice required all death sentences to be referred to the President of the Republic. From the beginning of the war to the events of 1917 there had been an average of twenty-two or twenty-three condemnations to death every month, of which the

President pardoned fifteen or sixteen. Now, by a decree of 8 June 1917, the President renounced his powers of pardon for condemned soldiers, leaving the matter entirely up to the military. Some French historians accept that swift and exemplary justice was needed, others are more cynical and think that the reason for this renunciation was to allow the government to evade responsibility if it all went wrong. In fact the presidential pardon continued in practice if not in law, as many French deputies (members of Parliament) were serving in the army and would intercede with the President or the War Minister on behalf of their constituents or of soldiers under their command. Many of the contemporary documents are missing or were destroyed, and exact figures are hard to come by; but the most convincing account is that of Pedroncini who calculates that 476 men, nearly all private soldiers, were condemned to death for offences connected with the mutinies, and that thirty of them were actually shot. There may have been more executions, and there is some anecdotal evidence that at the beginning of the troubles men were shot summarily, leaving no trace in the archives.[8] Many incidents that have passed into legend are, however, doubtful at best. At one stage it was claimed that a rebellious Senegalese division was herded out into no man's land and shelled into submission by French artillery. A colonial division was indeed shelled by its own artillery, but this was in the early days of the offensive in April, and was the fault not of over-zealous enforcers of military discipline but of a straightforward miscalculation by the gunners. (One of the problems found during the offensive was that liaison between infantry and artillery was poor.) Even if as many as forty-eight mutineers were shot, which some French historians think is possible, it is a very small number for actions that amounted to a complete disruption of the military system and that could have led to losing the war.

The French generals were convinced that the ringleaders were out-and-out bad hats: political agitators, Communists, anarchists, German agents, men deliberately setting out to bring down the French army. In fact there seems to be no evidence for this. Of those condemned to death, that is those considered most culpable, the majority were good soldiers with no previous record of political activism or of civil or military offences. The largest civilian profession represented was peasant farmer (*cultivateur*) (eighty-eight), followed by employees of tradesmen (nineteen). There were also twelve miners, twelve mechanics, ten bakers, ten labourers, two students, one policeman and one lawyer's clerk. Neither in age, profession, social class, education or place of residence or birth is there any indication that this was a concerted movement by any one group. The conclusion must be that the mutinies of 1917 were a spontaneous reaction to poor conditions, lack of welfare facilities and the dashing of hopes raised too high, with discontent being aggravated by deliberate anti-war propaganda and incitement from sections of the home front.

In a book that deals with British participation in this war I make no apology for devoting half a chapter to the events of 1917 in the French army, for all that happened to the British in the ensuing Third Battle of Ypres is directly attributable to the state of the French. The condition of the French army made it imperative, if France was to stay in the war and the Germans were not to win it, for the British to mount a major offensive unaided, and to continue that offensive, whatever the cost, until such time as the French army was once more ready to take the field. Staying on the defensive and waiting a year for the Americans was no longer a viable policy.

It had always been the intention of the British to begin their post-Nivelle attack in early June. The aim had been to break out of the Ypres salient, that flat, waterlogged bit of western Flanders where the British had spent over two years constantly overlooked by the Germans, and then to drive into the Douai plain and get back to mobile war. A further imperative was now urged: unrestricted submarine warfare had been again declared, and the Royal Navy wanted the army to break through to the Channel coast and prevent the Germans from using the Belgian ports as bases from which their U-boats could raid Allied commerce. While there would now be little or no French help, much could still be achieved, even if it was only to gain the high ground around the salient so that the British could overlook their enemy and not vice versa.

Before anything much could be done from the salient, the Messines Ridge, held by the Germans since 1914, had to be taken. At the bottom (south) end of the salient the British firing line ran east to west through Saint-Éloi, the scene of much mining and countermining throughout 1915

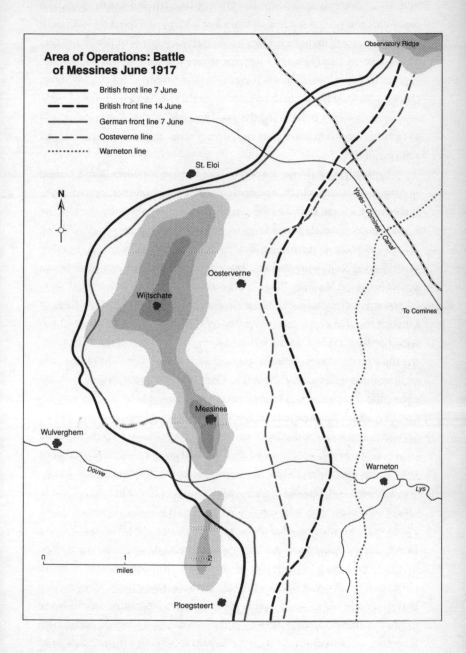

Area of Operations: Battle of Messines June 1917

British front line 7 June	
British front line 14 June	
German front line 7 June	
Oosteverne line	
Warneton line	

N

Observatory Ridge

St. Eloi

Oosterverne

Wijtschate

Ypres - Comines Canal

To Comines

Messines

Wulverghem

Douve

Warneton

Lys

0   1   2
miles

Ploegsteert

and 1916. West of Saint-Éloi the British line turned south. South of Saint-Éloi and east of the British front line a long, narrow ridge ran north to south, running up to the village of Wijtschate (known to British soldiers as Whitesheets) and along to Messines, where it sloped back down to meet the British front line again at Ploegsteert (Plugstreet). This ridge – about three miles long from north to south and three-quarters of a mile wide from east to west – overlooked the southern end of the Ypres salient, and the British front line down as far as Armentières. It was what soldiers call vital ground.

The British had always wanted to take out the Messines Ridge, but up to now there had been other priorities. Mines had, however, been in place under the German defences for a year, checked regularly by men of the tunnelling companies Royal Engineers to ensure that they had not been discovered and that the fuses and detonators would still work. Altogether twenty-one mines were dug and one million pounds of explosive put in position. On the Messines Ridge feature were six German divisions, totalling 75,000 men, and 630 guns. Their defences were based on three lines of bunkers, sited in depth and connected by trenches covered by wire obstacles. The first line was on the forward slope, the second on the ridge itself, the third on the reverse (east) slope, and a final line – the Oostaverne Line – about three miles east of the ridge. The Germans knew an attack would come; the British aim was to conceal when it would be.

The attack on Messines Ridge was the responsibility of the British Second Army, commanded by General Sir Herbert Plumer. Plumer's portly figure and large white moustache (his hair had gone completely grey since 1914) made him the model for the cartoonist Low's 'Colonel Blimp', but he was a superb and detailed planner, and a great believer in limited, easily identifiable objectives – 'bite and hold' tactics. It was decided to attack on 7 June 1917, a few days earlier than originally planned, and the Royal Flying Corps and the Royal Naval Air Service established complete air superiority, bringing back air photographs of the German positions and denying German aircraft opportunities for observation. A seventeen-day artillery bombardment began on 21 May, with three and a half million shells being fired in the last seven days alone. On the evening of 4 June the 16th (Irish) Division, John Redmond's Irish Volunteers, held an officers' dinner at

Locre. Lieutenant Colonel Buckley of the Royal Leinster Regiment proposed a toast to the division and to its success in the forthcoming operation, which was replied to by Major Willie Redmond, MP, 6th Battalion the Royal Irish Regiment, younger brother of the Nationalist leader and at fifty-seven probably the oldest company commander on the Western Front.

All day and during the night of 6 June 80,000 assaulting troops moved into position, covered by artillery and machine-gun barrages. A hot meal was served out at midnight, and the usual spoonful of rum was issued at 0230 hours. At 0310 hours the mines were blown. Nineteen went up with a deafening roar, and in Lille, twelve miles away, the German authorities thought it was an earthquake. One, the Spanbroekmolen mine, in the centre of the objective, exploded some twenty seconds late, and a few British soldiers who had just started to move from their jump-off positions were killed by falling rocks. Nine divisions, supported by seventy-two Mark IV tanks, moved forward towards the ridge behind a creeping barrage. To the north X Corps (23, 47 and 41 Divisions) attacked through Saint-Éloi; in the centre IX Corps (19, 16 (Irish) and 36 (Ulster) Divisions) went straight up the ridge at Wijtschate, while in the south II ANZAC Corps (25th, the New Zealand and the 3rd Australian Divisions) were responsible for Messines.

Using fire and movement, the first wave took the German forward line, which had been badly mangled by the bombardment and was now but lightly held. The second wave passed through and drove on up the slope. The 16th Irish and the 36th Ulster Divisions attacked side by side, their objective being Wijtschate village with the church as the interdivisional boundary. The Ulster Division had long since given up wearing orange sashes, and relations between the divisions representing the two opposing traditions in Ireland were now extremely good. Shortly after the taking of the first German line, Willie Redmond was badly wounded. His commanding officer had ordered him to be part of the 'left out of battle' party, but he protested, and was eventually allowed to accompany the attack on the understanding that he returned after the first line had been taken. The Irish Nationalist MP was tended and carried off the field by Protestant stretcher-bearers of the Ulster Division, but died of his wounds shortly afterwards. When the battle was over, the Nationalist Party in

Dublin opened a memorial fund for Willie Redmond; Major-General Oliver Nugent, commanding the Ulster Division, who had known Redmond and liked him, made a donation from his division's welfare funds. This led to uproar in Belfast, where the division's welfare committee, composed of hard-faced civilians who had done well out of the war, protested that Nugent had misappropriated money raised for the welfare of Protestant troops. Nugent was safe – he had consulted his Protestant soldiers before making the donation – but the incident showed that however well the different faiths cooperated in war, there was precious little reconciliation at home.[9]

By 0530 hours the second wave of attackers had reached the crest, and the New Zealand Division captured Messines itself. There was then a pause while the ridge was secured and guns moved forward, and by 1200 hours the third German line, on the reverse slope, was taken. Now three fresh divisions – 24, 11 and 4th Australian – were brought up and at 1510 hours they were hurled at the Germans' final defence line, the Oostaverne line, which was now overlooked by the British on Messines Ridge. By midnight it was firmly in British hands.

The attack had been a huge success. In one day the British had advanced over three miles on a five-mile front, and even more ground was made on 11 June when the Germans pulled back another mile to the Warneton Line. German casualties are estimated at 25,000, including 7,300 prisoners and 10,000 missing – many of whom were never found, or were blown to bits by the mines. The total of German dead was probably in the region of 8,000. Total British casualties were 24,500, including 3,500 killed. A disproportionate number were from the ANZAC Corps, some of whose losses were 'own goals' when the men crowded onto the ridge and overtook their own artillery barrage. Of the seventy-four tanks employed, eleven were knocked out by German fire or broke down, a far better record than that of the year before. As the attacker is calculated always to take more casualties than the defender, and as the average mortality in the twelve divisions taking part (nine in the assault on the ridge, three on the capture of the Oostaverne Line) was 292 per division, or less than three per cent, this was not only an outstanding victory but a cheap one too.

The comparison between the Somme and Messines is obvious. Instead of an inexperienced force where all ranks were learning their trade and where tactics were only as sophisticated as the leaders and the led were capable of executing (i.e., not very), this was an army that had learned from 1916, that had refined its tactics and methods and honed them in the Arras battles earlier in 1917, and in which every man knew what he had to do and had confidence in his capacity to achieve it. It was a triumph of all-arms planning – there was excellent cooperation between engineers, infantry, artillery, tanks and aircraft – and of detailed briefing of all ranks with clearly distinguishable objectives and sensible use of phases. It is true that the morale of the Germans on Messines Ridge was not as high as it had been the previous year, and that their staff work fell below its usual high standards; but this was still the highly competent, well-trained and well-equipped German army, and it had been resoundingly beaten.[10]

With the capture of Messines Ridge the British now had far more freedom to move unobserved in the south of the Ypres salient and behind their new front line. Now was the time to strike, while the German army was still reeling from its defeat. It was not to be, and there was a six-week delay before the next phase could start. Partly this was due to political interference. Lloyd George, only slightly mollified by the recent success and its refutation of his opinion regarding British leadership on the Western Front, still had to be convinced that the BEF should continue on the offensive, particularly as virtually no French support would be available. There was now less pressure from the Admiralty to strike for the Belgian coast, as it had emerged that the U-boats were operating from home bases and not, after all, from Channel ports. Winston Churchill, now Minister for Munitions, was increasingly of the view that the British army should hold, and continue to hold throughout 1918, until the Americans could take the field. Haig knew better. Aware that in the short term it was only the BEF that could keep France in the war, he knew that a major offensive had to happen. The French generals were insistent: the restoration of the French army's will to fight was still a long way off. Even Lloyd George's alternative sources of military advice – Sir John French and Sir Henry Wilson – sided with Haig, and eventually, late in July, the Cabinet sanctioned further offensive operations by the BEF.

There was another factor, however, that prevented Haig from dealing

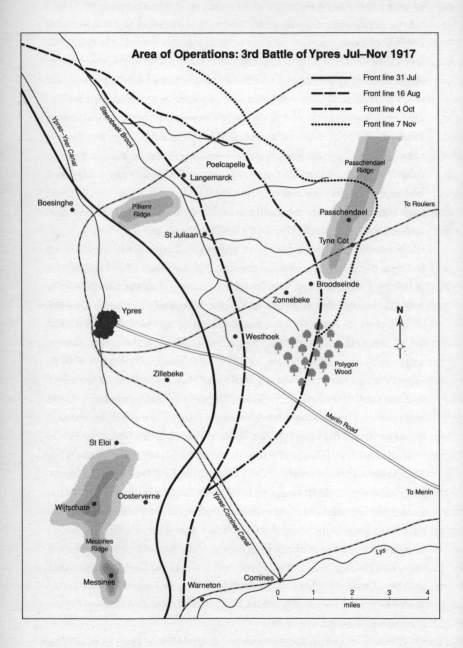

Area of Operations: 3rd Battle of Ypres Jul–Nov 1917

Front line 31 Jul
Front line 16 Aug
Front line 4 Oct
Front line 7 Nov

Ypres-Yser Canal

Steenbeek Brook

Poelcapelle
Langemarck

Passchendael Ridge

Boesinghe

Pilkenr Ridge

To Roulers

Passchendael

St Juliaan

Tyne Cot

Broodseinde

Zonnebeke

Ypres

Westhoek

N

Zillebeke

Polygon Wood

Menin Road

St Eloi

Oosterverne

To Menin

Wijtschate

Ypres-Comines Canal

Messines Ridge

Lys

Messines

Warneton

Comines

0   1   2   3   4
miles

his next blow hard on the heels of that struck at Messines. The British army simply did not have the assets to conduct two major operations at once. The engineering effort for Messines had left little over for the rest of the salient, and the guns had to be moved, the ammunition stockpiled and the men trained on mock-ups of the German positions. The next phase of the offensive was to be a series of hammer blows all around the Ypres salient, and was the responsibility of General Sir Hubert Gough, commanding the British Fifth Army. At last, by 31 July, he was ready.

On the 30th the weather broke, and when nine British infantry divisions attacked behind a creeping barrage at 0350 hours the next day between Zillebeke and Boesinghe, they did so in mist and driving rain; conditions worsened as the day wore on. In the north progress was good, and the Guards, 38 and 51 Divisions advanced about two and a half miles, well beyond the Pilkem Ridge, just short of Saint-Julien and almost to Langemarck. Next door, 39, 55 and 15 Divisions got even further, to the Langemarck–Zonnebeke road by 1300 hours, before being pushed back to the Steenbeek brook by last light. South of the Ypres–Roulers (Flemish Roeselare) railway progress was not so good, but significant advances were made.

The Germans too had been learning. They were now organising their defences in depth and basing them not on lines of trenches alone, but on concrete strongpoints linked by trenches. The idea was to exhaust the attacker by drawing him further and further into successive zones of elastic defence, and when he was exhausted to counter-attack with specially formed counter-attack divisions. The weather deteriorated progressively, and off-road movement, particularly of guns, was becoming very difficult for the British. It was to be the wettest summer for seventy-five years. On 10 August Westhoek was captured by 74 Division, and on 16 August in the Battle of Langemarck eight divisions went into action, with the 16th Irish and 36th Ulster once more side by side. But the ground was terrible; the drainage system had broken down completely as a result of constant shelling, the tanks could hardly move and the attack was a failure. South of the salient, Hill 70, north of Lens, was captured by the Canadian Corps on 15 August and there were minor advances south of Langemarck between 19 and 22 August, but even so the offensive was in danger of becoming bogged down (in many places literally). Haig now decided that a fresh approach was needed. He called a temporary halt and handed the battle over to Plumer and his Second Army. While the pressure on the Germans was kept up all along the line, no major attacks were launched for three weeks. As the weather improved, the ground began to dry out and the troops trained and rehearsed. On 20 September two Australian and four British divisions attacked either side of the Menin road, and once more the British tasted considerable success. Further advances culminated in the capture of Polygon Wood on 26 September.

The British were now consuming German divisions faster than they could be replaced. The advent of the counter-attack divisions had been a shock; but the British quickly adapted, using bite-and-hold tactics, whereby a limited objective was captured and then speedily put into a state of defence to await the counter-attack. When the counter-attack divisions appeared they were being repulsed with very bloody noses. At the Battle of Broodseinde on 4 October the British advanced one and a half miles and captured Poelkapelle, Zonnebeke and Broodseinde. There followed a series of frenzied counter-attacks, all beaten off with heavy German losses, and then the British advanced again. Ludendorff described 4 October 1917 as 'the black day of the German army'.[11]

The British were now poised to take Passchendaele, the last ridge before the plains and the last line of German defences around the salient. The chances of a breakthrough and breakout were now recognised as remote; but if the Passchendaele Ridge could be captured before winter set in, the BEF would have good, well-drained land for their front lines and – for the first time in the Ypres salient – it would be they, and not the Germans, who would hold the commanding heights. At this point, however, the weather broke again. In the entire month of October there were only seven days without rain, and they were overcast with no oppor-tunity for the ground to dry. Rainfall for the month was only just over four inches, which may not seem much; but in a low-lying area where the drainage was bad and the water-table high at the best of times, and when the rain was continuous rather than delivered in short, sharp bursts, it had an increasingly adverse affect on operations.[12] While lurid tales of men drowning in mud are mostly fiction (although it did happen, and wounded men who fell into waterlogged shell holes had to be pulled out quickly), the degeneration of the ground slowed everything, from the delivery of rations to the moving-forward of guns, to the speed at which infantrymen could cover open ground.

Had things on the Western Front been normal – whatever that may be in a war – Haig might well have decided in early October that his men had done enough, and closed the offensive down. His main task, however, was to keep the Germans away from the French, and Pétain still needed time before the French army could be fully operational again. Between 4 and 12 October Tyne Cot was captured across a sea of mud, but it was another three weeks before Passchendaele was taken by the Canadians on 7 November; three weeks of fighting in appalling conditions with temperatures rarely above fifty degrees Fahrenheit (but, contrary to received opinion, never below freezing).[13] With the taking of the Passchendaele Ridge the Third Battle of Ypres ended. Now the French mutinies had stopped, courts martial of the ringleaders were in full flow, conditions had been improved, and the French army was once more ready to play its part in the war, although morale remained brittle until the end.

Third Ypres cost the BEF a quarter of a million casualties, of whom around 53,000 were killed, and gave rise to the largest Commonwealth War Graves Commission cemetery in the world, with 12,000 graves. That more was not accomplished on the ground was due to political dithering, delay after Messines Ridge, and the weather, but there was genuine achievement. Considerable ground was gained, and the British were in a far better position after the battle than they had been before it. The Germans saw it as an unmitigated disaster for their army. Third Ypres pulled in eighty-eight German divisions, over half the total on the Western Front, and all, including the special counter-attack divisions on which the German generals had placed so much hope, were severely mauled. They could not move any divisions eastwards to face the Kerensky offensive, Russia's last attempt to fight in this war. Their butcher's bill was enormous, far higher than that of the British, and it was this savaging, coupled with the knowledge that the American army was coming on stream, that persuaded Ludendorff to chance all on the 'Kaiser's offensive' of 1918 – a decision that cost Germany the war. But more important than anything else, by launching the Third

Battle of Ypres, and by continuing it in the face of political opposition, mounting casualties and appalling conditions, Haig and the BEF kept the Germans away from the French. The French front was untroubled throughout the British offensive, and this gave the French generals the time they needed to reconstitute their army. For this reason, if for no other, Third Ypres had to be fought and had to be persisted with, whatever the cost to the British themselves.

Given that the conditions under which the British were attacking – mounting casualties, worsening conditions, gains less than expected – were not dissimilar to those that had precipitated the French mutinies, those who do not know the British soldier might ask why it was that the British army did not also dissolve into a mutinous rabble. At no time during Third Ypres, or at any other time in the war, was there anything approaching collective indiscipline in the British army, nor was there ever a crisis of morale. One reason was the British practice of regular and frequent rotation through firing, reserve, support lines and billets, whereas the French tended to put a division in the line and leave it there until it was exhausted. British welfare facilities and food were much better than those of the French, the pay was much better, leave was more generous and the arrangements for men to take leave worked. British medical services were always able to cope, and men knew that if they were wounded they would receive attention.

It was not that the French generals were uncaring or callous, but rather that their long experience of a conscript army had bred an outlook in which there was no need to worry about such things: since the Revolution at least, Frenchmen did their time in the army whether they liked it or not, and whatever conditions were provided. The British had always had a volunteer army, which men would not join unless the terms were acceptable, and in which they would not remain unless they felt that they were being properly looked after. A large conscript army can afford to be profligate with men's lives; a small regular army has to be husbanded. The BEF was now a mixture of regulars, wartime volunteers and conscripts, but the pre-war paternalistic attitudes remained.

As has been said, French officers at unit level led from the front – literally – many of them still donning white gloves before going 'over the top', but once the battle was over they left everything to the NCOs.[14] They were, perhaps, not as closely in touch with their soldiers as were their British counterparts, whose men might moan at being constantly under the eye of their officers, but could not, and did not, claim that the latter were not interested in them.

The British army came out of the Third Battle of Ypres in good order, hardened, its morale undamaged, and ready in 1918 to be the only army capable of taking the offensive against the Germans.

NOTES

1 *Jour J* was the day on which an operation started. The British called it Z-Day, later changing it to D-Day.

2 A French infantry division was divided into two brigades, each brigade having two regiments. Each regiment had three battalions.

3 There is no equivalent of the Gendarmerie Nationale in Britain or in the USA. Usually thought of as police, they were and are part of the armed forces and come under the Ministry of Defence (Ministry for War in 1914–18). They do carry out some of the functions of a national police force but are also formed into battalions for garrison duty overseas.

4 See Jean-Baptiste Duroselle, *La Grande Guerre des Français 1914–1918*, Perrin, Paris, 1994, pp. 202–06.

5 John Williams, *Mutiny 1917*, Heinemann, London, 1962.

6 Russia supplied the French with two divisions, each of two brigades. One division went to Salonika, where it stayed until January 1918 when it was disbanded; those soldiers who wished were repatriated. The other division, 22,000 men in all, arrived in Marseille in the spring of 1916. In the Nivelle offensive of 1917 they were part of General Mazel's army and fought well from 16 to 20 April, taking 4,500 casualties killed, wounded and missing. When the news of the abdication of the Tsar (on 15 March 1917) came through, the men split into factions and a mutiny that broke out in the 1st Brigade on 17 September was put down by the French, assisted by the 2nd Brigade. Twelve Russians were killed. The brigades were then separated and put into camps well away from the fighting. After the second Russian Revolution, in October 1917, which brought the Bolsheviks to power and was effectively the end of Russian participation in the war, the surviving Russian troops were given a choice: internment in French North Africa or enlistment into the French army. Most opted to go to North Africa, where they were interned in Algiers and repatriated through Odessa in 1919. The remainder, about a battalion's worth, were formed into the Russian Legion, under French officers, and incorporated into the Moroccan Division. They fought well enough in 1918, and after the war were part of the French occupation force in Germany. Most then became émigrés in Paris. Until fairly recently British officers on the Russian language course spent a year with one of these families, thus becoming fluent in a form of Russian understood in the USSR only by the very old or by priests in hiding.

7 G. Pedroncini, *Les Mutineries de 1917*, Presses Universitaires de France, Paris, 1967 (reprinted with corrections 1999).

8 William Serman and Jean-Paul Bertaud, *Nouvelle Histoire Militaire de la France*, Fayard, Paris, 1998.

9 I am grateful to Mr Nicholas Perry, of HM Imperial Civil Service and probably the greatest living authority on the 36th (Ulster) Division, for his help with the history of this division.

10 For an assessment of the German defenders of Messines Ridge see Ian Passingham, *Pillars of Fire*, Sutton Publishing, Stroud, 1998.

11 According to Ludendorff the German army had quite a few 'black days', but this was undoubtedly one of their worst.

12 Chris McCarthy, *Passchendaele: The Day-by-Day Account*, Arms and Armour Press, London, 1995.

13 Tyne Cot was so called because the Northumberland soldiers thought that the Belgian houses looked like cottages on Tyneside.

14 About forty per cent of all French infantry officers were killed in the war, a far higher proportion than in the British army.

13

TOO LITTLE, TOO LATE

The United States of America wanted nothing to do with European squab-
bles and internecine conflicts, which much of her population had emigrated
to avoid. President Woodrow Wilson spent most of the war years in naïve
manoeuvrings trying to persuade the Allies to accept an impossible peace
based on the 'brotherhood of man'. America entered the war at the last
minute, contributed nothing, and became the only power to make money
out of it. The United States insisted on setting up the League of Nations,
which she then fatally weakened by refusing to join, before she returned to
an isolationism that was a major contributory factor to the Second World
War a generation later.

Such is the impression of American effort in the Great War as held by
a very large number of people in Britain and Europe today. It is a view
arising from an ignorance of the facts and a failure to understand America's
perception of herself, tinged with not a little resentment as America has
superseded the powers of the Old World as the arbiter of man's destiny.

America was vital to the United Kingdom's prosecution of the Great
War almost from Day One; she helped the Allies in a way that far exceeded
the obligations of a neutral. By the middle of 1918 there were as many
American soldiers in France as there were British, and they held a
longer sector of front. While America's casualties were slight compared to

those of the French and British, what she did do was done well and undoubtedly helped to shorten the war.

During the nineteenth and early twentieth centuries the United States settled her interior, secured her coastlines, acquired Hawaii, chased Spain out of the Caribbean, and built the Panama Canal. Since the 1890s she had been the world's greatest industrial power, with a steel output greater than that of Britain and France combined. With her rapidly increasing economic muscle America now had the potential to become a world power, but was unsure how to use that potential. Within the Republican Party there was a vocal and influential minority, led by Theodore Roosevelt (President from 1901 to 1909) and Senator Henry Cabot Lodge, and linked to business interests, that favoured an outward-looking approach to world affairs. This group became increasingly suspicious of Germany, which they saw as a rival in the snapping-up of spare colonial morsels in the Pacific. The mass of the American population, however, was uninterested in matters far from home, and only reluctantly accepted the acquisition of the Philippines from Spain. It is important for Europeans to realise that America is a huge country. A truism to be sure, but it meant that Americans saw no need to travel abroad and, apart from the East Coast elite, had little contact with, and less understanding of, foreign aspirations. Most American political activity was directed inwards: the scars of the Civil War took many years to heal, and the priority (and the votes) went to nation-building, not international affairs.[1] Even today, only fifteen per cent of Americans hold passports, and American schoolchildren learn Spanish, not French.

In 1912 Roosevelt, attempting to make a comeback, split the Republican Party with his novel approach to both home and foreign affairs. This led to the election of a Democrat – Thomas Woodrow Wilson – as President. Wilson is somewhat of an enigma. He was born in Virginia in 1856, the son of a Presbyterian minister, and grew up in Georgia and South Carolina during the Civil War and its painful aftermath. He qualified as a lawyer and was called to the Georgia bar in 1882, but his law practice was unsuccessful. He next attended Johns Hopkins University and became a teacher, firstly in Pennsylvania and then as a professor at Princeton, whose president he became in 1902. In 1910 Wilson was nominated as the Democratic Party's candidate for the governorship of New Jersey, and won the election in a landslide. In 1912 he stood for President of the United States and won with eighty-two per cent of the Electoral College votes.

Wilson is often described as being non-political, and as seeing himself as being an 'outside force' in politics. This is the image he wanted to portray, but his Ph.D. from Johns Hopkins was in political science and based on his book *Congressional Government*. At Princeton he taught political economy (as well as jurisprudence). Clearly he was deeply interested in politics, and no one, then or now, becomes President of the United States without the financial backing of one of the two parties. Wilson had strong religious convictions, rejected the views of the 'imperialist' school with its links to banks and big business, and believed (probably genuinely) that the moral imperative and the spirit of universal brotherhood should govern relations between nations. There was much about Britain that he disliked, but he admired the British system of government where power lay with a prime minister in Parliament, and his hero was Gladstone. On the other hand he was inclined to be dictatorial, introduced segregation to the US civil service, rarely listened to advisers and largely ignored his wartime ambassador in Britain, Walter Page, whose advice he considered to be tainted by being too pro-British.

When war broke out in 1914 Wilson declared for neutrality. He could have done nothing else: at this stage the American voters, as represented by the Congress, would never have tolerated their leaders' taking them into a foreign war. And he was re-elected in 1916 largely on the slogan that he had kept America out of the war (although he himself never said that). His Republican opponent in 1916, Hughes, was much harder on Germany and suffered at the polls because of it.

It has to be said that America did well out of her neutrality. In 1914 she was entering recession, and the war saved her from it, or at least postponed it. America was now able to dominate markets that the Europeans could no longer service, and the warring Allies' greatly increased demand for American products boosted production and profits as never before. While Britain's gold reserves were depleted by £42 million between 1914 and 1919, America's increased by £278.5 million.[2] Theoretically the United States sold to all the belligerents, but in practice most of her exports went to the Allies, as the British blockade prevented trade with Germany.

Increasingly, sales on credit to Britain and France gave American business a vested interest in Allied victory. While this was not the cause of eventual American involvement in the war, it was a sufficiently strong reason to lead to the passing of the Neutrality Acts of 1935 and 1936, so that in the Second World War only 'cash and carry' sales could be made, with no commitment of American money or ships.

Despite Wilson's preference for democracy over autocracy, relations with Britain actually declined up to 1916. As a trading nation America regarded the freedom of the seas as a paramount objective of her foreign policy. Britain blockaded Germany, blockaded German ships in American ports, and stopped and searched neutral shipping to ensure that no 'contraband' was being carried to the Central Powers. This irritated Wilson – America had gone to war with Britain in 1812 largely on this issue – and many were the notes of protest handed to the British ambassador. When relations became too strained, Britain either allowed goods regarded as vital to American exports to go through or, if the cargo was considered by Britain to be too important to be allowed to go to Germany (such as cotton), bought the entire output herself.

The Hearst press was openly hostile to Britain. Indeed, their correspondent in Berlin was later found to have been in the pay of the Germans, and the repression of the 'Easter Rising' in Ireland increased anti-British sentiment amongst the Irish-American community – feeling which was encouraged by German agents. There were a large number of Americans of German descent in the Midwest, with their own newspapers and clubs, many of which were under the influence of the German embassy. All of this meant that Wilson would have found it very difficult to go to war alongside the French and, particularly, the British in 1914. Nevertheless Britain relied on America as the provider of all manner of war materials that British industry could not itself produce. For horses, rifles, artillery pieces, ammunition of all types, aircraft, aero-engines and motor vehicles, the British government placed contracts with American suppliers and manufacturers, to say nothing of the thirty per cent of British foodstuffs that by 1916 were being imported from the United States. America was under no obligation, moral or legal, to provide any of this, and it would have taken but a nod and a wink from the US government to banks and industrial magnates for credit to dry up and contracts to be unfulfilled. That no such censure was ever hinted at was, of course, partly commercial good sense; but it was also partly a mark of unwritten sympathy with, and understanding of, British war aims. American industry and American governmental tolerance were essential to the British war effort long before the United States entered the war, and while Britain might still have won the war without them, it would have taken far longer and would have cost many more lives.

While America disliked the blockade, Britain could make strong legal arguments for it, and these were always more convincing to the US government than German use of the submarine, which was seen as a terror weapon. The British did not sink ships or kill their crews; increasingly, German submarines were to sink merchant shipping without warning. With the failure of the Schlieffen plan and the onset of what would be a long war, informed opinion in Germany moved to regarding Britain, rather than France, as the major enemy. Initially this was not because of the size of Britain's army but because of her navy. The British blockade had an increasingly deleterious effect on the German war effort, not so much because it prevented the import of war-making items (oil could be extracted from coal and rubber replaced by synthetics), but because Germany had always relied on imports of food, mainly from France and Russia but also from further afield. All this was now denied to her, and as the war continued rationing became more extreme. If the Allies held their nerve, then, short of a quick victory on land (which looked increasingly unlikely), Germany would eventually starve.

The answer was the submarine. At the beginning of the war submarines were restricted to coastal defence, but improvements in diesel engines soon made them capable of being used offensively. In February 1915 Germany initiated unrestricted submarine warfare in war zones. This led to vehement American protests – so much so that on 1 September 1915 Germany announced the cessation of unrestricted submarine warfare. Germany tried the submarine again in 1916, and on 21 February announced that from 1 March armed merchant ships would be treated as warships. More American lives were lost (mainly in British ships), and further vigorous protests from America led to Germany's once more abandoning her unrestricted campaign. By 1917 the situation had changed. Largely owing to their inability to switch sufficient reserves from fending off the British 1916 offensive on the Somme to defeat the French at Verdun, the German High Command saw little prospect of a victory on land. The British blockade was becoming increasingly effective, rations for civilians were not far above the bare minimum, and the only option seemed to be to force Britain out of the war by strangling her trade. Previously there had been too few submarines to mount a quick and overwhelming knockout blow; now it appeared that there were enough. The German High Command and the increasingly sidelined civilian government were well aware that this could bring America into the war on the Allied side, but considered that the war could be won before America was in a position to intervene decisively. In any event, they calculated, American attention could be diverted elsewhere.

Part of the process of consolidating the US as the major state on the American continent was the incorporation of Texas, California, Nevada, Utah, Arizona, New Mexico, Colorado and Wyoming at the expense of Mexico, who saw herself as the rightful inheritor of Spanish interests on the North American continent. In the years leading up to 1914, Mexico underwent a series of changes of government in which one dictator replaced another, usually by assassination or armed insurrection. America had large financial interests in Mexico, and the business world wanted nothing so much as stability, regardless of who actually supplied it. Britain too wanted stability, as most of Mexico's oil was British-owned and needed for the Royal Navy. Wilson, on the other hand, wanted democracy in Mexico, an unrealistic hope for a country where eighty-five per cent of the population were illiterate peasant farmers. The rise of the rebel Pancho Villa and his propensity to raid across the border into the United States eventually led to Wilson's reluctantly sanctioning military intervention in Mexico. From March 1916 four-fifths of the United States regular army, under Major General John J. Pershing, was tied down inside Mexico or on its borders. All this was grist to the German mill. Germany supplied arms and money to the various Mexican factions, and hoped that the US would be too preoccupied with her own borders to become involved in the European war.

Another factor that Germany hoped to use was Japan. Japan had declared war on the Allied side in 1914. She had annexed Korea in 1910 and was now able to seize German bases in China and to obtain markets that the Europeans could no longer supply. Japan played little part in the war on land, but the use of her fleet in the Pacific, the China Seas and the Indian Ocean allowed Britain to withdraw ships from the Far East for use in the Atlantic. Relations between Japan and America were, however, fragile. Japan had now come to be seen as the 'Yellow Peril', competing with the United States for trade and influence in China, and posing a threat to American interests in the Pacific. Relations worsened with American restrictions on Japanese immigration, particularly with the passing by the California state legislature of a law forbidding Japanese nationals to own or lease land in that state. Rumours of Japanese ships off the Mexican coast and Japanese officers with the Mexican army abounded.

Up to this point Wilson was attempting to mediate between the belligerent powers. His efforts were directed towards 'peace without victory'. They were well-meaning but naïve, and were coming to naught. The Allies refused to accept that both sets of belligerents should receive equal treatment – it was their territory that was occupied – and Germany would not countenance a settlement that left her with no gains.

American mediation efforts were not helped by the man who was deputed to make them. Eschewing the normal diplomatic channels, Wilson used a trusted crony, Colonel Edward Mandell House. House was a wealthy Texan who had been active in state politics and whose organisational abilities and social contacts had been largely instrumental in securing the election of a succession of Democratic governors of Texas. In 1911 House met Wilson and played a crucial role in uniting the Democratic Party behind this somewhat unusual presidential candidate. Having succeeded to the presidency, Wilson found House to have no political ambitions of his own and began to use him more and more, although without giving him an official government position. As Wilson's emissary to Europe before the war, House had discussions with all the principal governments, but his somewhat unsophisticated attempts to broker a solution to great-power rivalry came to nothing. Once war broke out House believed, as did Wilson, that it was in America's interest to stay neutral, although his (and Wilson's) sympathies were with the Allies. The Allied governments found House difficult because he did not fit the mould of the professional diplomat, a type with which they were used to dealing. The French and British generals assumed that his title of colonel implied that he had served in the American army, and thus understood the military imperative. When this was found not to be the case House's credibility was diminished, although Haig eventually formed the opinion that he was 'natural, sincere and capable'.[3] The French and British considered House's rank to be bogus, although this was a somewhat unfair description, as the conferring of honorary military ranks was common in the United States – Colonel Sanders of Kentucky being the best-known bearer of such today, at least in Britain.[4] House obtained his colonelcy from James Hogg, Governor of Texas in the early 1890s, and with it came a smart uniform, which House later said he had given away to a 'grateful darkie' in his employ.[5] In the spring of 1914 House sent a report to President Wilson describing his impressions of the European situation:

> ...It is militarism run stark mad...Whenever England consents, France and Russia will close in on Germany and Austria. England does not want Germany wholly crushed, for she would then have to reckon with her ancient enemy, Russia; but if Germany insists upon an ever increasing navy, then England will have no choice. The best chance for peace is an understanding between England and Germany in regard to naval armaments and yet there is some disadvantage to us by these two getting too close.[6]

The report was a mixture of misunderstandings and *Realpolitik*. France and Russia were in no state to 'close in' on Germany and Austria, whatever England might or might not consent to; and Russia was not England's ancient enemy – that accolade goes to France. House was quite right when he said that a naval armaments agreement was needed, something that England had tried very hard to get but which the Kaiser and the German government would not accept. No doubt House's worries that Germany and England might get too close was a realisation that a combination of the world's greatest sea power and the world's greatest land power would be unstoppable.[7]

In late 1916 the German High Command calculated that unrestricted submarine warfare would bring Britain to her knees in five months – far too short a time for America to intervene even if she could not be kept neutral. On 31 January 1917 Germany announced unrestricted submarine warfare to begin the following day. On 3 February the United States broke off relations with Germany in protest. American ships refused to sail, and ports became clogged with ships and cargoes that could not be moved. In mid-February Wilson introduced a bill in Congress to permit the arming of United States merchant ships; he still hoped to keep America out of the war and intended the Armed Shipping Bill as a last warning to Germany. The pacifist faction in Congress began to organise a filibuster against the bill.

And then occurred something so momentous that it is difficult to believe that any rational government – and the German government was rational – could have sanctioned it. Zimmerman, the German Foreign Secretary, sent a coded cable to the German ambassador in Washington, to be passed on to the German minister in Mexico. As the Royal Navy had long ago cut all German undersea cables, the Germans could initially communicate overseas only by wireless or through (pro-German) Swedish channels. Since 1915 Wilson had permitted the German government to use the US State Department cable for communications to and from the German embassy in Washington. This had been authorised by Wilson because the Germans had assured him that these channels would be used solely for matters pertaining to Wilson's search for peace terms. The British had long ago cracked both the German naval and diplomatic codes, and had been monitoring American cables, but rather than protest against this flagrant breach of American neutrality they were happy to decipher enemy messages sent by this means. It is ironic that it was from the State Department cable that they intercepted and decoded the 'Zimmerman telegram'. Translated into English it read:

> Foreign Office telegram 16 January 1917: strictly secret yourself to decipher. We intend from the first February unrestricted U-boat war to begin. It will nevertheless be attempted to keep the United States neutral. In the event that this should not succeed, we offer Mexico an alliance on the following terms. Together we make war and together we make peace. Generous financial support and understanding on our part that Mexico reconquer the lost territories of Texas and Arizona. Settlement of the details to be left to Your Excellency. You will inform the President of Mexico of the foregoing in

strictest secrecy. As soon as war with the US is certain it is suggested that Japan is added and that the President of Mexico should be invited to immediately negotiate between ourselves and Japan. Please point out to the President of Mexico that ruthless employment of our U-boats now points to the prospect of England being forced to make peace in a few months. Acknowledge receipt. Zimmerman.

The British naturally wished to pass on this information to the Americans, but had to do so in a way that did not expose British possession of German code books, or British ability to tap American government cable, wireless and telephone communications. Eventually they managed to lift the message again, while it was being transmitted from Washington to Mexico, thus giving the impression that they had obtained a decoded copy either in Mexico or in Washington. For the moment the message lay in the safe of the British Chief of Naval Intelligence in London.

On 5 February, after America had broken off relations with Germany, Zimmerman sent a further telegram instructing the German minister in Mexico to make the offer now, including Japanese participation, without waiting for America to enter the war. This too was intercepted and decoded by the British. On the same day Wilson finally withdrew the US army from Mexico.

It now appeared to the British that America might not enter the war after all, and there were fears in London that Wilson might even put economic pressure on Britain to make peace on disadvantageous terms. On 23 February the British gave the text of the Zimmerman telegram to the American ambassador in London, Walter Page, who sent it on to Washington on 24 February. Wilson was described as being 'indignant', and sat on the document until the following Monday, when he was due to address Congress on the Armed Merchant Ships Bill. Even as the President was speaking, news came in of the sinking of the Cunard Liner *Laconia*, with the loss of two American lives. Two days later Wilson, in order to defeat the filibuster against the bill, decided to publish the telegram. The story broke on 1 March 1917.

The initial reaction was mixed. For the pro-Allied party and the eastern press it was a godsend; to the Hearst press, the German Midwest and the pacifist faction it was a British fake. The filibuster succeeded and the Armed Ships Bill did not pass. Three-quarters of the American people were still indifferent to the war, and very few believed that the Zimmerman telegram could possibly be genuine.

Then Zimmerman did something that is still inexplicable – unless in terms of German arrogance. He publicly admitted, at a press conference in Berlin, that the telegram was authentic. This admission was the catalyst that changed American thinking about the war. On 9 March Wilson, using his executive authority, ordered the arming of American merchant ships. Goods began to move again. On 18 March three American ships were sunk without warning by U-boats. On 19 March the abdication of the Tsar of Russia removed one of Wilson's objection to the Allies – they were now all democratic.

On 20 March Wilson met with his cabinet and the decision was taken to enter the war. On 2 April the President announced the decision to Congress, and on 6 April 1917 America declared war on Germany (she did not declare war on Austria-Hungary until December). By this time British losses due to U-boat attacks had soared to 875,000 tons and Admiral Beatty calculated that Britain would run out of foodstuffs and essential supplies by July. In May the convoy system was instituted and the results were spectacular. British, and increasingly American, escort vessels were able to ensure the safe passage of more than enough supplies, and to sink more U-boats, which were now deprived of easy victims. Although shipping losses were over eight million tons by the end of the year, Allied ship-building more than replaced them.

In the spring of 1917 America was in no state to go to war. The American army, along with that of Argentina, ranked seventeenth in the world and was but 70,000 strong. It had 400 obsolete artillery pieces, 1,500 machine guns of four different and non-interchangeable calibres, and while there were 285,000 Springfield rifles in store, there was only enough ammunition for one regimental (three-battalion) attack. Although America had invented powered flight it was regarded as little more than a circus attraction, and the Aviation Section of the Army Signal Corps had only fifty-five obsolete aircraft and thirty-five pilots to fly them. The United States now had to raise an army. The enormous expansion required was achieved by conscription, although many Americans volunteered before they were called up. Despite American law's forbidding enlistment in foreign armies, Americans had crossed the border into Canada and joined the Canadian army; some had even joined the British army. There were American volunteer ambulance units on the Western Front and there was even a combat group of American flyers fighting with the French – the *Escadrille Lafayette* – but this was but a handful compared to what would be needed.[8] Having learned from their own experiences in the Civil War and the British experience of the present conflict, the American army eschewed territorial recruitment, and while the spearhead of the American Expeditionary Force (AEF) would be the few regular divisions and the United States Marine Corps, they would be followed by the National Guard (the equivalent of the British Territorial Force but recruited state-wide) and conscript divisions deliberately formed from men from all over the Union (known as National Army divisions).

Promotion in the tiny pre-war American army was painfully slow, and as promotion was in the hands of Congress, which wished to save money, there were only seven major generals in the whole army in 1917. The junior major general was John J. Pershing, selected to command the expeditionary force partly because of his record, but also owing to political contacts – his father-in-law was Chairman of the Senate Armed Services Committee. When telephoned and asked if he could speak French, Pershing saw what was in the wind and claimed to be fluent. America is a genuinely egalitarian society, and it loves a poor boy made good. Pershing was often referred to as the 'Missouri Ploughboy', and while he may have done some ploughing on his father's land, he was in fact well educated and his family, which originated from Alsace, had good political connections. Born in 1860 he was for a while a teacher, then decided to read for the bar until he received a nomination to West Point where he graduated in 1886. He was commissioned into the cavalry and took part in the Indian Wars, during which he was Chief of Scouts in the suppression of the North Dakota Sioux. He was still a second lieutenant at the age of thirty-two; he served as Captain of Cadets at Nebraska University, where he also took a law degree, and as a captain served in Cuba and the Philippines.[9] His nickname of 'Black Jack' may date from his command of a troop of Negro cavalry in Cuba (the US army was segregated until the early 1950s). Pershing so impressed Theodore Roosevelt, who fought as a volunteer in Cuba and was later President of the United States, that he was promoted from captain to brigadier general over the heads of 882 others, which must have enhanced his popularity. He spent most of 1915 and 1916 on operations on the Mexican border, during which his wife (a senator's daughter) and three daughters were burned to death in a fire at their married quarters (a son survived).

Pershing and his staff arrived in France in June 1917 to a tumultuous welcome from the French, who immediately whisked him off to visit the tomb of Lafayette.[10] Pershing never said, *'Lafayette, nous sommes voici'* – the words were uttered by Colonel C. E. Stanton, an officer on Pershing's staff – but Pershing was widely credited with them, and they were a shrewd comment that went down very well with the French. The French were very anxious to take the Americans under their wing. After all, they frequently proclaimed, it was France that had given America liberty, freedom and democracy. That neither Bourbon, Revolutionary nor Napoleonic France had been liberal, free or democratic was conveniently ignored.

The Allies, and Pershing, were well aware that it would take time for the American army to build up and be trained for warfare on the Western Front. The French suggested that building up a separate army was really not necessary – manpower was what was needed, and American soldiers could be incorporated into the French army. The British, who had the advantage of a common language, were equally in favour of having American units in the BEF; but when it swiftly became apparent that this was unacceptable, they came up with a better suggestion. To begin with, offered the British generals, there could be American battalions in British brigades. Once experience had been gained, American brigades could be put into British divisions (with American divisional commanders to avoid offence to American pride), and then American divisions into British corps, and American corps into British armies, until a separate American army could be formed. This made sound military sense and would have worked, but that it was proposed at all was to fail to understand the American psyche. The British had a long history of sending their tiny land forces to serve as members of a coalition, often under allied commanders. America was very reluctant ever to have her soldiers serve under a foreign flag, and she still is.[11]

Pershing saw the state of the French army in 1917, riven with discontent and mutiny, and to place his men under command of the British would be seen by the American public as a reversion to the colonial status that they had broken away from. Most Americans would have heard stories about the War of 1812, a forgotten campaign to the British, to whom the fight against Napoleon was what mattered, but important to the United States as their first foreign war; the President's official residence was a constant reminder of the episode, not having been the White House until after the British set fire to it.

It was not Pershing alone, however, who refused to integrate American troops into Allied formations. Wilson had been quite clear as to America's role in Europe. She was not an 'Ally' of France and Britain, but an 'Associated Power' – hair-splitting to some, but in fact a genuine indication that Wilson did not see French and British war aims as necessarily coinciding with his own. His instructions to Pershing were categorical: there was to be no American involvement in the fighting until there was an American force ready to take the field, with its own sector of front and operating as an army in its own right, and not under the command or direction of anybody else. This, of course, infuriated the French and the British, but from the American viewpoint it was reasonable and right. American soldiers were not in Europe to act as anybody's poodles, or to win the war for the French and the British. They were there to strike a blow in their own right, and to end the war in accordance with Wilson's principles of a just and lasting peace. Pershing did not necessarily agree with his commander-in-chief – indeed he said later that the inclusion of half a million Americans in the Third Battle of Ypres could have ended the war in 1917[12] – but he could not flagrantly disobey him, although he did bend the rules on a number of occasions by allowing American troops to help out.

America had no great difficulty in finding men for the American Expeditionary Force (AEF) but, like the British in 1914, they had a small regular army, and finding officers and NCOs was not easy. Nor was finding senior officers to command regiments, brigades and divisions. The final arbiter of promotions and appointments for the AEF was the Secretary of War, Newton D. Baker, who generally accepted Pershing's advice; but in the early days all sorts of highly unsuitable people who had seniority or political connections on their side were sent out. In a letter to the Secretary of War dated 4 October 1917, Pershing said: '…we have some general officers who have neither the experience, the energy, nor the aggressive spirit to prepare their units or to handle them under battle conditions…'[13] Pershing had to be hard, and he made few friends in the AEF by insisting that only the best was good enough. He irritated the doctors when he inspected a medical unit and found them under the impression that they were still civilian practitioners translated abroad. They were left in no doubt by Pershing that, doctors or no, they would wear uniform, stand to attention and salute – and be inspected again the next day. Brigade and divisional commanders were refused commands for being too old, too fat, or deficient in combat experience.

The Germans did not believe that American forces could ever reach Europe in sufficient strength and in time to make a difference, but a combination of the Royal Navy (which transported fifty-one per cent of US troops bound for France), American shipping and confiscated German ships stranded in American harbours delivered them in increasing numbers. The first American division (1 Division, the Big Red One), an amalgam of regular army units, arrived on 28 June 1917 and thereafter the build-up of the AEF is shown below:[14]

Table 13

Date	Strength of AEF (all ranks)
30 June 1917	14,359
31 July 1917	16,748
31 August 1917	36,658
30 September 1917	61,531
31 October 1917	81.055
30 November 1917	125,950
31 December 1917	174,884
31 January 1918	215,788
28 February 1918	251,889
31 March 1918	318,621
30 April 1918	429,659
31 May 1918	651,284
30 June 1918	873,691
31 July 1918	1,169,062
31 August 1918	1,415,128
30 September 1918	1,705,392
31 October 1918	1,867,623

By way of comparison, the strength of the BEF on 31 October 1918 was 1,859,246 (plus a further 84,000 in Italy).

It was, however, one thing to get the men across to Europe – a considerable organisational feat – and quite another to equip them and prepare them for all-out war. Although the factories of America were turning out all manner of weapons and equipment for the Allies, there was little capacity left over for their own army. It might be asked why American industry did not simply stop supplying the British and the French, and turn their capacity over to their own army instead. The answer is that, apart from the contractual implications, a shipload of ammunition delivered to the British would be fired at the Germans now, whereas if it were turned over to the Americans it would only be used when they were ready to fire it – which would not be for some time yet. Eventually the AEF used French artillery pieces, British rifles rebored to take American ammunition, British helmets, mainly French aircraft, British trench mortars and grenades, French Chauchat light machine guns (the American-designed Lewis, a better gun and in service with the BEF, had been rejected by the pre-war American military when offered to them) and French Hotchkiss medium machine guns. There was a shortage of boots, and many of the troops arriving in the early days could only be issued with shoes. There were insufficient horses, largely because available shipping concentrated on men and equipment, and because the United States had hoped to buy horses from Spain. The Spanish, in reprisal for American refusal to export cotton to them (which would then have found its way to Germany), refused to sell them any; British artillery gun teams had to be reduced from six horses to four so that the Americans could have at least some horses until enough could be obtained from other suppliers. The American army had a system of campaign medals, but no bravery awards except for the Congressional Medal of Honour (dating from 1862) and merit certificates. The Distinguished Service Cross and Distinguished Service Medal were therefore authorised by Congress, and the law was changed to permit American soldiers to accept French and British decorations. Promotions were a problem, as the Secretary of War and the Chief of Army Staff in America naturally wished to follow the normal promotion system, which was largely by seniority. Thus, when Pershing wanted to promote a deserving brigade commander to command a division, he was often thwarted by the despatch of an officer from the United States. Congress was, in any case, reluctant to sanction many substantive promotions: when the army eventually contracted to its peacetime establishment there would be no jobs for most of those promoted, but they would still have to be paid the salary or pension of their rank. This meant that officers commanding American formations were often several ranks below their French or British counterparts, even when granted acting rank for the duration.

In the autumn of 1917 a number of officers were sent to Europe to see conditions for themselves, spending twelve days with the British, twelve with the French and six with the AEF, so that they could then return to America and train their divisions for the Western Front. Pershing was not impressed by many of them: 'too old', 'in bad shape', 'infirm', 'very fat and inactive' and 'could not begin to stand the strain' were some of the more charitable remarks written about them.[15] One officer who was both too old – he was sixty – and too fat was Major General Hunter Liggett. Told by Pershing that he was quite unsuitable as a divisional commander, he faced the General down and was given time to prove the old curmudgeon wrong. To get fit and lose weight Liggett decided to take up riding. As he had never sat upon a horse before this was a precarious business, resulting in a series of horrific falls, many bruises and, on one occasion, concussion. Pershing relented and allowed him to stay. It was a wise decision, as Liggett turned out to be one of the most competent field commanders in the AEF. He rose, via a division and a corps, to command of the First American Army by the end of the war.

Major General William L. Sibert, Commander 1 Division, was not so lucky. In October 1917 Pershing wrote: 'Sibert. Slow of speech and thought…slovenly in dress, has an eye to his personal interests. Without any ability as a soldier. Utterly hopeless as an instructor or as a tactician. Fails to appreciate soldierly qualities having none himself. Loyal as far as it suits his purpose. Opinionated withal and difficult to teach. Has a very high opinion of his own worth…'[16] Secretary Baker accepted Pershing's assessment and Sibert was returned to the United States.

As with the British army in the early days, there were difficulties in finding enough staff officers. The American army did have a General Staff, but it was very small and not highly thought of by ambitious officers. Far more staff officers were needed than could be made available under the peacetime system, and so British staff courses were expanded to include American students. Training in France was done by setting up schools of instruction and by getting the French and British to help. Pershing was not entirely happy with the Allied training: he thought that the French were war-weary and too defensively minded, whereas he found the British concept to be much more aggressive, and more suited to American soldiers. At the same time he did not want his soldiers to be pale imitations of the British; he was convinced that he should be training his men not for the trenches, but for open warfare. In that everybody on the Allied side wanted open warfare, and that the war did, in the final stages, develop into that, Pershing was right; but his insistence on concentrating on open warfare and marksmanship handicapped his men when they found themselves engaged in the hard slog of close-range trench fighting until the last few months of the war.

Joint training with the British was generally regarded as a success. Americans preferred British rations to their own except that they preferred coffee to tea, and so coffee was supplied from America.[17] The British habit of issuing their men with a rum ration raised eyebrows in the American headquarters, until Pershing decreed that it would be bad for morale if his men, when training with the British, were not to have the same perquisites as their hosts.[18]

Winston Churchill once said that the British and the Americans were one people divided by a common language. There were misunderstandings. Prior to the Battle of Cambrai in November 1917, Pershing agreed to lend the British three engineer regiments (11th, 12th and 14th) to help. The Eleventh Engineers supported and fought with the British 20 Division; the 12th delivered artillery ammunition, and the 14th assisted with the operation of the light railway system behind the lines. One American engineer officer reported that he had detected a serious decline in British morale. A British officer had remarked to him that if the Germans wanted this particular bit of France they were welcome to it. Typically self-deprecatory British humour was not always understood.

While the AEF was building up, training and being equipped, individual units did take part in a number of actions despite Wilson's wish that they should not. Pershing, as a soldier, understood the military situation on the Western Front; and while he stoutly resisted continuing French pressure to incorporate American regiments in French divisions, he was prepared to lend troops to help out in emergencies, often under the pretext of training. While the Allies were more than happy to have American participation – indeed they constantly urged it – there were difficulties of organisation. The strength of an American division was 28,000 all ranks, twice the size of the French or British equivalent, so that divisional dumps of petrol, rations and ammunition established by the French and British could not cope with the demands of an American division.[19] Most administration, therefore, was perforce left to the Americans themselves.

In January 1918 President Wilson made his famous 'Fourteen Points' speech to Congress. He had not consulted the Allies, but on the face of it what he was proposing was entirely reasonable. Closer scrutiny, however, worried the Allies greatly. They could not agree to the abolition of secret diplomacy; nor were they entirely happy about the creation of an independent Polish state. Absolute freedom of the seas in peace and war was not acceptable to the British, who relied on blockade in the event of war; and for the French, that 'the wrong done to France by Prussia in 1871 in the matter of Alsace-Lorraine…should be righted' was not strong enough. Both the French and the British disliked the suggestion that the wishes of the colonial peoples should hold equal sway with the views of the imperial powers, and the suggestion that the possessions of the Ottoman Empire should be allowed autonomy did not suit Allied perceptions of the post-war shape of the Middle East. It was perhaps as well that the Germans did not immediately accept the Wilson proposals, for had they done so the Allies would have found themselves on a hook from which it would have been difficult to escape.

The AEF provided engineer support to the British at Cambrai, and when the 'Kaiser's offensive' fell on the British Fifth Army on 21 March 1918 on a fifty-mile front between La Fère and Arras, near the junction with the French Sixth Army, men of the 6th American Engineer Regiment who were employed on railway repair tasks swapped spanners for rifles and fought shoulder to shoulder with the British. Pershing offered three more regiments of engineers and two of artillery, which were gratefully accepted by Field Marshal Haig. At this time there were five American divisions in Europe. The Big Red One was put into reserve for the French First Army, and the other four relieved French divisions in quiet sectors, so that the French could support the sorely pressed British. Between 21 March and 6 April 1918, when the German offensive on the Somme tailed off, 2,200 American soldiers were in action, and another 500 fought on the River Lys between 9 and 27 April.

During the March retreat by the British army Haig became increasingly concerned that the French were not supporting the BEF sufficiently. Reserves promised by Pétain did not appear, and it began to look as if the French might abandon the agreed priority of maintaining contact between the British and French armies, choosing instead to fall back in order to cover Paris. Haig feared that the British army might collapse if support was not forthcoming, and on 25 March asked that 'General Foch, or some other determined general who would fight, should be given supreme control of the operations in France'.[20] This led to the appointment of Foch as 'Generalissimo' of the Allied armies, which is often taken to mean that Foch was now the Allied Supreme Commander in the same way as Eisenhower in the European theatre from 1944. What Haig wanted was unity of command in the military sense, not by way of Lloyd George's divide-and-rule ploy of the Supreme War Council. In fact Foch's brief was only to coordinate the actions of French, British and American troops on the Western Front. As a French general he could give orders to Pétain, commanding the French army, but not to Haig, and certainly not to Pershing. Foch could get nothing done except by persuasion and force of personality; nevertheless, this was a great improvement on the previous state of affairs, and did much to counteract Pétain's fear concerning the fragility of the French army and his reluctance to move troops away from defended localities. Even so, Haig had problems with French reinforcements, which were always slow in coming; but as the British army did not collapse, perhaps no great harm was done – except to Haig's private opinion of the French.

Haig and Pershing did their best to cooperate with Foch, but there were disagreements, particularly when Haig thought that the British army was being misused to bail out the French, or when Pershing detected attempts to dissipate American units to bolster Allied divisions.

The first major action by the AEF took place on 28 May 1918. The German offensive that began on 21 March had driven the British Fifth Army back nearly forty miles before being halted at Cantigny, about four miles north-west of Montdidier. Cantigny was held by the French First Army, still with the American 1 Division nominally in reserve – nominally, because the agreement with Pershing was that the French were only to use the American division to take over parts of the line temporarily, to allow French units to rest and refit. In the event, the Americans found themselves holding the front lines when the Germans shelled them heavily on 3 May. Some 15,000 artillery shells, both high-explosive and mustard-gas, rained down on the 18th Infantry Regiment, which had 200 men killed and 600 wounded. The mix of French and American artillery supporting the division replied, and in the next twenty-four hours fired 10,000 shells. The divisional commander, Major General Robert Lee Bullard, now decided that he had had enough of passive defence, and ordered patrols into no man's land and trench raids on the German positions; he was gleefully encouraged by the French. On 15 May the French asked Bullard to attack and recapture Cantigny. While this was not vital to the war effort, it was a limited objective and would be good practice for the Americans. Bullard asked Pershing, who agreed. The division spent thirteen days planning and rehearsing the attack.

At 0445 hours on 28 May there was a two-hour artillery bombardment of the German positions, and at 0645 hours the doughboys of 1 Division left their jump-off lines supported by French artillery, twelve French light tanks and French and British aircraft.[21] All the objectives were taken, and the Americans beat off three counter-attacks. The French, and perhaps more importantly Pershing, were now convinced that American troops could take part in offensive actions.

Although the first thrust of the German spring offensive of 1918 had been stopped on the Somme, in April a further attack was launched on the British in Flanders and was only halted at Hazebrouck, twenty-five miles south of Dunkirk. The Germans then made a feint attack against the French, south of the River Oise, from the Chemin des Dames. The 'Kaiser's offensive' had made considerable inroads into Allied territory, but had so far failed to split the French and British armies. If this could be achieved, the French would move to defend Paris while the British would see their priority as being the Channel ports; the two Allied armies would diverge even further, and could be dealt with one after the other. The attack south of the Oise was designed to force the Allies to move their reserves south, and by 30 May the Germans had reached Château-Thierry, only fifty miles from Paris. Field Marshal Haig was less than happy about the French conduct of the defence – he had sent them three British divisions that had been mishandled and virtually destroyed. Four French divisions had been badly knocked about, and thirty-five other French infantry divisions and six cavalry divisions were scattered, with the French XVIII Corps falling back in disorder. General Foch, coordinating Allied operations, knew that the German advance here was a feint – but now it looked as if the feint was turning into a success. Foch appealed to Pershing for help.

While all this was going on Pershing was in the British sector, visiting army schools and units attached to the British for training. Amongst the five American divisions in the area was the regular 3 Division. The men were spread all over the place with different British units, but the infantry – 17,000 men – were all in one place and were the nearest Americans to Château-Thierry. Pershing agreed with Foch that these infantrymen could be put into position behind the French to bolster them up.

Château-Thierry sits on the north bank of the River Marne. To the north of the town is a range of hills, and the old chateau itself dominates the town. At about 1700 hours on 31 May the first contingent of American infantry – Lieutenant John T. Bissell and fourteen men of the 7th (Motorised) Machine Gun Battalion – came up from the south and approached the bridge leading into the town across the Marne. They met a scene of utter chaos. The Germans were on the hills above and confused fighting was going on within the town. The roads leading south were clogged with retreating soldiers, stragglers and civilians trying to haul their possessions away from the advancing Germans. Bissell left his vehicles short of the bridge and, with his two Hotchkiss guns, crossed the bridge and disappeared into the narrow streets. The rest of the battalion were close behind: there was no question of their bolstering up the front line – they *were* the front line.

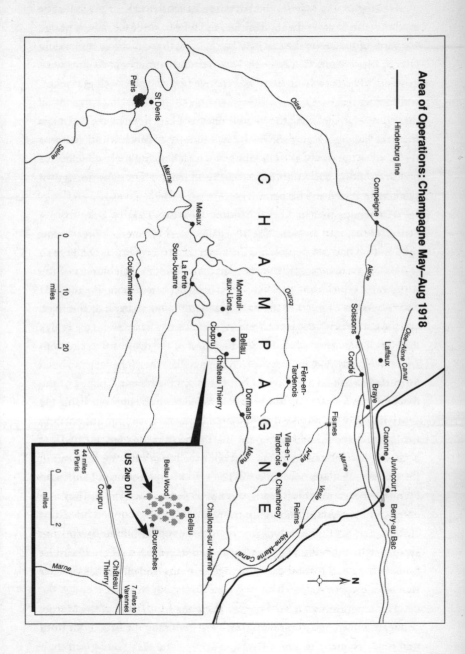

Area of Operations: Champagne May–Aug 1918

Hindenburg line

0 10 20
miles

Paris
St Denis
Seine
Marne
Oise
Compiegne
Meaux
Coulommiers
La Ferte Sous-Jouarre
Monteuil-aux-Lions
Coupru
Belleau
Château Thierry
Dormans
Ourcq
Soissons
Condé
Braye
Laffaux
Crucq
Fère-en-Tardenois
Ville-en-Tardenois
Chambrecy
Fismes
Ardre
Marne
Vesle
Reims
Aisne
Olse-Aisne Canal
Craonne
Juvincourt
Berry-au-Bac
Chalons-sur-Marne
Aisne-Marne Canal

C H A M P A G N E

N

Inset:

44 miles to Paris
0 2
miles

Coupru
Belleau Wood
US 2ND DIV
Bellau
Bouresches
Château Thierry
Marne
7 miles to Varennes

Halting on the Marne, the battalion executive officer placed eight machine guns to cover the road bridge, and nine to cover the railway bridge 500 yards upstream (to the east). By last light on that day the Commanding Officer, Major James G. Taylor, had arrived, and by midnight all guns were in place.[22] The crews dug three alternative positions for each gun team, and another that was 'secret' and known only to the crew. Unfortunately all these positions, including the 'secret' ones, could be seen by the Germans from the heights. During the next day, 1 June, the French withdrew from the town as the rest of the US infantry trickled in and took up defensive positions along the south bank of the Marne. There was no sign of Lieutenant Bissell and his band.

The troops that had been holding Château-Thierry were from a Senegalese colonial division. The Senegalese were famous as looters, information that had not percolated down to the Americans; as the French troops left, heading south, they helped themselves to the contents of the Americans' vehicles and packs that had been deposited along the road. At 2200 hours on 1 June the Germans reached the north bank of the river, and the last French troops withdrew. As they were halfway across the bridge the French engineers blew it up, sending most of the rearguard to kingdom come. Next day nothing very much happened – the Germans had been instructed to halt on the Marne – but that night Lieutenant Cobbey, of the machine-gun battalion, heard his name called from the opposite bank. He crossed by the railway bridge, which had been blown but not entirely demolished, and found Lieutenant Bissell and thirteen men. He had lost both his guns and one man, but had done well to get anyone at all out of the shambles that was now Château-Thierry. On the same night Lieutenant Flannery heard moaning from the north bank. With the unthinking courage of the young and inexperienced, Flannery stripped off all his clothes, tied his Colt revolver on top of his head with a bandanna, and swam across the river. He found a wounded French soldier, whom he brought back to the American bank. He later received the French *Croix de Guerre* for his action.

The Americans were now spread along the south bank of the Marne, and were mixed in with French units and generally messed about until mid-June. Then the rest of 3 Division arrived and they were given their own sector, about seven miles of the south bank of the Marne running from Château-Thierry to Varennes. The Americans had arrived just in time and in just sufficient numbers to dissuade the local German commanders from exceeding their orders and pushing on over the Marne. West of Château-Thierry the Marne turns south-south-west for about six miles before once more flowing westwards, and so to the west of the town the Germans were still pressing on to reach the river. While 3 Division were placing themselves as the cork in the bottle of Château-Thierry, more pleas for help from the French persuaded Pershing to agree to the US 2 Division being placed behind the French to the west of the town. Probably the most experienced division in the American army at that time, 2 Division had one regular army brigade and one Marine Corps brigade. The division left Paris on 30 May in stifling heat and moved to Meaux by train in the traditional French cattle wagons. From Meaux to La Ferté-sous-Jouarre the men and their kit were transported by a twelve-mile column of French lorries driven by Indo-Chinese who spoke not a word of any familiar language. The division spent the night in La Ferté, where the Marines found a brandy distillery. With a generosity not normally found between leathernecks and doughboys, the Marines shared their discovery with the army, and the entire division completed a jolly evening by looting the town.[23] It was a very cheerful division that marched the six miles to Montreuil-aux-Lions next morning; it was well provided with trussed-up chickens, and many soldiers sported booty in the form of ladies' hats. On 1 June the division, under command of the French XXI Corps, began to take up an eleven-mile front astride the Paris road, east of Coupru and behind the French. A German attack on 2 June broke through the French, but ran out of steam and withdrew when it hit the American front. The French had, however, lost Belleau Wood. By 4 June the US 2 Division were all in place but the situation was confused, not least because the French had neglected to issue the Americans with any maps. Disorganised French units were retreating through the Americans, and nobody seemed to know where German or French positions were. A French aviator saw troops on the ground running back and thought they were Americans. The French Corps Commander, General Degoutte, telephoned Colonel Wendell C. Neville, commanding the US Marine Corps Brigade, to ask why his men were withdrawing. Neville in turn telephoned Major Thomas Holcomb, Commanding Officer 6th Marines, the forward battalion, and received the reply, 'When I do any running it will be in the opposite direction. Nothing doing in the fall-back business.' Colonel Neville's message to General Degoutte has gone down in Marine Corps legend: 'Retreat? Hell – we only just got here.'

By the morning of 5 June it was clear that, far from the US 2 Division holding behind the French to bolster them up, there were now no French troops between the Germans and the Americans. General Degoutte – completely contrary to what had been agreed between Foch and Pershing – now ordered the Americans to retake Belleau Wood. The plan was for the army brigade to capture the woods looking north to Belleau Wood, after which the Marines would capture Belleau Wood itself. The battle went on from first light on 6 June until 25 June, and, for the Marines in particular, was a smaller-scale version of the Somme. Long-service soldiers though many Marines were, their service in Mexico or the Philippines had done little to prepare them for the Western Front, and all the mistakes of the British in 1916 were repeated by the Americans. Moving in straight lines, without using fire and movement and with poor coordination between infantry and artillery, the Marines moved across open ground and suffered heavily. Once the Germans reinforced the wood the battle became a bloody slog, Marine and army units relieving each other in turn, with advances measured in yards. Finally, after a night and a day of artillery bombardment, the wood fell to an attack by the Marines' 3rd Battalion. On the Marines' right on the first day of the attack, 6 June, the 23rd Infantry Regiment (of the army brigade) should have been protecting the right flank; but in their eagerness one battalion pressed on into the edges of the wood, had twenty-seven men killed and 225 wounded, and withdrew. One company of Marines got into the village of Bouresches, but were then cut off when the army brigade withdrew. There they stayed until 25 June, facing repeated German counter-attacks and mounting casualties. The Americans were particularly appalled to find that the original French garrison had been using an antique grandfather clock as the seat for the officers' latrine. An officer who visited the village some years after the war was intrigued to find the mayor driving around in a Dodge pick-up with

US Marine Corps markings. Asked where he had got it, the mayor explained that he had been sold it by a Marine during the siege in June 1918!

Belleau Wood might have been taken on 10 June, before the Germans reinforced it. On that day Lieutenant Colonel Wise, with the unfortunate nickname of 'Dopey', led an attack by the 5th Marines from the south end of the wood. Once in the wood he veered off to his right and emerged at the eastern edge overlooking the village of Bouresches. Thinking this was Belleau village, he reported the capture of Belleau Wood, and it was some time before the error was realised. As on the Somme, inexperienced officers were not using their compasses and were getting lost. Included in the American casualties were 334 men of the 23rd Infantry Regiment who had been gassed. Of these only two died, the rest being out of action for around two weeks. The battle for Belleau Wood was in some ways an unnecessary action, for the French could have regrouped and taken it themselves – or simply stayed on the defensive. It is probably an exaggeration to say that the action of the US 2 Division saved Paris, but it was by no means a wasted effort and, like the British on 1 July 1916, the Americans learned vital lessons which would stand them in good stead later on.

The German attacks on the Marne had not achieved their aim – to force the Allied reserves south, thus allowing the Germans to attack the British in Flanders. By July General Degoutte was commanding the French Sixth Army, defending a crescent-shaped line that ran from Château-Thierry twenty-five miles eastwards to Reims, with the US 3 Division still holding its seven miles along the Marne between Château-Thierry and Varennes. The Commander 3 Division was an unlikely-looking example of the American officer corps. Major General Joseph T. Dickman was portly, a lover of good food and wine and an amateur painter, but was a soldier to his fingertips. He had survived Pershing's dislike of fat officers, and as a cavalryman he was a far better rider than Hunter Liggett. Dickman realised that the Marne west of Château-Thierry was not suitable for a river crossing, and thought that if the Germans came they would come at his division. He decided to hold his sector with a lightly manned forward line along the river, with strongpoints further back from which counter-attacks could be mounted, and with his final defence line on the hills overlooking the river and about two miles south of it. The right of Dickman's sector was held by Colonel Ulysses Grant McAlexander's 38th Infantry Regiment, to whose right were elements of the US 28th Division (the Pennsylvania National Guard) interspersed with French units. General Degoutte did not like Dickman's dispositions and felt that far more of 3 Division should be concentrated on the river line. This layout would have been acceptable for French troops, whose tactic was to withdraw the forward line when heavily pressed and mount counter-attacks by fresh troops. Dickman, however, was well aware that his men were inexperienced and that a tactical with-drawal could easily turn into a rout; he intended his forward line to remain in place and the Germans, should they break through, to be held by his backstops. Degoutte went on his way and Dickman ignored the orders to concentrate forward. The French corps commander turned a blind eye.

Early on 14 July a French patrol near Reims captured a German major who was carrying a copy of a plan for a forthcoming offensive. It showed that the aim was as before: to force the Allies to move their reserves south, thus allowing the Germans to attack the British in Flanders. For Opera-tion 'Marne', an artillery bombardment was to start at 0010 hours the next day, 15 July, and at 0130 hours fourteen German divisions were to cross the Marne between Reims and Château-Thierry, with another fourteen divisions following up, and with eighty-three artillery battalions concen-trating on the US 3 Division sector alone. There would be a second German attack (Operation 'Reims') between Reims and Verdun with Châlons-sur-Marne, twenty-five miles south, as its objective. There would thus be two thrusts aimed at Paris; the Allies would have to move their reserves, and three German armies would fall upon the British in the north.

Was the captured plan real, or a German ruse? The Allied Generalis-simo, Foch, had little time to make up his mind but decided it was genuine, and so at 2345 hours on 14 July every available Allied gun between Château-Thierry and Reims opened up on likely German approaches, assembly areas and stores dumps. Had the captured plan been a plant, this would, of course, have given away the positions of the Allied artillery; but at 0010 hours, exactly as the plan had said, German artillery began to bombard the Allied lines, and an hour later German infantry stormed down to the river line. In McAlexander's sector they began to cross in boats and suffered terribly from the 28th Regiment's riflemen and light machine-gunners.

Although some got across to the south bank and through the American outpost line, they were stopped by Dickman's backstops supported by the divisional artillery on the reverse slopes. Lieutenant George P. Hays, an artillery liaison officer, had seven horses killed under him as he made regular sorties from the gun lines to the river. Eventually wounded himself, he survived. All day on 15 July the fighting went on, but the Germans could make no headway and by nightfall they were attempting to retreat across the river. They had not been as near to Paris since 1914, but they would get no nearer. McAlexander's regiment was rightly known thereafter as 'The Rock of the Marne'.

With the failure of Operations 'Marne' and 'Reims' the German army found itself in a seriously exposed salient, running from west of Soissons to Château-Thierry, Dormans and Reims. Ludendorff decided to withdraw; Foch decided to attack. The Aisne–Marne counter-offensive, as it was later known, lasted from 18 July to 6 August and involved nine American divisions under French command. When it was over, all the German gains of Operations 'Marne' and 'Reims', and most of those of 'Yorck' and 'Blücher', had been recaptured, and the Allied line ran from Soissons eastwards to Reims. The American divisions had done well, but it was not all plain sailing for them, partly owing to the French habit of issuing only the vaguest of orders. Major General Harbord, now commanding the US 2 Division (the original commander, Bundy, had been sacked by Pershing as lacking in grip) complained:

> A division...was completely removed from the knowledge of its responsible commander, and deflected by truck and by marching through France to a destination uncommunicated to any authority responsible for its supply, its safety or its efficiency in an attack but thirty hours away. General Berdoulat [Commander French XX Corps] and his people were unable to say where it would be debussed or where orders would reach it which would move it to its place in time.[24]

On the other hand neither was American staff work all it would become. The record of the headquarters French Sixth Army dated 22 July says: '1250 p.m. Arrival of a staff officer from the American 26th Division at Buire...This officer does not know the order in which the regiments are placed, neither does he know what elements they have had in action or what they have in reserve.'[25]

The French were still pressing for American units to be incorporated into their army, but Pershing and the headquarters of the AEF were becoming increasingly disillusioned about their major partner. At the same time they realised that despite the British officers' odd ways and constant making fun of themselves, it was the British who retained a fighting spirit. On 28 March 1918, during the worst days of the British retreat before the 'Kaiser's offensive', a report by the intelligence Branch of AEF headquarters read:

> The morale of the British officer and man is just what could be expected of the British soldier. They do not have the attitude of a year ago, but they do show that they are full of fight. One gains the impression that they are out to stay with it to the last regardless of cost and that they expect to be able to hold the Germans until the French arrive [French divisions were on their way to bolster up the British front. By the time they arrived the German advance had been halted], and that ultimately he [the Germans] will be stopped as have all the offensives on the Western Front heretofore. There is no air of gloom and in watching the soldiers moving to the front they seem to be taking it all in a day's work. Those coming back tell how many Boche they have killed and say that he [the Germans] can't keep it up. Their spirit is admirable.[26]

On the other hand, Colonel Fox Connor, Assistant Chief of Staff of the AEF, wrote to Pershing on 21 June 1918:

> ...there are two factors [factions?] among the higher French officers and staff officers. One faction has never abandoned the idea of drafting Americans into French units – the other realizes the necessity of forming larger American units but considers the morale of the French is so poor at present as to necessitate the dispersion of American units so as to bolster up failing French morale...There can be no doubt as to the necessity of bolstering up French morale...We are also face to face with another fact – many of our officers, and, it is believed, soldiers, are distinctly disgusted with French tutelage...we must never consent to permitting the French to

control the preliminary instruction of our troops. The French methods are
not suited to our troops, and we should not delay longer in telling the French
so in very plain language.[27]

To be fair, the British had not suffered wholesale mutinies in their army, and it was hardly surprising that French thoughts were now mainly on the defensive; but such impressions did strengthen Pershing's determination to form an American army as soon as he could. Up to now American divisions, or elements of them, had assisted the French and the British in emergency. Such measures, however, useful though they were, were only stopgaps. There were now over a million US troops in France, and on 30 August the First US Army was formed. For this purpose American divisions had to be recalled, which caused friction with the British. On 8 August the BEF's Fourth Army under General Rawlinson had launched a hammer blow on the Somme which ruptured the German line and advanced seven miles over a fourteen-mile front, taking 420 guns and nearly 30,000 prisoners with only light British casualties. This, the Battle of Amiens, was another of Ludendorff's 'black days'. One regiment of the US 33 Division had taken part in the attack, and the British were hoping to use some of the five American divisions training with them as they exploited their gains, but now Pershing asked for them back. Haig, who generally got on very well with Pershing, was furious, and in his diary of 12 August he wrote:

He [Pershing] came to see me. He stated that he might have to withdraw the five American divisions which are training with British divisions. I pointed out to him that I had done everything to equip and help these units of the American army, and to provide them with horses. So far, I have had no help from these troops (except from the three battalions which were used in the battle near Chapilly [Chipilly] in error). If he now withdraws the five American divisions he must expect some criticism of his actions...all I wanted to know was definitely whether I could prepare to use the American troops for an attack (along with the British) at the end of September against Kemmel. Now I know I cannot do so. When he was going he thanked me for being outspoken to him: 'at any rate I always know when I am dealing with you what your opinion is on the issue in question. This is not always the case with the French'.[28]

One can understand Haig's frustration. The British were now the only effective army on the Western Front: the French were exhausted and war-weary, the Americans inexperienced. The British had shipped over half the Americans to France and wanted some help from them in what was a critical battle. On the other hand, Pershing had already exceeded his instructions from Wilson, and the public and the press at home were beginning to ask if there would ever be an American army. Haig gave way gracefully and his relations with Pershing remained cordial, but on 25 August he wrote: 'The last American division started to entrain today. What will history say regarding this action of the Americans leaving the British zone of operations when the decisive battle of the war is at its height, and the decision is still in doubt!'[29] As it happened, the British coped perfectly well, and Pershing relented and let Haig have two American divisions, which were to stay with him and render excellent service until the end of the war.

The First American Army was given its own forty-mile sector around the Saint-Mihiel Salient, held by the Germans since 1914 and a quiet area up to now. The army consisted of 450,000 American soldiers and 110,000 Frenchmen in four French divisions and in the artillery. Pershing decided that a useful rehearsal for the new army would be to reduce the Saint-Mihiel Salient. Foch was unsure of the value of this operation – he wanted the First Army to take part in a joint offensive in the Meuse–Argonne area in late September – but agreed to it provided Pershing then took part in the joint attack.

The Germans had ten divisions in the salient, and Pershing planned to attack with nine American and four French divisions. He tried to procure 750 tanks from the British, but they needed all they had for their own offensive. Instead Pershing was given 267 light tanks by the French, half crewed by them, half by Americans, and the whole under command of the American Brigadier General Samuel D. Rockenbach, whose chief of staff was one Colonel George S. Patton, resplendent in cavalry breeches and sporting pearl-handled revolvers. Haig lent the Independent Bombing Squadron of the Royal Air Force,[30] and immediate air support would be provided by a French aviation wing and American pilots flying French aircraft. The Air Commander would be the American Colonel Billy

Mitchell. There would be artillery support from 3,020 French guns, half crewed by Americans. Pershing decided to attack on 12 September (incidentally his fifty-seventh birthday), and the deception plan consisted of sending Colonel Bundy (now down to his substantive rank after being relieved as a divisional commander) off to a comfortable billet in a French hotel with a good kitchen and telling him to prepare an attack through the Belfort Gap near the Swiss border. Pershing calculated – rightly – that German agents would go through Bundy's waste-paper basket and conclude that it was the Rhine Valley that the Americans were after.

After a four-hour artillery bombardment the attack began at 0500 hours on 12 September 1918, in drizzle and mist and under cover of a smoke-screen. The Germans had already decided to withdraw from the salient that day, and many of their troops were caught in the open by the bombardment. For all that, they fought well enough, particularly in fortified locations strongly protected with barbed wire. The American method of surmounting wire obstacles was to use long-handled cutters left over from the Spanish–American War, and then throw rolls of chicken wire over the entanglements to make a sort of causeway. The French, intrigued by this novel approach, concluded that it was all right for the Americans – they had long legs and big feet! By 18 September it was all over. The Americans were not allowed to capture Saint-Mihiel itself – that was President Poincaré's home town and had to be liberated by French troops – but they took all their objectives and captured 16,000 prisoners and 450 guns, at a cost to themselves of 7,000 casualties, of which about 1,500 were killed. It was an easy victory but a useful shake-out for the First Army, and it did wonders for both French morale and American confidence.

Pershing, however, was now having increasing problems with the Army Chief of Staff and Congress at home. He found that officers whom he had recommended for promotion did not receive it, while those whom he had specified as unfit for preferment (like Douglas MacArthur) were advanced. He had great difficulty in getting his corps commanders promoted to lieutenant general, as the pre-war American army had never been big enough to have such an appointment. Congress had voted pilots a fifty per cent pay bonus. Pershing thought this was wrong – pay should be for rank, not speciality – and tried unsuccessfully to have the windfall annulled. The

Army Chief of Staff objected to Pershing's dealing direct with Secretary Baker and thought Pershing was getting too big for his boots, an opinion shared by Colonel House. Nevertheless Pershing retained the confidence of the President and of Secretary Baker, though procedural arguments by cable and letter did not assist him in planning for the First Army's next engagement.

By now, all their spring offensives having failed, the Germans had pulled back to the Hindenburg Line. Their morale was suffering from a reduction in rations and from discontent in the ranks. Much of this was fanned by former prisoners of the Russians who had been infected by Bolshevik propaganda before being repatriated and sent to units of the Western Front. The men were aware that their relatives at home were not far off starving; the 'Kaiser's offensive' which was to win the war had manifestly failed; the British were attacking as if the war had only just begun; and now a seemingly inexhaustible supply of American manpower was flooding into Europe.

The Allied plan for the next stage was for the British to continue attacking on the Somme and in Flanders, and even the Belgians, supported by French and British divisions, would go on the offensive. Additionally the British, French and Americans were to mount a major offensive further south: the British would go north in the direction of Valenciennes, the Americans would attack up the valley of the River Meuse and through the Argonne Forest, and the French would hold to the east of the Meuse and attack west of the Argonne in the Aisne valley. The aim was to close all exits from France and defeat the German army before it could withdraw into its own territory.

There were still two American divisions – 27 and 30 – with the British at Saint-Quentin (where they were very useful in clearing the canal tunnels) and two – 2 and 56 – with the French. Otherwise, fifteen American divisions – seven from Saint-Mihiel, three from the Vosges, three from Soissons, one from Bar-le-Duc and one from a training area in the interior – had to be moved to their jump-off positions, ready to begin the new offensive on 26 September. The move began on the 20th. In six days the Americans had to move 428,000 men with their guns, tanks, stores and ammunition forty-eight miles across a network of very bad roads. Fourteen trains a day were

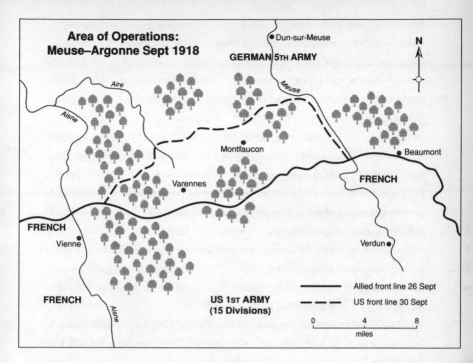

**Area of Operations:
Meuse–Argonne Sept 1918**

GERMAN 5TH ARMY

● Dun-sur-Meuse

N

Aire

Aisne

Meuse

Montfaucon

● Beaumont

FRENCH

Varennes

FRENCH

Vienne ●

Verdun ●

FRENCH

Aisne

US 1ST ARMY
(15 Divisions)

——— Allied front line 26 Sept

– – – US front line 30 Sept

0   4   8
        miles

needed for artillery ammunition alone, to be delivered to twenty-four
depots. The quartermasters needed nine depots, the engineers twelve;
there were eight depots for water, six for chemical-warfare equipment (gas
and smoke) and nine for petrol, oil and lubricants. Forage for 90,000 horses
and mules had to be pre-dumped, thirty-four casualty clearing stations
established and 164 miles of light railway built. It was a prodigious and
nearly impossible task; but the Americans managed it, overseen by a bright
young star of the staff, Colonel George C. Marshall (who would be
Chairman of the US Joint Chiefs of Staff in the next war).

Zero hour was 0520 on 26 September, and the First Army attacked
with three corps in line: I Corps (Hunter Liggett) on the left, Cameron's
V Corps in the centre and Bullard's III Corps on the right. They were supported by nearly 4,000 guns, about 1,500 of them French, and the
astonishing total of 40,000 tons of shells. The 1st Tank Brigade, of French
tanks with mixed crews, was now commanded by Patton, still looking as if

he had stepped out of a tailor's catalogue. There was a thick mist, but each infantry company was accompanied by an engineer officer or NCO with a compass. In general the German infantry made a show of resistance and then withdrew, except for the machine-gun detachments which held their ground and fought it out. In the centre, and a Day-One objective for V Corps, was the hill of Montfaucon. The plan was for 79 Division to go right (east), 91 Division to go left, and 37 Division (the Maryland and Virginia National Guard) to assault frontally. The men plodded five miles through the woods in heavy rain, and by late afternoon were around the slopes of the hill but could not get through the wire obstacles, which were stoutly defended. By this time virtually all of the tanks had been knocked out by German artillery and the crews were in comfortable ditches brewing coffee, no doubt speculating that for them the war – or at least this part of it – was over. Patton would have none of it. He toured bushes, ditches and houses, digging out the crews with his swagger stick, and then led them in a brave but hopeless attack on foot against Montfaucon. Patton was wounded and carried off the field. 'At least I'll get my DSC [Distinguished Service Cross],' he was heard to gasp. He did. Next morning the hill was taken by 37 Division in a first-light assault.

By 3 October the Americans had advanced ten miles, but now the offensive ground to a halt as roads became clogged and supplies and artillery could not be moved forward. Foch and Haig were disappointed, but it was not the Americans' fault – they were experiencing their Somme, though they were luckier in the quality of the enemy they faced. Pershing brought up more troops and created the Second American Army. Hunter Liggett was given command of the First Army and Bullard of the Second. By the end of the month, advancing more slowly now, the Americans had gained another five miles. Meanwhile, on 27 September the British had stormed the Hindenburg Line and by 5 October they were through the last portion of it. Simultaneously the Belgians and British swept out of Diksmuide and Ypres and drove the Germans back. By the end of October the British Third and Fourth Armies were over the River Selle. The French were moving more slowly, but all along the line the Allies and the Americans were advancing and the Germans retreating; now it was a question of following up a beaten German army, for peace was in the air.

On 6 October, as the German army began to crumble, the new Imperial Chancellor of Germany, Prince Max of Baden, asked President Wilson for an armistice on the basis of his Fourteen Points. When it was clear that neither the Allies nor the United States would negotiate with what was in effect a military dictatorship, Ludendorff resigned as Chief of Staff, being replaced by General Wilhelm Groener. At the end of October there was a mutiny in the German High Seas Fleet, which refused to sally out against the British for what the Kaiser and the admirals hoped would be a last glorious act of defiance. At the same time morale in the German army was at an all-time low, with some soldiers refusing to obey orders and a surge in desertions. At home there were riots in the streets and revolution, stirred by Communists, extreme socialists and advocates of stopping the war at any cost, broke out. Between 7 and 11 November a German civilian delegation (the army refused to take part) negotiated the terms of an armistice with Foch (a marshal since August that year).

All three commanders-in-chief, Pétain, Haig and Pershing, were asked for their views on the terms to be offered. An armistice is not a surrender, but merely a pause in the conduct of war, and all three were anxious to ensure that the armistice terms would put them in an advantageous position should the armistice not lead to a peace. Haig's suggested terms were the most generous – he thought that the German army still had some fight left in it and that the German government should be made an offer it could not refuse; the French, understandably for historical and geographical reasons, were in favour of harsher conditions. Perhaps surprisingly, Pershing was the lion of the three, wanting terms that would make it impossible for the Germans to resume hostilities. Although Haig was inclined towards leniency, he was concerned that the German army had been defeated not on German soil but inside territory that they had invaded, and that the German army was to be allowed to march home, the men with their rifles and the officers with their swords. This, he felt (as did Pershing), could give rise to a myth of military victory thrown away by political chicanery; and in due course the 'stab in the back' legend did indeed arise. In the event the French won, and Pershing's demands were watered down by Wilson. The Kaiser abdicated on 9 November 1918, and the armistice came into effect at 11 a.m. on the 11th. The war was formally ended by the signing of the Treaty of Versailles on 28 June 1919.

Once they had entered the war, the greatest service rendered by the Americans to the Allied cause was the message they sent to Germany: that a huge and so far untapped reservoir of manpower was willing, and would in due course be able, to take the field. Had the war gone on into 1919, as most French, British and American politicians and generals thought it would, the Americans would have had between eighty and 100 large divisions in France, a force larger than the combined armies of France and Britain. Germany could not possibly have held out against this swelling of the Allied ranks; it was that knowledge, combined with the hammering suffered by the German army at Passchendaele, that led Ludendorff to launch the 1918 offensive, a decision that lost Germany the war. The American army was inexperienced; its staff procedures were rudimentary at times and, as with the British when they first attempted to launch a mass army into the attack, its tactics were unsophisticated. When it finally engaged in operations as the First Army it was up against troops who were long past their best, but the Americans cannot be slighted for that. Their men fought with great gallantry and, increasingly, with skill. Pershing never had a chance to show whether or not he was a great commander: the war ended too soon. He was inclined to play his cards too close to his chest; he did not delegate enough, and tried to control every aspect of the AEF himself, which no one man could possibly do; he did not always appreciate other people's problems – particularly those of the War Department back in the United States – and he could never be accused of being tactful. For all that, he was an inspiring personality who largely succeeded in walking the treacherous tightrope between being a good military ally and adhering to the policies of his Commander-in-Chief, President Wilson.

While America's main role in the war was in the message her declaration and subsequent appearance in Europe sent to Germany, her military actions were not without cost. The American army had 204,000 battle casualties on the Western Front, of whom 53,000 were killed. There was an uneven spread: of the forty-three American divisions in France, the most affected were 1 and 2 Divisions, which had 2,996 killed and 17,324 wounded and 5,155 killed and 18,080 wounded respectively. Taking relative divisional strengths into account, this compares with the casualties of British divisions on the Somme. There were 591 killed in 93 Division, which arrived in March 1918, and 182 in 92 Division which arrived in June 1918. Nobody at all was killed in 8, 31, 34, 38, 39, 40, 76, 84, 86 and 87 Divisions. In addition to battle deaths the Americans lost around 30,000 dead from disease and accidents. Few died as a result of gassing, but the influenza epidemic hit them especially hard. No Americans were executed as a result of sentences passed by courts martial for military offences on the Western Front, but ten soldiers were executed for civil offences (rape carried the death penalty). While the American death toll could more easily be absorbed by the population of the United States than could far higher totals by the smaller populations of France and Britain, these deaths were significant to America because it was the first time she had sent a mass army to a foreign war. It is a sadness, and unfair, that her contribution to the war on the Western Front has been all but forgotten – even in America.

The First World War marked America's emergence onto the world stage. It was her first step towards becoming a superpower, but that status was to be delayed until another war a generation later. Having approved the Armistice and signed the Treaty of Versailles, President Wilson returned home. In 1919, however, there was a new Congress with a Republican majority, and it did not agree with the terms to which Wilson had subscribed. In particular it objected to collective security agreements (which might drag America into another war), and to the establishment of the League of Nations which had been agreed at Versailles. The United States did not ratify the Versailles treaty, but negotiated a separate peace with Germany. Wilson, worn out by his efforts to get the treaty accepted in America, fell ill and was unable to campaign for the 1920 presidential election.[31] It was won by a Republican, Warren G. Harding, and Wilson retired to Washington, where he died in 1924.[32] America reverted to isolationism – understandable for a country that can survive perfectly well without intercourse with foreign states – and would not reap her true destiny until after the next great world conflict in 1945.

NOTES

1 Some might say that the scars of the Civil War are not yet healed. The Royal Military Academy Sandhurst, Britain's West Point, once had an American lecturer on the academic staff. He was the obvious choice to teach the American Civil War, which is of great interest to

the British army. Problems arose when it was discovered that he was teaching 'The War of Northern Aggression'.

2 Colin Nicholson, *The Longman Companion to the First World War*, Pearson Education, Edinburgh, 2002.

3 Robert Blake (ed.), *The Private Papers of Douglas Haig*, Eyre and Spottiswoode, London, 1952.

4 The practice probably began with the colonial militia, and continued during the Civil War when local notables who raised regiments were given the rank of colonel, even though they may not have actually taken the field. Afterwards the rank was often conferred by state governors, generally in the South, on members of their staff or on prominent citizens. It is really not very different from our own practice of conferring knighthoods, so we British should not sneer at it too much.

5 I am grateful to Professor Hunt Tooley, of Austin College Texas, for his explanation of the origins of House's rank.

6 Jane Plotke, *WWI Document Archive*, http://www.lib.byu.edu, 1996.

7 It was never going to happen, although the Kaiser did once suggest it to King Edward VII. England was not interested in large-scale conquest on land; her concern was control of the seas to protect her trade and the security of the empire.

8 Although ninety American pilots transferred from the *Escadrille* to the American army, which was a tremendous bonus.

9 At that time officers of the US army could serve until retirement at the age of sixty-five (on three-quarters pay), and hardly any were promoted above the substantive rank of major (which saved Congress money). In the pre-1914 British army majors retired at forty-seven if not selected for promotion, and lieutenant colonels and colonels at fifty-two.

10 For British readers, Marie-Joseph-Paul-Roch-Yves-Gilbert Motier, Marquis de Lafayette (1757–1834), was a French general who fought on the American side in the Revolutionary Wars (1774–1783), when their Frenchmen beat our Germans.

11 Apart from the Korean War, which was technically a UN operation but in practice an American one, American soldiers have never donned the blue beret of the UN, nor have they been happy to place their troops under command of anyone other than an American. The Commander-in-Chief of NATO is always an American. Currently it is most unlikely that the US will agree to the provisions of the proposed International War Crimes agreement, which will allow soldiers to be hauled before courts not of their own nation. The British, being wetter in such matters, have indicated that they will agree, thus making the British army no longer responsible for its own discipline. Good for the USA, say I.

12 Except that there were not half a million American troops available for the 1917 offensive, and that number would not be in Europe until May 1918.

13 General John J. Pershing, *My Experiences in the First World War*, F. A. Stokes, New York, 1931.

14 Ibid.

15 Quoted in Donald Smythe, *Pershing, General of the Armies*, Indiana University Press, 1986.

16 Ibid.

17 American soldiers still prefer British field rations to their own. In the Gulf War the going

rate for an American camp bed (superior to the British version) was three British composite ration packs.

18 The American navy is still completely dry, the America army virtually so, and completely dry when in the field. When training with American troops this author found instant popularity through always being armed with several bottles of Gurkha rum.

19 An American division had two brigades, each of two regiments. A regiment had three battalions and a machine-gun company. A battalion had four companies each of four platoons. Each platoon had fifty-eight men divided into seven squads (sections). By now a British division had nine battalions, compared to the American twelve larger ones.

20 Blake (ed.), *The Private Papers of Douglas Haig*, Eyre and Spottiswoode, London, 1952.

21 The nickname 'doughboy' is thought to date from the American involvement along the Rio Grande in Texas, when the white dust adhering to their uniforms led to their being compared to bakers.

22 An American battalion was commanded by a major. The executive officer – exec – was a cross between the second-in-command and the operations officer in the modern British army.

23 The US Marines continued to wear a stock long after the army had abandoned that item of uniform, hence 'leathernecks'.

24 Ibid.

25 US Army Center of Military History, *The United States Army in the World War, 1917–1919*, Vol. 5, 1988–92.

26 Ibid., Vol. 3.

27 Ibid.

28 Blake (ed.), *The Private Papers of Douglas Haig*, Eyre and Spottiswoode, London, 1952.

29 Ibid.

30 It is unkind to remind the RAF that they were formed on 1 April 1918.

31 At that time a President was not yet limited by statute to two terms.

32 Harding died in 1923, before completing his term and just before the administration became embroiled in the 'Teapot Dome' scandal, in which land containing naval oil reserves was corruptly leased to private commercial interests.

14

EPILOGUE

The Great War did not, of course, end war. No war ever does, and in any case the cry was a politician's, not a soldier's. The Versailles Treaty of 1919 gave Alsace and Lorraine back to France; but the fact that the numerous memorials to Prussian regiments scattered across Alsace have escaped defacement, even after 1945, may indicate that the inhabitants had not necessarily been unhappy as Germans. The Treaty of Brest-Litovsk was annulled, and an independent Poland came into being. The Austro-Hungarian Empire collapsed and Czechoslovakia and Yugoslavia were born. The German High Seas Fleet was interned at Scapa Flow, where its crews scuttled their ships in a last gesture of defiance. Germany lost her colonies, and was required to admit war guilt and pay a huge indemnity; her army was reduced to 100,000 men, she was allowed no aircraft or submarines, and she was to abolish the Great General Staff. French and British troops occupied parts of Germany. In Russia, despite Allied and American military intervention, the Bolsheviks consolidated their hold on the country and the world's first Communist state was established. The League of Nations was set up to implement collective security measures that would make the waging of aggressive war everlastingly impossible.

In the 1920s the League was shown to be toothless. Raging inflation, the collapse of the economy and civil unrest in Germany led to the rise of extreme nationalism, the unravelling of the peace settlement and war again in 1939. It is often held that the climate that fostered the rise of National Socialism was created by the terms of the Versailles Treaty. Certainly the cutting-off the German eastern provinces by the Polish Corridor was always going to be a *casus belli*, as were the demilitarisation of the Rhineland and the existence of substantial ethnic German minorities outside Germany's borders. Nevertheless it was not just Germany but the whole developed world that went into economic recession in the 1920s, and the Germans can hardly be blamed for voting for a party that promised full employ-ment, a stable currency, the recovery of *Germania Irredenta*, good roads and trains that would run on time. The Nazi uniforms were smart too. All would-be dictators look for internal and external enemies, and Hitler had no trouble finding them: Germany had not been defeated on the field of battle, but stabbed in the back by traitors at home, aided and abetted by international Jewry, Bolshevism and faithless politicians. If Versailles had been kinder to Germany, then perhaps phase two of the Great War of 1914–45, as it has been called, might not have happened; but it is difficult to see how the terms could have been much different. France was determined to regain her lost provinces and wanted security against ever being invaded again; the nationalist aspirations of the Poles and the races of Austria-Hungary had to be taken into account; Britain had to ensure that she was no longer threatened by a naval arms race, and Germany was not a natural colonial power in any case. The war-guilt clause and the reparations were window dressing: Germany could not afford to pay, and after one instal-ment the reparations were forgotten. Had the First World War not happened there would almost certainly have been a Russian Revolution anyway, although power might have remained with relative moderates like Kerensky instead of being seized by the Communists, and Russia might have developed into a liberal democracy. Might have, because there is no democratic tradition in Russia.

Hangovers from the war of 1914–18 are still with us. Versailles failed to reconcile cultural and religious differences in the Balkans, which with the demise of communism have reverted to chaos and tie up increasing numbers of British troops today. The founding of the state of Israel flowed from the Balfour declaration of 2 November 1917. America had entered the war and the British Foreign Secretary, Arthur Balfour, promised a national home for the Jews in Palestine, his motive being to obtain Jewish support for the war effort. As the only country where Jewish opinion mattered was the United States, this was in fact a ploy to attract an influential section of American opinion. The declaration was abrogated by Chamberlain's government in 1939 as a result of Arab objections and Jewish terrorism, but it was too late. The terrible fate of the Jews in Germany during the Hitler era, to say nothing of American pressure, made it impossible for Britain to block the establishment of a Jewish state in Palestine, and Israel came into being in 1948. Israelis are a charming and hospitable people, and the British, with their natural sympathy for the underdog, are inclined to admire their courage and their ability to stand up to far stronger enemies. While it is not the purpose of this book to argue the validity of the Jewish claim to a state in Palestine – a claim based on their god's having supposedly granted the land to them at some time in the distant past – the fact is that there was, and is, no British interest in Israel. We buy nothing from her apart from Jaffa oranges, which would presumably grow there anyway, and we have no military understandings with her. Israel exists because of American subsidies. There was, and is, a major British interest in the Arab states – oil – and the troubles still raging in the Middle East today might not continue to threaten the peace of the world if Britain had stuck to her traditional Arabist policy, and not betrayed the Arabs at Versailles.

All this is speculation, and we cannot undo what has been done. Britain entered the war because she had to, and in 1918 it was the British army that made the major contribution to the defeat of the German army – and whatever the Germans later claimed, it *was* a defeat. The British army in 1918 was more professional, better organised and better led than it was in 1945; this is hardly surprising, because in 1918 it had been fighting the main enemy in the main theatre for four and a quarter years, whereas in 1945 it had been doing so only since the Normandy landings of 6 June 1944. Even then, it can be argued that in 1944–5 the major theatre was not Western Europe at all, but the Eastern Front, where the bulk of the German army was.

Field Marshal Haig, the *bête noire* of today's critics of Great War generalship, was congratulated by the King and lauded in the newspapers. For winning the war he was offered a viscountcy by Lloyd George, the same level of the peerage that had been given to Sir John French for not winning it. Haig refused any honours until the government agreed financial provisions for disabled ex-soldiers, which eventually it did. Then, after intervention by the King, he accepted an earldom. He remained as Commander-in-Chief of the BEF until April 1919 when he became Commander-in-Chief Home Forces, with Robertson assuming command of the Army of Occupation in Germany. When the Home Forces post was abolished in January 1920 Haig was still only fifty-nine, and might reasonably have expected to be appointed to a viceroyalty or a governor-generalship. Lloyd George was still Prime Minister, however (he had won a landslide victory in the 1918 election), and he was not going to do anything for a man whom he detested. Haig devoted the rest of his life to the welfare of ex-servicemen, and it was his prestige and powers of persuasion that managed to combine a number of mutually hostile and quarrelling ex-servicemen's organisations into the British Legion, not only in the United Kingdom but also around the empire. He died of a heart attack in January 1928, and was mourned by hundreds of thousands who had served under his command in the greatest war in British history.

'Wully' Robertson, who had done so much to put the British army and the management of the war on a professional footing, and had acted as the buffer between Haig and those politicians who were out to undermine him, was promoted to field marshal and created a baronet in March 1920. As another soldier whom Lloyd George disliked, he was offered no further employment, and left the active list. He became Colonel of the Royal Horse Guards in January 1928, a singular and deserved honour for a man who had started his military career as a private soldier in the line cavalry, and held the appointment until his death in 1933. Henry Wilson, the clever, devious, political soldier whom Lloyd George did like, at least initially, and who had taken over from Robertson as CIGS, saw his influence decrease when Foch, who did not trust Wilson, took over as Allied Generalissimo in 1918. After the war he fell out with Lloyd George when the Prime Minister announced the end of conscription as soon as the Armistice was signed, without consulting the CIGS. Wilson became a baronet and a field marshal in July 1919 and left the active list in 1922, being elected Unionist member of parliament for a Northern Ireland constituency. He was murdered in London by the IRA in July 1922.

Pershing went back to America and was promoted to General of the Armies, the first since George Washington, and the first actually to carry the rank.[1] He was nominated as a presidential candidate, flirted half-heartedly with the idea and was not adopted, and became Chief of Army Staff (equivalent to CIGS) in 1921.[2] As Chief of Staff he fought valiantly but largely unsuccessfully to preserve American military strength in a period of retrenchment and cost-cutting, and retired in 1924. His greatest legacy to the American army as its Chief was probably his reformation of the General Staff system, which developed into the branches of G1 (Administration and Personnel), G2 (Intelligence), G3 (Operations and Training), G4 (Matériel) and G5 (Civil Affairs), now used by all NATO armies. He established a War Plans Division in the War Department, and the schools system for peacetime training. In retirement he carried out various overseas visits and inspections on behalf of the government, and wrote *My Experiences in the First World War* – a mine of information but, it has to be said, not an easy read. He died peacefully in 1948.

Marshal Foch became a member of the *Académie Française* in 1920, and he and Marshal Joffre (not a member of the *Académie*) did little more than participate in ceremonial occasions until they died in 1929 and 1931 respectively. Marshal Pétain, the 'Saviour of Verdun' and the man who restored order to the French army after the mutinies of 1917, was appointed to the Military Advisory Council, was Minister of War in 1934, and became ambassador to Madrid in 1939. On 17 May 1940, with the German invasion of France a week old, Pétain was recalled as Deputy Prime Minister of France. On 10 June the French government left the capital, and four days later German troops entered Paris. On 16 June Paul Reynaud resigned as Prime Minister and Pétain took his place. The next day, with French resistance almost at an end and the British Expeditionary Force having beaten an undignified retreat back to England via Dunkirk and Cherbourg, the Marshal announced an armistice. The nation that had defied Germany for four and a quarter long years when Pétain last commanded her armies had been defeated in a mere six weeks. On 10 July 1940 the French National

Assembly voted 'all powers to the government of the Republic under the authority and signature of Marshal Pétain'. For four years Pétain headed the collaborationist Vichy regime, and when France was finally liberated the Free French government of Charles de Gaulle (who had been an officer in Pétain's old regiment and had been wounded and captured at Verdun in 1916) put the eighty-nine-year-old Marshal on trial for treason.[3] The finding was guilty and the sentence death, commuted to life imprisonment on the Île d'Yeu in the Bay of Biscay. Pétain died in his island prison on 23 July 1951. The Pétain story does not quite end there, however, for in February 1973 his tomb on the Île d'Yeu was opened clandestinely and the body stolen; spirited away by those who wanted to lay him to rest with his soldiers in the cemetery at Fort Douaumont, monument to the defence of Verdun and symbol of French defiance. The coffin was found in a lock-up garage in Saint-Ouen and reinterred on the Île d'Yeu, where, as far as we know, it still is.

The Kaiser spent his exile at Doorn in Holland. He rejected all overtures from the Nazis, realising that this arriviste party, that had sprung from the working and lower middle classes, was unlikely to restore the monarchy. Nevertheless he could not resist sending a message of congratulation to the German army when it occupied Paris; this irritated Queen Wilhelmina of the Netherlands and led to the sequestration of the Doorn estate after the war. This deprived not the Kaiser, who died on 4 June 1941, but his son, Crown Prince William, who died a dissolute and poverty-stricken rake in the arms of his mistress in Italy in 1951. The Kaiser's grandson died serving in the German army in 1940, and today's claimants to the Hohenzollern throne serve in the British army under the name of von Preussen. Field Marshal von Hindenburg became President of the Weimar Republic, appointed Hitler as Chancellor, and died in 1934. Ludendorff became an ultra-nationalist, marched with Hitler in the abortive Munich putsch of November 1923, was tried for treason but acquitted, and died in 1937.

Lloyd George remained Prime Minister of the United Kingdom until 1922, when he fell out with the Conservatives in his coalition, resigned and published a self-serving, exhaustive and exhausting account of his part in the Great War. The rest of his life was dogged by (well-founded) allegations of corruption while in office, particularly his enrichment by the sale of honours. He had an active sex life and Queen Mary advised her ladies-in-waiting never to be alone in a room with him. He was too unwell (and unwilling) to join Churchill's coalition government in 1940 and died in 1945.

After the war the British army was demobilised with almost indecent haste, leading to unrest when those considered essential to industry were released before others who had served for longer. The army itself settled down and appointed a committee under Lieutenant General Kirke to study the lessons of the war, with a view to putting things right for the next one. Whatever politicians might be saying on the hustings, the generals knew very well that there would always be wars. The committee, composed of officers who had all served in the late conflict, albeit in relatively junior posts, eventually presented its conclusions in voluminous detail in October 1932.[4] Much of it was common sense: the need for thorough training; the importance of good intelligence; the advantages of modern equipment, including tanks and aircraft (this was a time when the army considered it had insufficient tanks, lacked offensive air support and was concerned over proposals to save money by reducing the number of heavy artillery units); the significance of good food, welfare facilities and medical support in the maintenance of morale; the pointlessness of trying to capture ground for its own sake; the vital necessity for artillery and infantry to work together, and the recognition that cavalry did not have the capability to break through defended lines. The report was still, alas, trying to convince readers that shrapnel should be discarded completely in favour of high explosive. It highlighted the problems of communications, with some headquarters being too far back and the commanders ignorant of what was happening at the front. The answer to this was radio, but even in 1932 the army still did not have enough battlefield radios for its needs. Much attention was paid to the preparation and training of commanders, and the report insisted that they should be young, energetic and vigorous, able to 'grasp those fleeting opportunities which, if rightly used, can turn partial success into complete victory'. Recognising that the absence of flanks on the Western Front in 1914–18 made frontal assaults inevitable, the report nevertheless advocated surprise, attacking at night, and the use of smoke to mask movement.

It also bemoaned the likelihood that gas would be denied to the British army in any future conflict.

The next war would doubtless be different, said the report, but as one member, Major-General Kennedy, pointed out:

> ...in the class of major operations which our training contemplates [i.e., training for the next war] manoeuvre and mobility will play a leading part... I know too that the problems of such operations are being studied and applied in our training, and that there is no need to stress further what is already in our manuals. What these latter, of course, cannot picture, nor our training produce, are the real conditions of warfare – the disorder that must be controlled to make manoeuvre possible – the confusion that hampers mobility – or the shells and bullets under which opportunity dies...We must not forget the sordid details of the actual man-to-man struggles, which so often made manoeuvre possible. The most important object of our training must be to produce commanders with the character and ability to turn unfamiliar conditions to their own advantage, and who will neither be crushed by the unexpected, nor afraid of the unknown.

The report was no great traducing of the past, nor a visionary panorama of future war. It said that the Great War had been fought as well as it could be, given the situation and the manpower and assets available to the British army. Such criticisms as there were – like headquarters being too far back, and the need to deploy reserves quickly – were well known at the time and unavoidable given the difficulties of communication. Those who now deplore the generals' conduct of the war, particularly on the Western Front, might like to demonstrate how they would have done it differently, and how the results would have been better. This author, with a lifetime of army service and access to every worthwhile fountain of military thought, has to confess that, with the exception of individual errors to which all are prone, he cannot!

Far from being simply a series of mindless frontal assaults by massed infantry – not much different from previous conflicts except in scale – the Great War was in reality a revolution in the art of warfare. There were huge advances in technology. The first use of tanks, air reconnaissance and aerial photography, fighter aeroplanes and strategic bombing, artillery spotting by aircraft, mechanical transport, indirect fire by artillery, man-portable machine guns, trench mortars, radio, gas, plastic surgery, attack submarines and aircraft carriers – all these owe their development to the war of 1914–18. Many of these innovations were British, and those that were not were eagerly seized upon and developed by them – at the instance of the very generals who are supposed to have been so hidebound and resistant to new ideas.[5]

Whether the generals and the politicians did any better in the Second World War is a moot point. The two wars were very different because British participation on land was largely peripheral between 1940 and 1944. It is often claimed that the Second War generals, having learned their trade in the trenches of the Western Front, were determined that such casualties should never happen again; but to have casualties you have to fight. And when the British did fight, the casualties in the Normandy campaign, as has been shown, were every bit as heavy as they had been in the Great War, although absolute numbers were lower because there were significantly fewer troops involved. If casualty rates are to be the sole criterion for judging a general, then Montgomery was no less a butcher than Haig; and Montgomery was not facing the cream of the German army.

Political interference in the Second War was almost as dangerous as it had been in the First. Churchill was an honourable man, which Lloyd George indubitably was not, and Sir Alan Brooke had more success in controlling Churchill than 'Wully' Robertson had with Lloyd George; but it was Churchill's wild flights of fancy, and the old search for the 'soft underbelly', that led to disasters like Crete, which achieved nothing apart from dissuading the Germans from using parachute troops en masse again, and Dieppe, which achieved nothing except Canadian distrust of British competence.

The BEF that went to France in 1939 had been starved of money and resources until the very last minute; it lacked the professionalism of its 1914 predecessor and had very much the same equipment, but rather less of it. It was the British who had invented the tank, but the Germans who had taken note of it and developed the tank arm. German tanks in 1940 were no more advanced than those of their opponents, and fewer in quantity than the combined total of French and British; but what the

Germans had done was to perfect all-arms cooperation, with armour, infantry, artillery and air forces working together. It was not that French and British of the Second War did not understand these things: simply that the Germans did them better.

A democracy, and particularly a democracy that faces no immediate threat by land, such as Britain, will always be at a disadvantage at the beginning of a war. We do not wish, nor can we afford, large armies or universal conscription. There are no votes to be gained on defence issues in peacetime, and funding for education, health, welfare and public transport will inevitably take precedence over the armed forces. There will always be political interference in matters military, and that is the price we have to pay for living in a liberal, just, free society. Few would have it otherwise, but with that must go the recognition that there will always be a Somme, or a Normandy, when this nation puts a mass army into battle against a first-class enemy. Accept that, or do not bother to fight.

To those who aver that there will never be another war of the scale of the two great conflicts of the twentieth century, one can only reply that such contentions have been disproved over and over again in the history of this nation. It is difficult to see another war between the powers of Western Europe – the European Economic Community, and its successor the European Union, have bound their economies together too tightly for war to be possible – but Russia is as yet a halting democracy, and China still sleeps. The prospect of Arab unity at some time in the future is not entirely far-fetched, nor may the vast continent of Africa remain for ever a fragmented economic basket case ruled over by quarrelling and incompetent dictators. The next Somme may be ten years away, or fifty, or a hundred; but it will come. In the meantime we should do well to remember that the only nation able, and conceivably likely, to come to our aid in the event of a major conflagration is the United States of America. America is no longer populated almost exclusively by Englishmen abroad: it would pay to be nice to her.

In this book I have tried to show that the Great War of 1914 to 1918 was a just war, which Britain was right to join; indeed she had no other viable option, both in terms of morality and in terms of her own interests. As King George V said to Walter Page, the American ambassador to

London, when he asked the King why Britain had entered the war, 'Mr Page, what else could we have done?' Given that we had to fight on land, rather than simply blockade our enemy, the absence of universal military service before the war made it necessary to raise a huge citizen army – an army that had no experience, was short of men to train it, and lacked equipment of all types. The New Army's first encounter with all-out war on the Somme was inevitably shocking. The army learned, and improved continuously as time went on. I have emphasised that this was a coalition war, and that to look at it only from the stance of what the British army did is to miss the point. Haig and his generals may not have been the best team that the British army has ever produced, but they were pretty good, and did their best with what they had in a war whose like had never been contemplated. The men who served under them also thought the generals were pretty good, for had there not been trust between leader and led the British army would surely have gone the way of the French.

There are very few veterans of the First War alive in Britain today: perhaps 100, all at least a century old, and the number shrinks by the week. Within a year, or at the most two, there will be none left. Even the children of the men who fought in the Great War are in their eighties, and their grandchildren are mature adults. The British people have chosen to snipe, to sneer, to believe that all was a waste and achieved nothing. It is true that very many British soldiers were killed; but in the last analysis that is what soldiers are for. Everything has its price, and the price of victory in war is the death of many of the people who contribute to it. The Great War is an episode in our history, not an emotional experience. In 1918 the soldiers thought they had won a great and just victory. There was glory, and there was pride. In what those men did, and in how they did it, we too should feel pride today.

NOTES

1 The American forces do not normally promote above the rank of General. Pershing was eventually a general as commander of the AEF. In Washington the Chief of Staff of the army, its professional head, was only an acting general, and reverted to major general after the end of hostilities. A few officers (George Marshall and Omar Bradley amongst them) have been elevated to General of the Army (equivalent to field marshal). General of the Armies is superior to that, and the British have no equivalent.

2 American history has a habit of throwing up soldiers as Presidents in the aftermath of war:

George Washington, Andrew Jackson, Zachary Taylor, Ulysses S. Grant and Dwight D. Eisenhower. Pershing could have been adopted as the Republican candidate had he really wanted it, and had he bothered to campaign energetically; he would also probably have won the election. He might well have made a very good President.

3 Argument still rages as to the legality of the trial. The Vichy government, which controlled unoccupied France and those French overseas territories that had not declared for de Gaulle's Free French or been occupied by the British, was a legal government, and the USA, Canada and the USSR, amongst others, had accredited diplomats to it. The legal arguments that preceded the trial centred on the fact that Pétain exercised authority in the name of the 'French State', as opposed to the 'French Republic' whose powers he had been voted.

4 *Report of the Committee on the Lessons of the Great War*, The War Office, London, 1932 (Public Record Office, Kew, PRO WO33/1297).

5 See Jonathan Bailey, *The First World War and the Birth of the Modern Style of Warfare*, Strategic and Combat Studies Institute, Camberley, 1996. This pamphlet is particularly good on the development of artillery – the author is now (2002) the British army's Director Royal Artillery.

BIBLIOGRAPHY

Annual Register, The, 1914, 1915, 1916, 1917, 1918, Longman, London, 1915/16/17/18/19.

Alexander, Barrie, *War Underground*, Frederick Muller, London, 1962.

Anglesey, Marquess of, *A History of the British Cavalry 1816–1919*, Vols. 7 & 8, Leo Cooper, London, 1996, 1997.

Ascoli, David, *The Mons Star*, Harrap, London, 1981.

Ashworth, Tony, *Trench Warfare 1914–18*, Macmillan, London, 1980.

Atkinson, C. T., *The Seventh Division 1914–18*, Naval & Military Press (reprint), London, 1998.

Autin, Jean, *Foch*, Perrin, Paris, 1987.

Babington, Anthony, *For the Sake of Example*, Leo Cooper, London, 1983.

Bach, C. A., and Hall, H. N., *The Fourth Division: its Services and Achievements in the World War*, privately published, New York, 1920.

Baring, Maurice, *Flying Corps Headquarters, 1914–18*, G. Bell & Sons, London, 1920.

Barker, Ralph, *The Royal Flying Corps in France* (two vols.), Constable, London, 1994/5.

Barnett, Correlli, *The Swordbearers*, Eyre and Spottiswoode, London, 1963.

Baynes, John, *Morale*, Cassell & Co., London, 1967.

Baynes, John, *Far from a Donkey: the Life of General Sir Ivor Maxse*, Brassey's, London, 1995.

Bean, C. E. W., *The Official History of Australia in the War of 1914–18* (12 vols.), Angus & Robertson, Sydney, 1923–42.

Beaver, Patrick (ed.), *The Wipers Times*, Papermac, London, 1988.

Becke, Maj. A. F., *Order of Battle of Divisions* (six vols.), HMSO, London, 1945.

Beckett, Ian F. W., *The Great War 1914–18*, Longman, London, 2001.

Beckett, Ian F. W. (ed.), *The Army and the Curragh Incident 1914*, Bodley Head, London, 1986.

Bet–El, Ilana R, *Conscripts*, Sutton Publishing, Stroud, 1999.

Blackburne, Harry, *This Also Happened on the Western Front*, Hodder & Stoughton, London, 1932.

Blake, Robert (ed.), *The Private Papers of Douglas Haig*, Eyre & Spottiswoode, London, 1952.

Bogert, E. Alexander, *Let's Go!*, H. S. Crocker, San Francisco, 1927.

Bond, Professor Brian (ed.), *The First World War and British Military History*, Clarendon Press, Oxford, 1991.

Bond, Professor Brian, and Cave, Nigel (eds.), *Haig, a Reappraisal 70 Years On*, Leo Cooper, London, 1999.

Bond, Professor Brian, et al., *Look to Your Front: Studies in the First World War by the British Commission for Military History*, Spellmount, Staplehurst, 1999.

Boraston, Lt Col. J. H., and Bax, Capt. E. O., *The Eighth Division, 1914–18*, Naval & Military Press (reprint), London, 1999.

Bourne, J. M., *Who's Who in World War One*, Routledge, London, 2001.

Bourne, J. M., *Britain and the Great War 1914–18*, Edward Arnold, London, 1989.

Bristow, Adrian, *A Serious Disappointment*, Leo Cooper, London, 1995.

Brown, Malcolm, *The Imperial War Museum Book of 1918: Year of Victory*, Sidgwick & Jackson, London, 1998.

Brown, Malcolm, *The Imperial War Museum Book of the Somme*, Sidgwick & Jackson, London, 1996.

Brown, Malcolm, *The Imperial War Museum Book of the Western Front*, Sidgwick & Jackson, London, 1993.

Cecil, Hugh, and Liddle, Peter H., (eds.), *Facing Armageddon*, Leo Cooper, London, 1996.

Charteris, Brig. Gen. John, *Field Marshal Earl Haig*, Cassell & Co., London, 1929.

Cheseldine, R. M., *Ohio in the Rainbow (The Official History of the 166th Regt, 42nd Div. in the World War)*, F. J. Heer, Columbus, Ohio, 1924.

Clark, Alan, *The Donkeys*, Hutchinson, London, 1961.

Conte, Arthur, *Joffre*, Perrin, Paris, 1991.

Corns, Cathryn, and Hughes-Wilson, John, *Blindfold and Alone*, Cassell & Co., London, 2001.

Corrigan, Maj. J. G. H., *Sepoys in the Trenches: the Indian Corps on the Western Front 1914–15*, Spellmount, Staplehurst, 1999.

Cooksey, Jon, *Barnsley Pals*, Leo Cooper, London, 1996.

Crozier, F. P., *A Brasshat in No Man's Land*, Jonathan Cape, London, 1930.

Cuttell, Barry, *148 Days on the Somme*, GMS Enterprises, Peterborough, 2000.

Cuttell, Barry, *One Day on the Somme*, GMS Enterprises, Peterborough, 1998.

Davies, Frank, and Maddocks, Graham, *Bloody Red Tabs*, Leo Cooper, London, 1995.

Danchev, Alex, *Alchemist of War: the Life of Basil Liddell Hart*, Weidenfeld & Nicolson, London, 1998.

Davidson, Maj. Gen. Sir John, *Haig, Master of the Field*, Peter Nevill, London, 1953.

Davies, Pete, *Catching Cold*, Michael Joseph, London, 1999.

DeGroot, Gerard J., *Blighty: British Society in the Era of the Great War*, Longman, London, 1996.

Denman, Terence, *Ireland's Unknown Soldiers*, Irish Academic Press, Dublin, 1992.

Devlin, Patrick, *Too Proud to Fight: Woodrow Wilson's Neutrality*, Oxford University Press, London, 1974.

Dewar, George H., *Sir Douglas Haig's Command* (two vols.), Constable, London, 1921.

Dudley Ward, Maj. C. H., *The Fifty-Sixth Division 1914–18*, Naval & Military Press (reprint), London, 1998.

Duroselle, Jean-Baptiste, *La Grande Guerre des Français 1914–18*, Perrin, Paris, 1994.

Edmonds, Brig. Gen. James, *Military Operations France and Belgium, 1914* (two vols.), Macmillan, London, 1922, 1925.

Edmonds, Brig. Gen. James, *Military Operations France and Belgium, 1915* (two vols.), Macmillan, London, 1927, 1928.

Edmonds, Brig. Gen. James, *Military Operations France and Belgium, 1916*, Vol. I, Macmillan, London, 1932.

Edmonds, Brig. Gen. James, *Military Operations France and Belgium, 1917*, Vol. II, HMSO, London, 1948.

Edmonds, Brig. Gen. James, *Military Operations France and Belgium, 1918* (five vols.), Macmillan, London, 1935, 1937, 1939, 1947, 1947.

Edmonds, Brig. Gen. Sir James, and Davies, Maj. Gen. H. R., *Military Operations Italy, 1915–19*, Imperial War Museum (reprint), London, 1991.

Emdem, Richard van, *Tickled to Death to Go*, Spellmount, Staplehurst, 1996.

Falls, Capt. Cyril, *Military Operations France and Belgium, 1917*, Vol. I, Macmillan, London, 1940.

Falls, Cyril, *The History of the 36th (Ulster) Division*, McCaw, Stevenson & Orr, Belfast and London, 1922.

Farrar-Hockley, Gen. Sir Anthony, *Death of an Army*, Barker, London, 1967.

Farrar-Hockley, Gen. Sir Anthony, *The Somme*, Batsford, London, 1964.

Fayolle, Maréchal Émile, *Carnets secrets de la Grande Guerre*, Plon, Paris, 1964.

Ferguson, Niall, *The Pity of War*, Allen Lane, London, 1998.

Ferris, John (ed.), *The British Army and Signals Intelligence during the First World War*, Sutton Publishing, Stroud, 1992.

Fielding, Rowland (ed. Jonathan Walker), *War Letters to a Wife*, Medici Society, London, 1929.

Fischer, Fritz, *Germany's Aims in the First World War*, Chatto & Windus, London, 1967.

Foch, Marshal Ferdinand (tr. Col. T. Bentley Mott), *The Memoirs of Marshal Foch*, William Heinemann, London, 1931.

Formby, John (tr.), *Cavalry in Action*, Hugh Rees, London, 1905.

Foulkes, Maj. Gen. C. H., *Gas! The Story of the Special Brigade*, London, 1934.

French, Field Marshal Viscount, *1914*, Constable, London, 1914.

French, Field Marshal Viscount, *The Despatches of Lord French*, Chapman & Hall, London, 1917.

French, Maj. the Hon. Gerald, *French Replies to Haig*, Hutchinson, London, 1936.

General Staff, War Office, *Trench Fortifications 1914–18*, Imperial War Museum (reprint), London, 1998.

General Staff, War Office, *British Trench Warfare 1917–18*, Imperial War Museum (reprint), London, 1997.

Gliddon, Gerald, *VCs of the First World War: Arras and Messines 1917*, Sutton Publishing, Stroud, 1998.

Gliddon, Gerald, *When the Barrage Lifts*, Sutton Publishing, Stroud, 1994.

Glubb, John, *Into Battle*, Cassell & Co., London, 1978.

Godwin-Austen Maj. A. R., *The Staff and the Staff College*, Constable, London, 1927.

Griffiths, Paddy, *Battle Tactics of the Western Front*, Yale University Press, London, 1994.

Guéno, J.-P., and Laplume, d'Y., (eds.), *Paroles de poilus, Lettres et carnets du Front 1914–18*, Librio, Paris, 1998.

Harvey, A. D., *Collision of Empires*, Hambledon Press, London, 1992.

Hay, Ian, *The First Hundred Thousand*, William Blackwood, Edinburgh, 1916.

Haythornthwaite, Philip J., *The World War One Source Book*, Arms and Armour Press, London, 1992.

Headlam, Cuthbert, *The Guards Division in the Great War* (two vols.), John Murray, London, 1924.

Hendrick, Burton J., *The Life and Letters of Walter H. Page*, William Heinemann, London, 1924.

Henniker, Col. A. M., *Transportation on the Western Front*, HMSO, London, 1937.

Historical Committee Second Division, *The Second Division AEF in France 1917–19*, Hillman Press Inc., New York, 1937.

Hogg, Ian V., *Allied Artillery of World War One*, Crowood Press, Ramsbury, 1998.

Holmes, Richard, *Army Battlefield Guide: Belgium and Northern France*, HMSO, London, 1995.

Horne, Alistair, *The Price of Glory*, Macmillan, London, 1962.

Howard, James M., *The Autobiography of a Regiment – a History of the 304th Field Artillery in the World War*, privately published, New York, 1920.

Imperial War Museum, *Order of Battle British Armies in France*, Imperial War Museum, London, 1989.

James, Brig. E. A., *British Regiments 1914–18*, Naval & Military Press, London, 1978.

Jefferey, Keith, (ed.), *The Military Correspondence of Field Marshal Sir Henry Wilson 1918–22*, Bodley Head, London, 1995.

Jensen, Geoffrey, and Wiest, Andrew (eds.) *War in the Age of Technology*, New York University Press, New York and London, 2002.

Jervis, Lt Col. H. S., *The Second Munsters in France*, Gale & Polden, Aldershot, 1927.

Johnson, J. H., *1918: The Unexpected Victory*, Arms and Armour Press, London, 1997.

Johnston, Tom, and Hagerty, James, *The Cross and the Sword*, Geoffrey Chapman, London, 1996.

Joll, James, *The Origins of the First World War*, Longman, London, 1984.

Keegan, John, *The First World War*, Hutchinson, London, 1998.

Kiberd, Declan (ed.), *1916 Easter Rebellion Handbook*, Mourne River Press, Dublin, 1998.

Kipling, Rudyard, *The Irish Guards in the Great War* (two vols.), Spellmount, Staplehurst, 1997.

Laffin, John, *British Butchers and Bunglers of World War One*, Sutton Publishing, Stroud, 1988.

Laurent, André, *La Bataille de la Somme 1916*, Martelle, Amiens, 1998.

Lee, John, *A Soldier's Life: Gen. Sir Ian Hamilton 1853–1947*, Macmillan, London, 2000.

Liddell Hart, B. H., *The Real War 1914–18*, Faber & Faber, London, 1930.

Liddell Hart, B. H., *The Tanks: The History of the Royal Tank Regiment*, Vol. I, *1914–39*, Cassell & Co., London, 1959.

Liddle, Peter H., (ed.), *Passchendaele in Perspective*, Leo Cooper, London, 1997.

Lloyd George, David, *War Memoirs* (two vols.), Odhams Press, London, 1936, 1938.

Lloyd, Maj. P. S. (ed. R. J. Lloyd), *The Wood of Death and Beyond*, Oakham Books, Oakham, 1997.

Ludendorff, General Erich von, *My War Memoirs* (two vols.), Hutchinson, London, 1920.

Ludendorff, General Erich von, *The General Staff and Its Problems* (two vols.), Hutchinson, London, 1920.

MacDonogh, Giles, *The Last Kaiser*, Weidenfeld & Nicolson, London, 2000.

Mangin, Général Charles, *Lettres de guerre*, Fayard, Paris, 1950.

Marix Evans, Martin, *Passchendaele and the Battles of Ypres 1914–18*, Osprey, London, 1997.

Maude, Alan H., *The History of the 47th (London) Division 1914–19*, Naval & Military Press (reprint), London, 2000.

Maurice, Nancy, (ed.), *The Maurice Case*, Leo Cooper, London, 1972.

Maxwell, R. M., *Villiers-Stuart goes to War*, Pentland Press, Kippielaw, 1990.

McCarthy, Chris, *The Somme: the Day-by-Day Account*, Arms and Armour Press, London, 1995.

McCarthy, Chris, *Passchendaele: the Day-by-Day Account*, Arms and Armour Press, London, 1995.

Mead, Gary, *The Doughboys: America and the First World War*, Allen Lane, London, 2000.

Middlebrook, Martin, *The First Day on the Somme, 1 July 1916*, Allen Lane, London, 1971.

Miles, Capt. Wilfred, *Military Operations France and Belgium, 1916*, Vol. II, Macmillan, London, 1938.

Miles, Capt. Wilfred, *Military Operations France and Belgium, 1917*, Vol. III, HMSO, London, 1948.

Mitchell, Frank, *Tank Warfare, the Story of Tanks in the Great War*, Spa Books, Stevenage, 1987.

Mitchell, Maj. T. J., and Smith, Miss G. M., *Official History of the War, Casualties and Medical Statistics*, Imperial War Museum (reprint), London, 1997.

Morris, A. J. A., (ed.), *The Letters of Lieutenant Colonel Charles à Court Repington*, Sutton Publishing, Stroud, 1999.

Murphy, Z. A., and Thomas, R. S., *The 30th Division in the World War*, OM Publishing, Lepanto, Arkansas, 1936.

Neillands, Robin, *The Great War Generals of the Western Front 1914–18*, Constable Robinson, London, 1999.

Neillands, Robin, *Attrition: the Great War on the Western Front 1916*, Robson Books, London, 2001.

Nicolson, Colin, *The First World War in Europe 1914–18*, Longman, Harlow, 2001.

Nobécourt, R. G., *Les Fantassins du Chemin des Dames*, Éditions Bertout, Luneray, 1983.

O'Neill, H. C., *The Royal Fusiliers in the Great War*, William Heinemann, London, 1922.

Oldfield, Lt Col. E. A. L., *History of the Army Physical Training Corps*, Gale & Polden, Aldershot, 1955.

O'Rahilly, Professor A., *Father William Doyle, SJ*, Longman, Green & Co., London, 1920.

Oram, Gerard, *Death Sentences Passed by Military Courts of the British Army 1914–24*, Francis Boutle, London, 1998.

Ousby, Ian, *The Road to Verdun*, Jonathan Cape, London, 2002.

Palmer, Alan, *Victory 1918*, Weidenfeld & Nicolson, London, 1998.

Parker, Ernest, *Into Battle 1914–18*, Longmans, Green & Co., London, 1964.

Passingham, Ian, *Pillars of Fire: the Battle of Messines Ridge June 1917*, Sutton Publishing, Stroud, 1998.

Pedroncini, Guy, *Les Mutineries de 1917*, Presses Universitaires de France, Paris, 1967.

Pedroncini, Guy, *Pétain le soldat*, Perrin, Paris, 1998.

Pershing, General John J., *My Experiences in the First World War* (two vols.), F. A. Stokes, New York, 1931.

Pidgeon, Trevor, *The Tanks at Flers* (two vols.), Fairmile Books, Cobham, 1995.

Pollard, A. F., *A Short History of the Great War*, Methuen, London, 1920.

Powell, E. Alexander, *The Army behind the Army*, Charles Scribner's Sons, New York, 1919.

Prior, Robin, and Wilson, Trevor, *Passchendaele, the Untold Story*, Yale University Press, New York & London, 1996.

Prior, Robin, and Wilson, Trevor, *Command on the Western Front: the Military Career of Sir Henry Rawlinson*, Blackwell, Oxford, 1992.

Putowski, Julian, and Sykes, Julian, *Shot at Dawn* (seventh impression), Leo Cooper, London, 1998.

Raw, David, *It's Only Me*, Frank Peters, Gatebeck, 1988.

Rickard, Mrs V., *The Story of the Munsters*, Hodder & Stoughton, London, 1918.

Ritter, Gerhard (tr. A. & E. Wilson), *The Schlieffen Plan*, Oswald Wolff, London, 1958.

Robinson, Edgar E., and West, Victor J., *The Foreign Policy of Woodrow Wilson 1913–17*, Macmillan, New York, 1918.

Rogers, Col. H. C. B., *Artillery through the Ages*, Seeley Service, London, 1971.

Royal Engineers, Institute of, *History of the Corps of Royal Engineers*, Vols. V and VI, Institute of Royal Engineers, Chatham, 1952.

Royle, Trevor, *The Kitchener Enigma*, Michael Joseph, London, 1985.

Sambrook, James, *With the Rank and Pay of a Sapper*, Paddy Griffith Associates, Nuneaton, 1998.

Schindler, John R., *Isonzo, the Forgotten Sacrifice*, Praeger, Westport, Connecticut, 2001.

Schmidt, Bernadette E., *The Coming of the War*, Vol. I, *1914*, Charles Scribner & Sons, New York and London, 1930.

Second Division, Historical Committee *see* Historical Committee Second Division.

Selzbach, Herbert (tr. R. Thenger), *With the German Guns*, Leo Cooper, London, 1973.

Serman, William, and Bertaud, Jean-Paul, *Nouvelle Histoire Militaire de la France*, Fayard, Paris, 1998.

Seymour, William, *The History of the Rifle Brigade in the War of 1914–18*, Rifle Brigade Club, London, 1936.

Sheffield, G. D., *Forgotten Victory*, Headline, London, 2001.

Sheffield, G. D., *Leadership in the Trenches, Officer–Man Relations, Morale and Discipline in the British Army in the Era of the Great War*, Macmillan, London, 2000.

Sibley, Frank P., *With the Yankee Division in France*, Little, Brown & Co., Boston, 1919.

Simkins, Peter, *Kitchener's Army: The Raising of New Armies, 1914–16*, Manchester University Press, Manchester, 1988.

Smith, Maj. Gen. Sir Frederick, *A History of the Royal Army Veterinary Corps*, Ballière, Tindall & Cox, London, 1927.

Smythe, Donald, *Pershing, General of the Armies*, Indiana University Press, Bloomington, 1986.

Spagnoly, Tony, *The Anatomy of a Raid*, Multidream Publications, London, 1991.

Spears, Maj. Gen. Sir Edward, *Liaison 1914*, Eyre & Spottiswoode, London, 1930.

Spears, Maj. Gen. Sir Edward, *Two Men Who Saved France*, Eyre & Spottiswoode, London, 1966.

Stallings, Laurence, *The Doughboys: the Story of the AEF 1917–18*, Harper & Row, New York, 1963.

Strachan, Hew (ed.), *World War I, A History*, Oxford University Press, Oxford and New York, 1998.

Taylor, A. J. P., *The First World War: an Illustrated History*, Penguin Books, Harmondsworth, 1963.

Terraine, John, *The Smoke and the Fire*, Sidgwick & Jackson, London, 1980.

Terraine, John, *The First World War*, Hutchinson, London, 1965.

Terraine, John, *General Jack's Diary*, Eyre & Spottiswoode, London, 1964.

Terraine, John, *Mons: the Retreat to Victory*, Batsford, London, 1960.

Terraine, John, *To Win A War: 1918, The Year of Victory*, Sidgwick & Jackson, London, 1978.

Terraine, John, *Douglas Haig, The Educated Soldier*, Hutchinson, London, 1963.

Thomas, Shipley, *History of the American Expeditionary Force*, Geo. H. Duncan Co., New York, 1920.

Thullier, Maj. Gen. Sir H., *Gas in the Next War*, Geoffrey Bles, London, 1939.

Tiebout, Frank B., *A History of the 305th Infantry*, Wynkoop, Hallenbeck, Crawford Co., New York, 1919.

Tuchman, B. W., *The Zimmermann Telegram*, Constable & Co., London, 1958.

Walker, Jonathan, *The Blood Tub: General Gough and the Battle of Bullecourt 1917*, Spellmount Ltd, Staplehurst, 1998.

Warner, Philip, *The Battle of Loos*, William Kimber & Co., London, 1976.

War Office, The, *Statistics of the Military Effort of the British Empire during the Great War*, HMSO, London, 1922.

Westlake, Ray, *British Battalions on the Somme*, Leo Cooper, Barnsley, 1994.

Westlake, Ray, *Kitchener's Army*, Spellmount Ltd, Staplehurst, 1989.

Whitehead, Ian R., *Doctors in the Great War*, Leo Cooper, London, 1999.

Wilhelm, Crown Prince (*also* Foch, Joffre, Ludendorff), *The Two Battles of the Marne*, Thornton Butterworth, London, 1927.

Williams, Jeffery, *Byng of Vimy*, Leo Cooper, London, 1983.

Williams, John, *Mutiny 1917*, William Heinemann, London, 1962.

Winter, Denis, *Haig's Command*, Viking, London, 1991.

Winter, Denis, *Death's Men*, Allen Lane, London, 1978.

Winter, J. M., *The Great War and the British People*, Macmillan, London, 1985.

Wisconsin War History Ctte, *The 32nd Division in the World War*, Wisconsin Printing Co., Wisconsin, 1920.

Woodward, David R., (ed.), *The Military Correspondence of Field Marshal Sir William Robertson 1915–18*, Bodley Head, London, 1989.

Wyrall, Everard, *The History of the Second Division*, Naval & Military Press (reprint), London, 2000.

Wyrall, Everard, *The Nineteenth Division 1914–18*, Naval & Military Press (reprint), London, 1999.

Wyrall, Everard, *The Fiftieth Division*, Naval & Military Press (reprint), London, 1999.

Wyrall, Everard, *The Somerset Light Infantry, 1914–19*, Methuen & Co., London, 1927.

Zeman, Zab, *A Diplomatic History of the First World War*, Weidenfeld & Nicolson, London, 1971.

INDEX OF MILITARY UNITS

GENERAL INDEX

Figures in **bold** refer to diagrams and maps.

available from
THE ORION PUBLISHING GROUP

Jutland 1916
Peter Hart
0 304 36648 X ☐
£6.99

Weapons of Mass Destruction
Robert Hutchinson
0 304 36653 6 ☐
£7.99

Eisenhower
Carlo D'Este
0 304 36658 7 ☐
£9.99

Enigma
Hugh Sebag-Montefiore
0 304 36662 5 ☐
£8.99

Fire from the Forest
Roger Ford
0 304 36336 7 ☐
£7.99

A Storm in Flanders
Winston Groom
0 304 36656 0 ☐
£7.99

Churchill's Folly
Anthony Rogers
0 304 36655 2 ☐
£7.99

Rising Sun and Tumbling Bear
Richard Connaughton
0 304 36657 9 ☐
£7.99

Mud, Blood and Poppycock
Gordon Corrigan
0 304 36659 5 ☐
£7.99

All Orion/Phoenix titles are available at your local bookshop or from the following address:

Mail Order Department
Littlehampton Book Services
FREEPOST BR535
Worthing, West Sussex, BN13 3BR
telephone 01903 828503, *facsimile* 01903 828802
e-mail MailOrders@lbsltd.co.uk
(Please ensure that you include full postal address details)

Payment can be made either by credit/debit card (Visa, Mastercard, Access and Switch accepted) or by sending a £ Sterling cheque or postal order made payable to *Littlehampton Book Services*.
DO NOT SEND CASH OR CURRENCY.

Please add the following to cover postage and packing

UK and BFPO:
£1.50 for the first book, and 50p for each additional book to a maximum of £3.50

Overseas and Eire:
£2.50 for the first book plus £1.00 for the second book and 50p for each additional book ordered

---

BLOCK CAPITALS PLEASE

name of cardholder ....   *delivery address*
....   *(if different from cardholder)*

address of cardholder ....

....

....

postcode ....   *postcode* ....

☐ I enclose my remittance for £..

☐ please debit my Mastercard/Visa/Access/Switch (delete as appropriate)

card number ☐☐☐☐ ☐☐☐☐ ☐☐☐☐ ☐☐☐☐

expiry date ☐☐☐   Switch issue no. ☐☐

signature ....

prices and availability are subject to change without notice